THE POLITICAL ECONOMY OF SAME-SEX MARRIAGE

Same-sex marriage is now legal in twenty-nine countries and the subject of continued debate around the world. *The Political Economy of Same-Sex Marriage: A Feminist Critique* considers this debate from a political economy perspective. Rather than engaging directly in the now well-rehearsed social-movement and academic for-and-against debates, this book focuses on processes of institutionalisation of same-sex marriage and so-called "rainbow families" within (neo)liberal capitalist democracies. It examines how states and markets appropriate same-sex marriage and family to enhance their own political and symbolic capital, consolidating power and profit within existing systems of gendered and raced socioeconomic stratification.

Taking a radical feminist, heterodox, qualitative and intersectional approach, this book investigates the political economy of same-sex marriage across three axes: same-sex marriage as institution; same-sex marriage and the market; and the political economy of the "rainbow family". The examination of case studies from different countries and regions enables a comparative analysis that foregrounds cultural, political and economic path dependencies while at the same time highlighting a number of striking commonalities. In all the countries discussed in this book and in most respects, same-sex marriage has been integrated almost seamlessly into a mainstream/malestream political economy of marriage and family and its translation into added market and productive value.

The Political Economy of Same-Sex Marriage: A Feminist Critique will be of use to researchers and students alike, and indeed to all those who are curious about the mainstreaming of homosexuality within twenty-first-century capitalist democracies.

Bronwyn Winter is Professor of Transnational Studies at the University of Sydney, Australia, where she teaches in the European Studies and International and Global Studies programs. Her research lies at the intersections of gender, sexuality, race, religion, migration, conflict and the state, often in relation to international discourses and practices concerning gendered political economy, human rights and violence in a globalised world.

ROUTLEDGE IAFFE ADVANCES IN FEMINIST ECONOMICS

IAFFE aims to increase the visibility and range of economic research on gender; facilitate communication among scholars, policymakers, and activists concerned with women's wellbeing and empowerment; promote discussions among policy makers about interventions which serve women's needs; educate economists, policymakers, and the general public about feminist perspectives on economic issues; foster feminist evaluations of economics as a discipline; expose the gender blindness characteristic of much social science and the ways in which this impoverishes all research - even research that does not explicitly concern women's issues; help expand opportunities for women, especially women from underrepresented groups, within economics; and, encourage the inclusion of feminist perspectives in the teaching of economics. The IAFFE book series pursues the aims of the organization by providing a forum in which scholars have space to develop their ideas at length and in detail. The series exemplifies the value of feminist research and the high standard of IAFFE sponsored scholarship.

18 Global Women's Work
Perspectives on Gender and Work in the Global Economy
Edited by Beth English, Mary E. Frederickson and Olga Sanmiguel-Valderrama

19 Informal Women Workers in the Global South
Policies and Practices for the Formalisation of Women's Employment in Developing Economies
Edited by Jayati Ghosh

20 The Political Economy of Same-Sex Marriage
A Feminist Critique
Bronwyn Winter

21 Women's Economic Thought in the Romantic Age
Towards a Transdisciplinary Herstory of Economic Thought
Joanna Rostek

For more information about this series, please visit www.routledge.com/Routledge-IAFFE-Advances-in-Feminist-Economics/book-series/IAFFE

THE POLITICAL ECONOMY OF SAME-SEX MARRIAGE

A Feminist Critique

Bronwyn Winter

Routledge
Taylor & Francis Group
LONDON AND NEW YORK

First published 2021
by Routledge
2 Park Square, Milton Park, Abingdon, Oxon OX14 4RN

and by Routledge
52 Vanderbilt Avenue, New York, NY 10017

Routledge is an imprint of the Taylor & Francis Group, an informa business

British Library Cataloguing in Publication Data
A catalogue record for this book is available from the British Library

Library of Congress Cataloging-in-Publication Data
Names: Winter, Bronwyn, 1955- author.
Title: The political economy of same-sex marriage : a feminist critique / Bronwyn Winter.
Description: 1 Edition. | New York : Routledge, 2020. | Series: Routledge-IAFFE advances in feminist economics | Includes bibliographical references and index.
Identifiers: LCCN 2020033743 (print) | LCCN 2020033744 (ebook) | ISBN 9781138502673 (hardback) | ISBN 9781138502680 (paperback) | ISBN 9781315145013 (ebook)
Subjects: LCSH: Same-sex marriage. | Same-sex marriage–Political aspects. | Same-sex marriage–Economic aspects. | Democracy–Economic aspects. | Economic policy. | Social structure–History–21st century.
Classification: LCC HQ1033 .W56 2020 (print) | LCC HQ1033 (ebook) | DDC 306.84/8–dc23
LC record available at https://lccn.loc.gov/2020033743
LC ebook record available at https://lccn.loc.gov/2020033744

ISBN: 978-1-138-50267-3 (hbk)
ISBN: 978-1-138-50268-0 (pbk)
ISBN: 978-1-315-14501-3 (ebk)

Typeset in Bembo
by Taylor & Francis Books

For Véronique

CONTENTS

ACKNOWLEDGEMENTS

I had never planned to write a book about the political economy of same-sex marriage. It originally sat at the margins of my research agenda, but then a series of circumstances moved it from margin to centre.

It began in 2016, when I presented a paper on the political economy of same-sex marriage at the conference of the International Association for Feminist Economics (IAFFE) held at the National University of Ireland, Galway: so IAFFE are the first people to thank, collectively as an organisation for providing spaces for these sorts of feminist conversations. At that time, as a result of another somewhat coincidental encounter, I had ended up working as lead co-editor on an international anthology on the institutionalisation of same-sex marriage, published by Palgrave Macmillan in 2018. The IAFFE paper was prepared in the context of that other work, but was never meant to be more than a journal article at most. However, out of the blue, Emily Kindleysides, then a senior economics editor with Taylor & Francis, which publishes the journal *Feminist Economics*, emailed me prior to the conference expressing keen interest in the topic and asking if I was considering writing a book on it. I wasn't. The international anthology was really quite enough for me at that time and I was eager to move back to my usual transnational feminist themes. I had no intention of continuing to work on same-sex marriage.

But Emily's enthusiasm encouraged me to develop a book proposal, so here we are. During the preparation of the manuscript, Emily moved to another area within Taylor & Francis, and her successor, Kristina Abbotts, became my interlocutor. She and her assistant Christiana Mandizha have seen the book through multiple delays (my university workload, bouts of illness, a computer drama and then to cap it all off, the COVID-19 pandemic resulting in yet more university workload) with infinite grace and patience. So my thanks to all three—Emily, Kristina and Chrissy—and to production editor Jenny Guildford, to eagle-eyed copyeditor

Peter Stafford, and of course to others in Taylor & Francis whose names I do not know and who have helped this book make its final steps to publication.

I am also grateful to the research communities of which I am part. Many IAFFE members provided me with valuable tips, feedback and resources (among others, Lee Badgett—even though we disagree on same-sex marriages, Barbara Hopkins, Karin Schönpflug, Alyssa Schneebaum and Mansour Omeira). Within the School of Languages and Cultures where I work at the University of Sydney, I was able to run ideas past colleagues such as Fernanda Peñaloza and Cat Moir, who helped me fact-check cultural and linguistic references. Finally, a big thankyou to Robert Boncardo, for his excellent indexing work. Always a pleasure, Rob!

Bronwyn Winter

INTRODUCTION

"Decriminalization or marriage, where should Caribbean LGBT people focus?" read the May, 2020 headline on the Erasing 76 Crimes website, dedicated to the "human toll of 70-plus countries' anti-gay laws" and "the struggle to repeal them" (Tomlinson 2020, online). (Male) homosexuality remains illegal in most English-speaking island nations in the Caribbean. In 1962, Jamaica (the author's country of origin) introduced the world's first constitutional ban on same-sex unions. Maurice Tomlinson, the article's author, who petitioned the Inter-American Commission on Human Rights in 2019 to have the ban overturned, asks:

> Is our advocacy for LGBT human rights in the Caribbean missing a crucial element? Instead of exclusively campaigning to decriminalize gay sex should we also be showing that LGBT people are members of families? Could it be that a large part of the resistance to decriminalization is because many straight people find gay sex "icky" and still equate it with HIV and AIDS because of decades of religious miseducation?
>
> Should we therefore capitalize on the fact that nearly everyone can relate to the need for love and family while few people can appreciate a right to same-sex intimacy, even if done in private? Does the singular focus on decriminalization reduce LGBT people to a sex act in the eyes of the public, and discussing same-sex unions might help to humanize us? (Tomlinson 2020, online)

It is routinely argued by feminist critics of heteronormative intimate and social relations (e.g. Bergeron 2009) that homosexuality is disruptive of heteropatriarchal society and its family models, and even heteropatriarchal nationalisms (e.g. Peterson 2013), and thus feminist analyses of the family cannot be applied to same-sex relationships and families. In the very first issue of the journal *Feminist Economics*, Lee Badgett argued that "active rewriting of family definition and policy presents an important opportunity for feminists of all sexual orientations to affect what a 'family' means and does" (Badgett 1995, 124). Yet, Tomlinson's reflections suggest that the road to successful legalisation of same-sex marriage (with the concurrent outcome, in his context, of decriminalisation of homosexuality), is less about "actively rewriting" policy than about fitting same-sex unions, and homosexuals more broadly, into it. Placing same-sex unions in the frame of "truly unremarkable married life" (Tomlinson 2020) would make homosexuality less "icky" in the eyes of state and society, less about physicality and more about normative family values, and thus acceptable. Such assimilation was dubbed "the new homonormativity" by Lisa Duggan (2002): "a politics that does not contest dominant heteronormative assumptions and institutions, but upholds and sustains them while promising the possibility of a demobilized gay constituency and a privatized, depoliticized gay culture anchored in domesticity and consumption" (Duggan 2002, 179). Later, Jasbir Puar extended the concept to examine the appropriation of "LGBT rights" by Western states, the better to demonise the racialised Other, a practice she dubbed "homonationalism" (Puar 2007). This practice has also been termed "pinkwashing" in relation to the Israeli state in particular, but since extended to other countries as well, such as in Latin America (Winter 2017, ch. 5; Tabbush et al. 2019).

At the same time, Tomlinson, in wishing to homonormalise his relationship with his Canadian spouse in his native Jamaica, is also making a political claim. He wants LGBTIQ populations to be "humanised", in a country where they are not considered fully human because deprived of the rights and freedoms open to heterosexuals. As any feminist can testify, making a claim to be fully human in a world where one is not considered so is a revolutionary act in itself. It is thus not my intent here to dismiss or belittle the struggles of minorities in an often extremely hostile world. It is, rather, what happens *next*, once those struggles are homonormatively and homonationalistically appropriated and institutionalised within states and markets, that interests me in this book.

The sociopolitical debate on the pros and cons of same-sex marriage is now well-rehearsed and familiar to all concerned by the issue, and I do not intend to comprehensively revisit that particular debate here.[1] My purpose in writing this book is rather to critique the socioeconomic, cultural and political functions of the *institutions* of marriage and family as core elements of the malestream political economy. I consider how, and why, states and markets embrace same-sex marriage and rainbow families, my argument being that neither would do so were it not in their own interest. They similarly would not do so if "family" were not so fundamentally entwined with both, such that neither states nor markets could function effectively in their current form without it, or indeed, without each other. The three function as an interdependent triad, materially, ideologically and symbolically, across the varied national contexts that I discuss in this book. The main reason, in fact, that "nearly everyone can relate" to family (Tomlinson 2020), beyond or even outside considerations of "love", is because "family" is the core value and core structure around which, and upon which, our malestream political economies are built.

How has this state-market-family triad, then, incorporated same-sex family and its domestic economy into the national family and its political economy? What is gained or lost by doing so? Within the "equal marriage" frame, are some still more equal than others? How does the "global" same-sex marriage agenda intersect and interact with specific national path dependencies? What have been the mixed impacts of the concurrent development of a human-rights-and-equality turn and a neoliberal turn in global and domestic politics? These are the questions that I set out to explore in this book.

Same-sex marriage is now legal in 29 countries,[2] all of which are secular (neo) liberal capitalist democracies, which also means, in our contemporary world, that they remain heteropatriarchal, notwithstanding formal sex-egalitarianism. I will argue presently that this concordance between the political and economic system and the legalisation of same-sex marriage is not accidental. Three-quarters of the legalisations occurred in the decade since 2010, and some 40 per cent in the five years since 2015, which suggests a snowballing effect of policy convergence and/or transfer within these democracies. The most recent legalisation at the time of writing is Costa Rica (26 May 2020), the first in Central America. Except for South Africa and Taiwan, all of these countries are in Western Europe, Latin America and the Anglosphere five (in order of national legalisation: Canada, New Zealand, UK, US and Australia). These countries would thus appear to have satisfied Badgett's challenge that they "evolve" as concerns extending their legal and political understandings of marriage and family, yet, as Badgett herself concluded in her 2009 study of the Netherlands, heterosexuals and homosexuals have, in fact, remarkably similar approaches to marriage (Badgett 2009, ch.10). In fact, marriage has been in a process of evolution over the last two centuries, as among other things, the political, economic and social emancipation of women—albeit imperfectly realised to date—has been incorporated into legal and cultural understandings of the institution. Even so, societal norms, economic patterning and legal regulatory frameworks all continue to reproduce malestream understandings of how relationships and families function or should function, including in their class, race and transnationalised dimensions.

The term "malestream" was coined by Mary O'Brien, to describe and critique the masculinist ideology "that buttresses and justifies … male dominant culture" (O'Brien 1981, 5). Analysis of "the relation of the individual to cultures and collectivities", she argued, was thus rendered a more difficult and complex task for women, because the methodological and theoretical tools they were given to use were all developed on the basis of male experience and in response to questions that men found important. Or, as Audré Lorde put it around the same time, in comments on race, class and heterosexism at the Second Sex Conference in New York in 1979, women faced the difficulty of using "The Master's Tools" which were not fit for the task of "dismantl[ing] the Master's House" (Lorde 1984, 110). Marriage and the family are core elements of the ideological apparatus that O'Brien and Lorde were critiquing, and they continue to be so, even in a rainbowed world. We will see time and again in this book just *how* gendered the institutions of marriage and family remain, even in their same-sex forms. O'Brien's term thus remains highly relevant, and I will use it on occasion in this book as shorthand for "heteropatriarchal (neo)liberal capitalist democracies".

Within malestream politics, familialist rhetoric as a profoundly gendered discourse is so routinely deployed in framings of societies, economies, nations, and states that it passes almost unnoticed as an ideological framework used by both the left and right. Such rhetoric is indeed "fundamental" to "thinking right", (*penser à droite*) as Colette Guillaumin put it:

> Discourse concerning relations between the sexes does not follow the usually-drawn boundaries between left and right. To tell the truth there is simply no boundary. If political parties and movements are classified as right wing or left wing according to their opinions in those areas defined as "political", the consensus, fortunately for the clarity of their debates, is that the question of the sexes is left alone in the middle of the arena. For it is a fact that the "natural" politics of the sexes can be found just as easily in what is supposed to be the left as it is in the right and left-wing options do not go as far as questioning them … The ideology of the right is thus not the exclusive province of a movement or a party of the right or extreme right, it is present everywhere and constantly in relations of domination. (Guillaumin 1986, 40, 41)

In this book, I use an interdisciplinary approach that draws heavily on the analyses of Guillaumin and other radical and materialist feminist and lesbian theorists, as well as on the work of other feminist and lesbian political theorists, sociologists, and of course, feminist (political) economists, as well as the occasional queer or gay theorist. I will discuss various approaches more fully within the individual chapters of this book, as they apply to topics covered therein, but most of the scholars whose work I draw on share, in varying ways, this understanding of "thinking right", as informing the power structures of gender, race and class that characterise the malestream and continue to impact on and through "the family" in our societies.

I argue in this book that in supporting same-sex marriage, the principal concern of states and markets is not to make "family" more egalitarian or inclusive—although that may be the effect, and even the sincere motivation of a number of individual actors within state and market systems. The concern of states and markets is rather to ensure their own ongoing viability through consolidation of malestream power, which means more loyal citizens in the case of the state and more effective and better commodified participants in the relations of production and consumption in the case of the market. It also means preserving the family as the basis of social organisation.

Marriage rates in almost all OECD member countries have declined significantly since 1970 (OECD 2019). In the EU between 1965 and 2016, the marriage rate halved while the divorce rate doubled (Eurostat 2019). The EU's report pointed to the generalisation of other types of cohabitation, such as registered partnerships (including among couples having children, and including among lesbians and gay men), as partially explaining this trend. The trend in divorce rates is more patchy (partly because of its illegality, even for heterosexuals, until relatively recently in some countries such as Ireland or Chile), but has followed the EU trend in rising overall. The Chinese are the most likely among the OECD countries to marry, but only middlingly likely to remain so (which could lead to some rather fanciful speculation about what might happen for same-sex couples once Chinese heterosexuals start shunning the institution in greater numbers). I do not think it is coincidental that same-sex marriage legalisations are occurring within this context of declining heteromarriage, even if this decline, and related state anxieties over preservation of the institution, cannot be considered a unique or even primary causal factor.

Human-rights-democracy-and-the-rule-of-law

In the countries under discussion in this book, the legal framework for social regulation is primarily articulated around the family unit as the site of physical, social, cultural and economic reproduction. This truth holds whatever other values individuals and groups may attribute to family, and however they relate to family as a source of refuge, nurture, transcendence in a religious or spiritual sense, community and so on, and whether they perceive family as a site of personal safety or personal risk (the latter, as we know, often being the case for women and girls within the heterosexual family unit). The very building of the modern nation-state and its economic and rights structures has been intricately linked to the development of its family law. As Philomila Tsoukala (2010) has argued with relation to both Greek and European nation/supranation-building processes, family law has been considered a crucial element of unification processes and the basis for cultural identity claim-making. It is the structural corollary to the ideology of family in the construction of the nation, and normative understandings of "family" are embedded in state labour laws, fiscal regimes and welfare systems, among other things. This legal and economic framework bolsters the ideological one in creating two classes of citizen, symbolically speaking: those who are married and those who are not, with often significant material consequences for the individuals concerned.

In all countries in which same-sex marriage has been legalised and institutionalised, or is likely to be so in the foreseeable future, the laws relating to marriage pertain primarily to (a) accumulation and transfer of wealth through property ownership, fiscal benefits and inheritance; (b) enhancing productivity through, for example, various work arrangements (such as benefits for spouses or special conditions for relocation of workers); (c) the production, education and care of future citizens (children), for whom biological or adoptive parents retain responsibility until the age of the children's majority; and (d) more generally, the labour of care of the temporarily or permanently infirm. Almost without exception, different legal and fiscal arrangements are made for married and single people, notably as concerns assets, tax and inheritance, with the former group enjoying significant advantages—although there are some exceptions, for example as concerns the right to unemployment benefit in some countries, such as Australia and the UK. In these countries, the whole "family income", including income and cash reserves of spouses or de facto partners, presumed to be living in the same house, is means-tested for the purpose of assessing eligibility to receive the dole of any unemployed member of that perceived family unit.

This familialist system of social regulation is, paradoxically, the same system that gave us the idea of the individual in whom inhere rights, *as an individual*, independent of the social, economic or political relationships in which that individual is engaged. A common assumption is that values of individualism, human rights and freedom of speech, association and enterprise are uniquely Western, and they have been understood as favouring gender equality and LGBTIQ rights (L. Davis and Williamson 2019; A. Hildebrandt, Trüdinger and Wyss 2019). I will set aside the question of whether these principles are "uniquely" Western or not, but the Western-aligned malestream context has clearly been the one in which LGBTIQ rights, including same-sex marriage, have flourished.

Mary Nolan has described the international political and economic order of the second half of the twentieth century as one dominated by the US worldview, which was characterised by the triple vision of

> the discourses and practices, institutions, and values of the U.S. model of consumerist democratic capitalism … human rights with its focus on the delineation and protection of the civil and political rights of the individual; and market fundamentalism, which refers not only to neoliberal economics, but also more broadly to the belief that all areas of politics, society, culture, and knowledge can and should succumb to market logic. (M. Nolan 2011, 17)

It was also a period, she argues, during which the institution of family was "stabilized through laws, public policies, and cultural campaigns" (M. Nolan 2011, 16).

The "human rights" framework, which derives from French and US revolutionary models of the eighteenth century, is generally considered an advance and indeed has been used by LGBTIQ activists to advance rights, including the right to marry. However, the history of human rights, including some tensions between "European" and "American" (US) understandings, is also why the framework is flawed. First, it developed in a context of the emergence of a mercantilist middle class that wished to wrest authority from church and crown and enable (white male) individuals to go about their business unfettered in a secularised world. Human rights thus go hand in hand, historically, politically and economically, with the emergence of capitalism. Second, "human rights" at that time, although posited as universal, were selectively interpreted to apply to a fairly restricted class of people, and indeed remain so, as states routinely and with impunity deprive certain classes of individuals of rights (slaves, indentured labour, women, LGBTIQ, lower castes, ethno-religious minorities and so on)—which leads us to the third problem. Rights are conferred by states, whose sovereignty extends to the ability to flout the provisions of human rights treaties with occasional censure but extremely rare sanction, especially if the flouting state is a relatively powerful one in geopolitical and geo-economic terms. In any case, the treaties themselves are designed to serve the interests, not of the least powerful, nor indeed of the most, but of those who have sufficient social and cultural capital to assert and fight for them. This is not a cultural-relativist argument against rights, but rather an acknowledgement of how the institutionalisation of rights functions: the very systems and classes that deprive people of rights are charged with upholding and advancing them. Finally, the notion of the individual in whom inhere rights—which remains a liberatory concept—quickly tips over into the ideology of individual*ism*: individuals are considered both as atomised agents and as responsible for their own destiny. For example, unemployment and poverty become the "fault" of the unemployed and poor, and "welfare capitalism" (Esping-Andersen 1990) has been founded on the tension between the moral duty of the patriarch to care for the needy and the blaming of the needy for being needy in the first place (on this last, see Thompson 2020). All of these factors have resulted in multiple contradictions in the human rights system, not the least of which is the fact that what *deprives* people of the inalienable and indivisible rights they are assumed to have by virtue of being human (the original "French" idealistic conceptualisation) is rarely, if ever, articulated in human rights treaties and declarations.

Perhaps the most significant political paradox of our age is that those very states that most ardently defend "rights", especially through what has become the EU values-mantra of "democracy, human rights and the rule of law", are inegalitarian (neo)liberal capitalist states, many of them very powerful. That said, the political concept of universal human rights, its international legal architecture, and its leading values defenders of today (UN, EU and so on), along with the associated formal separation of religious and positive law, provide an important framework for the marginalised to seek both a protected public tribune from which they can have effective voice and access to a means of remedy. Of course, being able to *seek* these things is not in itself a guarantee that they will be found, especially in the case of remedy, but human rights are an important moral and legal framework for the recognition of all as equally human—including those groups who were not originally members of the human rights club of the late eighteenth century.

This is the arena in which the same-sex marriage battles are being fought (sometimes as part of wider battles against persecution of homosexuals, as in the Jamaican case discussed by Tomlinson [2020]), and indeed, for all their paradoxes and pitfalls, the one in which they are most likely to succeed.

Some methodological challenges

In attempting to fulfil the task I set myself in this book, I come up against some quite specific problems, not all of which can be resolved in the space of one volume. The first is the sheer dimensions of the issue. It is simply impossible, in one book, to discuss in detail 29 different national contexts, and then compare them all. I thus rely on case studies, on specific examples, on occasional snapshots or even passing references (I hardly discuss Taiwan at all, for example). Language presents another barrier. Even though there is a good deal of material available in English (for example, many non-Anglophone states provide online materials in both the country's official language(s) and English), there is also a good deal that is not. I have the good fortune to be able to read some of the main languages of the countries under study, but not all of them, and am more fluent in some than in others; there is thus surely some material that escapes my notice or understanding.

A further problem is the availability of data. The overwhelming majority of both quantitative and qualitative research conducted—by academics, think tanks, NGOs or government institutions—on same-sex marriage and families is done in relation to the United States, with the next most important body of research focusing on other Western Anglosphere countries. This concentration of research is related to Anglo dominance in academe and particularly to the hegemonic status therein of the US, as well as the role of privately funded US institutes such as the Williams Institute (WI) at the University of California Los Angeles, undoubtedly the world's most significant university research centre devoted to things LGBTIQ. The WI is a philanthropically-funded think tank on sexual orientation, gender identity, the law and public policy, named for its founder and original funder, Charles ("Chuck") Williams, who in 2001 provided a US$2.5 million grant to establish it. The Institute is a fount of knowledge, with fulltime and visiting academic and professional staff working across a range of disciplines. I draw heavily on its research in various parts of this book. The US is also the location of important think tanks such as the Pew Research Center, which produces a great deal of demographic research, opinion polling and other social sciences data, primarily focused on the US but also often reaching beyond its borders. This Anglo- and US-centrism of research and data-gathering makes my task even more difficult. A great amount of cross-cultural and plurilinguistic digging is required to find material—most especially demographic data and analysis—on non-Anglo countries, but it remains very thin either on or under the ground. I thus often find myself drawing on US case studies or analyses when I wish to explore a particular issue, try as I might to escape the hegemon's pull.

Even within the US, research on Anglo white couples and families dominates. A content analysis of the articles published in the first ten years of the newish *Journal of GLBT Family Studies* found that apart from a minimal focus on either the B or the T, the majority of articles were qualitative empirical studies on white, middle-class, employed gay and lesbian parents in the US (Bible et al. 2018). Yet as the authors noted, drawing on other research, over 40 per cent of the LGBT population does not identify as Caucasian and same-sex couples are more likely to be interracial than heterosexual couples. Moreover, ethno-racial minority same-sex couples are more likely than those in white couples to be raising children.

The article further pointed out that unemployment rates are higher among same-sex couples and in all research on LGBT populations, lesbian and bisexual women are underrepresented.

Thus, as we will see time and again in this book, the plethora of quantitative and qualitative research on the US case tends to orchestrate US understandings of same-sex marriage and family, their political framing, and their economic structure as the exemplar. Yet, in very many ways—and most especially as concerns the political economy of marriage, work, welfare and family—the US is a strikingly unique case, even in relation to the rest of the Anglosphere. First, dominant US culture has a particularly strong attachment to the idea of marriage and what one might call "traditionally nuclear" dual-parent families, even if the idea's connection to the demographic reality is tenuous at best (Kramer 2019). Second, US social policy is conspicuous by its relative absence, compared to the other countries concerned by this book—even within the Anglosphere. Even though, as we will see, the global neoliberal shift is pushing social policies of other states more in the direction of the US model, socioeconomic factors that have been extremely important in same-sex marriage campaigns there, such as employer-provided spousal health insurance, have not even been relevant in other countries. Other debates around same-sex marriage are also quite US-specific—such as the controversy over comparisons of same-sex marriage campaign of today and the black civil rights movement of the 1950s and 1960s, which I discuss in Chapter 6. The US is thus in very many ways a standalone example, which makes it all the more unfortunate that US understandings of, and research on, the issue have been so influential.

Other research published in English largely focuses on the Anglosphere, with the next largest body of research focusing on Scandinavian countries or the Netherlands. Even research in French or Spanish—the languages spoken in many countries concerned by this book or subnational regions thereof—is relatively sparse and mostly of it is qualitative. Notable exceptions include the Dutch Statistics Bureau, which regularly conducts demographic surveys of LGBTIQ populations. Certainly, this book is itself qualitative, as I have neither the in-depth skills nor the research funding to conduct statistically valid transnational demographic research myself. The sample size would run into the thousands, costing millions of dollars, to ensure a truly viable transnational and intersectional sample that would produce meaningful data. I have thus relied on data produced by national census bureaus and the European Union, which have in some cases yielded results worthy of discussion, although most of the detailed data is fairly recent and thus precludes a longitudinal appreciation of the development of same-sex marriage, divorce and parenting in the countries in question.

However, hardly any of the statistical material I have found, whether drawn from censuses or surveys, mentions race at all, although almost all has some level of disaggregation by sex, and some discusses income and parenting. Where ethnoracially disaggregated data on LGTIBQ populations exists, it is often not systematically cross-referenced with data on marriage, divorce and parenting.

Notwithstanding these many regrettable limitations, there are some transnational generalisations that one is able to make, and some conclusions that it is possible to draw, albeit tentatively in some instances, pending further research. For example, campaigns for same-sex marriage, the demographics of those who are marrying, and the ways in which states and researchers alike frame the issue, appear to be dominated by middle class whiteness, and often dominated by men as well (even though, statistically speaking, lesbians are as likely if not more likely to marry than gay men).

A third problem takes the form of another paradox. Since my focus is institutions and the market, much of the discussion in this book starts with, and is framed by, heteronorms, which in a book on same-sex marriage may seem odd. However, the processes of legalisation and institutionalisation have meant that same-sex relationships have, explicitly and implicitly, been incorporated into the malestream familialist model of production, reproduction and welfare that lies at the base of our socioeconomic system. It is thus impossible to avoid discussing them, and indeed it would not be illuminating nor even particularly meaningful to do so.

Structure of the book and some questions of terminology

This book is divided into three thematic parts, each one focusing primarily on one element of the state-market-family triad, in that order, even if there are inevitable crossovers, given that the triad is impossible to separate neatly into its component parts. Each part comprises three chapters.

Part I, "Same-sex marriage as institution", focuses, as its title suggests, on the institutionalisation of marriage and family in general and same-sex marriage in particular. In Chapter 1, "Marriage and family as value in liberal capitalist societies", I consider the family not only as the privately framed yet publicly regulated structural and economic basis of the nation and its ruling state, but also as *metaphor* for the nation, with the state as ruling parent (father). I close on a brief discussion of how welfare systems fit into the state logics of family. In Chapter 2, "From subversive challenge to liberal rights", I focus on the human rights framing of same-sex marriage and family, and discuss the use by states of rights and equality frames to discursively incorporate same-sex marriage into their national "brand". In the third chapter, I extend this discussion of state rationales to look more in depth at three quite different case studies: Germany, Argentina and South Africa. To do so, I use an approach that sits broadly within a feminist-informed neo-institutionalist framework (Mackay, Kenny and Chappell 2010; Krook and Mackay 2011), both historical (Pierson and Skocpol 2002; Pierson 2004) and discursive (Schmidt 2008, 2010). I examine the specific path dependencies that apply in each case and impact on the ways in which—and indeed the time at which—the state has mobilised and rhetorically framed the issue of same-sex marriage, and consider the political opportunities or obstacles that have presented themselves to both state and civil society actors.

Part II, titled "Selling same-sex marriage", looks at both the market-economics and the demographics of same-sex marriage, with a key focus on what rainbow "inclusion" looks like socioeconomically, and who it in fact *ex*cludes. Chapter 4, "Rainbowing the workplace", discusses both corporate strategies of "inclusivity" and the courting of corporations by same-sex marriage advocates. As the "corporate case" for same-sex marriage has been most enthusiastically embraced in the Anglosphere, much albeit not all of the discussion in this chapter will concern Anglo countries. The chapter will also expose the underbelly of inclusivity, showing that the same corporations that fly the rainbow flag are very unequal employers in many other respects. Chapter 5 ventures down a path that has been little explored in same-sex marriage research: the gay wedding industry and wedding tourism. It asks what the gay components of the wedding and wedding tourism industries share or do not share with the straight ones (there are in fact many commonalities, as one might expect), and examines the media framing and marketisation that operate to target this new arrival into the wedding club and assimilate it into the club's traditions and practices. Chapter 6 closes this section by shifting gears a little, to look at same-sex marriage intersectionally: both demographics and representation. What do we know about who is getting same-sex married (and same-sex divorced for that matter)? How do race, class and national location impact, not only on who is counted but also on who counts? The chapter closes on the question: who is same-sex marriage "for"?

Finally, Part III focuses on the political economy of "rainbow families", through three axes: the workplace and welfare (Chapter 7, "Working families"); the dynamics of same-sex households including the labour of care and the question of housing (Chapter 8, "Caring families); and the political economy of surrogacy in the light of demands by gay men for access thereto (Chapter 9, "Gay dads"). I examine surrogacy as a highly unequal relationship of commercial exchange in a transnational capitalist economy.

Before proceeding, a couple of comments on terminology are warranted. First, the political use of the term "liberal" to mean "progressive" or "left-wing" is specific to the US. Yet the eighteenth-century European philosophical origins and class base of liberalism place it more in the centre of the political spectrum, as it is to do with the dominant moral philosophy informing the operation of capitalist democracies: liberty, equality and the consent or collective political will that provides legitimacy to governments. It is this European understanding that informs my use of the term in this book: liberalism can just as easily sit to the (centre-)right of politics as it can to the (centre-)left. (In Australia, the transatlantic confusion is amplified by the fact that the main conservative party has the name Liberal Party, resulting in the development of the expression "small-l liberal" to denote someone with broadly liberal philosophical and social values.) I also on occasion add the prefix "neo" in parentheses, to suggest that even beyond the US and the broader Anglosphere, contemporary liberal capitalist democracies are increasingly *neo*liberal in a globalised political economy dominated, as Mary Nolan (2011) has suggested, by The American Way.

Finally, I would like to make it clear that in this book, I am focusing on lesbians and gay men, because I consider both components of the term "homosexual" to be meaningful, and directly relevant to discussions of same-*sex* attraction and same-*sex* marriage. I thus set aside discussions of gender identity and its relationship to either sexuality or marriage for the purpose of this book. Such discussions are today complex and often extremely fraught, and as such are certainly deserving of further scholarly exploration, but I will leave that exploration to others. That said, I routinely use the now-familiar set of initials LGBTIQ (lesbian, gay, bisexual, trans*, intersex and queer/questioning), in acknowledgement of the fact that they have become discursively inscribed within discussions of all things "queer", broadly understood. Exceptions are cited material that may be limited to only some of the initials (usually LGBT). My primary focus is, however, the L and the G, even if I necessarily end up including, in the discussion of state and market logics that I undertake in this book, another letter that is normally not part of the acronym (for it is, in fact, the norm): S, for "straight". Out of heteronorms grow homonorms.

Notes

1 See for example Donovan 2004; A. Prasad 2008; Badgett 2009, 2020; Barker 2012; Y. Joshi 2012; Bernstein and Taylor 2013; Barker and Monk 2015; Richardson-Self 2015.

2 I include Mexico in this country count even though there is, at the time of writing, no federal legalisation of same-sex marriage. Marriage is regulated by states and municipalities, not all of which have legalised same-sex marriage, but the matter has progressed incrementally, with all states, even those that have not legalised same-sex marriage, recognising same-sex marriages performed in other states. In 2015 the Supreme Court ruled that same-sex marriage bans were unconstitutional, and in December 2019 the government introduced a constitutional amendment that would legalise same-sex marriage nationwide. That amendment has not yet been passed at the time of writing, no doubt in part because the COVID-19 pandemic has resulted in many matters going on hold.

PART I

(Same-sex) marriage as institution

1

MARRIAGE AND FAMILY AS VALUE IN LIBERAL CAPITALIST SOCIETIES

If "family" is the foundational unit of our national economies and polities, it is also the foundational *metaphor* for the nation and by extension the state apparatus that gives the latter political identity, as well as a primary focus of international rights treaties and related public and private international law. Family-as-value permeates our social, cultural and economic relations to such an extent that it is considered natural rather than ideological (c.f. "gender"). Although political movements for sex equality since the late eighteenth century and more recently for LGBTIQ rights have introduced more egalitarian conceptualisations of marriage and family life, the basic ideological and structural function of family in heteropatriarchal relations of ruling and the justifying ideologies of nations has, in fact, changed very little. In this opening chapter, I will first consider "family", and its related heterosexual and gendered kinship concepts, as metaphor for the nation. In the second part of the chapter, following second-wave feminist analyses, I will discuss the functioning of marriage and the family in heteropatriarchal patterns of socioeconomic and cultural reproduction, including capitalist notions of welfare and associated socioeconomic stratification.

Nations and states as families

The family as fundamental value underpins the structures and rhetoric of nations, and the symbolic value of citizenship within them. Family is a key metaphor for national belonging (fatherland, motherland) and even communities of nations (family, brotherhood, kin) as well as for any type of relationship or grouping that one wishes to connote as synonymous with the types of affective, moral or cultural virtue that are the ideal-type of social relations. Moreover, just as families have heads, so do nation-states, and the use of "family metaphors to establish the marks of authority" has characterised the symbolism of leadership in Western political history (Jones 1993, 119).

Brian Duff has suggested that "[i]t was an argument over the political significance of parenthood that gave birth to liberal-democratic political theory", via John Locke's response to Robert Filmer's defence of the "omnipotent fatherhood" of the monarch (B. Duff 2010, 1). "Over these centuries" that followed Locke, Duff argues, "theorists, politicians, and citizens have repeatedly returned to parenthood as the central experience informing citizenship" (B. Duff 2010, 1). Although Duff does not decline "parent" in the masculine, the conversation over statehood and citizenship has largely concerned fatherhood, for, until very recently in modern history, women were not considered to possess the faculties permitting the mental development that would make of them full citizens.

Yet this modern conceptualisation of the family and its parenting functions as the bedrock of society, economy, polity and law is rooted in an ancient one. For Aristotle, the family was the fundamental grouping from which the polity grew, and the site of the ethical and intellectual development of citizens. It was a privately owned institution controlled by its male head, to whom wives, slaves and children were all subservient. Even if he noted that "half the free persons in a state are women", in the same section he stressed, citing a poet, that women were inferior to men and that "silence is a woman's glory" (Aristotle 350 BCE, Book One, online; and for feminist critiques, see e.g. Millett [1970]1978; and Okin 1979, ch. 4).

Aristotle's view was seized upon with gusto by many, indeed most, Enlightenment philosophers, who more generally drew inspiration from classical philosophy, and who saw in the "natural" sexual division of labour the proper foundations for a moral society. Even Rousseau, who was of a more Platonically *Republican* leaning in his distaste for private property (Plato 360 BCE), took a more Aristotelian turn in his desire to keep women firmly in their familial nurturing place. Thus, the same philosopher who famously and ironically stated in his *Discours sur l'origine et les fondements de l'inégalité parmi les hommes* that "the first man who, having enclosed a plot of land, took it into his head to say: This is mine, and found people who were simple enough to believe him, was the true founder of civil society" (Rousseau 1755, online, my translation), also famously stated, in Book V of *Émile*, that "If woman is made in order to please and be subjugated, then she ought to make herself pleasing to man rather than provoke him" (1782, online, my translation). He went on to argue at length that, being made different from men—having the primary purpose of producing and rearing the children of their husband, to whom they owe obedience and fidelity, and for whom they should be entertaining—women should also have a different education. The cultivation of Émile's female counterpart Sophie must be with the aim of developing this art of pleasing (music, languages, dance), rather than the art of governing and public life, which, according to Rousseau, would simply force women into being men, and in doing so "lead to the most intolerable abuses", subverting "the most tender sentiments of nature" (1782, online, my translation). Rousseauldian morality necessitates that Sophie devote her energies to the *petite patrie* (little fatherland/nation) that is productive of the "good" (male) citizens of the *grande patrie* (greater fatherland/nation).

Rousseau's imagined founder of civil society was thus also the founder of *familia*: that fundamental grouping within the enclosed "plot of land", where the business of production and reproduction went on. As French materialist feminist Christine Delphy reminds us in her foundational essay "L'ennemi principal" (the main enemy), first published in 1970, in a special issue of the French journal *Partisans* devoted to the theme of "Women's liberation":

> historically and etymologically the family is a unit of production ... *Familia* in Latin designates the collection of land, slaves, women/wives and children subjected to the power (then synonym of property) of the father of the family. (Delphy 1998a, 37, my translation)

Rousseau and his Enlightenment contemporaries got round the problem of equality within the modern polity by retaining the ancient definition of family and excluding women from citizenship, through a strict separation of the public and private spheres and relegation of women to the latter. His framing of the *petite patrie* and *grande patrie*, and of Émile's and Sophie's respective roles within them, makes explicit the relationship between *family* as social kinship unit and *nation* as extension of that unit, with the *father* as the head of both in a process of material and ideological reproduction.

Benedict Anderson's famous "imagined communities" in the modern political framing of the nation (1983) remain at their base "imagined extended families". Even if, in its foundational French and United Statian modern conceptualisations (1789 *Déclaration des Droits de l'Homme et du Citoyen*, 1776 Declaration of Independence), the nation is formed out of the collective political will of "the people", it remains founded on the ambitions of its founding *fathers*: the very term "Founding Fathers" is part of the national mythology of the United States. Moreover, "the people" has always been declined in the masculine. Even if women are now admitted fully fledged to the category, for "the people" to be "the people", its significant component remains men. Men-without-women can still arguably be discursively synonymous with "the people"—groups of men are certainly considered synonymous with groups of ordinary "people" (minus the "the"), but women-without-men almost never are.

In our modern polities, the state then becomes the Father of the national *familia* (or "people"), and the citizens' love of the Fatherland remains a positive value, often explicitly promoted by states. For example, "patriots" (a term derived from the same Latin root as *patrie*) are, in United Statian political discourse, those "good" citizens who love their country and all that is good about it, and will defend it in speech and action. Gary Johnson has argued that the language of kinship is a core feature of patriotic discourse, in that it cues "altruistic dispositions" among citizens, a metaphorical bond to a human grouping symbolically configured as family, and that it appeals to a "reciprocity-based duty that is created by the benefits one enjoys as a citizen of one's country" (Johnson 1987, 169). Although I disagree with Johnson's evolutionary-biologising, conservative and patriarchal view of social and political organisation, the configuration of nation-as-father to which the national family pledges loyalty and obedience continues to run through even our modern egalitarian capitalist democracies. In contrast, "nationalists" (a term derived from the Latin *natio*, meaning "birth"), are those "bad" citizens who exhibit a feeling of ethno-political superiority and a negative and exclusionary attitude to those who are considered not to be members of the national community.

In Latin America, the term *patria* takes on a broader meaning of cultural and political unity in the face of hegemonic Western powers: the expression *Patria grande* refers to a continental unity that has, historically and today, generally been deployed by the left. It has been associated in particular with revolutionary and anticolonial figures such as Simón Bolivar and José de San Martín.

Outside these particular political framings of patriotism which ostensibly cross political divides and unite "the people", often in the face of threats to that same "people", notions of *fatherland* and the hierarchical relation between men and women that such notions encapsulate are usually assumed to linger only within conservative or even far-right worldviews. The idea of fatherland (*Vaterland*) is no doubt most closely associated with Nazi ideology in the Anglo-world imaginary, but its origins as a celebration of the German nation and its associated state apparatus go back much further. (Likewise the German phrase *Kinder Küche Kirche* [children, kitchen and church], now enduringly associated with Nazi ideology, is believed to have first been pronounced by Kaiser Wilhelm II, the last King of Prussia, in the late nineteenth century.) The term *Vaterland* notably features in the German national anthem, which today is the third verse of the *Lied der Deutschen* (Song of the Germans), composed by Joseph Hadyn and first performed in 1797, with lyrics by the poet August Heinrich Hoffmann von Fallersleben added in 1841. Fallersleben was a proponent of German unification, which occurred following the Prussian victory in the Franco-Prussian war, in 1871. Thus, again, the idea of *patria* is associated with national unity and solidarity. The lyrics celebrated this nationalist zeal, but with the advent of Nazism the beginning of the first verse, "Deutschland, Deutschland über alles/ Über alles in der Welt" (Germany, Germany above all / Above all in the world), became indelibly associated with Nazism, which resulted in post-World War II German leader Konrad Adenauer officially dropping all but the third verse. Unfortunately, the retention of the idea of fatherland remained unproblematic for him. The verse goes as follows:

> Einigkeit und Recht und Freiheit (Unity and right and freedom)
> Für das deutsche Vaterland! (For the German Fatherland)
> Danach lasst uns alle streben (Towards these let us all strive)
> Brüderlich mit Herz und Hand! (Brotherly with heart and hand)

In 2018, this third verse of the anthem also came to pose a problem in a now-egalitarian Germany, with Kristin Rose-Möhring, the equal opportunity commissioner for Germany's Family Ministry, proposing that *Vaterland* be changed to

Heimatland (homeland) and "brotherly" be replaced with "courageously". In doing so, she followed a trend set in both Austria and Canada, which had already replaced masculinist language in their own anthems with gender-neutral terms—although the question is begged as to whether such a change will truly reflect a fundamental reconfiguration of the ideological apparatus of the nation-state, in Germany, Austria or Canada. The original language remains in the German anthem at the time of writing.

Even following their emancipation as citizens in formal terms, women have continued to be mobilised primarily as mothers or spouses of (future) citizens rather than autonomous agents. Some of the great male emancipators of women, such as Jules Ferry in early Third Republic France in the late nineteenth century, who opened up public secular schooling to girls and encouraged training of women as primary school teachers, or Kemal Atatürk in post-World War I Turkey, who granted Turkish women full citizenship, did so in the interests of the nation and its governing state far more than in the interests of the women themselves. The emancipated woman in these modern scenarios was as much mother and wife of the nation as the traditional *Kinder-Küche-Kirche* wife-and-mother of German imperial imaginings—or indeed Rousseau's subservient and designed-to-please wife of the modern citizen. Although the specific symbolism and role of the nation's mothers served a different political agenda for these more emancipationist figures of Ferry and Atatürk, it nonetheless remained a heavily masculinist one.

Ernest Renan, author of the famous *Qu'est-ce qu'une nation?* (what is a nation?), first delivered as a lecture at the Sorbonne in 1882, characterised the nation as formed out of the collective "moral consciousness" of a people who had together made sacrifices for that nation and thus developed a sense of solidarity (Renan 1882): in short, the patriots. For Renan, it is the memory of those sacrifices by our ancestors—those heroic "great men"—that are the bedrock of the nation: "the cult of the ancestors is the most legitimate of all; our ancestors [those "great men"] have made us what we are" (Renan 1882, part III, my translation). The father is the heroic ideal-type of the nation, whether it be the modernist democratic French or United Statian versions, or their authoritarian alter-ego of the Nazi *Vaterland.*

As concerns mothers and mother-symbolism, the idea of "motherland" has rarely, if ever, been deployed as a direct metaphor for the nation-state, national unity or citizens' presumed pride in their national belonging, but rather as a metaphor for the nurturing home-and-hearth of one's childhood. If men build nations and national consciousness through their real or imagined heroic acts, women's role is to *reproduce* them, both biologically and symbolically. In their introduction to one of the iconic feminist anthologies on women, nation and state, a work titled, as it happens, *Woman-Nation-State*, Floya Anthias and Nira Yuval-Davis noted that women "are a special focus of state concerns as a social category with a specific role (particularly human reproduction)" (Anthias and Yuval-Davis 1989, 6). As the "biological reproducers of members of ethnic collectivities" women become, by extension, "reproducers of the boundaries of ethnic/national groups" and guardians and transmitters of the collectivity's culture (Anthias and Yuval-Davis 1989, 7). Women's dress, behaviour and wifely and—especially—mothering activities become intensely important to the men in their communities and to ruling institutions (or revolutionary movements) at times of national (identity) crisis, whether real or perceived (Enloe 1990; *Moghadam 1994*; Yuval-Davis 2006). Women reproduce the nation, both biologically and symbolically, and transmit its values within the political economy of the family—but the nation does not "belong" to them (Meyer 2000).

The mothering of the nation thus has an inward, nurturing focus: mothering the nation is about consolidating its values and ensuring its cohesion and ongoing protection. Fathering the nation is about being tough and strong to the outside world. The "Mommy" versus "Daddy" framing in politics has been developed notably in relation to the Democrat-Republican divide in the US, and has been famously theorised by George Lakoff as "moral politics" (1996, 2002). Lakoff contrasts the conservative worldview—the Strict Father model—with the liberal (progressive) worldview—the Nurturant Parent model. In using this nomenclature, Lakoff gender-neutralises the Nurturant model, implying that the conservative worldview is strictly gendered while the liberal/progressive worldview is not. Lakoff's sleight-of-vocabulary is worrying in that it creates the impression that the left of politics is not gender-demarcated in its functioning and that the qualities of empathy, strong social ties and good communication, which he associates with the Nurturant Parent model, are not *also* typically associated with women and mothers. Moreover, Lakoff's half-gendered framing is not reproduced in US political commentary more broadly; the latter explicitly associates "Daddy" with the Republican Party and "Mommy" with the Democrats. What Lakoff does recognise, however, is that these are "two different forms of family-based morality" and that "what links them to politics is a common understanding of the nation as family, with the government as parent" (Lakoff 2002, 35).

Duff has suggested, however, that "when parenthood is imagined to summon a confidence in our political virtues, it often reveals profound insecurities" and that "when parenthood is thought to instill the openness to contingency and change appropriate to democratic political contest, it often produces unexpected fundamentalisms and stagnation" (B. Duff 2010, 3). Lee Edelman has further argued that US political discourse is framed around what he calls "reproductive futurism", in which "our children" not only inherit the social order we construct, but provide the ideological authorisation for its imposition. "[T]he [idealised fictional] Child", he writes, "has come to embody for us the telos of the social order and come to be seen as the one for whom that order is held in perpetual trust" (Edelman 2004, 11). He further notes that some gay men, lesbians and transgender people are "psychically invested" in this reproductive futurism, which he nonetheless sees as associated with "heteronormative mandates" (Edelman 2004, 17). The citizen-as-parent is to the imaginary child within its imaginary family what the government-as-parent is to the "imagined community" (family) (Benedict Anderson 1983) of the nation's citizens. It is a framing upon which is built the rhetoric of order, harmony, certainty, refuge—and investment in projecting one's ideas thereof into an imagined future—whether the rhetoric follows "Strict Father" or "Nurturing Parent/ Mother" lines, or any one of a number of hybrid variants thereof, including gay and lesbian ones. Further, we will see in Chapter 7 that "working families" has entered political discourse within discussions of wage justice and so-called "work-life balance" (as if working sat somewhere outside living, which makes it, symbolically speaking, a kind of repeated temporary death).

In fact, the logics and metaphors of family are so deeply ingrained, and extended so readily to national, subnational or political communities, that second-wave feminists have not hesitated to pick up the terminology, positing a "sisterhood" of flesh-and-blood women as a counter-metaphor to the "brotherhood" of abstracted-universalist "Man". Laudable, even revolutionary, as the gesture may seem—and certainly seemed in 1970, when the famous early-second-wave anthology *Sisterhood is Powerful* was published in the US (Morgan 1970; see also Morgan 1984, 2003)—the term is nonetheless problematic. "Brothers" have historically been, and continue to be today, political and moral actors within and across nations. Indeed, Lakoff's "moral politics" notwithstanding, the "fraternal" liberal-democratic model has largely supplanted the "paternal" pre-democratic/pre-mercantilist model, with accompanying privatisation of family life to fit a new individualisation of participation in the nation (Pateman 1988; Tetreault 1992). As Carole Pateman put it in her celebrated book *The Sexual Contract*,

> the two spheres of civil society [private and public] are interwoven in a very complex manner … The civil individual and the public realm appear universal only in relation to and in opposition to the private sphere, the natural foundation of civil life. (Pateman 1988, 113–14)

"Brothers" are lawmakers, history-makers, groundbreakers, revolutionaries—hence the appeal of a mirror-image of "sisterhood" to feminists. "Sisters", however, continue in wider society to carry the baggage of submission: to brothers and fathers within the family and to a religious authority outside it. Nurses came to be called "sister" precisely because the first hospitals in the Christian West, such as they were, were run by Churches, and Catholic women religious did the nursing. They did not, after all, have their "own" children to care for, and were moreover the only women allowed to work outside the domestic economies of wives, daughters and servants in mediæval times. Nurses only, in fact, stopped being called "sisters" relatively recently, when the greater professionialisation of nursing started to attract men into the field (although the latter remain a minority: around 15 per cent on average in Europe and the Americas [Boniol et al. 2019]). I am thus not convinced that feminist reclaiming of the terms "sister" and "sisterhood" as an expression of feminist solidarity and a would-be subversive riposte to "brother" and "brotherhood" succeeds in ridding the terms of this baggage of family and servitude.

Families as privatised yet state-regulated economies: gendered ordoliberalism?

The "different education" of Rousseau's Sophie, with a view to the realisation of a different "natural" purpose, has meant that for women, marriage and childbearing have enduringly been central to their sense of self-definition and to their social value. As Simone de Beauvoir put it in *The Second Sex*:

> To this day, most women are either married, have been married, are preparing to be married or suffer from not being married. It is in relation to marriage that single women are defined, whether they are frustrated, in revolt or even indifferent with regard to this institution. (Beauvoir 1949, vol. 2, 10, my translation)

Seventy years later, the same observation can still be made. Even if, as Beauvoir herself noted, the institution of marriage has become more egalitarian, it remains nonetheless the case that marriage "presents itself in a radically different manner for women and for men" (Beauvoir 1949, vol. 2, 11, my translation). Although in same-sex marriage the traditional heterosexual patterning does not obtain in the same way, we will see in subsequent chapters that there nonetheless remain significant gendered differences in women's and men's experiences on the one hand and in institutional expectations, commercial targeting and media framings on the other hand.

Carole Pateman has further argued that, notwithstanding the fact that "most of the reforms to marriage law demanded by feminists in the nineteenth century have now been enacted … the marriage contract diverges in significant respects from other contracts" (Pateman 1988, 163). Although there now exist in many countries legally binding marriage contracts for the regulation of ownership, distribution and inheritance of assets during the marriage and after its possible dissolution, there exists no legally binding contract for the regulation of personal relations and domestic and affective labour within the marriage. Pateman provides the example of domestic labour, which I paraphrase here to encompass same-sex marriage: a married couple cannot contract for one spouse to be paid by another spouse for her or his labour within the home (Pateman 1988, 165). Although Pateman was discussing heterosexual marriage and her and many other feminist analyses of domestic labour (e.g. Beauvoir 1949; Oakley 1974; Waring 1988) remain within a heterosexual frame, the issue of paid and unpaid domestic labour and its gendered and raced implications does not go away in same-sex couples. That said, as for other issues also affecting heterosexual couples, such as domestic violence (briefly discussed below), the question of domestic labour presents somewhat differently (see Chapter 8). Pateman also reminds us of the legally and economically idiosyncratic nature of a marriage contract by stressing that for it to exist, all that is necessary is an act of performative speech ("I do"), duly recorded in a signed register, plus the "consummation" of that act through sexual relations (Pateman 1988, 164), although even the latter is now not strictly necessary in most countries.

The singularity of the marriage contract and unregulated privatisation of relations within it results in a number of experiential and legal singularities, which generally operate to women's detriment within heterosexual marriage. Among other things, the family is the site in which the most grievous and violent oppression of women occur, and therein lies a profound contradiction in the international human rights system, which affords strong protections to "the family" (Universal Declaration of Human Rights, discussed at the end of this chapter and in Chapter 2). Even the Convention on the Elimination of All Forms of Discrimination Against Women (1979), produced following much international lobbying by feminists, unfortunately reproduces the "family" framing, even as it tweaks it to be more "egalitarian", with particular attention to access to health services related to reproduction and children and to welfare benefits. The far more radical Declaration on the Elimination of Violence Against Women (1994) explicitly acknowledges that the family is a key site of physical and psychological violence against women, although, not being a treaty, it unfortunately does not create legal obligations for UN member states.

Notwithstanding these developments, we seem to continue in a state of denial as to the systematicity of these oppressions, even in our more egalitarian times. For example, as I write these words in May 2020, political and news commentators, and unfortunately some academic commentators, around the world have expressed alarm at the sudden spike in domestic violence (DV) since COVID-19-related lockdowns began. Much of the commentary frames the increase in number and seriousness of DV attacks on women as somehow "caused" by the pandemic. For example, philosopher Dalia Nassar, during a discussion on Australian national radio inspired by Italian philosopher Giorgio Agamben's suggestions that the lockdown may be creating worse problems than the virus, opined that the lockdown was putting women's lives at risk because "they are stuck at home with abusive partners" (in ABC Radio National, *The Minefield*, 13 May 2020). She did not seem to consider that it was male entitlement and the social condoning thereof, which existed structurally and ideologically well prior to the pandemic, that was putting women's lives at risk. Comments such as these are, unfortunately, widespread, but have, fortunately, come in for trenchant criticism. Writing in *The Conversation* in mid-May, Emma Williamson, Nancy Lombard and Oona Brooks-Hay denounced the "unhelpful narrative" that framed recent spikes in DV killings as "COVID-19 murders" because

> it masks the reality that perpetrators are ordinary people. These men are not monsters; they have the veneer of respectability as your mate down the pub, the devoted dad or the family man next door … [The narrative] implies that we are in a situation that will dissipate after lockdown when, in reality, domestic violence and abuse existed before COVID-19 and will be there after it. In the middle of such a crisis, it is crucial that we continue to see the dynamics of domestic violence as both a pattern of abusive behaviours and a product of the unequal world we live in, rather than viewing it as a reaction to

> a specific event. All that does is make it harder for victims to be seen and to get the proper help and support they need. Worse, it shifts the blame from those who should be held accountable for the violent abuse of their partners. (Williamson, Lombard and Brooks-Hay 2020)

It is tempting to treat the issue of domestic violence, along with the institutionalised heterosexuality of marriage more generally, as a problem confined to heterosexuality and thus of limited relevance for same-sex couples. Yet domestic violence does exist in same-sex couples, and has attracted growing attention among academics and policymakers (see e.g. the contributions to Ristock 2011, some of which are referenced here). It is a troubling issue for lesbians in particular, as one would like to think that once the male oppressor is removed, the violence will disappear. It does not. However, it functions differently: if power and control remain central, the ways in which they operate within the relationship are less likely to be unidirectional and more closely bound up with the impact of (heterosexist) social institutions, including internalised lesbophobia (Kierrynn Davis and Glass 2011). The particular dynamics of violence within lesbian couples (and indeed gay male couples) thus both share and do not share aspects with intimate partner violence in heterosexual couples, but in both cases heteronormative social and economic institutions are a major factor impacting in domestic settings. In both cases, also, the singularity of the marriage/domestic partnership "contract" as it operates in the private/privatised sphere means that the dominant social-services approach to intimate partner violence relies on models of individual pathology rather than approaching it as a structural issue (Poon 2011). The structure in question remains heterosexist and privileges a dominant race-class narrative of conformity and deviance, to the extent that "healthy relationships" models used in prevention and training programmes, even those aimed at "queer" populations, still privilege heteronormative "white and middle-class nationalist agendas" of neoliberal societies (Holmes 2011, 227). Indeed, the obtaining of funding to run such programmes depends on a high degree of conformity to such narratives.

To return to the issue of "consummation", in rare cases, such as that of the UK, it is still possible to have an unconsummated marriage annulled, although interestingly, this ground for voiding a marriage is not available to same-sex couples there.[1] Although the reason for this British distinction is not made clear, it tends to foreground the ongoing ideological and legal weight given to the procreative function of heterosexual marriage. In France, it is not possible to void a marriage for non-consummation but it *is* possible if either partner is unable to have children. However, the process is legally cumbersome and it is not clear whether this possibility is open to same-sex couples, although I suspect it is unlikely. In most other countries, non-consummation or infertility are no longer grounds for annulment. As no-fault divorce is now readily available in many countries, and annulment, even where possible, is difficult outside situations of bigamy, false identity or close blood ties, the reason for going down the path of annulment rather than the generally less complicated path of divorce would appear to be primarily to do with either financial arrangements (which would be immediately cancelled at the time of annulment) or traditional customs. In France, for example, the Civil Code provides for annulment if there has been an error concerning the "essential qualities" of one of the spouses (Article 180), such that consent to the marriage could not have been given in good faith. A 2008 decision to annul a marriage between two people of North African background because the wife was not a virgin and had lied about it gave rise to considerable controversy because of its combined sexism and cultural relativism. The decision was overturned on appeal, as the court rightly deemed that virginity was not an "essential quality" (L.D. 2008), which left divorce as the only option should either spouse wish to dissolve the marriage.

What this discussion on marriage, consummation and grounds (or not) for annulment of course highlights is that who says marriage also, of course, says family—specifically, procreation, as the two remain closely linked. They are linked not only legally and in the public imaginary (including the same-sex imaginary), but also, importantly, economically.

As feminist economists have long argued, the framing of "family" as a discrete, private and homogeneous unit disappears not only the structural and systemic violence I discussed briefly above but also, and more broadly, differential access to power and resources. In particular, as feminist sociologists and economists have argued, it disappears different levels and types of labour required, among the individuals within the family, to maintain the family as a cohesive, *reproductive and productive* unit (e.g. Agarwal 1988; Waring 1988; Delphy [1970]1998a,b;), and the low value attached to caring labour (Folbre 1994, 2001; Folbre and Bittman 2004; Nelson 2013). State rhetoric and regulatory mechanisms for recognising and controlling the family have largely ignored it as a productive unit, focusing rather on its reproductive functions through the accumulation of assets, the production, ownership and rearing of children (including, importantly, inculcation of societal values), and the transmission of assets to those children in due course. The progressive legalisations of same-sex marriage in (neo)liberal capitalist democracies have done little to shift this discursive and regulatory framework.

I gave this section the perhaps provocative title of "gendered ordoliberalism", with a nod to the postwar German regulation of a so-called "social market economy", in which the state intervened to ensure "fair" competition in the capitalist market, along with provision of a social welfare safety net. The term, coined by Hero Moeller in 1950, has become synonymous with the postwar German political economy. I appropriate it here—and generalise its use beyond the German context—to highlight the fact that although the family is considered a private entity and economically self-sustaining, it is heavily regulated by the state, to keep it within acceptable norms and within state understandings of "fairness". The welfare system, of which the history and logic(s) are discussed in the next section, intervenes in quite similar ways as it does within the broader ordoliberal economy, to support the family when the government-regulated yet privatised "family market" proves insufficient to do so.

To take just one small example of the embedding of the logic of family, including in its egalitarian framings, within political systems and mechanisms of regulation: a tour of ministerial nomenclature and portfolios of governments reflects both constants and shifts within state thinking. Although the example may seem anecdotal, the discursive and structural configuration of government legislative and policy responsibilities tells us a great deal about how "family" and "gender", and their associated social and economic policies, are constructed in our polities. Until relatively recently, many, even most, governments maintained ministerial portfolios for *family*, to which matters of concern to women were often attached and to which welfare matters were always attached. Some governments even continue to contain such portfolios. In the fourth Merkel cabinet in Germany, Franziska Giffey is, at the time of writing in mid-2020, Minister for Family Affairs, Senior Citizens, Women and Youth, whereas in Taiwan, "social and family affairs administration" is part of the portfolio of the Minister for Health and Welfare, while there is no ministerial portfolio or sub-portfolio for "women", "gender" or "equality".[2] In Canada, the portfolio of Families, Children and Social Development (which, unusually, is held by a man rather than a woman, as women more often head up such "soft" ministerial portfolios pertaining to social welfare and disadvantage), is separate from the portfolio of Women and Gender Equality. Similarly, Sweden separates family and welfare matters, attached to the Ministry of Health and Social Affairs, from Gender Equality, which is a sub-portfolio of Employment, indicating that the primary or even only area in which "gender equality" is considered to be an issue in need of ongoing government intervention is the workforce. (Interestingly, and rather curiously, Sweden also has a Ministry for Democracy, a sub-portfolio—also curiously—of the Ministry for Culture. The site of the Ministry includes "human rights" in this sub-portfolio.)[3] In a number of other countries, children's and women's welfare are variously attached to social affairs, education, health or employment, and are often not cabinet ministries or are subministries: that is, they have lower status within the government. In the UK, the ministerial portfolio for "Women and Equalities" is, at the time of writing, bizarrely tacked on to the responsibilities of Elizabeth Truss, Secretary of State for International Trade, which makes it appear as somewhat of an afterthought. In yet other cases, "women's" ministerial portfolios have become replaced by "gender" or "equality" portfolios with the aim of including LGBTIQ issues, such as the Minister for Equality in the Australian state of Victoria. At the same time, who is *not* covered by the portfolio of "equality" can be as illuminating as who *is*. In Victoria, "equality" is in fact code for LGBTIQ, while "women" sit in the same ministerial portfolio as "Aboriginal Affairs".

Social stratification and welfare: the state as parent

Barbara Hopkins reminds us that "human beings in capitalist economies are dependent on all three sources of provision: market, family, and state" (Hopkins 2013, 97). These three sources do not exist independently of each other, and the forces shaping them are neither entirely material nor entirely ideological. They are also cultural—and indeed religious, for the former is informed by and imbricated with the latter to greater or lesser degrees (Winter 2006; see also, on the links between religious norms and the welfare state, Siaroff 1994; Avraham 2016). The ways in which they develop and interact will thus contain cultural components, which are co-constitutive, along with political and economic regimes, of specific national path dependencies. In all cases, however, notwithstanding national specificities, the national family emerges as an extension of the private family, the latter constituted as both primary locus of socialisation and provisioning, and feeder and consumer of the market.

If "parenthood is the central experience informing citizenship" (B. Duff 2010, 1), with the state as father to whom the citizens owe their obedience and loyalty, it is also at the core of the development of modern welfare systems, although the term "welfare state" is not used everywhere, and different terms have been used at different times in history. The contemporary welfare state is generally conceptualised as having its origins in the late nineteenth and twentieth centuries (Bismarck, Beveridge), although its origins go back further. In western medieval societies religious and guild communities supplied forms of welfare to members or to the needy, but the origin of the first "legal right to relief" in the modern West has been traced to English common law: the 1601 Poor Relief Act. Lorie Charlesworth has characterised the longstanding existence of this right as "largely forgotten, often denied and hence underestimated" (Charlesworth 2010, 2). Although poor relief and contemporary welfare do not operate, legally or structurally, in the same way, and the notorious 1834 Poor Law Amendment Act paved the way for the "pathologisation" of poverty (Charlesworth 2010, 5) that continues to this day, a legal framework for relief of material need was nonetheless in place from the beginning of the seventeenth century. Moreover, Derek Fraser has argued that even the Poor Law was not as uniformly detrimental to the poor as its popular image suggests, and the contemporary Beveridge welfare state remains in "uncomfortable harness" with it (D. Fraser 2019, 29). The "uncomfortable harness" in question is due to the original and continued tension between the pathologisation of "pauperism" and the both anterior and subsequent conceptualisation of the rights of the needy to relief—that is, of welfare as a moral duty and a social good.

Welfare states thus appear either alternatively or simultaneously as Nurturing Parent (the welfare-as-social-good model) or Strict Father (the welfare-as-punishment-for-pauperism model). In both cases the framing is invariably masculinist, even when terminology such as the "Mommy state" or the "Nanny state" is used by conservative oppositions to denigrate the "nurturing parent" side. From its beginnings, the "very project of the [modern] welfare state … has constituted the 'state subject' in a gendered way, that is as essentially male in its capacities and needs" (Anthias and Yuval-Davis 1989, 6). The worthy welfare recipient is the breadwinner head of Rousseau's *petite patrie*, whose worthiness is demonstrated, first, by his maleness, and second, by his desire to work, which has been somehow thwarted by circumstance. This logic was thrown into sharp relief in the context of the 2020 COVID-19 pandemic, with millions of employees worldwide laid off or stood down, and governments taking a variety of approaches to supporting them. In Australia, where government subsidies for struggling businesses and workers have been, if not perfect, at least much better than in many places, those subsidies have been accompanied by a government rhetoric concerning workers who lost their jobs through "no fault of their own", which "it made clear that the *already* unemployed were somehow at fault" (A. O'Brien 2020, online, italics in original). Similarly undeserving are those who do not conform to normative family models. In capitalist economies, lone mothers and their children are among the most likely to live below the poverty line, with that risk exacerbated along race lines in most cases. Particular difficulties are faced by lesbian sole parents, who conform to neither the model of affluent, dual-parent, self-sustaining families nor the expectations of "compulsory heterosexuality" (Rich 1980; Lapidus 2004).

In short, welfare legislation has been tied from the outset to conceptions of the national good, the survival of the (hetero-)nuclear family, and normative sex roles and sexuality, such that to qualify for welfare, one has needed to be perceived as morally acceptable and thus appropriately deserving. Social policy is thus core to the ongoing materiality of the subordination of women and other marginalised populations. It helps construct what counts as family as well as circumscribing who has access to welfare and other social services (MacKinnon 1989; O'Connor et al. 1999). Historically, women who had children outside marriage were long prohibited from access to many welfare programmes or when granted support, received less than widowed mothers. Today, single mothers, whatever their sexual orientation, continue to be stigmatised in media representations of them as "welfare queens" or rendered disposable in popular discourse (Hancock 2004; Taylor and Bloch 2018). They have even been dubbed "brides of the state" by neoliberals in particular, according to whom

> brides of the state are engaging in illegitimate rent-seeking behaviour, encouraged by benefits superior to the returns they could obtain in the market or in more traditional forms of marriage … The image of women "marrying the state" assumes that financial provision is a male function, whether undertaken by heads of households or by the welfare state. (Sawer 1996, 131)

As for gay and lesbian parents, their parental rights are still not recognised in all state social policy and welfare programmes, even where same-sex marriage is legal, or have lagged considerably behind marriage recognition (Bernstein and Harvey 2018; see also Chapter 8). Feminist welfare state analyses and intersectional feminist research further demonstrate, among other things, the ways in which class-based social regulatory processes are gendered and racialised (Quadagno 1994: Abramovitz 1988; Hancock 2004).

To return to the Rousseauldian analogy, the *grande patrie*, the state, ensures the unity and allegiance of all the *petites patries* through its provisioning system. Indeed, the French translation of "welfare state" is *état providence*: literally, the providence state, which puts the accent on the state as all-powerful provider of material well-being, as the original meaning of "providence" relates to God's acts of creation. Which leads us directly to France's supposed Bismarckian partner in welfare conservatism: Germany.

The first use of the term "welfare state" can be traced to progressive German philosophers of the 1840s (*Wohlfahrtsstaat*), although it was also, at that time and subsequently, used in a denigratory way to characterise the French state (Petersen and Petersen 2013, 39 ff.). In its early German statist framing, it became one component of the "perfect state": "[t]he perfect state was the state in which the three parts formed an inseparable unity: an eudemonic welfare state ('Wohlfahrtsstaat'), a state of law ('Rechtsstaat') and a cultural state ('Culturstaat')" (Petersen and Petersen 2013, 40). The term progressively gave way, however, to the idea of *Sozialstaat* (its framing post-1945), via the peculiarly Bismarckian conceptualisation of *Staatssozialismus*. In a newly unified Germany seeking to distance itself from both British industrial capitalist liberalism and the impact of French Revolutionary liberal egalitarianism, and to calm working class unrest expressed during and after the so-called "People's Spring" of 1848, *Staatssozialismus* became Bismarck's way to provide (male) workers with some social protection and thereby ensure their adherence to the state. The Bismarckian state was strongly authoritarian and informed by Christian morality: Bismarck himself famously referred to his welfare measures as "practical Christianity" (cited in Avraham 2016, 154). He also saw it as his moral duty as the God-entrusted patriarchal ruler to provide for the needy.

Welfare is considered to sit within the third stage of citizenship rights—social rights—as presented in T.H. Marshall's classic work on citizenship and social class (1950), the first two being civil rights then political rights. Feminist have taken Marshall to task for the Anglocentric (Siim 2002) and gender-blind (Orloff 1993; Walby 1994) aspects of his analysis. They have pointed out, among other things, that women had access to many social rights—largely through welfare provisioning but also through workplace regulation for female industrial workers—long before they obtained the right to vote in European countries, contrary to what was the case for men. Feminists have similarly criticised Gøsta Esping-Andersen's typology of "welfare capitalism" (1990): the conservative or Bismarckian (Franco-German) model, the liberal or Beveridge (Anglosphere) model and the social-democrat (Nordic) model (for examples of such critiques see J. Lewis 1997; Orloff 1993, 1997; Sainsbury 1994, 1996, 1999).

In any case, the neoliberal turn, exacerbated by the financial crisis of the late 2000s (Taylor-Gooby, Leruth and Chung 2017), begs the question of the extent to which the model remains applicable. In France, classified by Esping-Andersen in the "conservative" worker insurance-based welfare model, Romaric Godin has characterised president Macron as abandoning the previous government's social-policy tempering of neoliberalism in favour of a more aggressive neoliberal approach. Godin argues that Macron is using an authoritarian leadership style to push through measures that weaken or dismantle many aspects of its social protection system, in the face of a plural and vocal opposition (Godin 2019; see also Rouban 2018). (Such authoritarian leadership combined with aggressive neoliberalism is already in evidence in much of the Anglosphere, notably, at the time of writing, the US, the UK and Australia.)

As for social-democrat models, which are generally characterised positively as resisting the neoliberal turn quite well (e.g. Hänninen et al. 2019) and maintaining a relatively egalitarian and high level of welfare protection, this protection comes at a triple cost. First, the ideology of the work ethic is strong, because as even Esping-Andersen—who himself favours the "Nordic" social-democrat model—pointed out:

> … the enormous costs of maintaining a solidaristic, universalistic and de-commodifying welfare system means that it must minimize social problems and maximize revenue income. This is obviously best done with most people working, and the fewest possible living off social transfers. (Esping-Andersen 1990, ch. 1, Kindle edition)

Second, the image of Nordic countries as the most gender-equal in the world is often belied by the reality, not only in the tying of "gender equality" to both national and heterosexual norms but also in ongoing inequalities in family and working life and built in to the social insurance system (see, on Sweden, Martinsson, Griffin and Nygren 2016). Third, access to welfare is tied to national belonging and citizenship, legally (Sainsbury 2006), ideologically and structurally (V. Barker 2018), and institutionally (Eliassi 2015). Vanessa Barker, writing in the context of the so-called European refugee "crisis" of 2015, has suggested that this preservation comes at the price of "penal nationalism". Focusing on Sweden, that paradigmatic example of the Nordic social-democrat model, she argues that the social-democrat welfare regime is protected only by a securitarian logic that both penalises deviance from the national moral and class order and walls off the country from non-members of the national welfare community (V. Barker 2018). Similarly, Barzoo Eliassi, drawing on his research among Swedish social workers, argues that even though the Swedish welfare state "has served as an exceptional model for its extensive welfare policies based on social democratic ideas", social workers reproduce an institutional othering of immigrants accessing social services (Eliassi 2015, 554). He found that social workers tend to disproportionately attribute to "culture" the problems of those immigrants accessing Swedish welfare services.

Esping-Andersen's model has come under further critique in that it is not easily applicable to non-European contexts—or even some European ones, as a Mediterranean typology has also been considered as distinct from the Bismarckian one. The Mediterranean model is characterised both by the relatively recent entry of the main so-called Mediterranean (European) states (Portugal, Spain, Italy and Greece) to liberal-democratic capitalism and by their related historical and ongoing heavy reliance on non-state welfare through extended family networks, with low female labour-market participation and high domestic time-use disparities (Gálvez-Muñoz et al. 2011). Alan Siaroff (1994) has also noted the preponderant impact of Catholic and Orthodox Christian views in the gendered stratification of Mediterranean societies. At the same time, the Mediterranean states have until recently had a relatively high level of employment protection more consistent with the Bismarckian model.

As for Latin America, it shares with the Mediterranean model the Christian conservatism and associated familialist welfare networks, as well as, in many cases, the legacy of dictatorships, but the continent has in addition a varied legacy of colonialism and decolonialism and socialist or social-democrat revolutions or transformations that have both preceded and succeeded dictatorial regimes. In addition, the continent has historically experienced tensions between neoliberal capitalism (and associated national debt to the Global North) on the one hand, and moves towards some sort of state-funded egalitarianism on the other hand. The region nonetheless remains historically characterised by high levels of informal labour and low levels of state protection. Juliana Martínez Franzoni, drawing on the work of Filgueira (1998) and Rudra (2007), presents three clusters: state protectionist, which favours labour decommodification in the sense understood by Esping-Andersen and thus protects citizens from the market; state productivist, which has a high level of commodification and thus encourages citizens to enter the market; and non-state familialist. The first cluster, which includes Brazil and Mexico, is the most heterogeneous, and both of these countries' systems were typified as "dual" by Filgueira, while the second, which includes Argentina, discussed in Chapter 3, is the most homogeneous (Martínez Franzoni 2008; see also Barrientos 2004). Sonia Fleury (2017) suggests that in the Latin American context, social rights have been fragilised through a combined legacy of military dictatorships and neoliberal economic trends, with trade unions and state bureaucracies having become debilitated through the uneven process of democratisation (p. 3). She argues that in the Latin American context, the concept of citizenship is particularly pertinent to discussion of welfare regimes, as the sense of belonging to a national community and ensuing rights and obligations conferred by/towards the national state is not historically anchored in the same way as it is in more long-standing democratic capitalist polities. At the same time, as we saw above in the case of Sweden, "citizenship" is pertinent to both the framing and operation of welfare regimes even in more established nations.

Feminist critiques of Esping-Andersen's model have highlighted both the gendered socioeconomic stratification of welfare systems and the lack of attention, within masculinist analyses of welfare capitalism, to the fact that "the family has historically been the largest provider of welfare [in all types of regimes] and its importance in this regard shows no sign of decline" (J. Lewis 1997, 162). Without the family, the system cannot function. Moreover, the notion of labour commodification and decommodification on which Esping-Andersen's and subsequent analyses are based—including many of those applied to Latin America as discussed briefly above—is inadequate for analysing women's place within welfare capitalism and the impacts of welfare systems upon them (Orloff 1993; Siaroff 1994). Not only is women's labour in family-based production and reproduction largely invisibilised, but their capacity for labour-market participation is constrained and regulated by state and employer-based family and child welfare policies, as well as by various taxation and unemployment benefit regimes that attach to married couples and family units. Moreover, the development of the welfare state occurred at a time when women did not exist as independent political or economic beings, and the road to them becoming so has been slow. Among other things, laws restricting (hetero-)married women's employment and property rights remained on the statute books until the 1960s and even 1970s in many capitalist democracies.

The above-mentioned feminist critiques have largely centred on the material impacts on women's lives of the legal regulation of heterosexual marriage and family, including through social provisioning. The extent to which they remain relevant within lesbian and gay couples and families is less clear, and has to date been less extensively researched. That said, many of the above-discussed constraints on heterosexual women with children are also relevant to a significant extent for lesbians, both single and living in couples, who, first, are far more likely than gay men to be raising children, and second, are generally significantly poorer than both gay and straight men, as will be discussed later in this book. As concerns state policy, it can be argued that welfare legislation does not ask questions concerning the sexual orientation of the unemployed, the disabled or the parent, although it generally *does* ask questions concerning the marital status or the previous or current employment of the welfare recipient, and in most cases, the recipient's sex as well. In other words, the fundamental commonality between the hetero-married and the gay-married, and the hetero parents and the gay parents, is the impact of malestream familialist ideology underpinning not only the socioeconomic arrangements and impacts of welfare, but "the very project" of welfare capitalism itself as constitutive of political, social and economic actors and the relations between them.

Conclusion: family as (a) right

The family as absolute moral value and as the foundational structure of society is internationally benchmarked in what are considered to constitute the "international bill of rights": (Universal Declaration of Human Rights [UDHR], 1948; International Covenant on Civil and Political Rights [ICCPR], 1966; and International Covenant on Economic, Social and Cultural Rights (ICESCR), 1966), which draw heavily on Western understandings of rights and social organisation, as well as in the Convention on the Rights of the Child (CRC, 1989). The UDHR, which although technically not a treaty, unlike the other UN documents mentioned here, nonetheless derives directly from the UN Charter (1945) and carries significant moral weight. Its provisions, many, even most, of which are reproduced in other international and regional treaties, national constitutions and national laws, spell out very clearly the high value stakes represented by the family. It stipulates that the family is the "natural and fundamental group unit of society" and "entitled to protection by society and the State" (UDHR 1948, Article 16[3]). Article 10(1) of ICESCR, which Karel Vašák (1977) categorises as belonging to the "second generation" of human rights—economic, social and cultural rights, with a key focus on positive rights—extends this protection to the "widest possible protection and assistance" (Winter 2018b, 110). Thus, not only is the family ideologically constructed as belonging to the realm of *nature* rather than as a sociocultural phenomenon, and as constituting the basis and the core of all social organisation, it is also granted symbolic personhood in its *entitlement* to the "widest possible" protection and assistance. It is the only entity prior to the so-called "third generation" of human rights (Vašák 1977)—namely, collective developmental and self-determination rights—to be granted a *group right*.

This benchmarking of the family as a group entity in which inhere rights has been carried into the two core European rights documents—the European Convention on Human Rights (Council of Europe, 1950) and the European Union's Charter of Fundamental Rights (2000, attached to the Lisbon Treaty in 2007 to become an integral part of EU law from its application in 2009)—as well as into the two other regional human rights conventions: the American Convention on Human Rights (1969) and the African Charter on Human and People's Rights (1981). It is also encoded in a number of national constitutions. These documents all posit the family in UDHR terms, as the fundamental unit of society and as deserving of protection by the state. Existing human rights declarations that concern sexual orientation and gender identity reproduce this UN framing. It is to those documents that I will now turn in Chapter 2, followed by a discussion of how the issue of same-sex marriage and family has played out in regional human rights jurisdictions and how these rights understandings have been incorporated into state legislation and logics.

Notes

1 Information provided to the public by the UK government, accessed 21 May 2020. https://www.gov.uk/how-to-annul-marriage
2 https://www.taiwan.gov.tw/3866.php?xq_xCat=2, accessed 13 June 2020.
3 https://www.government.se/government-policy/democracy-and-human-rights/, accessed 13 June 2020.

2

FROM SUBVERSIVE CHALLENGE TO LIBERAL RIGHTS

The logical place to begin the discussion of the normalisation of same-sex marriage within a liberal equality-rights-justice paradigm is within international, European and Inter-American human rights instruments and regional human rights courts. Following that discussion, I will consider the mechanisms by which states appropriate the issue of same-sex marriage in their own national, political or indeed economic interest, as a prelude to the more specific case-study discussion in Chapter 3.

As noted in Chapter 1, Article 16(3) of the Universal Declaration of Human Rights (UDHR) foregrounds the family as the "natural and fundamental group unit of society". Paragraphs (1) and (2) of that same Article state that

(1)
Men and women of full age, without any limitation due to race, nationality or religion, have the right to marry and to found a family. They are entitled to equal rights as to marriage, during marriage and at its dissolution.

(2)
Marriage shall be entered into only with the free and full consent of the intending spouses (UN 1948).

Although the logic informing Article 16(1) was heterosexual (given that male homosexuality in particular was illegal in most UN signatory countries in 1948, including practically all of the Western ones), the Article does *not* state that the right only applies to men and women marrying *each other*, and is thus open to interpretation that any adult should have the right to marry any other adult. It is this open interpretation that LGBTIQ movements have privileged in pursuing rights claims to same-sex marriage.

The first international declaration to make this claim was the Declaration of Montreal (2006), issued at the close of what was branded as the "largest-ever international conference on LGBT issues" with 1,500 attendees from over one hundred countries, held from 26 to 29 July 2006 (Declaration of Montreal website). It was also the first international conference to focus explicitly on "LGBT" *human rights*, a concept that had slowly gained currency, including in institutional fora, since the creation of the International Gay and Lesbian Human Rights Commission (IGLHRC), now rebadged Outright Action International, in New York in 1990, and the lobbying of the UN by gay rights activists, such as in the case of *Toonen vs the State of Tasmania.* In 1991, Nicholas Toonen petitioned the UN Human Rights Committee (HRC) because he claimed that the Australian state of Tasmania, in its laws prohibiting homosexuality, breached the International Covenant on Civil and Political Rights. The HRC agreed, and its 1994 decision paved the way for a change of law in both Tasmania and in Australia nationally, as well as opening up a space in which UN institutional actors could take up the cause of LGBT(IQ) human rights. For example, in a statement to the fifty-eighth session of the Commission for Human Rights in 2002, the UN Special Rapporteur on Violence Against Women, Radhika Coomaraswamy, characterised the rights of persons who faced violence on the basis of their sexual orientation or gender identity as "the last frontier of human rights" (cited in SRVAW 2009, 38).

The 2006 Montreal Conference was held immediately prior to the first World Outgames, which came into existence following a split with the Gay Games. (The Outgames continue to have conferences attached to them, while the Gay Games do not: the last Gay Games to have associated conferences were held in Sydney, Australia in 2002.) The Declaration had been drafted prior to the conference by the two conference co-convenors, Joke Swiebel (Dutch Member of the European Parliament 1999–2004) and Robert Wintemute (Professor of Human Rights Law, Kings College London), and approved unanimously by the 37-member conference committee. The Declaration, which included claims to the right to marry and found families (including "every option" for parenthood), was an important step along the road to the establishment of LGBT(IQ) rights as part of the core business to which the UN now needed to turn its attention. The keynote speaker at the Montreal conference was Louise Arbour, a native of Montreal and then UN High Commissioner for Human Rights, who was instrumental in progressing the LGBT (IQ) rights agenda at the level of the UN Human Rights Council.

Some three and a half months after the Montreal conference, independently of the conference itself but as part of the same expansion of the "human rights" frame on LGBT(IQ) issues, the International Commission of Jurists, the International Service for Human Rights and other international human rights experts met at Gadjah Mada University, Yogyakarta on the Indonesian island of Java, to produce the "The Yogyakarta Principles: Principles on the application of international human rights law in relation to sexual orientation and gender identity". They were launched at the UN Human Rights Council on 26 March 2007, and presented at a UN event in New York, co-sponsored by Argentina, Brazil, and Uruguay, on 7 November 2007. Principle 24 concerns "the right to found a family" and non-discrimination against any family "on the basis of the sexual orientation or gender identity of any of its members" (Yogyakarta Principles, 2007). Even though the document stops short of setting out an explicit right to marry, limiting itself to a basic equality provision in those "States that recognise same-sex marriages or registered partnerships" (Article 24[E]), it has, along with the Montreal Declaration and the UDHR, ICCPR and ICESCR, become the standard for rights on the basis of sexual orientation and gender identity (now commonly abbreviated as SOGI within LGBTIQ human rights fora).

On 18 December 2008, the first-ever SOGI rights declaration by states to be made within a UN forum was presented to the UN General Assembly, read by Argentina. This declaration was at the initiative of France and the Netherlands, and was endorsed by 66 member states (not including the US). The following day, however, Syria read a counter-declaration initiated by the Organisation of the Islamic Conference. The first UN resolution on SOGI rights came three years later, adopted in 2011 by a slim majority (including the US this time) at the Human Rights Council. Acting on this resolution, the Office of the High Commissioner for Human Rights prepared the UN's first report on "Discriminatory laws and practices and acts of violence against individuals based on their sexual orientation and gender identity" (UNHRC 2011).

However, there is to this day no international treaty on SOGI human rights, and the only regional treaty that explicitly mentions them at the of writing is Article 21 of the European Union's Charter of Fundamental Rights (2000), incorporated into the Treaty of Lisbon in 2007 to become part of EU law (from the time of the Treaty's entering into force at the beginning of 2009). The Article is a basic negative-rights statement: prohibition of discrimination on a number of grounds, which include sexual orientation.

Nor is there any international human rights court that LGBTIQ rights advocacy groups or individuals can petition. They have thus pursued the matter of same-sex marriage at the level of regional commissions and courts, which have also on occasion been petitioned by states as well:

- the European Court of Human Rights (ECtHR) of the Council of Europe (CoE): an international organisation with 47 member states which is separate from the European Union, and which is the body to which are referred matters arising under the European Convention on Human Rights (1950);
- the European Court of Justice (ECJ), part of the Court of Justice of the European Union (CJEU), which advises and rules on EU law as encoded in its core treaties: Treaty on European Union (TEU, originally the Treaty of Maastricht, 1992) and Treaty on the Functioniong of the European Union (TFEU, originally the Treaty of Rome, 1957), updated and grouped together under the 2007 Lisbon Treaty, which supersedes earlier treaties. The 2000 Charter of Fundamental Rights is part of this body of law since 2009, as indicated above;
- the Inter-American Commission and Court of Human Rights (IACHR and IACtHR), set up in 1979 to deal with matters arising under the American Convention on Human Rights (1969, effective 1978) of the Organisation of American States.

There are also an African Commission on Human and People's Rights and a Court of Justice and Human and People's Rights of the African Union, which deal among other things with matters arising from the African Charter of Human and People's Rights, but these institutions have not to date been petitioned in matters relating to same-sex unions and families. It has been suggested that in the current political climate on the African continent, such an action could be counterproductive, with a high risk of decisions that would reinforce discriminations rather than remove them (Ibrahim 2015). Even slimmer prospects of success are offered by the Cairo Declaration on Human Rights in Islam (CDHRI) adopted in 1990 by the member states of the Organisation of Islamic Cooperation (formerly Conference) (OIC), and based on sharia law. As for (Southeast) Asia, three years after ASEAN set up its Intergovernmental Commission on Human Rights (AICHR) in 2009, it adopted a much-criticised Human Rights Declaration (ADHR, 2012), which reproduces some of the cultural-relativist provisions and concessions to national sovereignty contained in the earlier Bangkok Declaration produced by Asian states in the lead up to the 1993 World Conference on Human Rights held in Vienna. A number of national, international and regional civil society organisations denounced the ADHR as "a declaration of government powers disguised as a declaration of human rights" (Aliansi Masyarakat Adat Nusantara et al. 2012; see also Gerber 2012; Renshaw 2013; Duxbury and Tan 2019). The setting up of an Asia-Pacific Human Rights Court has been mooted but has not materialised, even in preparatory stages, at the time of writing.

The Council of Europe and ECtHR

Although the ECtHR has been petitioned on same-sex marriage, it unequivocally ruled in 2016, in the case of *Chapin and Charpentier v. France* (brought in 2007), that marriage was a matter for states to decide and that the ECtHR had no jurisdiction in this matter. (The applicants had married in the Bordeaux suburb of Bègles 2004, in a high-profile ceremony—the nation's first—performed by Greens Mayor and gay marriage advocate Noël Mamère, but the then illegal marriage was rapidly annulled by a Bordeaux court.) In so ruling, it referenced a number of previous decisions along similar lines and reiterated that Article 12 of the Convention ("Men and women of marriageable age have the right to marry and to found a family") could not be interpreted as opening marriage rights to same-sex couples, for the rest of the sentence in this article reads "according to the national laws governing the exercise of this right" (ECtHR 2016). It thus ruled that Article 12 "does not impose an obligation on the Contracting States to grant same-sex couples access to marriage", and that the Court had "repeatedly held that marriage confers a special status on those who enter into it. The exercise of the right to marry is protected by Article 12 of the Convention and gives rise to social, personal and legal consequences" (ECtHR 2016, para 106).

Perhaps most importantly as concerns the case for same-sex marriage, the Court appeared to consider access to civil unions such as the French PaCS (Pacte Civil de Solidarité) to be a good enough alternative for homosexual couples:

> Nor can a right to same-sex marriage be derived from Article 14 [non-discrimination] taken in conjunction with Article 8 [respect for private and family life]. Where a State chooses to provide same-sex couples with an alternative means of legal recognition, it enjoys a certain margin of appreciation as regards the exact status conferred. (ECtHR 2016, para 106)

Of course, and ironically, by the time the ECtHR had ruled in the *Chapin and Charpentier* case, same-sex marriage had already been legal in France for three years, which indicates the heavy caseload of the ECtHR, resulting in a years-long time lag before rulings are handed down.

As concerns adoption by same-sex couples, an Austrian lesbian couple petitioned the Court, also in 2007, and also under Articles 14 and 8 of the ECHR (ECtHR 2013). In its 2013 ruling, the Court recognised that "the relationship of a cohabiting same-sex couple living in a stable de facto relationship falls within the notion of 'family life' just as the relationship of a different-sex couple in the same situation would" (ECtHR 2013, para. 95). In doing so, it referenced a previous admissibility judgment (*Gas and Dubois v. France*)—that is, a ruling on whether or not a case could proceed to hearing by the Court under the terms of the ECHR. In that earlier ruling, the Court found that the relationship between two lesbians in a civil partnership (the French PaCS) and the child borne by one of them via assisted reproduction constituted "family life" (ECtHR 2012, 2013). However, in the case of *Gas and Dubois*, the Court finally ruled against the applicant in 2012, because under French law, second-parent (non-biological parent) adoption was not open to unmarried heterosexual couples either at that time (ECtHR 2012). Thus, national law prevailed because there was no discrimination in this instance between heterosexual and homosexual couples. In contrast, under Austrian law, second-parent adoption was allowable for heterosexual partners of biological parents in unmarried couples; it is also possible for single homosexuals. The Court thus found there to be discrimination; moreover, it found the Austrian law to be "incoherent" and judged that the Austrian courts had not properly considered the circumstances (ECtHR 2013).

Apart from the primacy given to national law in ECtHR cases, a significant dissuasive element is the cost for individuals of petitioning the Court, and most cases do not get as far as the ECtHR for this reason. Normally, the ECtHR is a last resort once all national juridical avenues have been exhausted. Thus, Sue Wilkinson and Celia Kitzinger, who had brought a case against the UK government in 2006 for not recognising their legal Canadian same-sex marriage, decided not to pursue the case at the ECtHR due to lack of funds (Winter 2018a).

The European Union and the CJEU

The purpose of the Court of Justice of the European Union (CJEU) is to interpret EU law and ensure its uniform application across and between member states; this work includes resolving conflicts between EU institutions and national governments. As the EU, including its legal framework, has always been a work in progress, the CJEU has been referred to as an "activist" court (Dawson, De Witte and Muir 2013; Craig and De Búrca 2015). Its case law has contributed significantly to constitutionalising EU law (Björnsson and Shany 2014), rendering the aspirational statement of "ever closer union" encoded in the EU treaties a more coherent legal reality. Given that the EU's *raison d'être* and ongoing primary purpose has always been economic, based on the "four freedoms" of movement of goods, capital, services and labour within the Union, the majority of the CJEU's work has concerned areas such as trade, agriculture, competition law, workplace law and so on. However, as the EU has progressed from being solely an economic entity to becoming a more fully developed political entity and a values actor within its territory and beyond, the CJEU's work has gradually expanded to include the area of fundamental rights, even before the CFR was formally incorporated into EU law through the Treaty of Lisbon (Muir 2013).

The CJEU comprises two courts: the European Court of Justice (ECJ), which handles requests for preliminary rulings from national courts, as well as certain actions for annulment and appeals; and the General Court, which rules on actions for annulment brought by individuals, companies and, in some cases, EU governments. Although individuals and private companies may petition the CJEU directly through its General Court, they can only do so in the case of damage to them brought about by the actions or inaction of an EU institution. In the overwhelming majority of cases concerning the rights of individuals, the matter is referred to the ECJ by national governments.

In international discussions on LGBTIQ rights more generally and same-sex marriage in particular, the EU has a particular status. It is the world's only supranational entity (notwithstanding ongoing tensions between intergovernmentalism and federalism in the EU's ever-developing structure), and as noted above, its body of law includes a basic non-discrimination provision on the basis of sexual orientation (Article 21[1] of the Charter of Fundamental Rights [CFR]), the only such law in the international arena to date. (Article 21 is silent on gender identity, but is increasingly interpreted to include it, and the ECJ has ruled in a number of cases involving access for transgender persons to pensions and employment protections.) Notwithstanding Article 21, and notwithstanding the ECJ's aforementioned "activist" credentials, it has nonetheless tended to take a similar stance to the ECtHR in the area of same-sex marriage and adoption in that recognition of marital or family status and adoption rights remain the province of national legislation. States thus maintain a right to decide who can get married and who can adopt.

However, in 2018 the ECJ ruled on what has been perceived as a landmark case. It concerned recognition by a member state, where same-sex marriage is not legal, of a marriage of a binational same-sex couple contracted in a member state where same-sex marriage *is* legal. The matter was referred to the ECJ by the Constitutional Court of Romania, concerning the right of residency of Robert Clabourn Hamilton, a US citizen, who married Romanian-American binational Relu Adrian Coman in Brussels in 2010. The matter concerned Hamilton's right, as Coman's spouse, to reside in Romania for a period of longer than three months. The decision hinged on the ECJ's interpretation of one of the EU's abovementioned "four freedoms" that are core to its values and identity: that of movement of people. Article 21 of the TFEU (not to be confused with Article 21 of the CFR) concerns the right of free movement of EU citizens, as does Directive 2004/38/EC of the European Parliament and Council "on the right of citizens of the Union and their family members to move and reside freely within the territory of the Member States". The ECJ's interpretation of the word "spouse" in this second document was also crucial: the court ruled that the Directive did not specify that "spouse" referred explicitly to heterosexual marriages. The provisions on non-discrimination and respect for private and family life of the Charter of Fundamental Rights were referenced as well.

In ruling in favour of Hamilton's right of residency in Romania as Coman's spouse, the ECJ nonetheless concluded that

> the obligation for a Member State to recognise a marriage between persons of the same sex concluded in another Member State in accordance with the law of that state, for the sole purpose of granting a derived right of residence to a third-country national, does not undermine the institution of marriage in the first Member State, which is defined by national law and … falls within the competence of the Member States. Such recognition does not require that Member State to provide, in its national law, for the institution of marriage between persons of the same sex. (ECJ 2018, paras 45 and 46)

The Court thus recognised *both* the marital and residential rights of the binational, same-sex, legally married couple *and* the right of the country of residence to maintain its sovereign right to legislate on marriage.

The decision was nonetheless hailed by some commentators as "a landmark ruling of great constitutional importance which has the potential of changing the legal landscape for the recognition of same-sex relationships within the EU", as Alina Tryfonidou put it, writing on the EU Law Blog a couple of weeks after the decision. She further remarked on the shift in ECJ's position over 15 years, and on the symbolic importance of the ruling in that "the EU's supreme court made it clear that it considers same-sex marriages as equal to opposite-sex marriages" (Tryfonidou 2018, online). Other commentators were less glowing, pointing out that the ECJ ruling had no impact on state legislatures and excluded all same-sex couples who did not get married in the EU or indeed did not get married at all, thus favouring the marriage institution (Neidhardt 2018).

Interestingly, the Romanian gay rights organisation that had brought the case against the Romanian state alongside the Coman-Hamilton couple is called "Accept", which is indicative of the sort of vocabulary that civil society actors have used in their incrementalist approach to changing attitudes and laws. The framing of "acceptance" has generally been a precursor to the more "hard-law" frame of "rights" and "equality" and is indicative of the political context in Romania, which is in the dual position of being marginal in the EU socioeconomic context (its second-poorest country), as well as its political one. Among other things, it is one of the most corrupt countries in the EU and has come under censure for refusing travel rights to former anti-corruption prosecutor Laura Codruta Kövesi, whose appointment as the EU's first Chief Prosecutor was confirmed by the European Parliament on 17 October 2019. It is also the home of the EU's largest Roma population: the most racialised and marginalised ethnic Europeans. On LGBTIQ rights, Romania was ranked fourth-last in the EU by ILGA-Europe in 2019, ahead of, in decreasing order, Bulgaria, Poland and Latvia (ILGA-Europe 2019).

The Romanian backlash was significant but ultimately unsuccessful. A citizens' petition called for the Romanian government to organise a referendum to change the Constitution, limiting marriage to heterosexuals. The Coalition for Family obtained signatures of 3 million Romanians to support the initiative, which was also supported by the Orthodox Church. Despite representations to the Romanian government by MEPs (members of the European parliament) urging it not to proceed with such a referendum, it went ahead in October, 2018. A strong NO campaign to boycott the vote appeared to have had some success, as only 20.4 per cent of eligible Romanian voters cast their vote, falling well below the 30 per cent threshold necessary to validate the referendum (Hie 2018). The status quo thus continues to obtain, but the Coman decision may perform the quiet work of juridical incrementalism that has been successful elsewhere (see e.g. Smith 2018).

The IACtHR

As for Latin America, the American Convention on Human Rights, adopted in 1969 in San José, Costa Rica, makes no mention of sexual orientation, and only 23 of the 35 members of the Organisation of American States (OAS) are active parties to it. The Convention nonetheless spurred the creation of two human rights bodies within the OAS: the Inter-American Commission on Human Rights (IACHR) and the Inter-American Court of Human Rights (IACtHR). In May 2016, the IACtHR was petitioned by the Republic of Costa Rica on the issue of same-sex marriage (along with the issue of gender identity). Costa Rica gave as its reason for petitioning the Court the great diversity of situations in the countries covered by the Inter-American human rights system, and thus sought a ruling as a way of setting an Inter-American standard to which OAS member states would be obliged to conform (IACtHR/CIDH 2017, 4). The Court handed down its advisory opinion on 24 November 2017 (rendered public on 9 January 2018), affirming the right to change gender identity and stating that

> States must ensure full access to all the mechanisms that exist in their domestic laws, including the right to marriage, to ensure the protection of the rights of families formed by same-sex couples, without discrimination in relation to those that are formed by heterosexual couples. (IACtHR/CIDH 2017, 88, official translation)

In doing so, it explicitly referenced the Yogyakarta Principles, several times. It also explicitly applied the pro persona principle (also called pro homine principle) that it has generalised in Latin American human rights law (Pinto 1997; Rodiles 2016; Rodarte Berbera 2017), and affirmed that "at the current stage of development of international law, the fundamental principle of equality and non-discrimination has entered the domain of *jus cogens*" (that is, law from which no derogation is permitted) (IACtHR/CIDH 2017, 32, para. 61, my translation). However, the Court has also come under fire for its zealousness in making frequent *jus cogens* determinations (Rodiles 2016, 161 ff.).

The pro persona principle, which is derived from jurisprudence in the ECtHR, has exerted a particularly strong influence in Latin America (Rodiles 2016, 161). It is

> a hermeneutic criterion that informs all human rights law, in accordance with which one must have recourse to the most comprehensive norm, or the most extensive interpretation, where recognition of protected rights is concerned, and, conversely, the most restrictive norm or interpretation when it is a matter of establishing permanent restrictions to the exercise of rights or their extraordinary suspension. (Pinto 1997, 163, my translation)

The principle has been invoked by both state courts and the IACtHR with particular reference to Article 29 of the American Convention on Human Rights, which prohibits states from introducing any measures that may restrict the exercise of rights protected by the Convention and other human rights instruments. In its advisory opinion on same-sex marriage, the Court applied this principle to an expansive definition of "family" as protected by the American Convention, noting that none of the norms established by that Convention "contained a strict definition of what should be understood by 'family'" (IACtHR/CIDH 2017, 73, para. 174, my translation). The Convention's Article 17 on the family very closely parallel's Article 16 of the UDHR.

The IACtHR has been seen as proactive in establishing human rights norms "in a region with a poor human rights record" (Rodiles 2016, 161), not only in applying the pro persona principle but also in exercising a "conventionality control", that is, "demanding that national judges apply the American Convention over domestic legislation as interpreted by the Court", which, it has been argued, "positions the Inter-American Court as a kind of inter-American constitutional court" (Dulitzky 2019, 48)—cf. the constitutionalising role of the CJEU, discussed above. Through these approaches, the IACtHR has also benchmarked human rights norms during a period of post-dictatorship constitutional transformations in

Latin America, sometimes called new constitutionalism (García-Sayán 2011; Nolte and Schilling-Vacaflor 2012). However, the human rights norms ushered in during processes of post-dictatorship constitutional changes have been approached with some caution as to their applicability. First, their constitutionalisation within individual states has been seen as overly aspirational, setting out "shopping lists" of desirable rights without effective means to make them a reality (Nolte and Schilling-Vacaflor 2012, ch. 1). Second, the global new constitutionalism processes of which the Latin American transformations have been a significant part, corresponding to a supposed "left turn" there, have developed during a period of neoliberal economic and ideological expansion, which further begs the question of the enforceability of rights protections in a context of significant socioeconomic inequality (Gill and Cutler 2014; Falleti and Parrado 2017; see also Chapter 3 on the "Pink Tide").

The then Costa Rican president, Luis Guillermo Solís, had referred the matter to the IACtHR to provide legal and moral weight to a push for legalisation in Costa Rica, which he supported, notwithstanding strong anti-gay-marriage opposition. At the time the IACtHR decision was made public, in January 2018, Costa Rica was in the lead up to its presidential and legislative elections. LGBTIQ rights were a key issue in the campaign, and the second-round runoff in April delivered a resounding victory to the progressive Carlos Alvarado Quesada, whose vice-president Epsy Campbell became "the first woman of African descent to hold such a post anywhere in continental America" (Zaglul 2018). A few months later, in August, the country's Supreme Court aligned with the IACtHR decision in ruling the existing ban on same-sex marriage to be unconstitutional, and would automatically cease to legally exist in 18 months, even if no legislative action were taken (Sala Constitucional de la Corte Suprema de Justicia de Costa Rica 2018). Same-sex marriage became legal in Costa Rica on 26 May 2020.

States and same-sex marriage

The movement towards a normative human rights approach to same-sex marriage on an international or regional level has worked in tandem with nationally focused campaigns and political strategies. Whatever the motivations of those campaigning for same-sex marriage, states have invariably used its legalisation to position themselves as progressive, inclusive and just, and as moving with the times and "the people" as they have incrementally incorporated same-sex unions into the national institutional order. As Jan Duyvendak put it in relation to the Netherlands, "success" in achieving LGBTIQ rights outcomes

> often depends on how our agenda fits into a broader one—not necessarily transforming the social mainstream but fitting in, sometimes even reinforcing its main characteristics … [I]n the case of the Netherlands, the first country to open marriage to same-sex couples … acceptance of homosexuality has become a defining feature of the Dutch national self-image. (Duyvendak 2016, 289)

The Netherlands case is far from unique: there has in fact been a marked congruence among government positions in support of same-sex marriage, regardless of the political leanings of the governing party or the political system in place in each country, and notwithstanding some significant country-specific rhetorical framings that have to do with the political and cultural history of each country, as we will see in Chapter 3.

There are three main ways in which this national branding exercise is evident. First, governments have needed to assert their authority in the face of opposition to same-sex marriage (sometimes from within their own parties), by embedding it within a narrative of the nation and its history, around which all true patriots can rally. Same-sex marriage becomes a logical—almost inevitable—next chapter in that history, one that moves the national project further forward towards realisation of its full potential. Some version of this narrative has been present in all cases, but it has been particularly striking in countries where the debate over same-sex marriage has become imbricated with a contest over the values underpinning the national project as the nation advances into Big History, and the ultimate coherency of that project. In these cases, the debate over same-sex marriage has become a debate over the very identity of the nation. This has been the case, for example, in France, South Africa, Argentina and Ireland.

Two main strategies are used to demonise the opposition to same-sex marriage. First, governments have positioned themselves as promoting a "modern" and "inclusive" understanding of "family" (Lakoff's "nurturant" model) in opposition to the retrograde and patriarchal logic of (usually Christian) conservatives. Second, they have positioned themselves as being in lockstep with "public opinion" or "community standards", simultaneously presenting themselves as representing a majority stance while marginalising anti-gay-marriage campaigns as out-of-touch, insignificant and/or extremist minorities. Government responses to the deployment of ideas of religious morality have been particularly interesting in that they have used their support for same-sex marriage as a means of re-affirming liberal-democratic secular values in the face of the resurgence of fundamentalisms, while at the same time contextualising their responses within the political history and mood in their country. For example, in France, where Christian-fundamentalist oppositions to same-sex marriage were strident and in some cases violent, as was witnessed through the demonstrations of La Manif pour Tous ("demo for all", a play on words on "le mariage pour tous": marriage for all), the state reaffirmed the values of the secular Republic (Winter 2014, 2018b). In Ireland, the debate was informed by competing understandings of the role of Catholicism in the contemporary world in general and in constitutionally Catholic Ireland in particular (Winter 2018a). In the UK and Australia, conservative governments used their liberal-inclusive understanding of "family values" to simultaneously placate their own constituency and marginalise fundamentalist opponents (both Christian and Muslim). And so on.

A second important way in which governments have associated same-sex marriage with the national self-image has been to reaffirm the importance of marriage and family as the bedrock of the national community (national family), as that *natural and fundamental group unit* upon which the nation is built. As we saw in Chapter 1, the institutional and economic apparatus of marriage and filiation, which gives the family material and legal form, is the microcosm of the institutional and economic apparatus of the state, which gives the nation material and legal form. Single-parent families are still constructed, rhetorically, legally and economically, as unrealised or diminished in relation to the nuclear family of couple-plus-children. The couple as the nucleus of the family is both economically and morally necessary to ensure survival of the system. If governments were disinclined in the first instance to give same-sex partnerships the same status as heterosexual marriage, for fear, among other things, of undermining the marriage institution, they later came to see same-sex marriage as *preserving* rather than undermining that institution. This was famously the case of then Conservative Prime Minister David Cameron in the UK, who stated in 2011 that he supported same-sex marriage because family constituted "the ties that bind us" and that he thus did so not *despite* being a conservative but *because* he was a conservative (Cameron 2011; see also Winter 2014; Barker 2015). Some years later, in 2017, then Australian Prime Minister Malcolm Turnbull cited Cameron's words during a parliamentary debate on same-sex marriage, thus explicitly identifying himself with the moderates in his party (Liberal Party—the main conservative party in Australia) just as Cameron had done, while at the same time inscribing gay marriage within a socially conservative agenda (Winter 2018a and b).

The third aspect to the national branding exercise is the need for political leaders to align same-sex marriage with the values and traditions of *their own political party*, while not detracting from the broader national(ist) framing. In this way, same-sex marriage becomes a value-add for the party in question: a means of shoring up its political capital and hopefully, attracting more votes from the electorate. Typically, if same-sex marriage is inscribed within the Big History of the nation, the party is framed as representative of that nation: its values, its political traditions, its emblems.

Yet, paradoxically, even as they position themselves as values leaders in the area of same-sex marriage, governments have generally followed public opinion in this area rather than necessarily seeking to shape it, and have invariably adopted an incrementalist approach. This is the case for most issues considered to be matters of morality, notably women's reproductive rights and homosexual rights, where governments have tended to advance cautiously—even timidly. Parliaments in a number of countries, notably albeit not solely in the Anglosphere, have often used free votes or "conscience votes" rather than party-line votes when these issues arise, as both support and opposition on such "moral" issues tend to cross party lines. For example, same-sex civil unions and/or marriage in the UK, Northern Ireland, Australia, Canada, New Zealand and Germany were passed by a free parliamentary vote.

The cases of Australia and Germany are emblematic: neither government moved on same-sex marriage until it faced a groundswell of public opinion, fuelled by legalisation in comparable democracies (Canada, New Zealand, the UK, the US, and Ireland as concerns Australia, and practically every other country in Western Europe as concerns Germany). Governments have tended to move on the issue when there is strong enough middle-class dominant-culture civil society support, and usually when this support broadens beyond LGBTIQ movements. In other words, government support for the legalisation of same-sex marriage is as much if not more pragmatic as it is ideological. Where ideology has come into play, against the tide of public opinion, it has usually taken the form of strong state *opposition* to legalisation, as seen very strongly under the Howard and Abbott hard-right Liberal governments in Australia—and even, paradoxically, the centre-left Gillard government, but for different ideological reasons. Similar trenchant government opposition characterised various state administrations in the US prior to the 2015 Supreme Court decision in *Obergefell v. Hodges*. Other state oppositions to same-sex marriage, such as among increasingly illiberal governments in Eastern Europe, have tended either to flow *with* the tide of public opinion or intervened strongly to shape it, or both (see e.g. Forest 2018; Kuhar and Paternotte 2017). These interventions have invariably taken the form of laws explicitly restricting marriage to heterosexual couples (e.g. Australia 2004), or attempts to introduce them (e.g. in Haiti, Guatemala and, as discussed above, Romania). In some cases, where same-sex marriage had previously been legalised, a change of regime has opened the possibility that the law might be repealed; this is notably the case, at the time of writing, in Brazil, where ultra-conservative Jair Bolsonaro was sworn in as President on 1 January 2019.

However, there is no state that has *legalised* same-same marriage in opposition to a groundswell of public opinion, although states have very frequently legislated in other areas against such groundswells (e.g. changes to welfare regimes or retirement ages; securitisation of the refugee issue; development of coal or uranium mining or fracking for gas; and so on). Even where there has been very visible opposition to legalisation, as has been the case almost everywhere, the movement *for* same-sex marriage has been equally strong if not stronger. Such opposition has even, paradoxically, often helped get legislation over the political line in that governments, sometimes newly elected, and sometimes having included same-sex marriage in their electoral platform, have wished to distance themselves from the conservative, even fundamentalist, ideologies fuelling anti-same-sex-marriage campaigns, and in doing so, heighten their own moral authority.

State pragmatism in legislating on same-sex marriage is further characterised by the staged approach that has been adopted in almost all jurisdictions, itself informed by an ongoing dialogue between state and civil society. LGBTIQ civil society organisations were not necessarily themselves pushing for same-sex marriage at the time civil unions were first being debated and adopted, and even as states began legislating on same-sex marriage, civil society actors remained divided on the issue of the desirability of marriage as a framework for institutionalising lesbian and gay relationships. Both civil society and state actors have operated within, and in response to, the specific political and juridical frameworks that have at times provided political opportunities—for example, legal and juridical incrementalism within federal systems where marriage is a state matter, such as the US, Canada and Mexico—while at others they have imposed constraints, such as in systems where marriage legislation is a national matter or indeed, in the case of Ireland, governed by the Constitution. (For a comparison of different institutional and discursive path dependencies and the ways in which social movements and states have responded, see for example Boele-Woelki and Fuchs 2017; Winter, Forest and Sénac 2018; Friedman 2019.)

State and political responses to the issue of same-sex marriage have developed over time, in pragmatic response to both local activism and global shifts in LGBTIQ rights paradigms. With these shifts, the rhetoric deployed has also changed. Institutional framing in support of same-sex partnerships and, later, marriage has typically followed a pathway from a discourse of "tolerance" or "acceptance" to the equality-rights-justice frame, with "inclusion" also featuring along the way. This discursive development has been reflected in the legislative or juridical incrementalism adopted; it also reflects broader shifts in the political context, which provide new discursive and legislative opportunity structures. Jens Rydstrom analyses these developments in Scandinavian countries as linked to the emergence of socialist left parties "that broke with either the Moscow-influenced Communist hardliners or the Social Democrats and could therefore harbour pro-gay standpoints in a more libertarian socialist tradition" (Rydstrom 2011, 92). For example, in Denmark, the first country in the world to legalise same-sex civil unions (in 1989), the leader of the Socialist People's Party, Poul Dam, commented as early as 1968 during a parliamentary debate around a proposed registered partnerships law, that

> those that really exist will get a better, a more humane life, if society tells them that "yes, we know you are there, we not only tolerate you, but we also see that you have certain problems that we would like to help you solve by legislation". (cited in Rydstrom 2011, 92)

Rydstrom notes that although "this liberal and understanding attitude contrasts sharply with the homophobic campaigns just a decade earlier … it is also an example of a benevolent speech concerning tolerance and help instead of rights" (Rydstrom 2011, 92).

Around the same time, the Social Democrat parties also started reviewing their definitions of "family", and Rydstrom credits "the radicalisation of the feminist movement" with a large part of the impetus for this change. For example, a discussion document on family politics circulated by the Danish Social Democrats in 1969 defined "family" as "a group consisting of adult people with or without children; extended families and homophile marriages are thus included in this concept of family" (cited in Rydstrom 2011, 98). The feminist influence was even clearer in Sweden: in 1974 the Women's League of the Social Democrat Party published a pamphlet on "Family Politics of the Future" proposing new "cohabition laws … based on a view of the family as a voluntary union of economically independent members" and the recognition of a variety of family models including "extended families, sibling households, homosexuals and others" (Rydstrom 2011, 98).

An important intermediary step in many cases, between decriminalisation of (male) homosexuality and legal recognition of same-sex partnerships, was the uniformisation of the age of consent to bring that for (male) homosexuals into line for that for heterosexuals. In this case also, the idea of "public readiness" was deployed. For example, in 1997, when this issue was being considered in the Australian state of New South Wales, a parliamentary briefing paper foregrounded both government caution and the perception of attitudinal readiness in the population at large:

> The Crimes (Amendment) Bill 1984, which led to the legalisation of homosexual activity between consenting adults, was the fourth major attempt to bring about that reform since November 1981. As such it was put forward as a "rather conservative" reform, with the clear expectation that it would be reviewed at a later time, in the light of contemporary community standards. (Simpson and Figgis 1997, 14)

The paper went on to explain how those "community standards" had changed since the 1980s:

> Homosexuality *per se* is no longer regarded as unlawful or as a deviance, or psychological disorder which should be treated or modified; rather it is recognised as an acceptable and natural choice of sexuality practised by a section of humankind since time immemorial. (Simpson and Figgis 1997, 14)

Even when in favour of homosexual law reform, states continued to err on the side of "rather conservative" reforms as concerned partnership recognition, for fear of a backlash because sections of the public opinion (and particularly the governing party's own constituency) were not perceived to be "ready" for the move. Most of them thus preferred an incrementalist approach, putting forward legislation that would have a chance of passing in the first instance. It may also partly have been because the governments themselves, or significant sections thereof, considered same-sex partnerships to be lesser forms of coupledom than heterosexual marriage and thus wished to grant them a different legal status, tempering a desire for "inclusion" with a concurrent desire to maintain a hierarchy between heterosexual and homosexual partnerships.

Even the "pioneering" Danish state, like the many that would follow it, waited for the lead of public opinion before making a move to legislate on same-sex couple recognition. The Danish registered partnerships law, which the *The Wilson Quarterly* characterised a quarter of a century later as "a giant step in the fight for equality" (Krieger 2014), was only put to the parliamentary vote following a 1988 opinion poll, which showed a majority of Danes in favour of a same-sex registered partnership law. This showing of public opinion made it easier for the Social-Democrat-dominated government to quell its own more conservative elements in supporting the law (Rydstrom 2011, 99). Interestingly, notwithstanding the abovementioned feminist influence, the partnerships law seemed to be very much a male affair in the first instance, with the first 11 couples to register their partnerships in the Copenhagen Town Hall the day the law came into effect all being male (Krieger 2014). Even *The Wilson Quarterly*'s retrospective on the ongoing reverberations of the Danish law retains a masculinist framing in its headline, which reprises moon-landing astronaut Neil Armstrong's now-hackneyed phrase "one giant leap for mankind" (Krieger 2014). This masculin(ist) political and media framing of same-sex couple recognition was to be reproduced in many jurisdictions over the decades that followed, as we will see further in subsequent chapters.

Legal frameworks for couple recognition (whether marriage, de facto or civil union) involve two main aspects: those connected with procreation, filiation, adoption and parental rights, and those concerned with fiscal and financial arrangements: assets, tax and inheritance. Civil partnerships laws have typically focused on the latter (albeit sometimes differentially from marriage, for example as concerns fiscal arrangements), but have in most albeit not all cases excluded most or all of the former, beyond the legal recognition of birth mothers, which is the same for all women, whatever their marital status (with the exception of legal surrogacy arrangements in some countries, which will be discussed in Chapter 9).

So it was with the 1989 Danish law, which excluded adoption, and so it was ten years later with the French Pacte Civil de Solidarité (PaCS: Civil Solidarity Pact). Passed in 1999, the PaCS introduced a third legal relationship framework (the other two being marriage and de facto unions, called *concubinage* in French), and the only one that provided for legal partnerships between people who were not romantically involved. Any two adults of the same or different sex can *pacser*, on the condition that they are not already married or *pacsé*, and are not members of the same close family bloodline. Of the three types of registered relationship, de facto is the loosest and members of the couple retain complete financial independence. Couples who are *pacsés* benefit from the same taxation advantages as married couples but not the same automatic inheritance rights, nor the same automatic residency rights for foreign-born partners of French citizens (although they can apply for them). As concerns assets, the default position for *pacsés* is separation of these while the default position for marriage is *communauté des biens:* shared assets. For a different regime to apply, a legal agreement must be drawn up, in both cases. *Pacsés* do not automatically inherit from their partners while spouses do (although even here, biological or adopted children take priority, according to set legal parameters). For *pacsés* to inherit, they must be named in the will. Only married couples have the right to adopt children together, or to legally adopt the children of the biological-parent partner.

In legalising the PaCS, the French state was keen to point out that it did not encroach upon the meaning of marriage and "family". In 1999, during the second reading of the PaCS bill by the Assemblée Nationale, after it had been sent back by the Senate, which required changes, then Justice Minister Elisabeth Guigou criticised the Senate's position, stating:

> How many times do I need to remind people that the PaCS, which is a contract by means of which two people organise their life together, is neutral with respect to the family and to marriage? … The family contains a *temporal, procreative dimension* that the Pacte Civil de Solidarité does not. *The latter does not prohibit, nor does it confer, any of the rights attached to the family and to the descendants it includes.* The Pacte Civil de Solidarité is neutral with regard to the law on filiation, adoption, medically assisted reproduction and parental authority. It does not change these rules: medically assisted reproduction is prohibited for homosexuals, just as joint adoption is prohibited for de facto couples. The Pacte Civil de Solidarité will not lift these prohibitions. Nor does it constitute a factor likely to impact on the exercise of parental authority, which is subordinate to one interest: that of the child. It will not allow substitution of a partner's surname for that of a child. (Guigou 1999, my translation, emphasis added)

Across the Channel, the United Kingdom did not impose this level of distinction between civil unions and marriage, but nonetheless gave civil unions a different symbolic status in that only marriage involved a formal exchange of vows and only marriage could be conducted as a religious ceremony. Also in contrast to the PaCS, the Civil Partnership Act (CPA) of 2004 was introduced *only* for same-sex couples, giving them essentially the same rights as heterosexual couples (including parental responsibility). Curiously, following the legalisation of same-sex marriage in 2013, *heterosexuals* claimed discrimination, lobbying for civil partnerships to be opened to all. In 2017, Rebecca Steinfeld and Charles Keidan petitioned the UK Supreme Court, claiming that the restriction of civil partnerships to homosexuals infringed their rights under article 14 (on non-discrimination) read in conjunction with article 8 (on respect for private and family life) of the European Convention on Human Rights (ECHR). Interestingly, the same articles, along with Article 12 (on the right to marry), had been cited by Celia Kitzinger and Sue Wilkinson in petitioning the UK High Court over a decade earlier, in 2006, for recognition of their 2003 *marriage* entered into in British Columbia, Canada (Winter 2018a). Kitzinger and Wilkinson lost their case at that time, but Steinfeld and Keidan won theirs. The UKSC ruled that barring heterosexual couples from entering into civil partnerships did indeed breach the ECHR (UKSC 2018), and legislation opening up civil partnerships to heterosexuals was passed in March, 2019. In handing down the UKSC ruling, presiding judge Lady Hale stated that she

> would allow the appeal and make a declaration that sections 1 and 3 of CPA (to the extent that they preclude a different sex couple from entering into a civil partnership) are incompatible with article 14 of ECHR taken in conjunction with article 8 of the Convention. (UKSC 2018. 20)

This is precisely the *opposite* ruling from that handed down by presiding judge Mark Potter in the Kitzinger and Wilkinson case of 2006. At that time, Potter "rejected the petitioner's claim that the right to marry and respect for family life could be reinterpreted outside the bounds of existing British law" (Winter 2018a, 155; see also Potter 2006). Yet discrimination against *heterosexuals* was disallowed in 2017, even though the "bounds of existing British law" at that time limited civil partnerships to homosexuals. Thus, even as the UK normalised its marital and civil union regimes to bring each into step with the other as concerned equality between gay and straight couples, the judicial history of this normalisation shows a hierarchy, in legal thinking, between heterosexuality and homosexuality.

In the next chapter, we will explore further, through the three quite distinct case studies of Germany, Argentina and South Africa, how this hierarchy continues to operate—politically, culturally, economically and in the case of South Africa, legally as well—even as states use same-sex marriage as an exercise in national and political branding. Each case presents a political specificity of state logics with relation to same-sex marriage: the logic of continuity with a grand historical narrative in the case of Argentina; the logic of rupture with an oppressive past and mapping out an inclusive present in the case of South Africa; and, in the case of Germany, with which I will begin the chapter, the historical and ongoing effects of political and religious path dependencies, political compromise, policy convergence, political opportunity and opportunism, and the role of an influential leader in the most powerful state in the world's only supranational entity.

3

STATE RATIONALES

Three case studies

Convergence, constitutionality and political paradoxes in Germany

At the time Denmark introduced the world's first same-sex registered partnerships law in late 1989, Germany was undergoing a major transformation. What was to become known as the *Friedliche Revolution* (Peaceful Revolution), or *die Wende* (turning point, or change of direction), began in the German Democratic Republic (GDR: East Germany). Waves of emigration to the West via Hungary and Czechoslovakia occurred over the summer and early autumn and weekly pro-democracy protests took place from early September in the main cities of the GDR. On 9 November 1989, during a press conference, GDR central committee spokesman Günter Schabowski inadvertently pre-empted the application of a new law allowing direct migration into West Germany, resulting in the almost immediate fall of the Berlin Wall and the beginning of German reunification, which was completed less than a year later. This peculiarity of German history is one factor, albeit not the only one, in explaining why Germany lagged behind many of its Western European neighbours in legalising same-sex unions.

Germany has historically been a paradox as concerns LGBTIQ rights and freedoms. On the one hand, it has a reputation, both in the past and now, of being a place of both flourishing gay urban counterculture and gay political activism (Whisnant 2016). The very term *homosexual* originated in Germany in the 1860s in the context of campaigns against the anti-sodomy law of the time (Beachy 2014), although it was popularised as a medical term denoting a pathology in psychiatrist Richard von Krafft-Ebing's 1886 book *Psychopathia Sexualis* (Krafft-Ebing 1939). Magnus Hirschfeld's Scientific-Humanitarian Committee, founded in 1897, is widely credited with being the world's first homosexual rights organisation (Dose 2014; see also Hirschfeld 1914; R. Moeller 1994).

On the other hand, imperial Germany was a place of statist and nationalist conservatism—the same conservatism that led to the formation of the Bismarckian welfare system. The notorious Paragraph 175 (§175) outlawing homosexuality was introduced, not by the Nazis, with whom it became indelibly associated, but at the time of the German unification and the creation of the *Kaiserreich* following the Germanic alliance's victory in the Franco-Prussian war in 1871. Bismarckian social conservatism became particularly strong from 1890 (Puhle 1978), during which time police surveillance of (male) homosexuality increased—even if "same-sex sociability" was tolerated (Beachy 2012).

The paradox became even more pronounced during the years of the Weimar Republic, when German cities and most particularly Berlin became legendary sites of a flourishing gay culture (Beachy 2014), and what Laurie Marhoefer characterises as "probably … the freest queer press in the world" (Marhoefer 2015a, 76). The later years of the Republic, however, and notably from the time of the Great Depression, saw the rise of opposition to state liberalism from a range of hardline conservatives, including the Catholic Church and the Catholic Centre Party, elements of the Protestant Church and of course the Nationalsozialistische Deutsche Arbeiterpartei (National Socialist German Workers' Party, abbreviated to Nazi Party in English), founded in 1920 (Pretzel 2012; Marhoefer 2015b). After it came to power, the Nazi Party extended the reach of §175, which was to become the main legal framework for persecution of homosexuals under the Third Reich (Epstein and Friedman 2000).

The paradox continued after the end of World War II and the partition of Germany. Both the GDR and FRG (Federal Republic of Germany: at the time West Germany) faced the task of social, cultural, political and economic rebuilding after the devastation of World War II and Germany's role therein. Both faced the moral vacuum left by that devastation and a new crisis of patriarchal values (usually referred to in the literature as a "crisis of masculinity"). As concerns their approaches to homosexuality, the FRG was initially much more conservative than the GDR, which became what Florian Mildenberger has characterised as an "outlier" in the Soviet bloc in that it introduced a number of social reforms including "the depathologization of homosexuality" (Mildenberger 2014, 216). For example, the Berlin Court of Appeals decided in 1950 to reinstate the pre-1935 version of §175, which only criminalised anally-penetrative sex acts while the Nazi version had had much wider application (Taylor 2014, 308). This reform has been foregrounded by some as evidence of a more liberal—or at least lenient—stance in the GDR in comparison to the FRG (J. Evans 2010; Taylor 2014), which retained the Nazi-era §175 in its entirety. However, Günter Grau suggests that it would be "rash … to deduce a liberal or enlightened attitude" from this measure (Grau 1999, 7), as the regime's intent was primarily to distance itself from the oppressiveness of the Nazi regime. Moreover, the GDR encouraged a culture of "healthy" heterosexuality through "social eugenics", sometimes influenced by the former Nazi associations of members of the medical profession (Mildenberger 2014). The nation's (male/heterosexual) youth were framed as "'the bearers of hope for the Party' (*die Hoffnungsträger der Partei*)"—the party in question being the Sozialistische Einheitspartei Deutschlands (SED: Socialist Unity Party of Germany) (J. Evans 2010, 555).

At the same time, there was a push, including within the government at the time of the reform of the Penal Code, to decriminalise homosexuality altogether, and lobbying by gay psychologist and sexologist Rudolf Klimmer, who pursued the Hirschfeldian argument of a biological basis for homosexuality. Although §175 was retained in the 1958 code, there were few prosecutions after that time, and it was repealed altogether in 1968—primarily, according to former East German gay activist Jürgen Lemke, as "a propaganda move for the benefit of West Germany" (Lemke 1993, 35). Until the 1980s, however, the subject of homosexuality remained taboo in the public sphere, prohibitions of certain types of associations and publications continued (Grau 1999), and Stasi infiltration of gay and lesbian organisations was an ongoing risk (Davidson-Schmich 2017, 534).

Meanwhile in the FRG, "[b]etween 1953 and 1965, the police reported 98,700 violators of §175; nearly 38,000 of these were found guilty and sentenced", which according to Robert Moeller was more than during the Nazi era (R. Moeller 1994, 427), although the sentences were clearly far less severe. Although §175 was repealed in the FRG in1969, §175a, which dealt with "lewd and lascivious acts" performed through compulsion or prostitution or with minors, remained in force until 1994.

It was in the GDR, again, that "the first major German judicial decision stating that homosexuals enjoy the same civil rights as other citizens" was made (Hillhouse 1990, 588). In August 1987, the Supreme Court lowered the (male) homosexual age of consent to 14, the same as for heterosexuals, and in doing so affirmed homosexuals' equality with all other citizens under socialism and their right to protection from "all attacks on their integrity", whether physical, moral or judicial (cited in Hillhouse 1990, 588). This shift occurred in the context of a broader liberalisation and individualisation of rights, and the building of successful coalitions between the gay and lesbian movement and other organisations, notably sections of the Lutheran Church, which benefited from a degree of official recognition following the Church-State Agreement of 1978—a support that also benefited the feminist movement of the time (Ferree 1994, 602).

So, for lesbians and gay men, reunification was not an automatic emergence from a prison of silence and oppression in the GDR (although those also existed) into a freedom of liberation and equality in the FRG. It was, rather, the convergence of two different styles of activism (and oppression). On one side of the wall was the Western context of economic affluence along with the sexual liberation and women's liberation that began in the late 1960s. These movements, like the rest of the radical left, were characterised by diverse forms of political organising, with often heated debates over politics, separatism, reformism versus revolution, and so on. On the other side of the wall was a lower key and perhaps more concerted style of organising and activism, based on a different history and different political aims. After reunification, some Easterners expressed difficulty fitting into the "scene" in West Germany. One East German lesbian commented in the pages of *Gay Community News* (US) in 1991 that the "lesbian community in East Germany, by contrast, was open, friendly and together" (Hechler 1991, 16). Others decried the hedonism, consumerism, self-aggrandisement and internal bickering of the West German gay movement: "often we find ourselves missing emotion, we have a need for solidarity and closeness" (Lemke 1993, 36). Eastern lesbians and gay men also entered a society where they found themselves economically disadvantaged (more so if they were female), along with almost everybody else from East Germany at that time. At the same time, that Eastern "solidarity and closeness" led to the creation of an East German political organisation: Schwulenverband der DDR (SVD: GDR Gay Association) in 1990, in the lead up to formal reunification. Its first task was to ensure that §175, still in force in the FRG, would not be extended to the Eastern Länder, where it had been repealed. They succeeded. Following reunification, the joining up of a number of West German activists, and a name change to Lesben- und Schwulenverband in Deutschland (LSVD: Lesbian and Gay Association in Germany), the group became the major German LGBTIQ organisation by the end of the decade and a major driver of the same-sex partnerships and then marriage campaign (Davidson-Schmich 2017).

East German lesbians and gay men also found themselves moving into a political context dominated by the Christian centre-right: the CDU, Christian Democratic Union, the party of which Eastern-born Lutheran pastor's daughter Angela Merkel was to become leader. At the time of reunification, the FRG was led by the CDU's Helmut Kohl, who had been Chancellor since 1982 and was to remain Chancellor of the reunified republic until 1998, when the CDU was defeated by the SDP (Social Democratic Party). The SDP leader Gerhard Schröder, who was a member of the international "Third Way" group most famously personified by Tony Blair and Bill Clinton, became Chancellor, his party governing in coalition with the Greens until the CDU returned to power in 2005, under Angela Merkel's leadership. (The "Third Way", of which the intellectual driving force was Anthony Giddens [1998, 2001], was, in the late 1990s and early 2000s, a centre-left attempt to marry social-democrat values such as equality, human rights and social participation with a free-market capitalism that many saw as indistinguishable from neoliberalism [e.g. Romano 2006]. German ordoliberalism nonetheless ensured ongoing state involvement in market regulation and welfare protections.)

However, the German state did move relatively quickly after reunification—no doubt in great part in response to pressure by the newly (re)organised gay and lesbian movement—to address and unformise LGBTIQ rights in a number of areas. Thus, in 1994, §175 was finally struck off the statute books, and the age of consent was equalised between homosexuals and heterosexuals. In 2001, Germany legalised registered partnerships for gay men and lesbians, and a subsequent series of law reforms under successive governments, including that led by Merkel, plus rulings of the Constitutional Court, brought same-sex partnerships much closer to marriage. "Indeed", notes Samuel Fulli-Lemaire, "the Federal Constitutional Court has been from the outset a prime mover for bringing the legal regime of the registered partnership closer to that of marriage … by declaring discriminatory provisions to be unconstitutional" under Article 3 of the Basic Law (German Constitution: Federal Republic of Germany 1949) on equality of all persons before the law (Fulli-Lemaire 2017, 25). In fact, by the time same-sex marriage was legalised in Germany in 2017—later, sometimes much later, than most of its Western European neighbours—homosexual couples in registered partnerships enjoyed almost all the rights that married heterosexuals did. So what was blocking the move to legalisation?

The original registered partnerships law is seen to have been adopted as a compromise between the strong advocacy of gay marriage by many social groups and some political parties, and the social and religious conservatism present in many sections of society and represented politically by the CDU. That compromise position continued to be defended by the ruling coalition, and two legalisation bills presented by the Greens in the Bundestag (Federal parliament) in 2012 and to the Bundestag by the Bundesrat (Federal Council representing Germany's 16 Länder) in 2013, both during Merkel's leadership, were defeated, with the CDU continuing to vote along party lines. Finally, in 2017 Merkel, who herself continued to be opposed to legalisation, allowed a free vote in the CDU, which enabled the latest bill to pass.

I see three factors as contributing to this shift. The first is policy convergence. Germany, as the most powerful nation in the EU, and its largest economy, is not usually a follower in terms of policy convergence but more likely to be a leader. Yet Germany found itself lagging behind practically all of its Western European partners on legalisation of same-sex marriage. If Italy's and Greece's continuation as Meridional outliers can be explained by the continued weight of cultural (and religious) traditionalism, Germany had more difficulty explaining away its continued resistance to the Western European trend. In addition, the strong push for legalisation by both social movements and the political class, and the fact that by that time, civil unions bore very little ongoing difference to marriage anyway, made continued resistance to legalisation a politically untenable position.

Second, Germany's own particular path dependency meant that same-sex marriage was both encouraged and blocked, almost simultaneously, with the compromise civil union law. On the one hand, as noted above, the "clean break" with the Nazi past led to very strong equality provisions in the Basic Law of 1949, and reunification led to law reform on LGBTIQ matters. On the other hand, religious and social conservatism among both the political class and sections of the population acted to block full recognition of equality in marriage. The road to same-sex marriage was thus a road to compromise, travelled through both juridical incrementalism via the Constitutional Court and federal dialogue among the Länder and within their federal council.

Finally, the story of same-sex marriage legalisation in Germany is one of both political opportunity and political opportunism (some media commentators have suggested that it is primarily the latter: see for example Schließ 2017). Amid the so-called refugee "crisis" of 2015–2016, and perhaps a little before, Angela Merkel emerged as a strongly moral leader in the EU (Mushaben 2017). I use the word "moral" here not in a conservative or religious sense, but in the sense of embracing "European values" of justice and equality. At the same time, Merkel's stance on refugees gave her considerable trouble with the right flank of her own party, and the left used the potential political weakening of Merkel as an opportunity. Following the CDU blocking, in 2015, of two more bills for legalisation, one from the Bundesrat and one from the Greens, following also the decisions by some regional Lutheran synods in 2016 to begin conducting gay wedding ceremonies (Gerdes 2016), the Greens, the SDP and FPD (Free Democratic Party) all separately issued an ultimatum to the Chancellor. On 17 June, 2017, in the lead up to the September federal election, the Greens pledged not to participate in any post-election governing coalition unless same-sex marriage was part of the deal. A week later, the other two parties followed suit. Within days, Merkel announced she would put the bill to a conscience vote in the Bundestag. On the last day of that month, the Bundestag voted the bill into law by a clear majority.

Although Merkel still came close to being unable to form a governing coalition after the 2017 election, the same-sex marriage vote certainly won her some support from the left—and, indeed, from sections of her own Lutheran Church. Although same-sex marriage was not discursively tied, in Germany, to the very identity of the nation and its ruling party in the same way as it had been in many other countries, it *was* tied to the political fortunes of both its ruling class and its leader, and the nation-defining religion to which that leader belongs: Lutheranism. Post-war German politics, nation-building and Europeanisation have been deeply tied to Christian Democratic humanism and to the party that represents it: Merkel's CDU. Co-founder and first leader of the CDU, Catholic Konrad Adenauer, was also considered one of the founding fathers of the EU. His centre-right humanism and Christian democracy have been core to the ideology of the postwar German nation (Royce 2017, ch. 8).

Although the Lutheran Church itself, which has both progressive and conservative elements, is divided over same-sex marriage, its more progressive synods played a culturally significant role in the push towards legalisation. At the height of the pre-legalisation debate in 2016, the first gay Lutheran wedding was held to much fanfare in that symbolic and historic home of both the nation's parliament and its gay counterculture: Berlin (The Local.de 2016). Of course, it was a marriage between two men, just as the televised first legal gay weddings in France and in Argentina had been: the significant difference is that in the French and Argentinian cases, the weddings were held in municipal offices (thus secular). In all cases, however, the emblematic figure of same-sex marriage remains white and male. And, in Germany, he gets married in a Lutheran church.

Peronismo, Cristinismo y emancipacionismo in Argentina

In the lead up to same-sex marriage legalisation in Argentina, neo-Peronist President Cristina Fernández de Kirchner (known in Argentina as CFK, in an initialisation oddly reminiscent of JFK [for legendary US president John F.

Kennedy]) explicitly distanced herself from the "medievalist" discourse of conservative Catholic opponents, notably through a war of words with Cardinal Jorge Bergoglio, then Archbishop of Buenos Aires and now Pope Francis (Fernández de Kirchner 2010a; Winter 2018a). In doing so, she located same-sex marriage within the secular tradition of the modern and culturally pluralist nation. She also positioned herself, and by association same-sex marriage, within the Peronist political tradition. In her speech promulgating the law, delivered on 21 July 2010, CFK opened with a direct reference to a woman who has become the icon, not only of her own Peronist political party (Partido Justicialista: Justicialist Party), but also of the Argentine nation itself: Eva Perón, known to the world as Evita. After having greeted "all those who have done so much for this moment"—members of the government and of parliament, representatives of civil society organisations and international organisations, and personalities from the arts and culture—Kirchner said:

> I do not know how she would have felt—and when I say she it is Eva Perón [*cheers from the audience*] when she presented the granting of women's political rights; 58 years ago we could not vote and here we are, look how far we have come. (Fernández de Kirchner 2010b, my translation)

The promulgation speech was delivered in the Galería de los Patriotas Latinoamericanos, inaugurated by CFK in the Casa Rosada (presidential palace) just two months earlier to mark the bicentenary of the Revolución de Mayo (May Revolution, 25 May 1810) that ousted the Spanish Viceroy and began the Argentinian War of Independence. In that gallery hung a large painting of Evita, copied from a well-known photograph of her taken, unusually, with her hair down and flowing, unlike her usual chignon. It was a "revolutionary" image fitting the intent of the gallery, in which hung also portraits of a number of other revolutionary and progressive leaders, including CFK's late husband and former president, Néstor Kirchner. As CFK mentioned Eva Perón's name in the opening of her speech, the television cameras flashed from her to this portrait of Evita.

Kirchner thus inscribed same-sex marriage within a linear progression of democratic modernity that began with women's suffrage and with *peronismo*. More importantly, she directly associated herself, as leading political advocate of same-sex marriage, with the legendary heroine of the Argentine nation in general and its poorer women in particular. It is difficult to overstate the significance of this positioning, predictable though it may appear.

The law giving Argentinian women the vote—"aptly" nicknamed the "Evita law" (Meyer-Stabley 2017, ch. 4) because Eva Perón is credited with giving the campaign the final momentum it needed to push the law over the line—was finally adopted on 23 September 1947. A historical overview published on the site of TeleSUR celebrates Evita's role, stating that she "took the lead on what Argentine women had been asking for a long time, and made it happen … Evita's role was decisive" (TeleSUR 2014). Marifran Carlson (1988) suggests that the reality was more complex: the suffrage movement was not, in fact, originally a unified front that rallied around *peronismo*. Juan Perón, while Labour Secretary under the 1943–46 military regime of the Grupo de Oficiales Unidos (GOU), had introduced a number of labour and welfare measures that gained him working class support, including among women. Carlson argues that it was mainly this working class support, in contradistinction to the class background of the "historical" feminists, that contributed to the popularity of Perón' wife Eva, who famously described herself as being a "bridge between Perón and the people" (cited in Christie 2015, 18). This self-given role and its material impacts have endured in collective memory: as Fernanda Peñaloza noted in 2019, Evita was "absolutely instrumental in being a bridge between the state apparatus and the mobilisation of the masses" (cited in Lozano 2019, my translation).

At the same time, both Evita and her husband were ambiguous figures: apart from their populism and their taste for the grandiose, they also came under heavy criticism for having granted refuge to Nazi war criminals and anti-Semitic factions have been identified within Peronism (Besoky 2018). In response to this criticism, in 1997 Peronist President Carlos Menem set up the Comisión por el Esclarecimiento de las Actividades del Nazismo en la Argentina (CEANA), which in 1998 issued two reports, the second of which found that 180 Nazi war criminals had safely entered and lived in Argentina during the Perón regime (CEANA 1998a, 1998b).

Many have described Evita as a mythicised figure in Argentine history (e.g. Rosano 2005a and b; Ballent 2010; Fridman 2010; Navarro 2012): that iconic "empty signifier" (Laclau 2008) that groups a plurality of meanings under a hegemonic populist banner. She has become synonymous with the "spirit" of Argentina, as its first and only *Lider Espiritual de la Nación* (spiritual leader of the nation), the title bestowed upon her by the Argentine Congress in May 1952, less than three months before her death from cancer at the age of 33. She epitomises at once the *pueblo* (people) where it lives—the imagined *decamisados* (shirtless ones) whose cause she took up—and the rags-to-riches aspirations of that same imagined *pueblo*, particularly its female members, towards a life of glamour and luxury.

Evita has long since eclipsed her husband as the iconic symbol of modern Argentina, partly because of the institutionalisation of her political presence during her lifetime, notably via the wealthy Fundación Eva Perón set up in 1948 to assist poorer neighbourhoods and children. Following her death, the symbolism and institutionalisation of Evita as "Spiritual Leader of the Nation" has endured in part because of the efforts of her family, who in the 1990s set what was to become the Instituto Nacional de Investigaciones Históricas Eva Perón, now under the auspices of the National Secretariat for Culture. The national Eva Perón museum in Buenos Aires was created as part of this Institute in 2002. The Institute's website states that "Argentina entered the modern age thanks to Peronism", yet at the same time, cites Juan Perón as stating that

> dignifying women moral [*sic*] and materially is the equivalent of strengthening the family. To strengthen the family is to fortify the nation because the family is its first cell. To create a true social order one must begin with this basic cell, the Christian and rational basis for all human groups. (cited in Vázquez 2007)

Peronist modernity, then as now, even as it "dignified" women and finally granted them full citzenship, remained anchored in the family as society's "fundamental group unit". Indeed, for all her championing of women's rights, and as a both symbolically and materially enabling figure for women because of her high political profile and charitable works, Evita remained a resolutely *feminine* figure, devoted to her husband and her people.

Fast forward from Evita to her would-be direct descendant, politically speaking: Cristina Fernández de Kirchner, who at the time of writing has recently been re-elected, not as president this time, but as vice-president beside president-elect Alberto Fernández (no relation, but former Chief Cabinet Minister under Néstor Kirchner's presidency). CFK shares with her Peronist heroine a taste for designer clothes and a very feminine look. On the day she promulgated the same-sex marriage law, she wore a pale frilly dress with a pale pink fitted cardigan, pointed-toe white heeled shoes, and a triple-strand pearl necklace. Her hair was carefully styled and she wore heavy makeup. In short, she incarnated an entirely feminine image of which Evita would surely have approved. Before she began her speech, representatives of the Federación Argentina LGBT presented her with a golden plaque that read "To the President of the Nation Doctora Cristina Fernández, for her commitment and courage in defending equality and in building a nation for all [todas y todos]" (my translation). Not quite the nation's *lider espiritual*, and not quite *el pueblo* either, perhaps, but the presentation of this plaque amplified the effect of CFK's self-positioning mere moments later in relation to Evita and the latter's role in ushering in equality for women.

Like the Peróns before them, Cristina Fernández de Kirchner and her presidential predecessor and late husband, Néstor, have had a political -ism named for them, *kirchnerismo*, although in both cases it is the wife rather than the husband who has the most enduringly symbolised the *-ismo* in question. In both cases also, the *-ismo* and the couple that personified it constituted a "populist rupture" with the regime that preceded it (Cantamutto 2016, 2017). Kirchnerism developed out of the majority faction of the Justicialist Party in coalition with other left and centre-left groups to form the Frente para la Victoria (Front for Victory: FPV), and has been described as left-wing populist.

Luiz Carlos Bresser-Pereira (2011) has described Kirchnerism as neo-developmentalist. He places neodevelopmentalism between the "old" developmentalism of Peronism on the one hand and, on the other hand, the Washington Consensus neoliberalism of the presidency of Carlos Menem—himself from the Justicialist Party (1989–99). The latter was characterised by financial deregulations, state budget cuts, privatisations of some state-run enterprises and lifting of trade restrictions, while the former was inward-focused or "export pessimist" in terms of economic development, with a high level of state protectionism and interventionism in controlling the economy (Bresser-Pereira 2011). Neodevelopmentalism shares with Northern hemisphere Third Way politics its embracing of free-market capitalism, but it supports state intervention to control commodity exports and thus keep the exchange rate down. That intervention also encourages the development of manufacturing for export and provides "the general conditions for capital accumulation, such as education, health, transportation, communications, and power infrastructures" (Bresser-Pereira 2011, 118).

Throughout Néstor Kirchner's presidential campaign and after his election, he publicly distanced himself from neoliberalism and rolled back many of the changes introduced by Menem. That rollback included renationalisations of some industries, although most significant renationalisations occurred during CFK's time (Féliz 2016). At the same time, Kirchnerism, notwithstanding the social justice and populist-left rhetoric, set about neutralising trade unionists and *piqueteros* (organisations of the unemployed that took to the streets with pickets to protest Menem's neoliberal policies of the 1990s), in part through discourse and strategies of unification, in part by creating employment programmes and in part by co-opting some factions of them into government positions (Escudé 2007; Pérez and Natalucci 2010; Kaese and Wolff 2016; Quiroga, Brizzio and Forlani 2018).

CFK, who was elected to the presidency in 2007 after her husband declined to run for a second term, continued this combination of economic and social policies, but came up against two significant obstacles. The first was the global crisis in neoliberal capitalism that began in 2008, and the second was the "internal contradictions particular to the neodevelopmentalist project [which] were translating into ever growing barriers: high and sustained inflation, growing fiscal deficit and increasing foreign exchange deficit, amongst others" (Féliz 2016, 99). Following the 2008 financial crisis and the "business protest" (Fairfield 2011) the same year by agricultural producers against a proposed increase in export taxes on soy beans and sunflower oil, and the ensuing Congressional vote against the increase, CFK introduced two significant measures. The first was changes to the regulations governing the central bank, enabling it to pay down fiscal and foreign debt, and the second was renationalisation of the social security system. The government also increased its populist appeal through a policy programme of "basic universalism" providing employment and welfare subsidies, at a time of lacklustre economic growth (Féliz 2016, 102). Income inequality between the richest and poorest sectors of the population halved between 2003 and 2010, and economic growth improved from 2008, but at the cost of galloping inflation (IMF 2016, 9). Another popular move was Audiovisual Communication Services Law Number 26.522 of 2009 limiting media monopolies. The law, introduced to democratise media in a world region notorious for media oligarchies and monopolies, was ferociously combated by the powerful Clarín Group and the Inter American Press Association (IAPA), among others (Repoll 2010; Sel and Gasloli 2014).

The crisis of 2008 nonetheless fuelled a rise in the right and centre-right opposition, including *Propuesta Republicana* (PRO), the party of Mauricio Macri, who was to be elected president in 2015. The impact was that in 2009, CFK's coalition lost its majorities in both lower and upper houses in midterm legislative elections, to parties to both its left and its right.

It was during this period, in this economic and political climate, and in the lead up to the 2011 presidential election, that Law 26.618 modifying the Civil Code to allow same-sex marriage was voted in by the Senate on 14 July 2010, by a majority of only six votes and after nearly 15 hours of debate. Despite this narrow win, the popularity of the law on *matrimonio igualitario*, combined with CFK's above-mentioned socioeconomic equality policies, economic growth, and, in October the same year, national mourning and personal sympathy for the death of Néstor Kirchner, all boosted CFK's support base and she was re-elected president in 2011, with 54 per cent of the vote.

CFK has been both criticised and praised for being "the wife of", in the dynastic framings so often characteristic of women's rise to political leadership, and in association with Evita (Christie 2015). Although such historical comparisons risk becoming conflations, in which the later figure (CFK) is perceived as simply a latter-day clone of the earlier (Evita), and is consequently diminished as an actor in her own right, CFK herself has deliberately cultivated the association, and not only on the day she promulgated the same-sex marriage law. She also did so through the elevation of Néstor Kirchner to the status of idealised revolutionary hero following his death (she wore black for three years)—much as Evita idealised Perón in her autobiography—and through a populist identification with Evita *luchadora* (fighter), the activist Evita who defended the *decamisados* as well as votes for women. Jane Christie (2015) has argued that CFK, like Evita, incarnates a gender-role based, strong yet feminine leader, whose primary identification is with *el pueblo* (the people) rather than explicitly with *las mujeres* (women), and any "feminism" she exhibits remains within that safe zone of populist appeal.

The singular difference between Evita and CFK is, of course, that the latter has acceded to and consolidated political power in her own right following her husband's death: first, in the 2011 landslide victory, and second, in a 2019 comeback as vice-president next to her namesake Alberto Fernández. The team was elected on 27 October, exactly nine years to the day after Néstor Kirchner's death—which is pure coincidence, but the symbolism of the date has not escaped the press. Nor has the larger-than-life profile of CFK: for example, a Reuters report following the 2019 election characterised her as a "rockstar politician" (Garrison 2019). The same article also described her as a "fiery ... comeback queen", thus using used the "queen" framing discussed by Christie (2015) as frequently deployed to describe female political leaders. In fact, CFK's success is such that one perhaps should begin to speak of *cristinismo*, or *CFKismo*, rather than *kirchnerismo*, to give her status in her own right.

The same-sex marriage legalisation, and the televised announcement thereof, were an internationally celebrated feel-good moment in both Argentine and regional politics and the international LGBTIQ rights movement. It was the first country in Latin America to legalise same-sex marriage (although the Mexican subnational jurisdiction of Mexico City had legalised it there some six months earlier), the second in the Americas overall (after Canada) and in the Southern Hemisphere (after South Africa, discussed below), and only the tenth in the world. Yet, as Costanza Tabbush et al. point out, invoking the concept of pink-washing, "with the objective of being seen as progressive, [Latin American] Pink

Tide [left-wing] administrations made trade-offs between advances in some LGBT rights and setbacks or stagnation in policies central to feminism or human rights" (Tabbush et al. 2019, 83; see also Belgrano Rawson 2012; Lind and Keating 2013). They argue that advances in women's rights in Argentina during the Kirchnerist period largely corresponded to a maternalistic framing of helping women and poorer families, which "sidelined the gender-equality demands of adult women" (Tabbush et al. 2019, 83).

One of the most significant struggles of these adult women has concerned reproductive rights: it is telling that only a few days after same-sex marriage was legalised, women were demonstrating in the streets of Buenos Aires for abortion rights, which are severely limited in Argentina under a 1921 law that is still in force at the time of writing. In this respect, Argentina is comparable to Ireland, where contrary to what has been the case in many other countries, the legalisation of abortion has lagged behind the legalisation of same-sex marriage, with the latter then adding impetus to the campaign for the former. A national coalition of women's reproductive rights organisations in Argentina has long pushed for a Voluntary Termination of Pregnancy law, which was presented to the Chamber of Deputies four times between 2007 and 2014, but not put to a vote in Congress. During this period CFK publicly expressed her opposition to abortion, and feminist groups that were not malestreamed were sidelined and underfunded while the umbrella LGBTIQ rights group FALGBT gained access to institutional support (Tabbush et al. 2019, 87). More recently, in 2018, a bill to legalise unrestricted abortion up to 14 weeks of pregnancy was passed in the Chamber of Deputies—this time with the support of CFK who had changed her position—but defeated in the Senate after a 16-hour debate. Current president Alberto Fernández openly supported legalisation during his campaign, and on 1 March 2020 pledged to introduce a new bill to parliament within 10 days. The outcome is pending at the time of writing, but if the bill is passed Argentina will become the fourth Latin American country to legalise abortion on request (after Cuba, Uruguay and Guyana).

As Catharine MacKinnon argued in 1990, inequality between men and women is only permitted to be challenged "as long as the central pillars of gender as a system of power are permitted to remain standing" (MacKinnon 1990, 225). Even in those formerly Communist countries that legalised abortion and have not repealed those laws since, notwithstanding re-Christianisation in many cases, the ideology supporting women's contribution as productive members of the work-force, along with pragmatic measures to reduce "mouths to feed" in impoverished families (see e.g. Karpov 2005), rather than women's needs per se, are among the factors contributing to the ongoing legality of abortion there. In capitalist (neo) liberal democracies, including those where the Catholic Church is influential, the "equality" frame within which same-sex marriage and even "gender identity" can be accommodated does nothing to undermine the system of "sexist social meanings" in which it is far more difficult for women to obtain what they need if *only* women (that is, no males) need it (MacKinnon 1990, 219 and 225).

In Argentina, then, the emancipationist/equality frame, which is in keeping with the 2017 IACHR/CIDH pro persona interpretation of human rights discussed in the previous chapter, set within a particular path dependency of populist/social justice politics and the political opportunity created by the CFK regime, has led to the country becoming a perceived leader in LGBTIQ rights among Latin American "Pink Tide" democracies. This does not, however, mean, that deeper issues of socioeconmic inequality, notably concerning women (including lesbians), have been addressed, These and other contradictions demonstrate that the human rights and social justice politics of the (neo-Peronist) Argentine nation, despite some real advances, have had their limits, with cost-neutral social justice initiatives that win middle-class votes in a neoliberal world often taking precedence over more complex (and costly) social equality measures.

Transformative constitutionalism and unequal equality: the case of South Africa

I include South Africa as my last case study in this chapter because of its unique and paradoxical situation with regard to state political framing of same-sex marriage as congruent with its human rights rupture with an oppressive past and a state of exceptionalism to the heteronorms that characterise African-ness. On the one hand, South Africa, even more than Argentina, can lay claim to being a ground-breaker in LGBTIQ equality in its region and indeed the world. Its post-apartheid Constitution of 1996 contains the world's first constitutional protection of the rights of homosexual men and lesbians (Republic of South Africa 1996, Article 6, paragraphs 3 and 4), and it was one of the first countries in the world, and to date the only country in Africa, to have legalised same-sex marriage (in 2006). As such, South Africa has become a "beacon for sexual minorities throughout the world" (Robson 2007, 418) and its Constitution is still only one of ten national-level articulations of sexual orientation as a protected category under antidiscrimination provisions (that is, so-called negative rights [Vašák 1977]). On the other hand, South Africa is at the time of writing the world's most unequal country in socio-economic terms (Sulla and Zikhali 2018) and has become notorious for sexualised violence against women in general and so-called "corrective" rapes of lesbians in particular. As concerns same-sex marriage, the 2006 Civil Union Act, the result of a decision referred to the legislature by the Constitutional Court, forms part of a complicated and pluralist regime of matrimonial regulation and explicitly accommodates religious objections.

Moreover, Article 6's rather curious Paragraph 5 does allow for discrimination if it can be established that discrimination on any of the grounds mentioned in the previous articles is "fair" (Republic of South Africa 1996, Article 6, paragraph 5). The Constitution is silent on what might constitute "fairness" in this case. Its framing of non-discrmination is also weaker than that of the African National Congress's (ANC) Bill of Rights of 1993. Article 8 of the ANC document, titled "Gender Rights" reads as follows:

1 Discrimination on the grounds of gender, single parenthood, legitimacy of birth or sexual orientation shall be unlawful.
2 Legislation shall provide remedies for oppression, abuse, harassment or discrimination based on gender or sexual orientation.
3 Educational institutions, the media, advertising and other social institutions shall be under a duty to discourage sexual and other types of stereotyping (ANC 1993).

The ANC's Bill of Rights also includes a provision against domestic violence or abuse (Article 2, "Personal Rights", Paragraph 28) and non-gendered provisions on the right of "people" (rather than "men and women") to "live together with partners of their choice, and to marry" (Article 2, Paragraph 29). The Constitution ended up remaining silent on both matters, which are left to the domain of legislation.

Even watered down, the Constitution is nonetheless groundbreaking in its own right, all the more because it is explicitly framed in its Preamble as breaking with an oppressive past and moving forward on the basis of "democratic values, social justice and fundamental human rights" (Republic of South Africa 1996, 1). Guaranteeing rights for sexual minorities is seen as in keeping with that supposed clean break, and with a national narrative that presents a coherency of human rights, democracy and equality-in-diversity, this last being a key factor in South Africa's approach to both homosexuality and marriage.

Karl Klare famously termed the post-apartheid legal regime "transformative constitutionalism": "a long-term project of constitutional enactment, interpretation, and enforcement committed … to transforming a country's political and social institutions and power relationships in a democratic, participatory, and egalitarian direction … through nonviolent political processes grounded in law" (Klare 1998, 150). As part of that process, significant power has been given to the judiciary to interpret and adjudicate on rights, which has had both positive and negative consequences. One of the positive consequences has been in the area of LGBTIQ rights, as the National Coalition for Gay and Lesbian Equality (NCGLE) mobilised the human rights frame "to target the relatively strong and amenable judiciary" (Currier and Moreau 2018, 93). An early result of this strategy was the 1998 ruling of the Constitutional Court that existing prohibitions of male homosexuality and sodomy were constitutionally invalid and that thus effectively repealed those laws (*NCGLE v. Minister of Justice* [*MoJ*] 1998). As Pierre De Vos (2007) has noted, the Court upheld the spirit of the new Constitution in stating that "the desire for equality is not a hope for the elimination of all differences" (Ackermann J, *NCGLE v. MoJ*, para. 22). Justice Sachs added that "our future as a nation depends in large measure on how we manage difference. In the past difference has been experienced as a curse, today it can be seen as a source of interactive vitality" (Sachs J, *NCGLE v. MoJ*, para. 135).

The decriminalisation of homosexuality was thus framed as a logical consequence of post-apartheid commitment to human rights and equality-in-diversity.

Even as the right of those who opposed homosexuality "for reasons of religious or other belief" to hold their views was recognised, the Constitution "does not allow the state to turn these beliefs—even in moderate or gentle versions—into dogma imposed on the whole of society" (Sachs J, *NCGLE v. MoJ*, para. 137).

Eight years later, the stance of the Constitutional Court was less immediately proactive. In the case of *Fourie and Another v. Minister of Home Affairs and Another* (*Fourie* 2005)—the judgment concerning the final stage litigation, after the High and Supreme Courts, of a lesbian couple's petition for the right to marry—the Court ruled unanimously that not including same-sex couples within the legal framework of marriage was unconstitutional. In doing so, it reiterated the national rhetoric of "radical rupture with a past based on intolerance and exclusion" (*Fourie*, Sachs J, para. 59). However, it refused the remedy of simply reforming the 1961 Marriage Act (to add the word "or spouse" in addition to "husband" and "wife", or replace the latter two terms with the first). The majority ruling of eight judges was to refer the matter to Parliament (rather than rule immediately, which was the dissenting opinion of Justice O'Regan), for the reason that a "secure" remedy was required through "enduring and stable legislative appreciation" (*Fourie*, Sachs J, para. 136).

The Court similarly did not formally overturn the 1905 decision of the Transvaal Supreme Court in *Mashia Ebrahim v. Mahomed Essop*, assumed by many to be the "common law" definition of marriage. This latter decision specifies that marriage is "a union of one man with one woman, to the exclusion, while it lasts, of all others" [cited in *Fourie*, Sachs J, para. 3]). However, as the Constitutional Court pointed out in *Fourie*, it has no legal effect without the provisions of the Marriage Act also being invoked. In other words, there is no such legal entity as a "common law marriage" in South Africa: the import of *Ebrahim v. Essop* is thus conventional—and ideological—rather than legal. Its main import has been to give interpretive weight to the Marriage Act, which does not explicitly *prescribe* heterosexuality, although it is often assumed to (Currier and Moreau 2018, 95). The only explicit reference to heterosexual marriage is the Act's Article 28 regulating marriage between widowers and widows and the relatives of their deceased husband or wife.

The resulting law adopted by Parliament was the 2006 Civil Union Act, which provides for both homosexuals and heterosexuals aged 18 or over to enter into partnerships that they can decide are "marriages" or "civil partnerships". There is no significant (or any) legal distinction between the two, so the nomenclature is primarily symbolic, although according to some commentary it opened up the way to providing different models of interpersonal relationships, and as such was transformative (Bilchit and Judge 2007, 485 ff.). However, the Act is problematic for a number of reasons.

First, marriage in South Africa is now subject, not to two legal regimes but to three, governed by the 1961 Marriage Act, the 2006 Civil Union Act, and the 1998 Recognition of Customary Marriages Act (RCMA)—in roughly that symbolically hierarchical order. All three are mutually exclusive: one marries (or civilly partners) under one of these laws only, and cannot then have the marriage validated under either of the other two. The RCMA is explicitly between heterosexuals and recognises multiple customary marriages—but only polygynous ones. There is no provision for women to take more than one husband. As Elsje Bonthuy (2007) and Nicola Barker (2011), among others, have pointed out, the RCMA sits within a

> hierarchy of family forms [that] has at its apex the institution of civil marriage, associated with monogamy and procreation and accorded full legal recognition and protection, while at the lowest level it fails to recognise and attach legal consequences not only to unmarried heterosexual and same-sex relationships, but also to Muslim marriages. Somewhere between these poles lie customary marriages. (Bonthuy 2007, 527)

In deciding not to repeal the Marriage Act, the South African state kept that particular form of intimate partnership at the "apex", maintaining the symbolic hierarchy of Western-style heterosexual marriage as taking precedence over all other forms. Moreover, as Bonthuy further argues, the primacy of Judeo-Christian marriage and civil unions over customary marriages (and Muslim marriages, which have no distinct legal framework) reproduces the tradition vs modernity dichotomy. This dichotomy—and the solely heterosexual framing of the RMCA—also silence the history of customary frameworks in which same-sex unions have been accommodated (Bonthuy 2007, 532 ff.). Indeed, the lived reality of South African lesbians and gay men does not map neatly onto the civil marriage model, which frames them as what Ruthann Robson has termed a "model minority" (Robson 2007). The complexity of family structures in South Africa, with their raced, gendered, class and cultural dimensions, and the diversity of ways in which sexual minorities in the country live and articulate their relationships, is sidelined. This sidelining also occurred within the social-movement discursive framing. Moreover, as Ashley Currier and Julie Moreau have put it, "the movement for same-sex marriage … did not generate a discourse capable of adequately addressing South Africa's complex socioeconomic inequality, of which sexual inequities are only one element" (Currier and Moreau 2018, 98).

Second, the complex legal framework around marriage in which heteronormavitiy and cultural relativism both play a part, plays into what Currier and Moreau (2018) have called a "discursive anxiety" over homosexuality as a threat to traditional culture and religion. As an apparent concession to that anxiety, the Civil Union Act not only explicitly excludes same-sex marriage from the regime of customary marriage but also provides for a "conscientious objection". The pre-existing Marriage Act already grants any marriage officer "holding a responsible position in a religious domination or organization" the right to refuse to conduct a marriage "which would not conform to the rites, formularies, tenets, doctrines or discipline" of the religion in question (Article 31). The Civil Union Act, the only law that explicitly allows same-sex marriage, also provides for marriage officers to object "on the ground of conscience, religion and belief to solemnising a civil union between persons of the same sex, whereupon that marriage officer shall not be compelled to solemnise such civil union" (Article 6). Conservative religious opposition to legalisation of same-sex marriage was evident in public debate and consultation in the years leading up to the law, as documented, for example, by the South African Law Reform Commission, which recommended legalisation of same-sex marriage (SALRC 2003). Notwithstanding the Court's commitment, such as in *NCGLE v. MoJ* 1998, cited above, to not allowing religious beliefs to become the basis for discrimination, societal objections to homosexuality remain strong and their expression is particularly—and violently—punitive towards lesbians, as discussed below. The religious exemption and the mutual legal exclusivity of civil unions and customary marriage also exacerbates the impact of socioeconomic inequalities, notably between urban and rural lesbian and gay populations, among other things because the latter are less likely to be able to find registered marriage officers to marry them (Currier and Moreau 2018, 96).

Third, as concerns socioeconomic issues more broadly, post-apartheid South Africa has remained deeply inegalitarian: "[t]he post-apartheid distributional regime displays strong continuities from its predecessor, the late apartheid distributional regime, because the biggest losers under both [particularly the unemployed and the rural poor] have remained politically weak" (Seekings and Natrass 2005, 375). The abovementioned World Bank Report, which shows South Africa to be the most unequal country in the world, also shows that this situation has in fact *worsened* since the end of apartheid in 1994 (Sulla and Zikhali 2018). According to Jeremy Seekings and Nicoli Nattrass, writing a decade after the end of apartheid, the post-apartheid economic distributional regime tweaked the existing neoliberal regime with some social justice reforms rather than fundamentally changing it. In particular, the exacerbation of inequality since the end of apartheid contrasts starkly with the aspirational constitutional narrative of breaking the chains of an oppressive past. Seekings and Nattrass argue that the race frame rather than a class or socio-economic frame has dominated political conversations in the post-apartheid regime, and suggest that the various factions of the ANC have been most responsive to those with the resources to mobilise effectively, and the power to ensure their election or otherwise (Seekings and Nattrass 2005). Within this context of inequality, the "model minority" of same-sex wedded couples remains urban, male, middle class and white, reinforcing the counter-narrative of homosexuality as "un-African" and a "colonial import" (Naidoo and Karels 2012a and b; Morrissey 2013; Currier and Moreau 2018), "despite a body of evidence to the contrary" (Naidoo and Karels 2012b, 614).

The Civil Union Act is also presumed to be consistent with the narrative of sex and gender equality in South Africa, yet the latter is radically at variance with the reality of women's lives. This disjuncture between rhetoric and reality was even embedded in the South African process of peacemaking, as Tristan Anne Borer (2009) has pointed out with relation to the Truth and Reconciliation Commission.

Borer argues that the parameters given the Commission, which privileged violations of civil and political rights and excluded violations of economic and social rights, and was gender-neutral in its approach to truth gathering, meant that "the TRC was not terribly successful at uncovering the truth about women's experiences, specifically of sexual violence, under apartheid" (Borer 2009, 1170). Although after feminist urging the TRC did alter its truth gathering practices to gather women's testimony, and did note that women suffered sexual violence, there was no testimony by perpetrators and the TRC's final report provided no analysis "of how such violence functioned politically" (Borer 2009, 1179), nor were specific reparations for women recommended. Although since that time South Africa has introduced many mechanisms for protecting women's rights, including a Commission for Gender Equality, legal rights mechanisms do not in themselves guarantee the enactment of such protections. In this respect, the TRC set a very bad example. The privileging of civil and political rights over economic and social rights, notably those of rural black women, continues to this day within the narrative of "marriage equality" (Scott 2013).

In the case of rape, transformative constitutionalism may in fact have undermined efforts to develop a more holistic approach. Lisa Vetten has argued that South Africa's policy response to rape, which has been driven by both its post-apartheid visionary constitutional commitments and its lamentable reputation as concerns the material reality of violence against women, has been overly focused on judicial processes, with an accent on cleaning up crime, and less focused on support for victims and preventive processes (Vetten 2011). As concerns lesbians more specifically, Currier and Moreau argue that one effect of the LGBTIQ movement working with and within the normative institutional framework and discourse of human rights "has separated discussions of anti-lesbian rape from broader discussions of misogyny and socioeconomic injustice" (Currier and Moreau 2018, 99).

Early in the 2000s South Africa, which had already been dubbed "the rape capital of the world" in 1995 (cited in Jewkes and Abrahams 2002, 1231), began developing notoriety for so-called "corrective" or "curative" rapes. Young lesbians interviewed for a 2003 report jointly authored by Human Rights Watch and the International Gay and Lesbian Human Rights Commission (now Outright Action International) told of fear of sexual abuse and of a widespread belief in the "curative" power of rape to make lesbians "normal" (HRW and IGLHRC 2003, 109 ff.). Butch lesbians are particularly targeted (Naidoo and Karels 2012a; Swarr 2012). The issue developed national and international notoriety following the brutal rape and murder of Eudy Simelani, a soccer player for the national women's team, on 28 April 2008 (Martin et al. 2009; Bucher 2009), less than a year after the adoption of the Criminal Law (Sexual Offences and Related Matters) Amendment Act of 2007. A number of national and international reports dubbed these rapes hate crimes and debate ensued over whether a specific hate crime amendment should be added to the 2007 Act or some other legislation introduced (Naidoo and Karels 2012b; Koraan and Geduld 2015).

Kamban Naidoo and Michelle Karels have argued that the introduction of legislation providing for retributive justice for hate crimes will not on its own solve the problem and may introduce others, including the added difficulty, in an already tough prosecutorial terrain, "in securing a successful conviction for a crime committed with a specific state of mind or mental *animus*" (Naidoo and Karels 2016, 74). Sentencing behaviours also vary widely across the country, and the risks to the victim are significant throughout the process, including that of being "outed" to family and friends, which creates a fear of secondary victimisation and drives the women further underground rather than encouraging them to report the crimes. The authors conclude that "[u]nless South Africa deals with the roots of hate, such as patriarchy and misogyny, hate-crime legislation, whether substantive or sentence enhancing, may simply become another 'white elephant' on the statute books" (Naidoo and Karels 2016, 79). Indeed, many scholars and NGOs investigating "corrective rapes" have commented on the low reporting rate (in the case of those who survived, as many were also murdered), as of rape more generally (Naidoo and Karels 2012a,b; Du Toit 2005, 2014). The state has also been called to account for its role in worsening an already disastrous situation: among other things, Thabo Mbeki's denialism concerning the incidence of both rape and HIV/AIDs during the decade of his presidency (1999–2008) and the acquittal of the man who would become his successor, Jacob Zuma, on rape charges in 2006.

Certainly, the South African case is not unique: rape and sexual abuse of women and girls in general and lesbians in particular are so widespread in our societies that they appear as the norm rather than the exception, notwithstanding ubiquitous human rights rhetoric and (almost) universal institutional consensus that this violence against women and girls is A Very Bad Thing and must be eradicated. Even where there is a relatively good legislative framework and a professed state commitment to addressing the issue, state responses generally remain piecemeal if not downright half-hearted. Moreover, institutional and political actors tend to adopt specific rhetorical frames that remain masculinist in their register, such as muscular combats against crime, or protection of the weak and vulnerable, without providing either the material resources or the structures that provide real possibilities for victims to have a meaningful voice, effective protection and appropriate redress, or that enable comprehensive and transformative measures in the medium to longer term. As Louise Du Toit has put it:

> As long as circumstances make it reasonable for women to conclude that it is useless to report rape, then … the state and its structures are complicit in sustaining and perpetuating a culture or social ethics of rape which systematically humiliates and paralyses far more than half of its population. (Du Toit 2005, 267)

In the case of South Africa, then, the political and juridical discourse of collective "rupture" with an oppressive past to move towards a regime of human rights and equality-in-diversity for all, has, paradoxically perhaps, led to the creation of a new normative frame in which some are more equal, more modern and more deserving of consideration than others. Notably, lesbians, especially if black, poor, rural and butch-looking, are currently punished rather than protected by South African law and society, and marginalised within LGBTIQ movements (Scott 2013; Judge 2014). Moreover, the state and the courts, while insisting that religious dogma should not dictate law or undermine equality, continue to enable that dogma to flourish through the "conscientious objection" provision in the Civil Union Act. The deep, enduring and intersecting inequalities of class, race and gender are smoothed over, as is the real diversity of life situations and personal and political choices of lesbians and gay men who do not fit the "model minority" criteria for acceptance into the Rainbow Family of the Rainbow Nation.

PART II

Selling same-sex marriage

4

RAINBOWING THE WORKPLACE

Introduction: hashtag-inclusive

The social capital and presumed purchasing power of LGBTIQ minorities (and most particularly that of the "G"), have prompted businesses to incorporate support for "diversity" in general and same-sex marriage in particular in their brand. (I use the term "social capital" in a Bourdieusian sense of individuals and groups being able to capitalise on more or less institutionalised networks in order to obtain advancement (Bourdieu 1980a).) Some research has shown that US businesses including same-sex partner health benefits and other LGBTIQ-inclusive policies show an improvement in profit-making performance and/or employee satisfaction and loyalty (Li and Nagar 2013; Badgett et al. 2013; Webster 2018; Badgett 2020, ch. 4; Hossain et al. 2019), even though these results do not hold uniformly for all companies at all times. Be that as it may, large multinationals have been eager to use promotion of same-sex marriage and what I call "rainbowing" more generally as a marketing tool. The issue has even made it on to the agenda of the World Economic Forum (see for example Carmingnani 2017); one can thus read on the corporate blogsite of Microsoft, which refers to the 2015 WEF, that "[d]iversity and inclusion help drive our business and our bottom line", in both marketing and recruitment terms (Microsoft corporate blog 2015).[1]

Today, corporate and public-sector employers throughout the Western-aligned liberal capitalist world routinely feature LGBTIQ "inclusivity", notably support for same-sex couples and families, in their brand—albeit to differing degrees and framed in different ways to suit the cultural context. This "inclusivity" has even become a core element of now-fashionable corporate social responsibility (CSR). The concept of CSR is not new—its origins can be traced to a 1953 book by Howard Bowen (Bowen 2013)—but it has become the corporate buzzword of these first decades of the third millennium. Various corporate scandals, from massive oil spills to exposure of near-slavery conditions in garment and footwear factories in the Global South, have led to demands that corporations become ethically, socially and environmentally accountable. The LGBTIQ inclusivity aspect of CSR has become a relatively cost-neutral selling point for companies, presumed to give them a market advantage in both recruitment of skilled labour and increased market value, as companies build rainbow credentials in a growing market of upwardly mobile homosexuals with homonormativist aspirations. This chapter explores that branding exercise—that rainbowing—as a form of pink-washing. Much of the discussion here focuses on the Anglosphere, notably the US and Australia, where corporate partnering with LGBTIQ rights groups and/or same-sex marriage campaigns has been very prominent.

IBM uses the hashtag "#inclusiveIBM" to promote its "diversity-and-equality" credentials. When I last consulted the #inclusiveIBM website in late 2019, it featured a photograph of a young white woman with very closely cropped hair, seated in a relaxed position and smiling at the camera. She was dressed neatly in a short-sleeved shirt and dark trousers, wearing a large watch on one wrist and a leather band on the other: a certain image of the "corporate lesbian". We were told that the woman in the photograph was called Ella and that she joined IBM in 2014. The website's header claimed, presumably citing Ella: "I can be my best being myself". Underneath was the text: "Working at IBM, Ella is able to be herself every day, while building on IBM's history of an inclusive diversity culture". (#inclusive IBM website).[2] In a band below the header and the photograph, the page features the subhead "The Power of Inclusion" and the text:

> IBM has a long-standing commitment to diversity and inclusion, recognizing the unique value and skills every individual brings to the workplace. We believe that innovation comes from seeking out and inspiring collaboration in all dimensions. Consciously building inclusive teams and encouraging diversity of ideas helps us make the greatest impact for our clients, our colleagues, and the world. (#inclusive IBM website)

The website also provides a link to download a "diversity and inclusion" brochure, produced in 2015. On another tab, one can find a timeline of IBM's passage from "civil rights" to "diversity". It states that in 1984 it became one of the first companies to include sexual orientation in its equal opportunity policies (although at that time it was expressed as "sexual preference").[3]

Another early action by IBM was to introduce same-sex domestic partner health benefits for US employees, in 1996. It was a significant step: the US is one of the few countries in the liberal capitalist world without a universal public health care system: in fact, it is the worst in that respect. I will more thoroughly explore this question in Chapter 7, but the attraction of same-sex partner/spousal healthcare benefits offered by IBM and other US corporations needs to be stressed here, particularly at a time when the US state was retreating from even its own relatively minimalist welfare system. Partner health benefits have thus been used as a key element of corporate rainbow-branding in the US, and are a core component of the "Corporate Equality Index" published by the Human Rights Campaign that has, every year since 20.02, rated US corporations on their performance with regard to LGBTIQ employees.

Throughout the Anglosphere, the corporate world realised early on that supporting same-sex marriage would be good for the bottom line. In the US in 2011, 70 companies had signed on to a legal brief to defeat The Defense of Marriage Act, while in 2015, 379 of them signed on to the *Obergefell v. Hodges* brief that led to the US Supreme Court decision legalising same-sex marriage (Cadei 2015).

In Northern Ireland in 2018, Businesses for Love Equality, which included both local and multinational companies, published an open letter in support of the application there of the UK Marriage (Same-Sex Couples) Act, passed in 2013 and applied in England and Wales from March 2014 (Amnesty International 2018). Both Scotland and Northern Ireland, because of their semi-autonomous status, required separate acts of their respective parliaments to extend the legislation there. The Scottish Parliament adopted the law in 2014, but in Northern Ireland the ultra-conservative Democratic Unionist Party has consistently blocked it. In 2019, in the context of a collapsed Northern Ireland Executive, the UK passed the Northern Ireland (Executive Formation etc.) Act, which set a non-negotiable deadline of 13 January 2020 for the extension of same-sex marriage to Northern Ireland. (The Act also provided for the extension of the UK abortion law to Northern Ireland, which was passed on 21 October 2019.) The first legal same-sex marriage took place in Northern Ireland on 11 February 2020. The next section will focus on the Australian case.

"A happy workforce is a productive one": the Australian corporate campaign for same-sex marriage

The sentence cited above is taken from an Open Letter by Australian business leaders in support of same-sex marriage in Australia, published on the Australian Marriage Equality (AME) website at the time of the campaign for legalisation there. The letter is not dated, and no longer accessible via the AME website, but one of the few websites where one can still find it, that of the Health Informatics Society of Australia, put the number of business supporters of the campaign at 2,071 when it joined that number on 2 October 2017. The full paragraph reads:

> Not only is marriage equality the only truly fair option, it is also a sound economic option, given that a happy workforce is a productive one. To remain competitive and to attract top talent globally organisations – and nations – must create a fair and respectful environment for all. Equality in the workplace works; discrimination does not.[4]

The business campaign was spearheaded by AME, an advocacy group set up by long-time Tasmanian gay rights activist Rodney Croome in 2004, when the federal government passed the Marriage Amendment Act, explicitly limiting marriage to heterosexuals only. In 2014, businesswoman Janine Middleton came on board as a volunteer, and took over as AME co-chair in 2015, driving the corporate campaign that led to those 2,071 signatures. Middleton was lauded in the media in 2017, the year during which the Australian debate reached fever pitch. A proposed plebiscite on the issue, blocked by the Senate in November 2016, ended up being downgraded to a nationwide voluntary postal survey run over September and October 2017, amid urging on one side to just have the vote in parliament, given that a majority of Australians, already polled many times, supported legalisation, and on the other side, an anti-gay-marriage campaign by religious conservatives (Winter 2018a). (By this time, Croome had resigned as national director of AME, the organisation he had founded, as he opposed any sort of accommodation of a plebiscite, preferring to lobby for a direct parliamentary vote.)

As a "self-confessed 'very old-fashioned' Mrs Mosman: a Liberal-voting Catholic who knits, irons her husband's shirts, has 'fur babies' and never leaves the house without her pearls on", (Tang 2017), and a former managing director of investment banking company JP Morgan in London, Janine Middleton had all the qualities that would appeal to the business sector and the centre-right. (Mosman is one of the so-called "leafy suburbs" of Sydney, and one of the richest suburbs in Australia. Located on the affluent Lower North Shore of Sydney Harbour, its demographics are mostly white European, upper middle-class, well-educated and conservative. Middleton, the daughter of a working-class Labor voter, is against type in this area notorious for its old-money, old-school tribal mentality [Craze 2012]). She explained her choice to campaign for same-sex marriage through her experience at JP Morgan, where she noticed gay staff she supervised "editing" their lives, being selective about situations in which they would be "out", and where the company itself was moving to introduce more LGBTIQ-friendly policies (cited in Tang 2017). After her return to Australia in 2012, it was the 2014 coming out of Olympic swimming champion Ian Thorpe that was, she says, the "line in the sand" prompting her to join the same-sex marriage campaign (cited in Tang 2017).

The apparent contradictions in this story do not end there. The corporate campaign began when Middleton "wrangled an agreement from the establishment Catholic Sydney law firm of Gilbert + Tobin, which acts for the Catholic Church in the sexual abuse royal commission, to host a breakfast of corporate CEOs to discuss same-sex marriage" (Clark 2017). (The Royal Commission in question was a national commission of enquiry into sexual abuse of children within Catholic institutions, which took place from 2015 to 2017. Gilbert + Tobin were appointed to advise the Church's Truth, Justice and Healing Council, which had adopted a policy of not cross-examining abuse victims, a practice not respected by Cardinal George Pell, who appointed his own counsel to cross-examine. Pell was found guilty of child sexual abuse in December 2018 but later acquitted on appeal.) So, a Catholic law firm that had just been retained to help the Church "clean up its act", so to speak, found itself hosting a meeting of some 200 business leaders on an issue to which the Catholic Church was mostly extremely hostile.

On 29 May 2015, 50 of those corporations, including Gilbert + Tobin, took out a full page advertisement supporting same-sex marriage in the right-leaning daily newspaper *The Australian* (the flagship Australian publication of Rupert Murdoch's News Corp empire). Headed "Join the growing list of Corporate Australia supporting Marriage Equality", the ad featured the names and logos of Australian, US and European corporations, many of them multi- or transnational. The Australian-based signatories included airline Qantas; three of the "big four" Australian banking groups: Commonwealth, ANZ and Westpac; the main telecommunications company Telstra; the Foxtel media company co-owned by Telstra and News Corp; Slater and Gordon (one of the country's largest law firms, which also operates in the UK); Football Federation Australia; and upmarket department store group David Jones (although this last was taken over by South African group Woolworths in 2014). Others included US technology giant Google; ice cream company Ben and Jerry's (US-founded but now owned by British-Dutch group Unilever); both P&O Cruises and its parent company Carnival (UK); chemicals giant Dow Inc (US), Swedish fast fashion company H&M; and the management consultancy Boston Consulting Group (US). At the time the ad was published, AME Director Rodney Croome suggested that one of the motivators for corporate support was the reputational damage Australia would suffer if it did not "catch up" to other countries in the Anglosphere (with the implication that Australia's reputational damage would have a knock-on impact on brand reputation) (cited in ABC News 2015).

Corporate support grew over the subsequent two years thanks to the efforts of Middleton and others—including some academics such as Mark Humphery-Jenner of the University of New South Wales, who, in article published in *The Conversation* in 2016, drew on examples of US states that introduced religious exemptions to restrict same-sex marriage following the 2015 Supreme Court decision (he cited Indiana, North Carolina and Mississippi). He warned that like these states, Australia could face economic risks that "could include boycotts, adverse consequences for tourism, and undermining the ability to attract top talent to Australia", but by legalising same-sex marriage the Australian government would "help to highlight to the international business community that Australia is a welcoming country" (Humphery-Jenner 2016).

In March 2017, in the context of then Prime Minister Malcolm Turnbull's determination to proceed with a plebiscite, 34 of the pro-same-sex marriage corporate leaders went public again, this time writing to Turnbull to urge him to proceed directly to legislation without further ado. "As business leaders", they wrote, "we believe marriage equality is important for a number of reasons:"

> It is good for our employees – People are a company's most important asset …
>
> It is good for our customers – In the globally competitive marketplace, customers are becoming more discerning and are selecting products and services from companies that better represent their values …

> It is good for Australia – Australia's global reputation as a welcoming and inclusive nation helps to attract international talent and foreign investment …
>
> It is good for our business – Equality and diversity are strategic business issues. It has been well demonstrated that businesses that embrace workplace diversity and inclusion are more innovative and outperform in organisational effectiveness and profitability. Corporate social responsibility is becoming a critical factor to a growing number of global investors and the capital markets. (Bernhard et al 2017)

Seven of the signatories, or a little over 20 per cent, were women, which is much higher than the representation of women among the CEOs of Australia's top 200 companies (in 2019, this was 6 per cent, down from 7 per cent the previous year, which suggests that women may be going backwards in the corporate world [Ryan 2019]).

The letter caused a stir in both parliament and the business world. One corporate executive anonymously told *The Australian* that the corporate campaign to urge business leaders to sign the letter to Turnbull could be seen as "corporate bullying" of smaller companies and that other business priorities (such as lobbying for changes to taxation law or legislating for more "flexible" labour standards) were being neglected (cited in Shanahan 2017). Immigration Minister Peter Dutton lambasted the CEOs on several consecutive days, stating that the government would not be "bullied" and telling the CEOs to "stick to their knitting" instead of focusing on "fringe" issues and "jamming politically correct views down [people's] throats" (cited in Anderson and Smith 2017; Koziol 2017). Dutton, who at the time of writing remains in his post under current Prime Minister Scott Morrison, with his portfolio expanded and redubbed "Home Affairs", is one of the most powerful and most conservative members of the government. His criticisms of corporate support for same-sex marriage came in the wake of a furore over independent brewery Coopers' sponsoring of a Bible Society video called "Keeping it Light" in which two conservative members of parliament debated same-sex marriage "in a light-hearted way" according to the Coopers branding. This video accompanied the release of a "limited edition" of Coopers light beer sporting Bible verses on the packaging, in commemoration of the Bible Society's two hundredth anniversary. Some pubs and bars immediately boycotted Coopers and the company was roundly taken to task by both consumers and other companies—and satirised on social and mainstream media. After two press statements that attempted to justify the video were not effective in damage control, Coopers backpedalled, withdrawing the video, publishing an apology and issuing a statement in support of same-sex marriage (Winsor 2017). This incident was surely uppermost in Peter Dutton's mind when he claimed that "[s]ome companies are morally coerced into supporting campaigns in fear of being extorted by an online social media push to boycott their product and it is simply unconscionable" (cited in Belot 2017).

The controversy around the Coopers boycott and Dutton's reactions demonstrated that Humphery-Jenner's words in 2016 were prophetic: Coopers risked significant brand damage, which could have jeopardised the small company's survival.

Two of the corporate leaders specifically targeted by Dutton's comments were themselves openly gay: Business Council of Australia chief Jennifer Westacott, and Qantas CEO Alan Joyce, both of whom were very outspoken on the issue and actively campaigned for a "yes" vote in the 2017 postal ballot. Both also appeared in a list of 50 "outstanding LGBTI executives" compiled by Deloitte and the *Australian Financial Review* and published in December 2016. In an interview for that article, Westacott told of being "incensed" at talk of sexuality being a "lifestyle choice":

> I would not have chosen this like I was taking up tennis or chess or something. When I was a young person, this was the most confronting thing that could ever happen to you. It was just crippling loneliness and isolation because you couldn't talk to anyone. (cited in Gray 2016)

Joyce, for his part, urged "good businesses" to support the "yes" vote and donated AU$1 million to the cause, contrary to most companies, which had supported the campaign discursively but donated little to no money (Karp 2017). As CEO of the "Flying Kangaroo", Joyce told the media that he was proud to be an Australian citizen and part of the Australian "meritocracy", saying: "Where else in the world would an openly gay Irish man become the CEO of one of the biggest brands, if not the most iconic brand?" (cited in Cockburn 2017).

The support of business leaders, including openly gay ones, chimed with the wider demographic. An analysis of data from the Household, Income and Labour Dynamics in Australia survey (HILDA) showed that support of same-sex marriage in Australia (by well over two thirds of the population by 2017) was "significantly greater" among women, the well-educated, city dwellers, native speakers of English and those on higher incomes. Support was also, unsurprisingly, greater among the young, the gay and the non-religious (Perales and Campbell 2017).

When the "yes" vote won, it was hailed by the *Australian Financial Review* as a "rare win for the big end of town", at a time when "business [had] not had a good year" (Smith 2017). The author cited not only corporate Australia's failure to get what it wanted in terms of tax cuts or industrial relations reforms but also the fact that "[t]he populist backlash against the banks and energy companies in particular [reflected] a lack of trust globally in big institutions" (Smith 2017). (In fact, a Royal Commission on Misconduct in the Banking, Superannuation and Financial Services Industry was established within days of the same-sex marriage law being adopted in parliament in December 2017. The Commission handed down a damning report in 2018. As concerns energy companies, the issue remains a vexed one at the time of writing, both because of high prices and because of the continued coal-dependency of the energy economy, as well as the government's climate-change-denial stance.) So, getting a "yes" for same-sex marriage appeared to be as much a corporate success story in Australia as a social movement one, not the least because the two had openly joined forces in campaigning for it.

Corporate equality and inequality

Four years before IBM ventured to include the term "sexual preference" in its equal opportunity policy, Steve Endean set up the Human Rights Campaign Fund (HRC) as a Political Action Committee (PAC). (A PAC is a tax-exempt organisation that finances political campaigns in the US.) "The Fund's mission was to provide financial support on behalf of the gay and lesbian community to political candidates who supported gay civil rights legislation" (HRC website).[5] The Fund grew very quickly, and in 1995 it extended its work, dropping the word "Fund" from its name. It is today the country's largest LGBTIQ organisation and runs various advocacy, research and education projects. It has a large number of corporate partners, ranked Platinum, Gold, Silver or Bronze, depending on how much they donate. Platinum partners include Microsoft, Coca Cola, American Airlines and Apple; Gold includes Deloitte, Nike and Pfizer; in the Silver group one finds British Petroleum, Citi and MGM Resorts; while Amazon, Goldman Sachs, Shell, Whirlpool, Google and IBM are among the Bronze partners.

Every single one of these corporate partners has come under scrutiny for one or more of the following: exploitative employment practices including in their supply chain; environmental degradation; or corrupt business practices. For example, Deloitte, whose name crops up elsewhere in this chapter in relation to studies positively profiling LGBTIQ people in business and supporting same-sex marriage, is one of the so-called "Big Four" accountancy and consulting groups, the other three being PricewaterhouseCoopers, Ernst & Young and KPMG. These Big Four have been implicated in tax avoidance schemes, benefit from significant taxpayer-funded government contract, and lack transparency, yet they also, paradoxically, have a legitimacy-conferring role for clients with whom they work (Duff 2017; Brooks 2018: Tadros 2018a,b, 2019).

Since 2002 the HRC has produced the Corporate Equality Index. Points are awarded in four categories: "non-discrimination policies across business entities"; equitable healthcare, retirement and other benefits "for LGBTQ workers and their families"; "internal education and accountability metrics to promote LGBTQ inclusion competency" (which includes competency training and existence of an employee resource group, diversity council or similar); and "public commitment to LGBTQ equality" (which includes external engagement with the LGBTQ community) (HRC 2018a, 4). In 2002 18 companies achieved the top score of 100 per cent, while in 2020 this number had grown to 686 (HRC 2020). IBM has scored 100 since 2003, and other companies sporting that perfect score are Amazon and Uber, both publicly and trenchantly criticised in recent years for their labour practices. They sit amid a range of multinational companies with exploitative employment practices either directly within the company or within the supply chain (the food and garment industries, some of which such as Starbucks and Nike feature on the HRC's 100 per cent list, being notorious for offshore and supply chain labour exploitation as well as environmentally unsustainable practices).

There is a plethora of literature detailing these abuses,[6] in a labour economy that is increasingly globalised and informalised, and in which traditional workplace legislative and union protections do not operate, creating a new "precariat" (Standing [2011]2016; see also Prassl 2018; De Ruyter and Brown 2019). As Keith Cunningham-Parmeter has noted, "[t]his persistent uncertainty impacts an ever-expanding list of businesses in retail, service, home care, construction, information technology, and the burgeoning on-demand economy" (Cunningham-Parmeter 2016). In this economy, workers are not workers but "contractors", not hired but "crowdsourced", not doing a job but picking up a "gig". Employers in the on-demand economy spin a narrative of flexibility, innovation, independence and creativity for the workers but the reality is that workers are very poorly paid and constantly policed in terms of performance and behaviour, and are quickly "deactivated" (Uber's word) if they do not comply (Cunningham-Parmeter 2016; Prassl 2018).

One example of the digitally crowdsourced economy is Amazon's Mechanical Turk or MTurk platform, set up in 2005. Amazon took the name from a hoax invention produced in 1770 by Hungarian Wolfgang von Kempelen to impress Empress Maria Theresa of Austria, the last of the Habsburg rulers and the only female one. The Turk, an elaborate structure that sported a life-size artificial head of a "Turk" in Ottoman garb, was supposedly an automaton that could play chess. In fact, the "automaton" was a chess master concealed inside the box, using a system of numbered squares, magnets and strings to see the board and move pieces around. The machine was developed and named at a time when both mechanical modernity (Tresch 2011; Voskuhl 2013) and *turqueries*—a fascination for all things Turkish, from clothing to visual arts to music in a shifting love-hate relationship with the Ottoman Empire (Deringil 2007; Hadler 2017)—were all the rage, against a background of Enlightenment thinking that was making its presence felt, even in the Holy Roman Empire of the Habsburgs (Evans 2008, ch. 3).

Amazon's use of the name is a nod to the illusion created by Kempelen, in an advertising pitch that not everything can be completely automated: a range of mostly repetitive and low-level mechanical tasks still need discerning humans to do them effectively. At the same time, those humans are remote and invisible to the corporate users (called "requesters" by MTurk), who thus do not need to be troubled by the working conditions of those performing the digital tasks. Amazon boasts—on a simply-formatted website with no images of actual people—that MTurk "enables companies to harness the collective intelligence, skills, and insights from a global workforce to streamline business processes", in order to "optimize efficiency" by outsourcing repetitive "microtasks", "increase flexibility" through access to "a global, on-demand, 24x7 workforce" and "reduce cost" by "leveraging the skills of distributed Workers on a pay-per-task model" (Amazon MTurk homepage).[7] To workers, Amazon's pitch is "Make money in your spare time: Get paid for completing simple tasks" (Amazon MTurk worker page).[8] To the right of the page, one sees a pretty young woman of colour (but light-skinned none-theless), dressed casually in jeans and a sleeveless top, sitting cross-legged in front of her laptop with a big smile on her face. Below this opening image, one can scroll down to see the list of available tasks, accompanied by simple graphics. The list comprises various tasks under the four headers "Image/Video Processing", "Data Verification and Clean-up", "Information Gathering" and "Data Processing". Under this list is the closing text "Become an Amazon Mechanical Turk Worker: With thousands of available tasks, it's easy to find something that fits your skills and interests", and a "Get started" button. Reports detail very low pay and difficult working conditions, which include not only doing the task (for which sometimes workers are not paid if the results are rejected by the "requester") but also looking for tasks to do in the first place. Attempts by MTurk workers to organise within the digital landscape are regularly blocked by Amazon, for example by not admitting workers who subscribe to particular organising platforms (Hara et al. 2017; Semuels 2018; Schwartz 2019).

Even without venturing into the realm of crowdsourced, outsourced and off-shored labour practices, it is not at all difficult to find examples of exploitative labour practices in more traditional physical workplaces. Trade union density has been declining for some decades, in great part due to the abovementioned neo-liberal globalisation and informalisation of labour (Visser 2019), but it has never been very high in places such as the US—10 per cent density in 2016, according to ILOSTAT (2019)—and some corporations are openly hostile to unionisation. One of them, again, is Amazon, which applies two typical "localisation standards" for setting up its warehouses: "(a) proximity to freeways with favorable links to an international airport and (b) presence in structurally weak regions with a local labor market characterized by high unemployment" (Cattero and D'Onofrio 2018, 149). The overall precarity of work in the service sector in many countries (Cattero and D'Onofrio were looking at Germany and Italy) and Amazon's corporate structure (which in Europe consists of each distribution centre being an autonomous entity owned by a Luxembourg-based holding company), makes it very difficult for unions to organise workers across the different centres. However, this does not stop them trying: in 2019 workers in many distribution centres in the US pushed to unionise and protest the untenable pace of work, low pay and policing of employees—allegations Amazon routinely denies (Sainato 2019). Yet, even these appalling working conditions are considered by some commentators to be superior to MTurk digital piecework, to the extent that one journalist quipped darkly that working in Amazon's "fulfilment centres" may one day be remembered as "the good old days" (Mangan 2013).

Amazon has come under increasingly severe scrutiny in 2020 in the context of the COVID-19 pandemic. On 14 April, a court in the Parisian suburb of Nanterre handed down an emergency ruling limiting Amazon to trade in only essential goods (foodstuffs and medical supplies), until it was able to demonstrate that it had provided adequate protections to its staff, with an imposition of hefty daily fines for non-compliance. The company was also ordered to pay the court costs of the union Solidaires, which had brought the suit (Tribunal Judiciaire de Nanterre 2020). Amazon promptly responded by closing six French distribution centres, which at the time of writing are now gradually being reopened. In a country in which Amazon has long come under scrutiny (see e.g. Berthelot 2018), the 2020 court case represented what one press commentator termed an "unprecedented escalation", with Amazon becoming the focus of a "symbolic battle" in the midst of a health and economic crisis (Piquard 2020). In the meantime, Amazon CEO Jeff Bezos, the world's richest man and already its sole hectobillionaire (since 2018), is predicted to become its first trillionaire by 2026. The huge accumulation of wealth by Bezos at the expense of employees who work in oppressive conditions for very low wages has been termed a "policy failure" by one US commentator (Lowrey 2018).

As for IBM, the supposed pioneer of LGBTIQ-friendly workplaces, it has been the object of a number of lawsuits by workers. In 2006 "Big Blue" (as IBM is nicknamed) paid US$65 million to settle a class action lawsuit for unpaid overtime brought on behalf of some 32,000 current and former technical support workers. However, it then cut the base salary of those employees by 15 per cent to make up for the payout (Modine 2008). More recently, in 2019, it faced multiple age-discrimination lawsuits, including one class action, with evidence that it had fired up to 100,000 older employees over the previous few years. In a deposition in one of the cases, former vice-president for human resources Alan Wild told of Big Blue's push to look less like a "fuddy duddy" organisation and more like a "cool and trendy" one, attracting millennials (cited in Carville 2019)—perhaps more like young Ella, the woman featured on its hashtag-inclusive website, discussed above. The sackings did not, however, help in lifting IBM's brand value. In 2016 Big Blue had been seventh on the Forbes brand list, with a brand value of US$41.4 billion, while by 2019 it had slipped to twentieth place, with a brand value of US$31.5 billion, and was the sixtieth biggest company overall.[9]

Three years earlier, Alliance@IBM, a branch of Communication Workers of America set up in 1999 to combat redundancies as IBM laid off US workers and shifted jobs offshore, folded. National coordinator Lee Conrad cited "years of job cuts and membership losses" that had "taken their toll, [with] IBM executive management steamroll[ing] over employees and their families" (cited in Kunert 2016). In Argentina the following year, the union fared better, with stronger legislative protection. IBM was forced by the National Labour Court to recognise Unión Informática in the workplace and manage union membership contributions through payroll deductions for workers who were union members (Unión Informatica 2017).

Back in Australia, that outspoken corporate champion of same-sex marriage, Qantas boss Alan Joyce, has faced years of union protests over job cuts, low pay and exploitative working conditions. On 29 October 2011, he grounded the entire Qantas fleet and locked out staff in response to several months' industrial action by pilots, flight attendants, ground staff and engineers over pay, conditions and the offshoring of jobs. Two days later, the Australian industrial tribunal, by then misnamed Fair Work Australia, ordered the unions—at the request of the then Labor government—to cease all industrial action (Lauder 2011). Some weeks earlier, in the face of vociferous protest by the unions and some shareholders, the Qantas executive had awarded Joyce an AU$2.2 million bonus in shares, taking his then salary package to AU$5.1 million (ABC News 2011). Joyce continued with his offshoring plans in the face of ongoing union protest, and in 2015 he lashed out at protesting unions for "trashing" the Qantas brand (SBS News 2015). In December 2019, baggage handlers and ramp workers with Qantas's budget brand Jetstar went on strike once more over pay and conditions, which included dangerous overwork and understaffing, according to their union (ABC News 2019). In March 2020, as the airline industry began to feel the pain of the COVID-19 lockdown, Qantas and its budget subsidiary Jetstar stood down 20,000 employees (two thirds of the workforce) without pay, despite an AU$715 million government rescue package (Butler 2020a). On 25 June, Joyce announced that the airline would sack 6,000 staff and keep another 15,000 stood down (Butler 2020b).

Even statutory institutions that are normally supposed to provide impartial, evidence-based rulings on employment matters have been found to be biased in favour of employers and corporations more generally. For example, in the US, a report by the progressive foundation People for the American Way found the Supreme Court to favour corporations in its rulings on workplace disputes, to the extent that it had become a "Corporate Court" (PFAW 2010), while in Australia, the right-wing government has been accused of "stacking" the Fair Work Commission with pro-business appointees (Karp 2018).

For corporations as for states, then, same-sex marriage is very much a branding and marketing exercise, generating goodwill among some sections of the population—particularly the professional and executive workforce—while leaving entirely intact the systems of exploitation that these companies have become increasingly inventive in expanding and perpetuating. "Equality" and "inclusivity" in such companies, as understood by HRC, are truncated concepts: the focus is on the executive/professional end of town (and preferably youngish) rather than on quasi-slave labour in "fulfilment centres", digital micro-tasking, offshore factories and call centres, or the "contractor" gig economy.

HRC's 100 per cent list also included 127 law firms in 2018, "establishing law firms as the most represented industry among participants receiving a perfect score" (HRC 2018b, 1). Here again, however, the HRC's criteria prove to be narrow. The following year, the International Bar Association published a damning report on bullying and sexual harassment in the legal profession (Pender 2019). The study was based on the largest-ever survey on the issue, with 6,980 respondents, over two-thirds of whom were female, from 135 countries. The report also featured nine country case studies representing a diversity of geographical locations, reporting rates and legislative frameworks: Australia, Brazil, Costa Rica, Malaysia, Russia, South Africa, Sweden, the UK and the US. The US case showed "higher rates of both bullying and sexual harassment than the global average" (Pender 2019, 97), but also noted a higher rate of utilisation of workplace policies on harassment and bullying than in other countries. Seventy-one per cent of respondents reported the existence of such policies in their workplaces, and 46 per cent noted the existence of training programmes on the issues, but these training programmes had zero impact on the incidence of sexual harassment (Pender 2019, 98). Women reported, among other things, a male partner assigning work to junior women employees on the basis of their looks, or being sexually assaulted by an elected official in front of witnesses who did nothing to stop the behaviour (Pender 2019, 98). Although the report noted the existence of a "perception paradox" resulting in a higher rate of reporting in jurisdictions perceived as more progressive or having better legislation, it also noted that the higher rate of reporting is likely to more accurately reflect the actual rate of occurrence. In addition, the US was in 2017 "the epicentre of the #Metoo movement", leading to "unprecedented public attention" being paid to workplace sexual harassment (Pender 2019, 97). The report further noted that in order to correct for the "perception paradox" other indicators of gender (in) equality needed to be taken into account.

The US is the first country in the world to have introduced legislation on sexual harassment, following vigorous lobbying by feminists, via two landmark District Court decisions in 1976 and 1977 that extended the meaning of workplace sex discrimination in Title VII of the 1964 Civil Rights Act (Mackinnon and Siegel 2004). It also performs relatively well on the UN's Gender Development and Gender Equality indexes: it is tied with the UK in fifteenth position in both, although among the country case studies in the above-cited International Bar Association report it trails Australia in sixth place and Sweden in eighth (UNDP 2019, 312 and 316).

The IBA report does not name individual law firms but, given that two thirds of female employees and one third of male employees report bullying, while 54 per cent of female and 11 per cent of male employees report sexual harassment, it is entirely possible that some of the 127 firms on the HRC's "perfect score" list are rather less than perfect when it comes to sexual harassment and bullying. This likelihood is underlined by findings in New Zealand, where there is a system called "Rainbow Tick" comparable to the HRC's Corporate Equality Index, but run, like its Australian counterpart, by a collaboration of community NGOs and government health services. Law Firm Russell McVeagh, one of the most prestigious in the country, was one of the rainbow-ticked firms under the New Zealand system, but in 2015 and 2016 was the focus of a number of sexual harassment allegations that caused a public outcry and prompted an independent review in 2018. The review found four serious problems: a "work hard, play hard" culture involving excessive drinking and some "sexually inappropriate behaviour"; failings in the firm's governance systems, including a lack of code of conduct and poor response to the 2015–2016 allegations; "pockets" of bullying and overwork of junior lawyers, accompanied by a culture of fear of speaking out; a tendency of women employees to leave rather than progress to partnership due to sexism and unconscious bias, despite "progress in the LGBTI and diversity areas" (Bazley 2018). The same year, the Law Society of New Zealand published results of a study (cited by both the Russell McVeagh review and the IBA report) that found significant incidence of sexual harassment in law firms there (Adlam 2018).

Such findings are reproduced in law firms in other countries (see for example, in relation to France: Borgia, Remy and Roche 2018), and they suggest that "rainbow-ticking" is not by any means a guarantee that workplaces will not be sexist nor indeed that they will even be LGBTIQ-egalitarian (RNZ 2019). As I put the finishing touches to this book in June 2020, an inquiry by the Australian High Court (the country's highest court), found that one of its former judges, Dyson Heydon, "one of the nation's pre-eminent legal minds" and powerful figure in the legal hierarchy, had sexually harassed several female associates as well as higher ranking legal professionals, and that his behaviour had been "a open secret" for years (McClymont and Maley 2020, online).

To return to the US case, the "corporate equality" scores given by HRC become even more suspect when one subjects the HRC itself to a little scrutiny. In 2015, the organisation commissioned an investigation into its workplace practices. The findings were damning: they revealed a gay white male power structure, with female employees and "feminine-identified individuals" reporting on a sexist and judgemental working environment, and people of colour also reporting discriminatory treatment (Geidner 2015). HRC pledged to clean up its act, but more recent news about the types of candidates HRC supported in the 2018 midterm congressional elections showed the same prejudice—even worse, in fact, as in some instances centrist or republican straight white male candidates were supported over more left-wing gay candidates, some of whom were women of colour (Robinson 2018). When one considers that the HRC is the US's most wealthy and powerful LGBTIQ advocacy group, such reports, considered alongside the employment practices of corporations to which HRC gives its tick, suggest that some sections of the LGBTIQ population are more "equal" and "included" than others, to adapt yet again the famed Orwellian phrase (Orwell [1945]2001).

The symbolic versus the substantive in the "market for virtue"

In his book *The Market for Virtue*, David Vogel notes that "CSR is sustainable only if virtue pays off. The supply of corporate virtue is both made possible and constrained by the market" (Vogel 2006, 2–3). Angus Duff has noted, in his study on the operation of CSR among the Big Four accounting firms in the UK, a "dominance of the least durable and most easily attained pragmatic legitimacy at the expense of more robust but harder-to-attain levels of moral and cognitive legitimacies" (A. Duff 2017, 514). By "pragmatic legitimacy" Duff refers to the sorts of legitimacy practices that appeal to key constituents: "clients and potential clients … graduates as potential entrants to the industry; internal audiences represented by the firms' staff and partners; and other external audiences constructed as members of those local communities in which the firm operate" (A. Duff 2017, 513). In the area of support for same-sex marriage and "inclusivity" policies regarding LGBTIQ workers, firms attain what Duff calls "*influence legitimacy*, where audiences respond positively to the firm because it is perceived to act in their wider interests" (A. Duff 2017, 517: italics in original).

In Australia, exhibiting pro-same-sex marriage "virtue" was a legitimacy-conferring selling point in a country where in 2017 it was found that "customers from an Indigenous background, with a disability and identifying as lesbian, gay or bisexual were three times as likely to avoid an organisation and twice as likely to dissuade others because of an organisation's negative diversity reputation", and that a company's support for same-sex marriage was a major positive influence on customer behaviour (Deloitte/AHRC 2017, 25 and ff.). Getting a 100 per cent score or a rainbow tick, or being a corporate advocate for same-sex marriage, is thus a marketable "virtue" with little to no cost impact, whereas the virtue of coming clean about tax avoidance, for example, would do significant damage to the corporate bottom line, which is why most ardent defenders of same-sex marriage will not do that (Rhodes 2017). They similarly will not, for example, get involved in debates on, say, immigration, refugees or abortion, as their involvement in such debates is just as likely, if not more so, to lose them customers (and shareholder votes) as it is to win them (Ainsworth, Pekarek and Ghin 2018).

Rainbowing, on the other hand, sells, and it sells in different ways in different locations. In France, for example, during the same-sex marriage debate in 2013, Apple returned to the rainbow-apple logo it had abandoned in the late 1990s in favour of the monochrome, in order to show its support for same-sex marriage, but without making further branding statements—and two years ahead of its re-adoption of the rainbow logo in the US. As for French corporations, unlike those in the US or Australia, they were less interested in directly campaigning for same-sex marriage than in simply incorporating rainbow couples and families into their advertising. In 2011, for example, the company Eram sported an advertisement with two feminine-looking white women, dressed in close-fitting jeans and high heels, embracing each other and their black child, with the caption superimposed over part of the photograph: "As my two mums say, the family is sacred" (reproduced in Clavel 2013). The tongue-in-cheek ad was designed to make the well-known budget footwear, bag and accessory manufacturer appear ahead of its time in sex, sexuality and race terms, and enhance its appeal to younger buyers. Another tongue-in-cheek ad, made in 2010 for car manufacturer Renault's popular Twingo model, shows a video of a young woman in a white dress with a bouquet driving to a church with an older besuited man, whom one is led to presume is her father. They walk down the aisle together to a younger man waiting at the altar. The young woman then steps aside, wishing her father well, and the two men face each other to begin the wedding ceremony. The end of the ad shows the two men leaving the church together, the older man carrying a little girl who is possibly around six years old on his hip.[10] Both the Renault and the Eram ads reinforced the idea of the homonormalised (and possibly blended) "rainbow family".

In writing of these advertising campaigns, Geoffroy Clavel (2013) commented that French corporations seemed more to be jumping on the current affairs bandwagon for marketing purposes than developing the same level of political engagement as corporations in the Anglosphere. I would put it a little differently: the French companies were less interested in making a show of marketing "virtue" through policy statements à la IBM or campaigns à la Alan Joyce than in simply showing themselves to be already quite naturally in tune with the rainbow demographic. By appearing, in their marketing narratives, to take same-sex marriage and rainbow families for granted (albeit with comic surprise effect), as a no-fuss done deal, they branded themselves as ahead of the legislative game, without even having to weigh into the debate.

Rainbow-branding as a specific component of corporate social responsibility (or as a pointed advertising statement, as in the French examples), is, with few exceptions, a recent phenomenon, and even where it is present, it does not guarantee fair or equitable treatment of employees across the board. It certainly does not guarantee an end to systemic workplace sexism and racism. Some have made the argument that taking a stance on same-sex marriage is a "brave" and ethical stance on human rights (in line with, for example, taking a stance on abusive labour practices in another country with which the corporation has dealings) (e.g. Lazala and Bardwell 2015). Yet, gay cosmopolitanism and the mushrooming and mainstreaming of an LGBTIQ middle class has been part of Western cultures, and captured by its markets, for at least three decades. It is not, and has not been for many years, particularly "brave" for corporations—particularly in the Anglosphere—to sponsor Pride floats or support same-sex marriage, or use "gay" themes in advertising. Queer has well and truly become, in marketing and labour-hire terms, the new normal. As for the rest, it is business as usual.

Notes

1 https://blogs.microsoft.com/on-the-issues/2015/02/06/business-case-marriage-equality/, accessed 13 November 2016.
2 https://www.ibm.com/employment/inclusion/inclusive-ibm.html, accessed 17 December 2019.
3 https://www.ibm.com/employment/inclusion/our-culture.html, accessed 17 December 2019.
4 Accessed from the Health Informatics Society of Australia website, 18 December 2019. https://www.hisa.org.au/blog/australian-marriage-equality-open-letter/
5 https://www.hrc.org/hrc-story/about-us, accessed 18 December 2019.
6 For example, concerning the garment industry: Sobel-Read and Monaghan 2017; Stauffer 2018; Kara 2019.
7 https://www.mturk.com/, accessed 24 December 2019.
8 https://www.mturk.com/worker, accessed 24 December 2019.
9 Brand list 2019: https://www.forbes.com/powerful-brands/list/#tab:rank. Biggest companies list: https://www.forbes.com/global2000/list/2/#tab:overall. Brand list 2016: https://www.rankingthebrands.com/The-Brand-Rankings.aspx?rankingID=334&year=1053, accessed 19 December 2019.
10 Viewable on YouTube, accessed 20 December 2019. https://www.youtube.com/watch?time_continue=30&v=V0hGM7lh934&feature=emb_title

5

SAME-SEX WEDDING TOURISM

The wedding industry and its gay component

We saw in Part I that nations and their governments have used same-sex marriage as a branding exercise, incorporating same-sex marriage within their political traditions and reinvigorating and modernising the couple and the family as the bedrock of the nation. We are now about to see that this branding exercise is also a lucrative earner for both domestic and international wedding and tourism markets, and a key component of their growth. The gay wedding market includes both mainstream markets than have introduced "LGBTQ" themes into their advertising and events, and gay-specific wedding and wedding-tourism planners, which in some countries include gay-specific wedding shows such as those organised in Toronto and Montreal from 2004 and subsequently in Vancouver. I will start with an overview of the wedding industry, followed by a discussion of the targeted gendering of the same-sex wedding market, before moving on to a consideration of the political economy of homonormative (and gendered) wedding travel in the tourism industry of the global periphery and semi-periphery. Gay wedding tourism is a particularly strong growth industry, taking a larger share of the overall wedding tourism market than it does of the domestic wedding market, for reasons that are in part, but not solely, linked to the limited availability of legal same-sex weddings.

In 1999, Chrys Ingraham described the wedding industry as having reached "such proportions that it can be more accurately described as a wedding industrial complex" (Ingraham 1999, 26). It is difficult to obtain precise figures on the global value of this complex today: the figure of US$300 million has been cited since 2015 (e.g. Singh 2016; Bourque 2017), although it is probably much more than that now, due to rapid growth in both the gay wedding market and the Chinese hetero-wedding market (the world's third largest, after the US and India). The growing luxury market is estimated to represent a little over one-quarter of the total value of the wedding industry (Trade Arabia 2017), and is thus a significant focus for destination wedding planners in particular, given that roughly one-quarter of weddings are now also destination weddings, according to "travel expert" website TripSavvy (Sardone 2019: data based on US figures). The US market is considered to be the biggest driver of both luxury and destination weddings.

Most data on the market for same-sex weddings and the impact of same-sex wedding spending is compiled in the US and mostly concerns economic impacts of weddings held locally (or at most, interstate) by US nationals or residents. The research is conducted by organisations such as the Williams Institute (WI) and various wedding industry organisations such as digital wedding planning platforms WeddingWire and the Knot (now merged into one company). Both the WI and the wedding industry produced reports on trends in the US same-sex wedding market in the year following the 2015 *Obergefell v. Hodges* decision. The WI, drawing on a range of sources, found that spending over the previous year on an estimated 123,000 same-sex weddings across the US had "boosted state and local economies by an estimated $1.58 billion, and [had] generated an estimated $102 million in state and local sales tax revenue", supporting an estimated 18,900 jobs over one year (Mallory and Sears 2016, see also CMI et al. 2016). Only one-third of same-sex couples surveyed by CMI et al. (2016) received financial support for the wedding cost from parents, while over two-thirds of heterosexual couples received such support. Perhaps most tellingly, the survey found that the number of same-sex couples organising a formal wedding ceremony and reception had almost doubled since 2013 (CMI et al. 2016).

In the US as elsewhere, wedding planners seized the opportunity to go gay in the lead up to or following legalisation, with the online magazine *Pink Weddings*, for example, starting up in the UK in 2011. Another UK example is Gay Wedding Planner, set up by experienced wedding industry entrepreneur Petra Truneckova. Among other things, Truneckova has published a guide to the UK gay wedding industry, which sells for £9.99 at the time of writing. She also markets primarily to gay men, especially in the area of destination weddings, because, as she told *The Guardian* in 2015, "they tend to have a bigger budget, and are travelling more, and generally don't have children, and are bigger spenders than straight couples" (cited in Davies 2015). Australia, for its part, boasts several online same-sex wedding guides and planners, including Equality Weddings, Same Sex Wedding Guide, the Australian Same Sex Wedding Directory and dedicated wedding sections on other gay business sites such as Rainbow Flag Australia. *Business Insider Australia* predicted in September 2017 that the same-sex wedding industry could be worth AU$650 million annually to the Australian economy, where, according to *Financial Review*, the total wedding industry was valued at around AU$2 billion (Jacobs 2017; Misthos 2017). This is a large market share of almost one-third, compared to the US, which has 12 times the population and where in 2015 it was predicted that the same-sex wedding industry would boost the market of US$55–60 billion by less than 1 per cent (Avins 2015; Singh 2016). Of course, destination gay weddings within the US had already been part of the market since the Massachusetts legalisation of 2003.

Bridal paths: lesbians and the wedding market

Wedding ideology and the wedding industry have long been core to the institution of heterosexuality (Ingraham 1999). Women have been the main target of both, being routinely constructed, even today, as potential brides. Even market research on same-sex weddings has noted this trend: "many wedding traditions are focused around the bride only, which excludes both straight [and] gay men" (CMI et al. 2016, 20). Significantly, one of the biggest single items—if not *the* biggest—in the global wedding industry overall is bridal wear. Its value has been estimated as set to exceed US$80 billion by 2020, and specific fashion weeks are dedicated to all things bridal, from London to New York to Milan.[1] CMI et al. (2016) found that lesbians are far more likely than gay men to incorporate traditional "white wedding" rituals into their ceremonies, such as the bridal dress, the gift registry or the wedding shower/"bachelorette" party, despite having in general lower disposable incomes to spend on these rituals than the gay men.

Mariana Valverde, writing of the normalisation of the same-sex married couple in Canada, was struck by the media imagery from 2003, when same-sex marriage was legalised in Ontario and British Columbia, of "respectable" homosexual couples (Valverde 2006). This imagery was reinforced the following year by the mainstream media's coverage of Pride. In early 2004, when for a brief time lesbians and gay men could obtain marriage licences in the city of San Francisco, Valverde noticed the ubiquitous white wedding dresses worn by the lesbians, while the gay men featured by the media all wore suits and ties: "all were middle-class, middle aged, and white" (Valverde 2006, 158). She lamented the loss of the "sexual" in "homosexual": "bank loans, florists' bills, joint bank accounts, renovated gentrified downtown homes, and worries about the relatives are the homosexual entity that Canadian jurisprudence has helped to fabricate" (Valverde 2006, 162).

In contrast, Tina Fetner and Melanie Heath found that among 46 women they interviewed in Southern Ontario in 2008 and 2009, roughly two-thirds of the 27 heterosexual women participated in the "white wedding" rituals, while most of the 19 lesbians did not. They were more conflicted, and more likely to want to parody the marriage ritual if they followed it at all (which Valverde also suggested may have been the case in San Francisco in 2004) (Fetner and Heath 2016, 726 ff.; Valverde 2006, 157). They found that working class or racialised heterosexual women were also more likely to resist the white wedding conventions, albeit mostly due to the costs (Fetner and Heath 2016, 736–7). However, all their participants, whether heterosexual or lesbian,

> had to deal with the conventional wedding as a cultural ideal that shaped their choices. All viewed heterosexual marriage as a point of reference, either as the unquestioned standard that supports tradition or as a structure that must be negotiated and/or resisted when planning the big day. (Fetner and Heath 2016, 735)

Over the few brief years since Fetner and Heath published their research, the mainstream wedding market has increasingly incorporated LGBTIQ themes. In 2019, Victoria Park, a Brisbane, Australia golf driving range and function venue often used for weddings, published a webpage devoted to "LGBTQ wedding trends for 2019", in which "20 top wedding industry pros" were asked to provide their top three wedding predictions for this niche market. The responses were somewhat contradictory, with some professionals suggesting that "LGBTQ" couples "continue to throw wedding trends out the window", including in their attire, while others found that same-sex weddings were "starting to more closely resemble a traditional wedding", which one commentator found to be "a really cool shift".[2] A similar difference of opinion was in the area of scale: some found that same-sex weddings were usually more intimate that straight ones, while others found that same-sex couples were going "all out": splurging on a no-holds-barred wedding. Predictably, the two stereotypical wedding photographs featured on the site were, at the top, a male couple in dark suits being wed by a female celebrant, and further down, two blonde women in almost identical, close-fitting, strapless, embroidered white wedding gowns, and wearing tiaras. There was little on this advertorial page to distinguish the framing of same-sex weddings from, for example, the framing of a Millennials wedding, where traditions are "thrown out the window" only to come galloping back quickly enough.

There are many comparable mainstream sites—and indeed dedicated same-sex wedding sites. Almost all feature young white women in white dresses, but not usually as the banner image, the latter is generally of men. The ways in which the women are presented on these sites is normative, even heteronormative. To cite Chrys Ingraham again:

> The staging of weddings in television shows, weekly reporting on weddings in the press, magazine reports on celebrity weddings, advertising, and popular adult and children's movies with wedding themes or weddings inserted, all work together to teach us how to think about weddings, marriage, heterosexuality, race, gender, and labor. (Ingraham 2011, 304)

Ingraham's 2011 article is titled "One is Not Born a Bride", in an allusion to Simone de Beauvoir's famous sentence *On ne naît pas femme* (One is not born woman) (Beauvoir 1949, 285). The import of Beauvoir's often mistranslated sentence is that one is not born *this thing called "Woman"*: "Woman" is a socioculturally constructed entity, the becoming of which is inculcated into female humans from the time of their birth (Beauvoir's sentence opened the chapter of her book titled "Childhood"). Ingraham, in referencing this concept, argues that women similarly did not enter the world desiring white wedding dresses and all the rest of the paraphernalia and rituals associated with weddings, but learned to want them.

Many lesbians, particularly those involved in the feminist movement, had long been marriage resisters, finding all the rituals associated with weddings, marriage and the institution itself, patriarchal and hetero-oppressive. Now lesbians—including some of those former marriage resisters—are donning bridal dresses and engaging in those very same rituals. Even if the advertising imagery does not fully reflect the range of clothing or ritual practices lesbians engage in when marrying, the "white wedding" construction of the lesbian bride is ubiqitous, and is reproduced in popular culture. Kate McNicholas Smith and Imogen Tyler refer to this representation as part of the "now generic conventions of the lesbian normal", as epitomised by the lesbian wedding (in white dresses and conducted in a church) in a Christmas episode of the long-running British "working class" soap opera *Coronation Street* (McNicholas Smith and Tyler 2017, 322). Of course, being lesbian, they do have to be sacrificed at the altar: one of the intending newlyweds has doubts and the other flees the altar at the time of the ceremony. They nonetheless became the poster girls for lesbian marriage: figures brought into existence by "the unknotting of historical ties between lesbianism and feminist politics", during the same year in which David Cameron pronounced himself in favour of same-sex marriage not *despite* being a Conservative but *because* he was one (Cameron 2011; McNicholas Smith and Tyler 2017, 322). Even if these scenarios of "the lesbian normal" are often enacted for a straight audience, they are also remarkably successful among lesbians, as demonstrated, for example, by the popular series *The L Word*, which was the creation of lesbian filmmaker Rose Troche (and which also involves a jilting-at-the altar scene, in the final episode of Season 3).

In short, "arriving" in mainstream culture is always full of contradictions for marginalised groups, and multiply so for lesbians, particularly those coming from a feminist political culture, because "arrival" is almost immediately synonymous with assimilation and co-optation. White weddings sell, including to lesbians.

Gay wedding tourism

As David Coon has observed, "the promotional materials aimed at gay and lesbian tourists are situated at the intersection of discussions of sexuality, the market, representation, space, and citizenship" (Coon 2012, 512), and with the increased rate of legalisations of same-sex marriage, all of these aspects have been reinforced. According to the UN World Tourism Organisation (UNWTO), "the approval of [same-sex marriage] legislation sends a powerful brand image of tolerance, respect, progress and open-mindedness" (UNWTO & IGLTA 2017, 52). The UNWTO cites a YouGov study according to which "brands that consistently show support for the gay community have a strong public image across all consumers" (cited in UNWTO & IGLTA 2017, 53). The legality of same-sex marriage becomes code for an automatic guarantee of LGBTIQ-friendliness. In the consumer culture of contemporary liberal capitalist democracies, in which gay subjectivities and identities are "negotiated in the marketplace", as Alexandra Chasin put it in 2000 (p. 13), gay wedding tourism is folded into the marketplace aesthetics of "leisure spaces of constructed visibility" (Waitt and Markwell 2014, 19 ff.). It is a visibility that, like the gay tourism market more generally, remains deeply gendered,

Anglocentric, white and affluent. The now legal access to the "home and family" of one's own country is blended with the presumed cosmopolitanism of LGBTIQ minorities, which retains elements of its former edginess and avant-gardism.

The spaces that these minorities are represented as inhabiting and travelling to are above all urban. Cities have long been paradoxical places of refuge for the marginalised, providing opportunities to associate and create subcultures that are at once provocative and protective. However, in the late capitalist, post-gay-liberation era, gay urban spaces have become progressively "gay-gentrified" (Waitt and Markwell 2014, 248). This framing of affluent gay urban spaces as metonymic brand images of the supposedly progressive countries in which same-sex marriage is legal renders invisible the significant poverty rates among LGBTIQ populations, and the racial components thereof.

States have been quick to understand the market potential of same-sex wedding tourism, as the example of Canada demonstrates. On 15 May 2006, the Canadian Tourism Commission (CTC) launched a new marketing campaign, inviting lesbian and gay couples from the US to marry in Canada. At that time, the only place in the US where same-sex marriage was legal was Massachusetts, and Canada was only one of four countries in the world, and the only one in the Americas, where it was legal at a national level. It used—as it still does today (C. Glenn 2017)—same-sex marriage and LGBTIQ rights as a form of branding, positioning itself as a forward-looking and egalitarian nation. The campaign was spearheaded by an advertisement and lengthy article in the special "Wedding Destinations" issue (May, 2006) of the New York-based gay travel magazine *Passport*, "the most widely read gay travel magazine" in the country (Boswell 2012), albeit one that is visibly aimed at men. The CTC clearly understood the readership demographic, as its spiel included the text, under a photograph of a lively street scene in Quebec City: "Ready to tie the knot? Why not do it in a place that recognises love is love and a celebration is a celebration. Pack your sense of adventure, your curiosity and your *tuxedo* and come down the aisle" (cited in Boswell 2012, italics added). At that time, Montreal, Toronto and Vancouver, located in provinces where same-sex marriage had been legalised prior to national legalisation, were already favoured destinations for cashed-up and internationally-mobile lesbian and (especially) gay travellers (PR Newswire 2006).

The CTC's multi-thousand dollar marketing strategy, which included sponsoring cultural events such as film festivals in the US (Boswell 2012), was one of many that would become routine in the gay wedding tourism market. Gay wedding tourism now features regularly in mainstream travel services and travel guides such as *Lonely Planet* and *Fodor's*, discussed below, and is the object of special reports by business and international agencies such as the above-cited UN World Tourism Organisation (UNWTO). UNWTO has at the time of writing published two such reports in collaboration with the International LGBTQ+ Travel Association (then called the International Gay and Lesbian Travel Association and still known by its former initials IGLTA), founded in 1983. IGLTA, which in 2017 had a turnover of some US$1.2 million, partners with a number of major upmarket hotel and resort chains, national tourist boards, specialised travel services including Disney, Expedia, airline companies and Royal Caribbean Cruises. It attracted some controversy in 2017 because it includes among its membership three Trump-branded hotels (Villarreal 2017).

In many ways, the gay wedding tourism industry is exactly like the straight wedding tourism industry. They share the branding strategies and customer-targeting, the hype, the national or regional tourism boards vying for wedding-tourist dollars, euros, pesos or pounds, and some of the darker (neo)colonialist problems associated with the global tourism industry more broadly. Those critiques of tourism are well-known and well documented, and their substance is famously encapsulated in *A Small Place*, novelist and essayist Jamaica Kincaid's oft cited personal indictment of colonialism and neocolonialist tourism in her native Antigua, first published in 1988 (Kincaid 2018). The colonial history of gay male (sex) tourism has also been explored, such as in Robert Aldrich's history *Colonialism and Homosexuality* (2003). That history has left its traces in gay male travel guides such as *Spartacus* and—as has the history of heterosexual male sex tourism—in countries such as Morocco, Mexico, Thailand and the Philippines.

The same-sex wedding market does, however, present some peculiarities. First, if destination weddings represent around one-quarter of the total wedding industry (Sardone 2019), then for same-sex weddings that proportion appears to be much greater, given the limited legality of same-sex marriage internationally. In countries where same-sex marriage is now legal, destination weddings represent a little over half the market, according to a 2016 study by The Knot on US couples.[3]

Second, same-sex couples face all the legal restrictions faced by heterosexuals embarking on destination weddings, such as a minimum residency period, blood tests, provision and sometimes translation of key documents such as birth certificates and so on, but sometimes face added challenges as well. Taiwan, for example, one of the most recent countries to legalise same-sex marriage (in 2019) and the first and to date only one in Asia to do so, will only perform same-sex marriages for foreign nationals from countries where same-sex marriage is legal. Conversely, gay or lesbian nationals of countries where same-sex marriage is not legal who marry abroad may find their marriages are not recognised back home, as demonstrated by the Kitzinger/Wilkinson case in the UK, and as tested by the ECJ in the Comar case in Romania, discussed in Chapter 2.

Another legal peculiarity of same-sex wedding tourism is its development in countries where same-sex marriage is *not* legal. For example, Nepal has become reputedly one of the most gay-friendly countries in Asia since its transition to a republic in 2007, with explicit protections for "sexual minorities" in its 2015 Constitution. Its Pink Mountain travel company, located in much-romanticised Kathmandu, offers trekking and cultural tours aimed specifically at a gay market, including gay wedding packages (although the legal ceremony needs to be celebrated in the country of origin, the traditional Nepalese ceremony offered as part of the package having no legal status).

Third, as the abovementioned Canadian case demonstrates, the gay wedding tourism market is a business that in many cases mushroomed virtually overnight in the wake of legalisation, creating a "halo effect" on which tourism businesses are quick to capitalise (Guaracino 2007, 4). For example, gay wedding tourism businesses sprang up rapidly in Argentina following legalisation there in 2010 (Winter 2014), in a country that was already perceived as one of Latin America's most gay-friendly. Its capital city of Buenos Aires was described as having become a "gay mecca" in the region following legalisation of same-sex civil unions there (in the city, not nationally) in 2002. By 2007, it was estimated that 20 per cent of all tourists to the city were gay, drawn by attractions such as *tango queer* and gay sporting events, and spending some US$600 million of their so-called pink dollars there (Encarción 2016, ch. 4, online). In 2016 in New Zealand, where same-sex marriage was legalised in 2013, "49% of same-sex marriages or civil unions … were between overseas couples, and Australians accounted for 58% of these couples. Altogether, Australian couples comprised 29% of same-sex marriages or civil unions celebrated in New Zealand" that year (Gorman-Murray 2017). Although legalisation in Australia in late 2017 (effective January 2018) may impact in the medium term on these figures, New Zealand also regularly features as a desirable destination in travel guides for LGBTIQ tourism more generally and destination weddings in particular. However, travel experts suggest that the "halo effect" fades as "the rate of same-sex ceremonies held tends to fall back in line with the general population" after an initial surge (UNWTO & IGLTA 2017, 50). As "the general population" is already the norm, hetero-weddings have never been marketed as a time-sensitive niche in quite the same way.

Fourth, a particular idiosyncrasy of same-sex weddings has been the staged rollout of same-sex marriage legalisation to territories controlled by the legalising state. Thus, same-sex marriage became legal in Scotland several months later than its legalisation in England and Wales, and did not become legal in Northern Ireland until January 2020. Similarly, in September 2017, a British gay male couple who had planned for a quiet UK-legal wedding on the Faroe Islands (an autonomous territory within the Kingdom of Denmark) hit the news as the "accidental" first couple to get married on the Islands, where the 2012 Danish legislation was finally applied from July 2017. No locals had married on the islands during the two months since legalisation, hence the "accident" of the foreigners being the first ones (Duffy 2017).

Fifth, while heterosexual wedding and wedding tourism marketing is skewed more towards women, same-sex wedding marketing and particularly wedding tourism marketing is skewed more towards men.

Finally, as the abovementioned controversy over IGLTA and the Trump-branded hotels demonstrates, same-sex wedding tourism appears to be subject to specific political tensions, which extend beyond the debates over the very validity of same-sex marriage as a sign of progress. Are there particular ethical debates around same-sex wedding tourism that might be different from the ethical debates around straight wedding tourism? If so, what might they be? Are they *substantively* different from other ethical debates within and around the tourism industry?

Homonormalising the gay (male) adventurer

Gordon Waitt and Kevin Markwell have suggested that "the Western-constituted 'gay' identity" is to a significant extent "related to the spaces, meanings, performances, and activities of tourism" (2014, 10). That tourism forms a particular sociocultural and market niche in an industry that has become synonymous with what Joseph Pine and James Gilmore (2011) have termed "the experience economy". The World Travel and Tourism Council leapt on this aspect in its 2019 publication *World, Transformed* (rather cheesily picking up on the poetic postposition of the participle-used-as-adjective popularised by Susanna Kaysen's 1993 memoir *Girl, Interrupted* and the 1999 film of the same name). It identified five "megatrends" in the world of travel and tourism: "Reality, Enhanced" (combining "online and offline experiences"); "Life, Restructured" (largely to do with new "fluidity" in the tourism workplace, including the "gig economy"—all seen as a plus by the WTTC); "Data, Revolutionised" ("the Internet of Things"); "Power. Redistributed" (with the rise of Eastern and Southern middle classes); and "Consumption, Reimagined" (accent on "sustainable business practices") (WTTC, 2019a).

Same-sex wedding tourism definitely fits into this world of "enhanced reality", with promotions firmly focused on the total "experience" in a picture-postcard environment. Promotions overwhelmingly target Western Anglophone (and especially US-based) gay men, and most of the research on gay tourism and gay wedding tourism also focuses on gay men. Lesbians are occasionally mentioned (or photographed in tourism advertorials in wedding dresses, usually albeit not always white: both the women and the dresses), more often than not as part of the LGBT and sometimes LGBTQ+ acronym, but the target market, and target of the research, is male, Western, white and affluent (Waitt and Markwell 2014, 7 ff.), with, again, a focus on urban tourism. Mainstreamed gay (male) subcultures become part of the city's "enhanced consumer seduction … where the city itself is a commodity fetish-on-display, exhibiting and marketing its 'historic' sectors, and selling (selling-out) its 'alternative' neighborhoods and 'bohemian' lifestyles" (Chisholm 2004, 11). Gay (and subsequently LGBTIQ+) festivals have also been a tourist magnet in commodified gay urban bohemia, as cultures of protest develop into cultures of spectacle, or as a *Forbes* business magazine reporter put it in relation to Sydney Gay and Lesbian Mardi Gras, they go "from demonstration to dividend" (Stilinovic 2018).

Gay wedding tourism represents a new addition to these traditionally "gay" markets. It has also fuelled further development of the gay and gay-friendly resort-tourism market that is largely aimed at gay men, and often run by gay men as well. The history of this gay resort tourism dates back at least to the early 1970s, when the first gay bar opened on the Greek island of Mykonos. Such gay island resort "meccas" have proliferated in subsequent decades, although same-sex marriage not yet being legal in Greece—which has also suffered from economic, political and refugee crises over the last decade—Mykonos is no longer anywhere to be seen on the desirable destination list. Legalisations of same-sex marriage have, in contrast, boosted the appeal of many other European countries, their biggest or capital cities and their island territories as gay wedding or honeymoon destinations.

I will focus here on two mainstream travel guides freely available online: *Lonely Planet* (Zimmerman, dated August 2019, but probably first published mid-2010s and not updated since, as it mentions only 16 countries where same-sex marriage is legal); and *Fodor's* (Chauvin 2018). I have chosen them because they are two of the most frequently consulted travel guides and their lists are picked up by many other holiday/vacation websites, including gay ones, and because of the ways in which they frame same-sex couples and the destinations. Both same-sex wedding respectability and stereotypical national branding are much in evidence, as is the fact that the guides are pitched at the luxury end of the market and more specifically at gay men. For example, the *Lonely Planet* pitch for Hawai'i includes a suggestion that one can "ride horses with local cowboys" (an activity that would clearly be more appealing to gay men than to lesbians), while the *Fodor's* site provides a number of links to upmarket hotels, one of which, Le Pigonnet in Aix-en-Provence, has supplied a photograph for the entry on France, featuring two men in suits embracing and kissing in front of the door to what appears to be an eighteenth-century provincial manor (the original building of the hotel dating from that period).

Both also present a mix of cities, states or provinces, and countries. The *Lonely Planet* Guide features ten places: Hawai'i, San Francisco, Buenos Aires, Cape Town, Tahiti, Queenstown, New York City, Iceland, Vancouver, and Boston, in that order, accompanied by Getty Images-sourced views of the site in question. The *Fodor's* guide is more extensive: it features 18 destinations, accompanied by images sourced from a mix of stock tourist views of the location, hotel-provided images and images of same-sex couples getting married (men in blue or dark suits, and in one case crimson shirts, and feminine-looking women in long, mostly white and in one case frilly pink and orange dresses). The locations are, in order: Ireland, Sweden, Australia, Argentina, Iceland, Martinique, New Brunswick, Brazil, France, Cape Town, Puerto Vallarta (Mexico), Manchester (UK), New Zealand, Toronto, Tahiti, Spain, Germany and "The Middle of the Ocean" (with Celebrity Cruises). *Fodor's* list is rather odd because it features three sites that are actually "France": the European mainland, known in French as *la métropole*, which is called "France" in the guide, the overseas *département* of Martinique, in the Caribbean, and the island of Tahiti, which is part of the overseas territory of French Polynesia. The overseas *départements* have the same legal standing as the mainland departments, while the territories (now called *collectivités*) do not. The fact that these island destinations are distinguished from "France" in the guide reinforces their othering as somewhere that is not exactly "France".

Both *Lonely Planet* and *Fodor's* predictably foreground as selling points the beauty and romanticism of the locations, the culturally-specific and somewhat stereotypical national or local branding, and the ease with which one is able to get gay-married there. *Fodor's* is particularly upbeat, emphasising the merry party vibe of destination gay weddings: "Wedding bells are ringing for same-sex couples around the globe. Now that 26 nations are now pronouncing that 'love wins,' many a betrothal is followed by an even more daunting question: Where to get hitched?" (Chauvin 2018, online).

Both *Lonely Planet* and *Fodor's* foreground the typical tourist attractions of their chosen sites, with specific mentions of their iconic "gayborhoods" (Zimmerman 2019, online), but for the locations common to both sites, the accent is often placed on different aspects, with *Fodor's* more systematically drawing attention to the legal framework and recommending high-end resorts or venues. I will briefly discuss two examples here: Argentina and Iceland, and will discuss French Polynesia and other things "French" a little later in this chapter. As concerns Argentina, *Lonely Planet* focuses exclusively on "seductive" Buenos Aires, "one of Latin America's gay capitals", drawing attention to the historic and colourful La Boca neighbourhood (which is actually notorious for street crime), various gay-friendly neighbourhoods and, especially, queer tango. *Fodor's*, on the other hand, lists "Argentina" but then only discusses Buenos Aires, ignores queer tango and publishes a link to an upmarket hotel in the gentrified waterfront district of Puerto Madero. The development of that district from the beginning of the 1990s had been the result of "a topdown policy of class upgrading by segregating an important part of the city", and involved "the massive and immoral transfer [to private developers] … at a cost of roughly US$250 million … of public goods which could have been used to provide public spaces and housing for lower income groups" (López-Morales, Shin and Lees 2016, 1097).

Iceland is an interesting entry in both guides, as it is the only time that anything lesbian is foregrounded, primarily because at the time same-sex marriage was legalised, the country's then prime minister, Jóhanna Sigurðardóttir, was the world's first and only head of state or national government to be openly lesbian—a record she still holds. She and her partner were among the first to marry following legalisation in 2010. These facts are foregrounded by both sites, as is Iceland's lesbian-welcoming character, with both referring prospective newlyweds to Pink Iceland, a company founded by two lesbians in 2011.[4]

Iceland is an interesting example for another and more worrying reason. A tiny country with a population of roughly 360,000, which is less than the population of Cardiff in Wales, Iceland has become a major tourist attraction over the last decade, with 2.2 million foreign visitors in 2017 (up 400 per cent since 2010) earning the country some 42 per cent of foreign exchange earnings, according to the Icelandic Tourist Board (Óladóttir 2018). Although this surge helped Iceland recover from the impact of the Global Financial Crisis, it has created other problems, one of which is that the country is now heavily tourism-dependent. Yet it faces undersupply of accommodation (resulting in rising costs for all, and rapid construction of new luxury hotels and resorts), strains on infrastructure, policing and the health system, and, particularly, threats to the local ecosystem: "tourism affects the very environment most tourists come to experience" (OECD 2018, 73). In some ways this situation in Iceland resembles that of the tropical islands of the global periphery. Becoming the fashionable new winter wonderland destination for wealthy jetsetters in general and gay wedding tourists in particular is thus somewhat of a mixed blessing for this little country that has long had a big reputation for being feminist, gay- and, particularly, lesbian-friendly.

In addition to these dedicated sections in travel guides such as *Lonely Planet* and *Fodor's*, one can now find a plethora of gay destination wedding sites, either as features in *Passport* (US) or *Pink Weddings* (UK), as gay branches of mainstream online destination wedding planners such as Destination Weddings, or as part of dedicated gay travel sites such as Out of Office, which targets the gay male luxury travel market. Almost all of these gay-specific sites are US-based, and most of the others are elsewhere in the Anglosphere. It took quite a bit of searching to find sites that were not US-based, even when searching on Google sites of non-English-speaking countries using French, Spanish, German or Swedish. Many of the sites are other-language versions of Out Of Office or other US sites, or contain very similar information to those sites. French-language sites, for example, were mainly translations of US-based sites. In French Canada my search turned up an outdated article from Quebec City-based *Gay Voyageur*, but it was a brief advertorial about ten tourist destinations where same-sex marriage is legal and did not present any particular spin that was different from the English-language sites consulted.

Some exceptions to this US-driven dominance are the German site Gleich&Gleich (like and like), run by wedding planner Marco Fuß. When searching for *Hochzeitsort Schwule* or *Hochzeitsort gay* (gay wedding location) on the German version of Google I found a Gleich&Gleich feature on Italian upmarket villas, which is unusual as same-sex marriage is not legal there, but it was the only feature on destination weddings on that site.[5] I also found a short 2015 article in a Spanish-language online magazine called *Oveja Rosa* ("pink sheep"), which advertises itself as the "leading magazine for gay families (*familias homoparentales*) in Spain and Latin America".[6] The parent site of *Oveja Rosa* is the Spanish lesbian magazine *MiraLES* (literally, "look at them" but also a play on the word les[bians]).[7] When googling *boda de destino* (destination wedding) on the MiraLES site I found a number of articles on lesbian weddings, including wedding and honeymoon destinations, although most of the articles were similar to the English-language sites with the single main difference being that the articles were solely about lesbians, including fictional ones (*Coronation Street, Orange is the New Black*). One article featured five recommended lesbian holiday destinations, in order: San Francisco, Buenos Aires, Amsterdam, Tel Aviv and Rio de Janeiro, while a 2019 article proclaimed that lesbian weddings in Ireland are now all the rage (especially with the final application of the 2014 UK law in the North). The visuals featured photographs of relatively feminine-looking women dressed in white, with the occasional cross-dressing photo.

My search of gay-specific wedding travel sites in the hope that I just might find something a little out of the ordinary thus ended up being quite frustrating. Same-sex wedding planning and wedding travel sites are much "straighter" than all the

LGBTIQ-friendly marketing hype would have one believe. As Mariana Valverde feared in 2006, same-sex marriage has become very much a marketable commodity for the well-heeled and respectable.

Upmarket tourism and leisure labour

According to the World Travel and Tourism Council, the total travel and tourism sector was worth US$8.8 trillion in 2018 and "accounted for 10.4% of global GDP and 319 million jobs, or 10% of total employment", with almost 80 per cent being leisure travel (as opposed to business or personal travel) (WTTC 2019b, CEO's foreword). Leisure tourism represented some 6.5 per cent of total global exports and over 27 per cent of service exports. Growth in the industry is outpacing growth in other sectors, and although the US, China, Japan, Germany and the UK are the biggest markets, accounting for almost half the GDP earnings, the Caribbean accounts for 15.5 per cent of the market and "Oceania" (Australia, New Zealand and Pacific Islands), 12.2 per cent (WTTC 2019b, 1).

The WTTC's employment figure covers all employment either directly in the travel sector or in leisure and restaurant sectors frequented by tourists, accounting for some 125.5 million jobs or a little under 4 per cent of total jobs, with the remaining 193.5 million workers being employed in supply chain jobs (such as airline catering or fuel purchase, or provision of cleaning or IT services to hotels), work resulting from travel and tourism investment activity (such as aircraft or hotel construction) and government sector jobs (such as tourism marketing or provision of infrastructure to resorts).

The luxury tourism market is growing even more quickly than the wider market, and an overview provided by Statista places its global value in 2019 at US $831 billion, or circa 14 per cent of the global internal tourism revenue of US$5.9 trillion. Statista defines luxury tourism as "all acquisitions of consumer goods, services, and valuables for and during trips by individuals who have a net asset of over one million U.S. dollars".[8] While gay destination wedding and honeymoon tourism does not all fit this definition, a great deal of the growth market is nonetheless high-end resort tourism targeting largely middle class to affluent gay men from the US, by far the largest national market.

Part of this high-end growth sector is in cruise tourism, which is also a growth sector for destination gay weddings, as the *Fodor's* guide suggests. According to annual reports put out by the Cruise Lines International Association, the world's largest cruise industry trade association, there has been an upward trend in cruise activity, with passenger numbers rising to 30 million in 2019 and expected to reach 32 million in 2020 (although the COVID-19 pandemic may result in a downward revision of this figure), with 278 cruise ships of companies affiliated with CLIA scheduled to be in operation, of which 19 will be new (CLIA 2020). Roughly one-third of all cruises take place in the Caribbean, measured by percentage of passengers, followed by the Mediterranean with 17 per cent. The market share of Australia and the Pacific is 5 per cent. Almost half of all cruise passengers come from North America (mainly US), and an estimated 82 per cent of passengers are already, or are likely to become, repeat cruisers. The proportion of Generation X and Millennials on cruises is rising, although the reports do not provide precise demographics. The industry overall has a turnover of US$500 billion, and employs some 1.2 million people.

Three significant aspects of the development of the high-end resort-style market are the expropriation of land, the complexity and precarity of employment for hospitality workers and the impact of manufactured "authentic experiences" on local societies and cultures. I will discuss this last aspect in the next section, using French Polynesia, featured in both the *Lonely Planet* and *Fodor's* destination gay weddings guides, as a case study. As for the first, studies on land grabs in Latin America for the purpose of tourism development show significant levels of displacement of Indigenous populations, disruption of local economies including agriculture and fishing, lack of access to beaches and other local natural resources, and, often, environmental degradation, with the ironic impact of causing a downturn in tourism, as the cases of the Ceará coastline in Brazil and the Acapulco coast in Mexico have demonstrated (Diegues 2001; Vásquez Castillo 2004, ch. 6).

Many tourism operators have responded by making environmental considerations and ecotourism options part of their brand image, but the impacts of ecotourism are not always positive, with significant hidden costs for both Indigenous populations and the environment (Barnard 2013). This can even be the case when community-based tourism is part of the scenario: "[t]ourism has rarely been about empowerment or equity, especially at the grassroots" (Connell and Rugendyke 2008, 279). Moreover, as Jim Butcher (2007) argues, with Western companies and international NGOs being the main political and financial drivers of community-based ecotourism, fundamental contradictions arise between the hegemonic capitalist logic of "development", premised on economic and commercial expansion, urbanisation and resulting divisions of labour, and what he calls the "neopopulist" idea of community ecotourism, based on a relatively tight subsistence model kept separate from the transformations that the rest of the country may be undergoing. Neither model responds adequately to the needs of local communities, and outcomes end up being patchy. There are thus many ambiguities and complexities in such tourism initiatives, as local communities also become "players" in the tourism market, taking advantage of the economic opportunities community-based ecotourism presents while attempting to contain the role of commercial operators, at least to some extent (Ruiz-Ballesteros and Hernández-Ramírez 2010; Wang, Cater amd Low 2016).

Even more ambiguous and complex is the tourism and hospitality labour market. John Urry and Jonas Larsen have stressed that

> distinctions between hosts and guests are increasingly fluid in mobile societies where there is much travel for work and pleasure, and places are globally connected with wide-reaching cultural, social and economic networks. Tourist

> places are not unique, bounded and fixed "islands" that are subject to external forces producing impacts. They come into existence through relationships. Places float around within mobile, transnational networks of humans, technologies, objects, risks and images that continuously connect and disconnect them to other places. (Urry and Larsen 2011, 81)

Host-guest relations, then, come to involve "strange combinations of hospitality *and* hostility as the world's largest industry has utterly industrialised, commercialised and scripted" the practices of "hospitality" (Urry and Larsen 2011, 96).

Tourism and hospitality work are characterised by seasonality and precarity, and mobility (whether long-term or seasonal migrants or tourist-workers or even volunteers) inserted into a rigidity of the workplace (both in terms of where in the world or country, and in terms of the workplace constraints and hierarchies). It is also a workforce that is highly feminised and in which low-skilled and migrant labour dominates, particularly in terms of the "flexibility" required (e.g. Sinclair 1997; Vandegrift 2008; Zampoukos and Ioannides 2011; Jordhus-Lier and Underthun 2015; Lee et al. 2015; Costa et al. 2017). Service workers in hospitality and tourism who interact with the public perform in addition significant emotional labour (Hochschild 2012). As Arlie Hochschild has observed, hospitality and tourism workers constantly required to perform this labour undergo a particular type of alienation that she calls

> emotive dissonance, analogous to the principle of cognitive dissonance … Maintaining a difference between feeling and feigning over the long run leads to strain. We try to reduce this strain by pulling the two closer together either by changing what we feel or by changing what we feign. When display is required by the job, it is usually feeling that has to change. (Hochschild 2012, online, ch. 6)

Hochschild was discussing this "emotive dissonance" and worker strategies to deal with it in relation to female flight attendants. However, the discussion can easily be extended to the travel and hospitality industry more generally and most particularly to the resort industry, in which tourists enter manufactured and protected environments where everything and everyone is expected to be endlessly available, pretty and sunny. In gay resorts, many of these emotionally available and sexually pleasing workers may well be male, but the requirement that they perform emotional labour is no less a form of feminisation.

Steve French (2018) has argued that the employment conditions in the hospitality industry are so bad in the UK, in a context of neoliberalism, weak labour regulation and (then) impending Brexit (removing both EU labour and EU regulations), that they are opening a road to modern slavery. The intermingling of regular paid workers (both resident and migrant), seasonal workers (both resident and temporarily migrant), "working holiday" tourists on special visas and tourist volunteers further complicates the issue, as they are subjected to different regulatory regimes and do not all benefit from the same worker protections. Tourist volunteers working in the tourism and hospitality industry in various countries have no worker protections at all but often end up working long hours in difficult conditions as "trade" for accommodation, food and the tourist "experience" (C. Brennan 2018). As for those on so-called "working holiday" visas, they tend to be in a situation of liminality, taking the jobs to pay for their travels in between one life choice and another (in a post-school or post-university "gap year", for example). They are perhaps more likely to be white, but are also more likely to accept (and indeed be given) pay and working conditions that they may not accept back home, and are very unlikely to be unionised—as, for that matter, are seasonal workers (Underthun 2015; Terry 2018). They may also be routinely confused with visitors on regular tourist visas, the assumption being that they are not "real" workers but holidaymakers just like everyone else (C. Brennan 2014).

As concerns cruise workers, if hospitality and tourism workers are often highly mobile, cruise work "requires a high degree of mobility as a matter of vocation", as workers are away from home for long periods of time (Terry 2016, 124). Yet, ironically, they are also locked into immobility on board the ships, where the days are long (or sometimes, for the entertainers in particular, excruciatingly boring), the shared living quarters cramped, the hierarchy rigid and freedoms restricted (Terry 2016; Matousek 2019). While cruise work can be bread-and-butter for many entertainers, notably dancers and musicians, and pays better than the average income for the many cruise hospitality staff who come from lower-income countries, the polyglot environment on board cruises makes intermingling more difficult and keeps labour costs down. The mean income of cruise workers is estimated at roughly US$28,000 per annum—although the median sits much lower, at US$20,000 or less (Matousek 2019). Predictably, galley workers earn the least, while some workers providing activites or services for passengers such as gym classes are heavily reliant on commissions and often earn very little.

It is an inescapable fact that all travel and tourism, whatever the reason for travel and whatever the level of comfort or discomfort, are built on someone else's work. However, the ways in which that work is gendered, raced and otherwise hierarchised, and the degree of control or otherwise that the people who wait on us and entertain us are able to exercise, must necessarily be interrogated. The tourist industry—particularly at its higher end—has become dependent on the ability of workers in an often poorly regulated labour market to resolve their "emotive dissonance". As the gay tourism and destination wedding markets expand, the risks increase that the "rights" of the gay tourist to be out, proud, and married are enjoyed at the expense of the rights of those who create the context for that enjoyment, and that gay cosmopolitanism develops in a sanitised environment where the socioeconomic and cultural realities of the places visited are largely ignored or at best, poorly understood.

Manufacturing "authenticity" in (gay) resort tourism: the case of French Polynesia

In island resort destinations, "[i]nsisting on hospitality as a commodity that is produced through labor denaturalizes the link between hospitality and the putatively friendly native and makes room for questions about the ideological work of hospitality in the service of empire" (Vicuña Gonzalez 2015, 161–2). The tourist in search of "authentic" local experiences—as sources of wonder, pleasure, an escape from modernity, an insight into the local culture or even a sense of supporting a "traditional" local economy—is a willing, even eager, participant in the "experience economy", in which "culture is consumed, produced and dissolved in the service of social and economic development" (Robinson and Connell 2008, 95). This imagining of a tropical "authenticity" untouched by the corruptions of modernity extends to gay tourism, which "also relies upon colonial evolutionary narratives that pitch [islander peoples] as a remnant precapitalist society, living in a rich tropical environment and thus disarmed of homophobic prejudices" (Waitt and Markwell 2014, 107).

The presentation of Tahiti in the *Lonely Planet* and *Foder's* gay destination wedding guides is typical of that of island resorts in destination (gay) wedding literature more generally. Both guides in fact discuss Bora Bora, which is not the same island as Tahiti. Both are in French Polynesia, but referring to the islands collectively as "Tahiti" (and worse, referring to Bora Bora as "Tahiti") is a little like referring to the Hawai'ian islands as "Oahu", where Honolulu is located (although the largest island of Hawai'i, commonly referred to locally as "Big Island", has indeed become the metonym for the whole group). Both travel guides recommend upmarket hotels on Bora Bora: Le Méridien (*Lonely Planet*), a French luxury chain, and St Regis, Intercontinental or Four Seasons, all part of US luxury chains (*Fodor's*). *Fodor's* also mentions the fact that "Tahiti" (Bora Bora) is part of French Polynesia so one can get legally same-sex married there, and refers intending wedding travellers to Gay Destination Weddings (Chauvin 2018, online). *Lonely Planet* adds a little local colour by suggesting that "[y]ou'll likely run into *rae-rae*, cross-dressers or transgendered folks, who are a highly respected and integral part of the restaurant and hotel industries, as they have been for eons in this culture" (Zimmerman 2019, online).

Like most tropical islands in the Pacific and the Caribbean, the French Polynesian economy is heavily dependent on tourism, and most of it is in the resort sector. Tourists are "cocooned" into resort culture, with the effect that the islands end up being segregated, with the tourists being herded into the "pristine, beautiful, unique, untouched, authentic, and romantic" Tahiti of their imaginings in carefully controlled resort environments that maintain the fictional paradise (Kahn 2011, 201–2). In French Polynesia, as in many such tropical island "paradises", that control commences from the time the tourists arrive at Papeete airport, where they are greeted by Polynesian musicians and dancers and are given a lei: Miriam Kahn (2011) documents this practice and I experienced it myself when visiting Tahiti during the 2000s. In a prolongation of colonial-era privilege, tourists are sheltered from the often harsh reality of Tahitian life, where unemployment in 2017 was at 21 per cent, with over half of the unemployed being under 30, and with fewer women in the workforce than men (France Info 2019). As Fabien Piliu put it in 2014, French Polynesia is a "paradise for tourists [but] a nightmare for the young unemployed" (article headline, my translation).

The "pristine" and "untouched" environment into which tourists emerge is carefully engineered: lagoons are dredged to provide white sand beaches, coral is introduced to attract colourful fish. These introduced species must then be managed: without human intervention to maintain them, they would not survive. Hotel employees that the guests see are chosen first for their looks, to replicate the Gauginesque framing of "the Tahitian", and the sorts of "traditional" cultural events guests witness, such as dance performances, are carefully curated (Kahn 2011). These sorts of "authentic" local experiences are reproduced in resort hotels from Hawai'i to Vanuatu to Mauritius to Martinique, with little variation except slight changes to the style of costume or foods served.

There is nothing in the gay destination wedding advertising to suggest that the gay experience differs from the straight, except for *Lonely Planet*'s mention of *rae rae*, "highly respected … for eons in this culture" with a globalising reference to "transgendered folks" (Zimmerman 2019). The Tahitian reality is more complex than this framing suggests. First, "transgender" is a Western term and not applicable to traditional Polynesian and other Indigenous societies, where some men, known in French Polynesia as *mahu*, take on a "feminine" look and social roles normally performed by women (Elliston 2014; Mallol 2014). It is these men, not *rae rae* (who also exist but are part of a different history), whom one can find in civil service or hospitality roles, and who are socially venerated, to a quasi-mythical status (Lacombe 2008, 2013). There is no specific association with "homosexuality" (which is not to say that it did not exist) nor indeed "transgender". There are also some female *mahu* but they would appear to have emerged more recently (Lacombe 2013). In Western colonial eyes and Western travel writing about "Oceania", the *mahu* (whom *Lonely Planet* calls *rae rae*) are largely assimilated to the Western image of the *vahiné*, the young, servile and sexually available Tahitian woman, with one difference in that the *mahu* are considered not to engage in any sexual practices (Lacombe 2008). This presumed asexuality is considered part of their "authenticity" by Indigenous French-Polynesians (Elliston 2014), who are also heavily Christianised in both Catholic and Evangelical traditions: the *mahu* were tolerated by the Christian missionaries and continue to be by Indigenous French-Polynesians today (Lacombe 2008).

In contrast to the *mahu*, the *rae rae* are devalued and considered amoral in Tahitian society. Historically effeminate homosexuals, they are now increasingly chemically and surgically transgendered. They appear to have emerged as a discrete group during the arrival of US and French military during World War II, and have largely earned a living through street prostitution (Lacombe 2008; Mallol 2014), which did not exist prior to Western colonisation and developed considerably during the military presence: a common occurrence (Enloe 1990, 2000). In postwar French Polynesia, the *rae rae* appear to have been the majority of those working in street prostitution—and remain so—although the *mahu* were also solicited by the military for sex, but more "discreetly" and not in street prostitution (Elliston 2014; Mallol 2014). The *rae rae* also embrace a "mass-mediated Euro-American fashion-model femininity, beautiful in cover model ways", which works to undermine their bids for local legitimacy as self-affirming homosexuals rather than the "cowardly hypocrisy" of the *mahu* (Elliston 2014, 44–5). They are the product of "Tahitian modernity, with a different history and a different process of construction from the *mahu*, [and] characterised by the appearance of a sexual dimension and sexual commerce" (Mallol 2014, 95, my translation).

The *Lonely Planet*'s reference to *rae rae* thus conflates two discrete populations, demonstrating a singular lack of historical understanding of "queer" minority constructions in Tahiti and their layers of racialisation and marginalisation. To do so within a gay-cosmopolitan frame can only reinforce the globalised and commodified femininity performed by the *rae rae*, not to mention glorifying the practice of homosexual and transgender street prostitution in French Polynesia.

Cruising the periphery

The eighteenth recommended gay wedding destination in *Fodor's* is "the middle of the ocean". The guide provides intending newlyweds with a hotlink to Celebrity Cruises, which is a subsidiary of Royal Caribbean, the world's second largest cruise company after Carnival, which owns well-known brands such as P&O, Cunard, Princess and Costa. When I consulted it in late 2019, the LGBTQ+ cruise vacations page of Celebrity Cruises featured a photograph of two men, one black, one white, enjoying a picnic with wine on a manicured lawn. The page proudly proclaims that it won "LGBTQ+ Friendly Travel Company of the year" in 2016 at the prestigious TTG (Travel Trade Gazette) Travel Awards, and the title of "Best Large Ship Cruise Line for LGBTQ+ Passengers at the Cruizie [LGBTQ cruise-specific] Awards for four years running" (Celebrity Cruises website).[9] As Celebrity Cruises is based in Miami, marriages performed aboard Celebrity Cruise ships are now legal under US law. (This is not the case for parent company Royal Caribbean, whose ships are registered in the Bahamas, but symbolic weddings can be performed on the ships as well as, legally, ashore in places visited by the cruises where same-sex marriage is legal.)

In addition to onboard weddings, Celebrity Cruises organises annual at-sea Pride parties in June, with the 2020 party originally planned on the new liner Celebrity Apex at the Spanish resort island of Ibiza (subsequently transformaed into a virtual event due to the COVID-19 pandemic). In addition, the company offers "bespoke" LGBT+ cruises in partnership with LGBT+ cruise charter company Vacaya. The inaugural Vacaya seven-day cruise was organised in 2019 aboard the 2,200-passenger Celebrity Summit from New York to the Provincetown, Rhode

Island LGBTIQ carnival. Vacaya also takes over resorts, with the first resort holiday being in November 2019 in Riviera Maya on Mexico's Caribbean coast.

The promotional photographs featured by both Vacaya and Celebrity Cruises are mainly of white and mostly youngish men, with the occasional African American or Latino-looking man. When women are at times included in the Celebrity Cruises imagery, they are mostly accompanying the men, almost always white, and are very "straight-fem" looking, with skimpy attire. Vacaya imagery more often includes lesbians featured separately from men, but almost always photographed as couples rather than in groups. The price of Vacaya Cruise and resort holidays ranges from some US$3,000 starting price for a twin share in the cheapest stateroom on the 2020 Portugal River Cruise and Lisbon Resort holiday, to a some US$45,000 for sole occupancy of the most expensive suite on the 2020 Iceland cruise, on board the newest liner in the Ponant brand, Le Jacques Cartier (these cruises were subsequently cancelled, modified or postponed due to the pandemic). Ponant is owned by the Artemis Group, the holding company of French billionaire François-Henri Pinault. The holidays last a week to ten days, depending on the cruise, and the pricing does not include flights or airport transfers. The target market would appear to be primarily US.

Cruise tourism has in common with resort tourism its reserved enjoyment of private beaches, to which locals are not allowed access, but in cruise tourism the "private island" experience is amplified. It features prominently in Caribbean tourism in particular, where there is a thriving market in destination weddings catering to a "feted and pampered whiteness in a (post)colonial paradise" (Wilkes 2016, 193)—although to date a mostly heterosexual one as apart from overseas territories of the US or European countries, same-sex marriage is not legal in any Caribbean countries (although the Mexican Caribbean coast is a popular resort destination, and since the May, 2020 legalisation of same-sex marriage in Costa Rica, that country will surely follow suit).

One such private beach is Labadee on Haiti's north coast, leased from the Haitian state by Royal Caribbean for the exclusive use of its cruise passengers. It is fenced off and heavily guarded by private security, and includes a number of playground attractions for tourists. Some locals are allowed permits (for a fee) to sell souvenirs. Haiti is the poorest country in the Western hemisphere, with roughly 80 per cent of the population living in poverty. It is wracked by political instability and corruption associated with drug and arms trafficking, and has suffered significant environmental degradation, notably erosion resulting from deforestation and water pollution from untreated sewage, which is severely exacerbated following rains (frequent in the region) (Hersher 2017). Labadee is roughly 15 kilometres by land from Cap Haïtien, the major town on the north coast, but is not directly accessible by road. In 2010, Royal Caribbean came under fire for docking at Labadee only three days after the devastating earthquake that hit Haiti that year (Booth 2010). Bizarrely, some of the passengers were outraged at the decision to stop there following the earthquake (cited in Booth 2010). Yet the plight of this impoverished and troubled nation had not worried these passengers enough to stop them taking the cruise in the first place.

Conclusion

Same-sex marriage has become "a tourist attraction, an export commodity, and a marketplace activity through which gays and lesbians are schooled in how to participate in consumer culture and be good citizens" (Boyd 2008, 228). Cities, countries and companies use it as a branding exercise in which they show themselves to be progressive, inclusive and hip, yet their marketing of same-sex weddings, and wedding tourism, reproduces heteronormative and neocolonialist framings, from the portrayal of exotic and fun locations right down to the neatly groomed, traditionally dressed and gender-conforming (mostly male) models used in advertising.

Yet, as Jasbir Puar (2002a and b) has pointed out, it is not only those framed as "good homosexuals", and not only men, who travel, and they have a range of reasons for doing so. As concerns lesbian tourism, Puar (2002b) cites the example of Olivia Cruises, set up in 1990, although Olivia charters cruise ships complete with regular staff who are not likely to be lesbian and may not be particularly attuned to the needs of a Western (largely US) lesbian clientele. Puar further notes, as do Anette Therkelson et al. (2013), that lesbians are far more likely to travel with dependent children, and on smaller budgets, while less likely to seek out exclusively "lesbian" travel destinations. Not that such destinations exist in abundance in any case: in their 2007 study of lesbian spaces and activities in Manchester's "gay village", Annette Pritchard et al. found that gay enclaves are every bit as patriarchal as wider society and that it is difficult for lesbians to gain a foothold of any sort. They further commented that

> [n]otions of a homogeneous gay community and gay spaces … potentially obscure gay men's oppression of lesbians whilst reinforcing notions of a patriarchal society in which the male experience subsumes the female and becomes regarded as some gender-neutral "norm". (Pritchard et al 2007, 274)

If in this chapter I have primarily discussed the gay male wedding market, it is indeed because there is so little space given to lesbian wishes or lesbian experience—and lesbians simply have less disposable income to splash out on wedding tourism, and as such, are a less profitable target market for the gay tourism sector.

The increased visibility of a certain style of gay male tourism creates further political dilemmas at a transnational level. Puar (2002a) drew on the example of the contradictions thrown up by the refusal, in 1998, by the government of the Cayman Islands, a British territory, to allow docking privileges to a gay (male) cruise, sparking outcry by both gay organisations and the state in the US and UK. "I watched with confusion", she wrote, "hopeful that both former and current British possessions would tell Blair and the United States to mind their own business, but aware of my ambivalent solidarity with Caribbean activists" (Puar 2002a, 101). Some of those activists wanted to protest also, emphasising among other things the importance of gay tourist revenue for their countries, while others preferred to keep a low profile "for fear of the local exposure and a backlash against individuals as well as against nascent gay and lesbian and AIDS-related nongovernmental organizations (NGOs) that were barely surviving"' (p. 102).

Moreover, those working in the expanding gay tourism and wedding tourism industries are often themselves gay—and, occasionally, lesbian, as we saw in the Icelandic case. They are tourism entrepreneurs and wedding planners, they are marriage celebrants, tour guides, bar staff, galley staff, cleaners, entertainers. They fit, more or less seamlessly, into the raced and gendered cultures and socio-economic hierarchies of the gay wedding and tourism industry, but at the same time, they both experience and exude an "us-ness" of the gay (and, occasionally, lesbian) niche. How do the relationships between business owners and managers, workers and consumers play out within that niche? What sorts of gay mobilities and immobilities, visibilities and invisibilities, are thrown into question by these relationships? How does one grapple politically with circumstances in which a relatively conservative section of the LGBTIQ population becomes a symbol of radical visibility for activists in Global South, as in Puar's abovementioned example?

There has been much talk, for many years, of the market courting the "pink" dollar, and the wedding and wedding tourism market has predictably become part of that process. But in reality, dollars are dollars and the identities of those spending them only matter to the market insofar as the latter needs to adjust its pitch to attract new consumers. Once attracted, however, those new consumers are quickly assimilated into a normalised, sanitised and endlessly reproducible image of the ideal bride, groom and/or tourist in the "experience economy".

Notes

1 https://cpp-luxury.com/the-global-bridal-industry-tops-us-80-million/, accessed 4 December 2019.
2 https://victoriapark.com.au/lgbtq-wedding-trends-for-2019/, accessed 4 December 2019.
3 https://www.theknotww.com/press-releases/lgbtq-couples-wedding-spends-soar-as-does-family-acceptance-according-to-the-knot-lgbtq-weddings-study-2016/, accessed 8 December 2019.
4 https://www.pinkiceland.is/gay-weddings, accessed 4 December 2019.
5 "Say: 'YES' in Italy". https://www.gleichundgleich.com/destination-weddings/, accessed 14 December 2019.
6 http://ovejarosa.com/, accessed 14 December 2019.
7 https://www.mirales.es/revista, accessed 14 December 2019.
8 https://www.statista.com/study/67396/luxury-travel-and-tourism/?utm_source=Statista+PR&utm_campaign=ec0964380c-GEO+Outlook+2019+EN_COPY_01&utm_medium=email&utm_term=0_4271fcfa45-ec0964380c-306791561, accessed 14 December 2019.
9 https://www.celebritycruises.com/int/specialty-cruises/lgbt-gay-cruise-vacations, accessed 13 December 2019.

6

SAME-SEX MARRIAGE INTERSECTIONALLY

Gender, class and race dynamics

Four major issues arise when one attempts to discuss demographic and intersectional issues in relation to same-sex marriage. The first is to do with the risk of conflation of three foci: (1) on *representation* (whether discussing campaigns or discussing media representations or both simultaneously); (2) on *experience of discrimination*, which is not necessarily related specifically to same-sex coupledom, marriage or parenting; and (3) on actual *marriage demographics*: who is getting same-sex-married and who is not. It could be that they map onto each other, that the demographic of representation matches, by and large, the demographic of reality and that accounts of experience provide information from which demographic inferences can be made, at least tentatively. This mapping, however, needs to be borne out by the data, which leads us to the second problem: the paucity of statistics. Where statistics do exist, they may not be sufficiently disaggregated to enable meaningful discussions of intersectional and other demographic considerations. Those statistics also now need to include same-sex divorce: just as straight marriage is not always happy ever after, neither is gay marriage. Moreover, when we say divorce, we may also, in some cases, be saying ongoing parenting arrangements. That second problem leads us in turn to the third, already-encountered problem: the Anglo- and especially US-centrism of the data and research. The fourth problem is to do with the construction of a race divide concerning support for or opposition to same-sex marriage. Again, this issue has been most copiously discussed in relation to the US but is not absent from discussion elsewhere. The construction of this divide is in part grounded in observable and documented responses to the issue, but it also dovetails with a broader polemic about the politics of race, ethnicity, religion, immigration (in some cases), assimilationism and belonging, often coupled with a further discussion about class.

One could even add a fifth problem, which relates to the uses and abuses to which the term "intersectionality" has been put. Coined by Kimberlé Crenshaw

(1989), the term soon became mainstreamed, including within institutional fora. By the time of Crenshaw's address in Geneva to the UN Preparatory Session for the World Conference Against Racism held in Durban in September 2001, it had become a widely-used "buzzword", but often a confusing one (Kathy Davis 2008). Co-opted by the neoliberal academy, it became "whitewashed", with academics "dissociating it from its activist moorings and getting bogged down in extremely abstruse theoretical and metatheoretical debates" from which the very populations that "intersectionality" was supposed to be about were becoming excluded (Bilge 2015, 20, my translation). It also, in the neoliberal academy, became reduced to an "inert theory of identity that emphasizes difference over commonality, coalition, and contestation", combining with a "managerial discourse of diversity" that operates a "privatization of difference, a depoliticization of hierarchy, and a narrow construal of agency incompatible with all collective forms of struggle for social justice" (Mohanty 2013, 974). Indeed, in popular parlance the term is more often than not used as a serve-all marker for a range of assertions of individualised identity politics. For example, I have often noticed it used conversationally—and sometimes academically (e.g. Burnes and Chen 2012)—in relation to transgender, without the users of the term being particularly clear about the meaning they give it, beyond some vague equation with "shifting" or "multiple" individual identities. Yet, as the term's originator herself pointed out, "[i]ntersectionality is not primarily about identity; it's about how structures make certain identities the consequence of and the vehicle for vulnerability" (Crenshaw 2016). "Identities" do not pre-exist outside structures and relationships of power, as Nira Yuval-Davis (2006) has pointed out.

Who is getting gay-married?

Available statistics on same-sex marriage and families are patchy and with the exception of the US, mostly give only the numbers of marriages (and, sometimes, divorces): heterosexual, gay, lesbian (or in some cases, such as that of the case of South Africa, disaggregated by *type* of marriage or civil partnership law used). As concerns families including children, there is even less demographic data, although Argentina has announced that its 2020 Census will include this information, as well as gender identity. Occasionally, more comprehensively disaggregated data can be found. In the Netherlands, for example, the first country in the world to legalise same-sex marriage, the national agency Centraal Bureau van Statistiek periodically produces sex-disaggregated data on same-sex couples including income levels, same-sex divorce rates, adoption of partner's child(ren) and so on. In Australia, a 2018 Australian Bureau of Statistics "snapshot" of same-sex marriage taken six months after it was legalised showed that almost two-thirds of the married couples lived in New South Wales or Victoria, which are also the country's most populous states, but the proportion of the same-sex-married living there was higher than for the general population (57 per cent). The proportion of lesbians was also higher, which is comparable to data in a number of other countries, and their median age, at 39, was almost ten years younger than the median age of gay male newlyweds.[1]

Apart from these occasional snippets, there is little comprehensive data anywhere outside the US on same-sex couples disaggregated by major variables apart from sex, such as age, ethnicity, place of residence, or socioeconomic status, although sometimes one can infer certain patterns by correlating information from different datasets. Conclusions drawn from such inferences are necessarily, however, indicative at best. In some jurisdictions such as Mexico, where the legal framework is not uniform, data is available for some states but not others; in Argentina also, there is more statistical data available for Buenos Aires City and province, where most same-sex marriages are conducted.

In the EU, one can find various surveys and overviews of national data collection regimes, but the literature, there as elsewhere, often focuses on *experience* of LGBTIQ populations (notably concerning discrimination) and on legislative frameworks for equality and data collection on LGBTIQ populations more generally (e.g. Bell 2017), rather than intersectionally-disaggregated demographic statistics on same-sex marriage and households per se. For example, the EU's Fundamental Rights Agency conducted the first EU-wide survey of LGBT experience in 2012 (FRA 2014) and the results of its second survey, conducted in 2019, were released in May 2020 (FRA 2020).

So, although the situation in terms of disaggregated demographic statistics, sampling or targeted research on same-sex couples, marriages and households is rapidly evolving, so far the available information is very far from comprehensive. What one can generalise transnationally from the available data—albeit with a note of caution, pending further research—is that same-sex-married couples are more likely to be white, university-educated and in professional or managerial occupations. They are also likely to be urban dwelling, although there are gay enclaves in rural areas and some gay couples move to rural or semi-rural areas to raise children—although the risk of discrimination or denial of services may increase, depending on the area and the ethno-racial background of the couples (Australian Bureau of Statistics 2016; OECD 2019, ch. 1; The Other Foundation and HSRC 2016; Movement Advancement Project 2019).[2]

This data thus suggests at least some level of correlation between *representation* within same-sex marriage campaigns and the media, and the *reality* of who is getting married and who is not—and where they choose to live. One area where the representation and the reality are perhaps at variance is in the representation of men and women. Although men are slightly more likely than women to identify as gay or bisexual, and far more likely to be foregrounded in same-sex marriage campaigns (with a few exceptions), lesbians are more likely to marry: this demographic holds pretty much consistently across Europe, the Americas, and the Austral Anglosphere, the split being generally ±55 per cent versus ±45 per cent. A notable exception is Buenos Aires (city, not province), where most same-sex marriages in Argentina have been conducted: on average over nine years, there have been a little over three gay male marriages for every two lesbian ones.[3] Some data indicates that gay men are more likely to marry assortatively and in order to resource pool, while for lesbians the existence of or intention to have children is often a factor in marriage decisions (Aldén et al. 2015). For lesbians, protection of inheritance, especially where there are children from previous (heterosexual) marriages involved, or of other financial or fiscal benefits, may also be a factor.

Another reality that perhaps belies the representation is that where civil unions and marriage are both available, and the former predates the latter, many couples have chosen either not to convert their civil union into a marriage, or, when deciding what legal framework to give a new relationship, to opt for the civil union instead of the marriage. This tendency has been observed, for example, in relation to the UK, France and Sweden, discussed below. Moreover, in most countries where statistics are available over two or more years, we find that after an initial rush, there is a significant falling off in the numbers of people getting gay-married. While this falling off is predictable, the fact that civil unions remain equally popular suggests that the trend in same-sex unions *may* reflect the trend towards diminishing cultural and ideological value given to marriage more generally.

A counter-trend can be observed in Brazil, due to specific political circumstances there at the time of writing. Following the election of gay-hating Jair Bolsonaro to the presidency in October 2018, gay men and lesbians rushed to the altar to get married prior to Bolsonaro's inauguration in January 2019, fearing a possible overturning of the 2013 ruling of the Conselho Nacional de Justiça (National Justice Council) that legalised same-sex marriage (Kaiser 2018). The Instituto Brasileiro de Geografia e Estatística noted a jump in same-sex marriages of 61.7 per cent in 2018 (Estatísticas Socials 2019).

Statistics for England, Wales and Scotland, for example, show that a little under 3 per cent of all marriages are between same-sex couples, which, having increased to 2016, then plateaued, with the Scottish statistics showing a slight decline in 2017 and 2018 (National Records of Scotland 2019; Office for National Statistics 2019b). Conversion of same-sex civil partnerships to marriages began to taper off in 2016, but the numbers of same-sex couples choosing civil partnerships over marriage also dropped sharply after the same-sex marriage law came into effect in early 2014. In France, civil partnerships are on the rise whereas marriage is in decline for both heterosexual and same-sex couples. The Institut National de la Statistique et des études économiques (INSEE) reports that there are now four new PaCS (see Chapter 2) for every five marriages between heterosexual couples and that the trend is also away from marriage and towards PaCS for homosexual couples. In 2016, over two years after the new same-sex marriage law took effect, the number of new gay marriages and new gay PaCS was the same, at around 7,000, while in 2017 the number of new marriages dropped to 6,000, while the PaCS rate remained steady (INSEE 2019, 28).

Other national-level variations may be historical, cultural or an artefact of data-collecting methods; they may also rely heavily on individual self-identification, which may be more likely in some regional, national or age demographics than others.

Finally, in some data, the distinction between "couple", "married couple" and "household" may not be clear, particularly as Census data in particular presumes a "household" as the basic socioeconomic unit, and presumes that all those in intimate relationships live in some variation of a nuclear couple-and-family structure within "households". Alternative "households" (single people, people who dwell with unrelated others and not in a couple) are captured by some Census data, but non-normative intimate relationships are not. The normative assumptions concerning both "households" and intimate relationships on which Census data are based are likely to invisibilise a small but significant proportion of intimate relationships among both heterosexuals and homosexuals. However, the impact of this data-invisibility is arguably greater on homosexual and lesbian relationships, given that a significant number of lesbians and gay men have a political history and lived experience of challenging normative societal patterns, including within intimate relationships.

The greater amount and complexity of demographic data on LGBTIQ populations in general and same-sex couples in particular in the US is largely thanks, first, to the questions asked in US Census and community surveys (which include, notably, race, whereas those of many other countries do not, sometimes for specific political and institutional reasons), and second, to research centres such as the Pew Research Center and most particularly the Williams Institute (WI).

The latest available nationwide statistical analysis on same-sex couples that the WI provides, consulted at the time of writing in late 2019, is extrapolated from a number of statistical sources, including Census data from the early to mid-2010s and a large-sample Gallup poll conducted in 2017.[4] The analysis, which looks at *couples* in general and does not specify whether these couples are married or not, is nonetheless useful in that it is disaggregated by regional variations in population concentrations proportional to total households, income, age, race/ethnicity, sex, and whether or not the couple is raising children. The national mean shows that the country's 646,000 same-sex couples account for 5.56 per cent of all households, that they are mostly concentrated in the northeastern and west coast states, along with New Mexico and Hawai'i, that lesbians are getting married more than gay men (a little under 54 per cent of the total), and that the average annual income of same-sex households is US$56,200, which is some US$10,000 higher than the average for different sex-households. The state variations in incomes for same-sex couples map onto national averages in most cases, although there are some exceptions, such as New Mexico, where the same-sex household income is on a par with the state average. In numerical terms, the largest number of same-sex couples live in California, which is also the most populous state in the US, but as a proportion of overall households, the number is highest in the District of Columbia (DC) with 18.08 per 1,000 households; DC also has the nation's highest median household income, no doubt unsurprisingly. The proportion of same-sex households with children is highest in Maryland (20.3 per cent), followed by Georgia (19.6) and Vermont (18.6). Even the highest percentage is roughly half the average for the overall population, but by far the largest number of households with children is that of single mothers.[5] The average age of same-sex couples is lower than for different-sex: 44.7 versus 49.6, but it is possible that the older demographic among different-sex couples is due to changes both in legal frameworks for same-sex unions and wider social acceptance of same-sex relationships, which could mean that older gay men and lesbians are less likely to be in declared couple relationships—a presumption borne out by findings in another WI report (Choi and Meyer 2016). In both demographics, well over half the couples were in the Gen X and lower end of baby-boomer age range: 40 to 64. Same-sex couples in the US are also more likely to be university-educated (51 per cent versus 34 per cent), although the likelihood of being unemployed or having health insurance is quite similar to that of different-sex couples.

However, there are some variations in data analysis, depending on what, exactly, is being measured: the actual couple status of the people being surveyed, irrespective of employer approaches, or impacts of attitudinal shifts resulting from legislation. As concerns employment prospects, for example, the WI shows unemployment among same-sex couples running at 5 per cent versus the slightly lower rate of 4 per cent for different-sex couples, but Dario Sansone's state-by-state analysis using American Community Survey data (also one of the WI sources), showed that legalisation of same-marriage tended to *increase* employment prospects for gay men and lesbians (Sansone 2019). Although Sansone stressed that his model evaluated the impact of *legalisation*, and not marital status itself, his discussion nonetheless focused on labour market prospects and hours worked per week among same-sex couples. He argued that there was

> suggestive evidence that SSM legalization changed perceived social norms, improved attitudes in the population, and reduced (actual or expected) discrimination based on sexual orientation. This progress may have been the primary driver of the increased employment in same-sex couples. (Sansone 2019, online)

In the UK, a 2018 study found an income penalty for partnered gay men in relation to partnered heterosexual men but an income premium for partnered lesbians, in relation to both non-partnered lesbians and to partnered heterosexual women. However, the study was not disaggregated by race/ethnicity, nor by occupational sector (although it did look at the impact of residing in London or outside London, with the results not necessarily being those one might expect) (Aksoy, Carpenter and Frank 2018). A 2016 German study also found an income penalty for partnered gay men versus a premium for partnered lesbians (Humpert 2016). These findings contradict Dutch statistics, which indicate that gay male couples have higher incomes than either lesbian or straight couples. The analysis of the data by the Netherlands Statistics Bureau suggests that although gay men earn, on average, less than straight men, the significantly higher household earning would be explained by the fact that heterosexual women earn much less and this lower income drags down the heterosexual household average. However, when data is adjusted for age, education, country of origin and hours worked, the gay pay gap widens between individual gay men and individual heterosexual men, but reverses for lesbians and straight women: lesbians actually earn a little less. The positive initial average would be explained by the fact that lesbians, like gay men, are generally older, are less likely to have children, are more highly educated on average and are more likely to be working fulltime, although this last difference does not apply to gay men, who work fewer hours on average than straight men (Centraal Bureau voor de Statistiek 2019).

As concerns ethno-racial data in other Anglosphere countries (including, in this case, Ireland), they all maintain Census data on same-sex marriage, but to obtain more finely-grained data beyond sex-disaggregation one usually has to map this data onto other demographic statistics. The UK provides slightly more information than other Anglosphere countries outside the US, but the latest publicly available statistics on marriage in England and Wales (at the time of writing) date from 2016 (2018 for Scotland), while the latest statistics on sexual orientation date from 2017 (National Records of Scotland 2019; Office for National Statistics 2019a,b). As in the US, more lesbians than gay men marry, (56 per cent vs 44), and both lesbians and gay men are older than heterosexuals when they marry, although men are significantly so (Office for National Statistics 2019b). As for sexual orientation, the whole-of-UK statistics gleaned from the Annual Population survey show roughly 2 per cent of the nation's 52.8 million people (in 2017) identifying as lesbian, gay or bisexual (LGB), with the numbers being greater than in the previous decade and greater among men (Office for National Statistics 2019a, 3). A little under 5 per cent identify as "other": the Office for National Statistics notes that

> The "other" category captures people who do not consider themselves to fit into the heterosexual or straight, bisexual, gay or lesbian categories. It might also include people who responded "other" for different reasons such as those who did not understand the terminology or who are against categorisation. There is currently no further breakdown of "other" collected in the Annual Population Survey so no assumptions can be made about the sexual orientation or gender identity of those responding "other". (Office for National Statistics 2019a, 4)

The report further notes that self-identification as LGB is the highest among 16–24-year-olds (4.2 per cent), but that age group also had the highest rate of self-identification as "other" or "don't know or refuse" (Office for National Statistics 2019a, 6). The largest concentration of LGB is in London with the smallest in northeast and eastern England, and almost 70 per cent of them are single, with a little over 10 per cent being in heterosexual marriages, roughly 7 per cent being in same-sex civil partnerships and roughly 5 per cent being same-sex married (Office for National Statistics 2019a, 10). These statistics appear to indicate that the UK lesbian and gay population is hardly rushing to get legally partnered up, either civilly or maritally; one could assume that among the 70 per cent "single", a number might be involved in intimate relationships but choosing not to legally register that relationship in any way.

Who is getting gay-divorced?

In a 17 May 2017 interview with Charlie Pickering, host of the Australian satirical current affairs programme *The Weekly*, Canadian comedian DeAnne Smith commented on the longstanding legality of same-sex marriage in Canada by quipping "I got gay-married in 2005, then got gay-divorced in 2006". The remark was funny, particularly in the then Australian context of the heated debate over legalisation of same-sex marriage. It both normalised and banalised same-sex marriage and divorce at a time and place where the former was far from banal in Australia and the latter was not even on anyone's radar.

It was, however, on the radar of at least one couple in 2017. Smith's quip developed even greater ironic resonance when on 11 December 2017, two days after the Australian same-sex marriage law took effect, as hundreds of Australian couples were rushing to lodge their marriage applications, an Australian lesbian couple filed for divorce. The Perth women had been married in 2015, in a European country where same-sex marriage is legal, but were blocked from divorcing in Australia as the Australian state did not recognise same-sex marriage, and thus did not recognise same-sex divorce either (Hamlyn 2017).

In France, the first gay divorce also came quickly, but this time it was only four months after the marriage, when two Toulouse men who had married at the end of June, 2013, divorced at the end of October the same year (Le Monde, 2013). The couple's lawyer nonetheless downplayed the significance of this divorce, calling it an "epiphenomenon" in a country where half of all marriages end in divorce anyway (cited in Le Monde 2013). In Canada, where same-sex marriage was legalised in 2005, same-sex *divorce* was not available to non-resident same-sex spouses who had married in Canada and wished to divorce there, unless they had been resident there for one year. The problem was corrected by an amendment to the Divorce Act in 2013, after a lesbian couple, one of whom was from the US and one of whom was from the UK, and who had married in Ontario in 2005, challenged the constitutionality of the residency requirement in 2012 (Butler and Kirkby 2013). Similar legal anomalies and obstacles arose in different states within the US prior to nationwide legalisation in 2015 (Van Eeden-Moorefield et al. 2011).

Gay divorces make headlines, particularly when, as in the above cases, they are the first ones, happen quickly, or highlight anomalies or contradictions in legislation. After all the energy put into campaigning for "equal love" or "marriage for all" or "marriage equality", the very existence of gay divorces can seem somehow anomalous, as if a hard-won right had been suddenly trashed. For straight people and most particularly straight women in the Christian capitalist world, divorce has often been a liberation, and rights to equal, no-fault divorce have been a longstanding and yet-to-be-fully won feminist campaign. For gay people, on the other hand, it was marriage that was perceived to have that liberatory effect.

Some studies have borne out that liberatory expectation of same-sex marriage, at least as concerns well-being. They have shown that same-sex marriage prohibitions or legalisations have impacted on the mental health of gay men and lesbians. In Australia in September 2017, a number of mental health advocacy and research organisations, notably youth mental health organisations, launched an evidence-based "#mindthefacts" campaign supporting a "yes" vote in the postal opinion ballot on same-sex marriage.[6] Among the studies the campaign cited were a 2015 US study showing improved mental health among LGB populations in states that had legalised same-sex marriage (see also Badgett 2009). Even without marriage legalisation, one Australian study found that formalising their couple relationship in some way, through state-approved civil unions or through a private commitment ceremony, correlated positively with the mental health of study participants (Bariola et al. 2015). A large-scale study on suicide rates in Denmark and Sweden among the same-sex-married and heterosexually-married was more equivocal. The report noted the deleterious impact of minority stress overall on the mental health of LGB people, and found that even within marriage, the suicide rate for LGB was much higher than for heterosexuals, and more pronounced among women of all ages as well as young men in both groups (Erlangsen et al. 2020). The report did note a decline in suicide rates for the same-sex-married in recent years, and suggests that one factor may be growing societal acceptance, leading to a decrease in "stigmatisation, psychological stress and level of distress experienced by sexual minority people, thereby reducing their suicide risk. Nevertheless", it concludes,

> the finding that between 2003 and 2016, people who entered an SSM [same-sex marriage] in the relatively progressive countries of Denmark and Sweden continued to have a suicide rate that was around twice as high as that of people who entered an OSM [opposite-sex marriage] is worrisome [and] points to the critical need for better understanding of suicide risk and protective factors in sexual minority populations. (Erlangsen et al 2020, 80–1)

The jury thus remains out on the across-the-board health benefits of same-sex marriage in all countries where it is legal.

To return to the issue of same-sex divorce: if same-sex marriage means having access to being legally able to do what everyone else does, and so being (regarded as) "more like" everyone else, with one's homosexuality becoming a less salient factor in one's life (Badgett 2009), then logically, after "marriage equality" comes "divorce equality". In most countries for which we have data, same-sex divorce rates would appear to be higher than those for heterosexuals, with the exception of the US, where a 2014 study by the Williams Institute found that the same-sex divorce rate was *lower* than for heterosexuals (Badgett and Mallory 2014). This finding could, however, be in part at least an artefact of the unequal legalisation of same-sex marriage across the US at that time, which meant that couples who changed their state of residence after marriage could not divorce in that state. It may also be an artefact of the protracted and energetic campaign for same-sex marriage in the US, as well as of the high attachment that United Statians continue to have to the marriage institution—one of the highest in the OECD, compared to the low attachment on the part of, for example, the Dutch, French, Spanish, Italians or Argentinians (OECD 2019). However, the US attachment to the institution is greater among whites, Asians and Hispanics than among blacks, and it has been suggested that the US institution of marriage is patriarchally white in its representation and structure (Johnson and Loscocco 2015).

In the Netherlands, where same-sex marriage has been legal the longest, we know that just as lesbians are more likely to get married, they are also more likely to get divorced. By 2015, 30 per cent of the 580 lesbian marriages that were registered in 2005 had ended in divorce; this figure was 15 per cent for gay men and 18 per cent for heterosexuals (Centraal Bureau voor de Statistiek 2016). The likelihood of divorce in all groups was higher if people were married before their twentieth birthday or got married between the ages of 40 and 50. It was also higher if there was a significant age gap between the spouses—which in the Netherlands was more likely among gay-married men (and was also found to be in the case in Norway and Sweden [Andersson et al. 2006]).

Statistics elsewhere replicate those of the Netherlands. In a study on Norway and Sweden published in 2006, which also found higher gay than straight divorce rates, the authors suggested that a "higher propensity for divorce in same-sex couples is perhaps not very surprising given this group's lower exposure to normative pressure to maintain lifelong unions" (Andersson et al. 2006). In England and Wales in 2017, where heterosexual divorces were in decline (reflecting the longer-term decline in the marriage rate as well), the number of divorces for lesbians and gay men was, somewhat startlingly, triple that of the previous year, even though, as we saw above, the number of same-sex marriages was falling (Office for National Statistics 2018, 5 ff.). The lesbian divorce rate was a staggering two and a half times that for gay men, and "unreasonable behaviour" the most commonly cited reason (as it was for heterosexuals).

The UK lags behind most of the countries that are covered by this study as concerns its divorce laws: even Ireland voted by referendum in 2019 to get rid of the mandatory four-year waiting period in its 1996 divorce law. Whereas in countries as diverse as Australia, France, Germany, Mexico and South Africa, quick no-fault divorce has been available for decades, in the UK one must cite one of the following: adultery (only available to heterosexuals as a reason), unreasonable behaviour, desertion, living apart for at least two years with consent of the spouse to the divorce being required, or living apart for at least five years without consent being required. The Office for National Statistics did note that some of the 2017 divorces may concern marriages resulting from a civil partnership conversion, as the date of the beginning of the marriage for the purpose of assessing a divorce suit is taken to be the date at which the preceding civil union was entered into (Office for National Statistics 2018, 6). Attempts to introduce no-fault divorce in the UK 2019 failed, largely due to interruptions to parliament related to ongoing wrangles over Brexit. Although reintroduced in early 2020, the bill became stalled once again in committee after the onset of the COVID-19 pandemic.

Gunnar Andersson et al.'s study on Norway and Sweden and a later one on Sweden only also confirmed the higher divorce rates among lesbians (Andersson et al. 2006; Kolk and Andersson 2018). In both cases, the authors were at a loss to explain this higher rate, although Kolk and Andersson, citing previous research, suggest that lesbians are "more sensitive than men to different aspects of relationship quality" (Kolk and Andersson 2018, 25). A 2017 US study drew the same conclusion, adding that women are "socialized to place greater emphasis on intimate relationships" and that lesbian friendship networks may mean that lesbians are more likely to dissolve an unsatisfactory relationship, knowing they will have access to emotional support (Balsam, Rothblum and Wickham 2017, 254). Jen Bacon has argued that concern at lesbian divorce rates is indicative of heteropatriarchal thinking about what marriage is or should be, and she offers "an alternative to binary thinking about marriage in the sense that one is either married or divorced—connected or disconnected" (Bacon 2012, 162). She observes that lesbians are far more likely to remain friends with their exes, and have a greater investment in relational practices that involve empowerment, community and accountability. However, she did suggest that one possible negative consequence of the legalisation of same-sex marriage might be to engender more adversarial behaviours among lesbians upon splitting up (Bacon 2012). Anecdotal evidence from my own observations in various contexts suggests that whether or not, and the ways in which, lesbians engage with the continuity of community has a great deal to do with their feminist politics and practice, and their engagement with lesbian community more generally. Or it may simply be that lesbians, being women, were less attached to the marriage institution in the first place.

Counting intersectionally (1): self-identification and race/ethnicity demographics

It is difficult enough to "count" LGBTIQ populations in general and same-sex couples (married or otherwise) in particular, but those difficulties multiply when one attempts to do so intersectionally, particularly in terms of race/ethnicity. Even in the US, where data is disaggregated by race/ethnicity, interpreting the data, particularly in comparison to the population at large, is not a straightforward exercise. Among other things, how these demographics are "counted" is a historically path-dependent and politically fraught exercise. As a consequence of the history and politics, race/ethnicity both count and are counted differently in different countries, and are even *named* differently. This problem of nomenclature and categorisation is why I use the double term race/ethnicity here (except when citing literature that prefers one or the other), because the two terms present considerable overlap and confusion in the ways in which they are used. Another problem with "counting" the ethno-racial characteristics of same-sex couples has to do with self-identification within ethno-racial categories on the one hand, and as lesbian or gay on the other hand.

I use the term "race" advisedly here, not as a "scientific" term but as a political one, and one that is in fact still used in the US. The use of race in the US Census dates back to the history of slavery, and the famous (or perhaps infamous) Article 1, Section 2, paragraph 3 of the US Constitution, which originally restricted representation (and indeed counting) to "free persons".[7] "Free Persons" were of course white persons, and although the Constitution did not make this explicit, the Census did, from its first iteration in 1790 (Schor 2017, ch. 1). The term "race" continues to be a political and demographic marker used in both the US Census and the American Community Survey, but today it is considered an important demographic classification for other reasons, such as policy development and evaluation, measuring compliance with antidiscrimination laws, and targeted service provision.[8]

The stated motivation for asking the "race" question in the US has thus changed significantly, but the idea of "race" as a demographic marker is still taken for granted. In 1970 the concept of "origin" was introduced specifically for "Hispanics" or "Latinos" (both terms are now used), as their "ethnicity" did not necessarily have a colour, many Latin Americans in fact being white. They also get asked the "race" question and US Census data disaggregates the category "white" according to whether it includes Hispanics or not. This race/ethnicity dichotomy has been both confusing and controversial, with the members of the targeted Hispanic/Latino group not always identifying clearly with the Census categories (Cohn 2010; Taylor et al. 2012; Terry and Fond 2013; Schor 2017, ch. 17). At the time of writing, the questions targeting "Hispanics/Latinos" are being re-scrutinised for the 2020 Census (along with President Trump's proposed introduction of a new category of "Middle Eastern or North African origin") (Terry and Fond 2013; López 2018; Telles 2018). It is, however, taken as a given by many participants in the US debate that race and ethnicity are discrete concepts that describe different things, even if the law—and the Census—are not necessarily clear as to the distinction (e.g. López 2018).

The Census-reinforced notion that only Hispanics/Latinos have an "ethnicity" ("origin"), whereas all white non-Hispanics, all African Americans, all Asians and all other groups, including those who have to date been racially categorised as "other" in the US Census, apparently do not. In other words, most are defined by their "race" while some are defined by either or both of their "race" and their "ethnicity". Yet "race" is also a matter of perception: for example, some of "Middle Eastern ethnic background" may not have what is commonly imagined to be a "Middle Eastern appearance", or, in other words, their "street race" may be "white" rather than "of colour" (López, et al. 2018). Yet, as soon as they are identified as being "ethnically" Middle Eastern, they become perceived as not-white, and thus of Middle Eastern "race" (although this population is bundled into the "some other race" category on the US Census form that is current at the time of writing).

Across the Pond in Europe, there is a bewildering array of conflations and distinctions between "race" and "ethnicity", also for historical reasons, to do with the formation and disintegration of European empires and political blocs, the impacts of World War II, the history of colonisation and its accompanying ideologies, postcolonial immigration, and other specific national path dependencies. In her historical and legal analysis of the meaning of "ethnic or racial origin" under EU law, with particular reference to the EU's Racial Equality Directive (RED) (EU 2000), Lilla Farkas stresses that "[t]he abundance of terms and concepts applied to individuals and groups eligible for protection under the RED is overwhelming" (Farkas 2017, 124). In some countries, such as France, the terms "race" and "ethnicity" are considered equivalent in legal terms (although until a 2018 amendment the Constitution used the phrase "without distinction of race" in its Article 1 equality statement), while in others they are not: Swedish law outlaws the term "race" (as it considers it racist) but not "ethnicity". The term "race" similarly fell into disfavour in the UK, where the Race Relations Act, along with a number of other separate pieces of antidiscrimination legislation, was folded into the Equality Act of 2010, and UK case law now provides a discrete definition of "ethnicity". Farkas's report thus "purports to show that the quest for identifying differences between racial and ethnic origin has been futile and urges the legal profession to refrain from further pursuing such endeavours" (Farkas 2017, 125). Ethno-racial "counting" anywhere in Europe is thus even more fraught than in the US.

In Latin America, disaggregation by race/ethnicity relates to the history of settler colonialism. In Mexico, for example, "mestizo" was historically an official category in Census data, but is now not used, although most of those now self-identifying as "other" are probably what used to be termed "mestizo". In Argentina, Indigenous and Afro-descendant categories are included in Census data. In Brazil, the Instituto Brasileiro de Geografia e Estatística (Institute of Geography and Statistics, IBGE), has five distinct and somewhat controversial ethno-racial categories that are mostly colour codes: *branco* (white), *pardo* (brown), *preto* (black), *amarelo* (yellow, that is, "Asian"), and *indígena* (indigenous). The country made international news with its 2010 Census, which showed a majority of the population self-identifying as black or mixed race (primarily "brown") for the first time (Phillips 2011). The race divide maps onto the class divide in similar ways to the US, with the "black" category being the majority of the poorest group.

The enduring impact of Western racist worldviews on how populations are "counted" is nowhere more evident than in South Africa. Almost two decades after the end of apartheid, and notwithstanding the political discourse of "rupture" with a racist past, the South African Census has maintained apartheid-era racial categories to "count" its population. The last Census at the time of writing was in 2011, and its results classify the population as Black African, Coloured, Indian/Asian, White, and Other. Statistics on marriage and divorce classify the heterosexually divorced by the four main race groups but neither the heterosexually nor the homosexually married; I was unable to find statistics on same-sex divorce.

The dilemma of racial classification in law and politics, and individual and group self-identification, thus remains as deeply political in societies today as it did under European colonial empires, in the US in 1790, or in South Africa under apartheid.

Introducing terms such as "culture", "ethnicity" or "origin" does not resolve the dilemma but compounds it, all the more because the alternate terms tend to take on the same range of political meanings and usages, including racist ones. There is, in fact, no way to "count" people in terms of race/ethnicity without reproducing racialisation, as unfortunately the latter reflects a sociocultural, economic and political reality.

The above discussion provides the background to our first problem in this section: that of whether or not there is any ethno-racial breakdown at all in the way LGBTIQ populations in general or same-sex couples (married or not) in particular are counted. Mostly, there is no disaggregation of data by race/ethnicity and as usual, it is in the US that we find the most comprehensive information.

The Williams Institute (WI) uses seven "race/ethnicity" categories for its charts on LGBTIQ populations in general and same-sex couples in particular: white, black, Latino/a, "more than one race [general table]/mixed race [couple table]", Asian, "Native Hawaiian or other Pacific Islander", and "American Indian and Alaska Native" (the terms used by the Census bureau). All seven categories appear on the general table, but "Asian" disappears from the couple table, presumably because the percentage of the total is less than one and thus considered statistically insignificant. In both charts, the largest group is white, the second largest Latino/a, and the third black, but the proportion of whites to the other categories is significantly greater for the same-sex coupled, and the proportion of Latinos is halved: 74 per cent white, 11 Latino/a and 9 black in the couple chart versus 58, 21 and 12 in the general "LGBT" chart. The proportion of Native Hawai'ian/Pacific Islander in couples is also greater (3 per cent versus 1 per cent in the general chart).

This ethno-racial mix appears to be greater than among the general population, with proportions in all racialised categories except Asian being higher among LGBT than among the entire US population, and the proportion of *whites* being some 20 percentage points *lower*.[9] That said, some caution is needed in interpreting this comparison, as, first, the general population figures are based on estimates projected from the 2010 Census while the LGBT population figures are based on survey data up to 2017. Second, and more importantly, the Census data disaggregates white including Hispanics (76.5 per cent) and "white alone" (60.4 per cent), compounding the confusion around classification and counting of whites and Hispanics. The WI data is silent on whether "white" includes Hispanics who identify as white or whether the "Latino/a" category is all Hispanic/Latino counted either racially or ethnically. As concerns ethno-racial proportions of coupled (married and non-married) among the general population versus same-sex couples, clearly comparable statistics are difficult to track down, because the available Census data does not provide the proportion of the overall totals of couples along ethno-racial lines, only as a proportion within the particular ethno-racial group (Lofquist et al. 2012). In addition, 2010 Census data, from which WI figures are extrapolated, list all same-sex couples as unmarried (a small proportion would have been legally married at that time, in some subnational jurisdictions), while both married and unmarried heterosexual couples are listed. However, taking all that data in conjunction with a 2019 Pew Research Center study based for the most part on 2018 figures (Menasce Horowtiz, Graf and Livingston 2019), one arrives at the following very approximate mapping: the ethno-racial breakdown in percentages of same-sex couples among the total seems to approach that of different sex-couples, although the numbers are still slightly lower among whites, much higher among blacks, a little higher among mixed race, and very much higher among Native Hawai'ian/Pacific Islander.

A proportion of same-sex couples also appear to be interracial although it is unclear how big a proportion. A report prepared by the Pew Research Center suggest that interracial marriage overall is on the increase in the US, with the percentage of interracial *newlyweds* being 17 per cent in 2015. However, the Pew study comments that the percentage of same-sex marriages among these numbers is statistically insignificant: it is thus not counted as a discrete figure (Livingston and Brown 2017). Other research has suggested that there are ongoing structural and societal barriers to "interracial LGBTQ loving", including within white-dominated LGBTQ communities (P. Prasad 2018).

The main conclusion one might draw from these admittedly approximate mappings is that the self-identified LGBT population presents more ethno-racial diversity than the general population, but the tendency towards coupledom is far stronger among whites, albeit still lower than the general population. Unfortunately, this data does not tell us a great deal about comparative *marriage* statistics.

As concerns race and class, Coral del Río and Olga Alonso-Villar have found that race, sex and sexual orientation all impact on occupational distribution and income in the US, but with sex nonetheless being the most significant factor:

> White heterosexual men stand out as the group with the highest wage (about 19.2 per cent above the average wage of workers living with a partner) and gay men of any race earn much less … On the other hand, all female groups have wages below the average (except Asian lesbians, whose wage is around the average). The wage gap of women, with respect to the average wage of the economy, ranges between –7 per cent for white lesbians and –23.5 per cent for Hispanic heterosexual women. Moreover, the wages of heterosexual women of any race and that of black lesbians are much lower than the wages of any male group. (Del Río and Alonso-Villar 2019a, 726)

They further found that high educational qualifications and "lower immigration profile" give lesbians and gay men some protection in the US labour market (Del Río and Alonso-Villar 2019b; see also Badgett and Schneebaum 2019).

In the UK, Census data uses only the term "ethnicity" and tends to place reports on "ethnicity" under the umbrella of "ethnicity and religion". The "ethnicities" used in the Census are "white British, all other white, mixed/multiple ethnic groups, Asian/Asian British, Black/African/Caribbean/Black British", and "other ethnic group". Like the US, the UK mixes "ethnicity" and race, without explicitly using the term "race", and thus "black" and "white" become "ethnic" descriptors and not racial ones. The largest group by far is "white British", at a little under 80 per cent of the total, with the second largest being Asian/Asian British, at a little under 10 per cent (Office for National Statistics 2019c).

Interestingly, data from the UK Sexual Orientation Survey (Office for National Statistics 2019a) show that the largest proportion of ethno-racial self-identification among LGB people is not white, Asian or Asian British, black African or Caribbean or black British, nor even "other ethnic group", but "mixed or multiple ethnic groups", with "white" being the second largest group, although most respondents (over 80 per cent) to the 2017 UK survey appear to remain silent on ethno-racial self-identification. The report comments that ethnic self-identification is the least reliable and most frequently fluctuating figure for LGB populations, "due to small sample sizes … with notable uncertainty around LGB estimates for all ethnic groups except White" (Office for National Statistics 2019a, 10). Given the small percentages, it is impossible to map this data, even very approximately, onto same-sex marriage data, which is not ethno-racially disaggregated.

In Australia, Census data is broken down according to ancestry, country of origin or country of origin of parents, with the main ethno-racial demarcator being Aboriginal or Torres Strait Islander. This last is a routine question asked on a variety of administrative forms, for reasons linked to the specific history, status and needs of Australia's Indigenous populations and various institutional programmes set up to address them. Canada and New Zealand adopt similar demographic strategies, with Canada listing "ethnic and cultural origins" and New Zealand listing "ethnic groups", with the Indigenous populations forming a discrete group in each case. In none of these three countries is *colour* used as a term denoting "ethnicity", unlike the UK. In Ireland, it is the Irish Traveller population that is foregrounded as an Indigenous ethnic group with specific needs. And so on. However, nowhere outside the US is data on same-sex couples disaggregated by race or ethnicity, and any detective work on homosexuality and ethno-racial categories produces similarly frustrating results to the UK example above.

If in the Anglosphere one has little access to this sort of information, that figure drops to zero outside the Anglosphere, although some research gives data for rates of immigrant partners in the same-sex couple and suggests that this rate may be higher than the norm for heterosexuals (Andersson et al. 2006).

The problems are compounded when we consider our second issue announced at the beginning of this section: the difficulties in aligning national legal definitions of racial or ethnic categories and individual or group identifications or perceptions, as people may not recognise themselves under the labels they are given in law (Farkas 2017, 125). This problem also arises as concerns self-identification as lesbian or gay, and it has been suggested that the openly homosexual from higher socio-economic brackets are more likely to respond to surveys; inadequacy of Census questions has also been cited (Nathan and Pardo 2018, 9 and 16ff.).

The problem of self-identification is arguably greater for lesbians (at least since the decriminalisation of male homosexuality), due to the continued imposition of compulsory heterosexuality on women (Rich 1980), and the concurrent stigmatisation of lesbians, particularly those who are not feminine-looking. Research on lesbian self-identification in France, for example, has found that lesbians often find it easier to talk to others about their couple relationship with a girlfriend than to name themselves directly as lesbian (Chetcuti 2010), while lesbians from ethno-racial minorities may engage in strategies of invisibility to preserve both their lesbian lives and their family and community relationships (Amari 2018). Even if surveys, and to a lesser extent censuses, provide a measure of anonymity, respondents such as the women interviewed in France by Natacha Chetcuti and Salima Amari may not find answering questions on their sexual orientation or intimate relationships to be a straightforward exercise. As concerns same-sex couples more particularly, "there is no simple set of questions phrased in such a way that same-sex partners can easily identify themselves with no ambiguities in censuses or surveys" (Cortina and Festy 2014, 3). This is all the more the case in that there may be several administrative structures into which couples can fit, with some including both homosexuals and heterosexuals, such as in France, and some reserved for particular groups—including along ethno-racial lines, as in South Africa. This proliferation of regulatory frameworks means that Census questions on relationships within "households" become quite long and rather bewildering.

Another issue with data-gathering is that the relatively small numbers of persons who do self-identify as gay and lesbian and living in same-sex-coupled households may mean, first, that self-"mis-" identifications (for whatever reason) and small errors in data coding may take on more significance (a problem also noted by the Williams Institute), and second, that it is more difficult to meaningfully disaggregate data by other demographic characteristics (Cortina and Festy 2014). This difficulty is compounded when one has to rely on *survey* rather than Census data, as is the case concerning race/ethnicity in France, where it is illegal to identify people by race or ethnicity in national censuses, only by country of birth. So what we know about French ethno-racial minorities generally is extrapolated from that country of birth information and from regular surveys conducted by national statistics and demography institutes. What we know about those minorities among the same-sex-coupled or married is reduced to almost zero, and largely gleaned through qualitative ethnographies such as Amari's (2018), cited above, rather than through demographic surveys.

Counting intersectionally (2): who is same-sex marriage "for"?

The answer to the above question may seem obvious: same-sex marriage is for everyone who identifies as gay, lesbian or bisexual, whatever their biological sex and whether or not they see themselves as having a gender identity. Yet the debate continues concerning who same-sex marriage is "for" in terms of race, socio-economic status, and even sex. In this section, I will look at some other aspects of the demographic information, such as it is, and at debates around how same-sex marriage is marketed and campaigned for—that is, *represented*—including in terms of race/ethnicity. When one looks at this information and these representations, one begins to see that same-sex marriage would indeed appear to be "for" middle class white men, notwithstanding its formal legal accessibility for all.

Again, it is in the US that this debate has been the most extensively waged, around both race and class. First, in terms of race, some of the discursive framing around same-sex marriage has used both the black civil rights campaign and the groundbreaking 1967 *Loving versus Virginia* Supreme Court case on interracial marriage as a point of comparison. The *Loving* case even became known as the "Loving Analogy" and has been used as a frame for positioning same-sex marriage as a comparable civil rights and constitutional issue (Morrison 2007; Moran 2012). Adele Morrison, for example, stresses that the issue is not about "using" a civil rights matter as a comparator for gay rights, but argues for the status of *Loving* as a pivotal legal precedent in the areas of freedom of choice, antidiscrimination (importantly, in ruling that white supremacy was anti-constitutional) and the "fundamental right to marry" (Morrison 2007, 188). She further stresses that black people are *also* gay and as a socioeconomically marginalised population, stood to benefit financially from the legalisation of same-sex marriage (not the least because of health insurance, as pointed out elsewhere in this book). Finally, citing (with a slight paraphrase) the title of a famous work by bell hooks (1984), Morrison argues that interracial same-sex couples should be moved "from the margin to the center", not only because "countering subordination should be a common goal of all subordinated communities", but also because placing interracial same-sex couples at the centre of campaigns would enable the full potential of the *Loving* decision to be "truly realized" (Morrison 2007, 224). Rachel Moran argued, on the other hand, that the usefulness of *Loving* as a legal precedent was limited, because a number of state-level court decisions "explicitly rejected the claim that classifications based on sexual orientation, like those based on race, trigger the strictest constitutional scrutiny", due to the conservative legal argument that marriage first and foremost served a procreative function, which *Loving* did not contest (Moran 2012, 245ff.). Moran pointed out that campaigns that unlinked same-sex marriage from *Loving* were in fact more successful.

Beyond the legal and political arguments around the meanings and uses of *Loving*, race was part of the debate from the earliest days of the US same-sex marriage campaign. Three years before Morrison promoted the *Loving* analogy, black British journalist Gary Younge headed his article discussing US politics under George W Bush with the ironic title "gay is the new black" (Younge 2003). This is one of the earliest written records I can find of this phrase, yet, unlike critics of the race-homosexuality analogy in the US, Younge was using the expression to highlight the new targets of US conservatives, who formerly used race to rally the white Republican Party base. Writing in the lead up to the 2003 Massachusetts Supreme Court case *Goodridge versus Department of Public Health*, which led to the first subnational legalisation of same-sex marriage in the US, Younge concluded that "[w]hen it comes to finding a signifier for the indulgent excesses of liberal

Democrats and the Republicans' no-nonsense adherence to the values of middle America, gay is the new black" (Younge 2003, online).

In 2008 in the US, the sentence was again used as an ironic title (this time with a question mark) for Michael Gross's 16 November cover story in the well-known LGBTIQ magazine *The Advocate* in the wake of both the election of Barack Obama to the US presidency and the state of California's adoption of a state constitutional amendment known as Proposition 8, or "Prop. 8", outlawing same-sex marriage. The article discussed the fallout from the huge African American vote in favour of Prop. 8, after the manipulation of the race issue by anti-same-sex marriage campaigners (largely funded by the Mormon Church), who spread misinformation that Obama supported the amendment (Gross 2008). Gross lamented the wedge politics being operated, pointing out that African Americans actively supported LGBTIQ rights even though white gay people were not as eager or quick to support black rights. He similarly criticised the simplistic appropriation of the black civil rights movement as a symbol for the anti-Prop. 8 campaign: "Signs at protests said, 'I have a dream too,' 'Welcome to Selma,' and 'Gay is the new black'" (Gross 2008). He echoed Younge's 2003 analysis in writing that gay people were at that time "the most socially acceptable targets for the kind of casual hatred that American society once approved for habitual use against black people", and that this was the only sense in which "gay is the new black" was meaningful. However, he warned against facile and insulting reductionism that made light of the oppression of black people by the system of white privilege and wealth.

And so it went on. In fact, the US civil rights movement was routinely invoked—even before the Bush II era (see e.g. Hutchinson 2000)—as a point of comparison with the same-sex marriage campaign. This comparison was not limited to the *Loving* analogy but invoked various civil rights figures, imagery and slogans—including "gay is the new black"—prompting a great deal of critical analysis of the postracialist stance adopted by the white people at the forefront of the same-sex marriage movement (Robinson 2014; see also Stone and Ward 2011; Wadsworth 2011; Kearl 2015). "Postracialism" has been defined as an ideological framework that considers race to no longer be a structural factor in social, economic and political organisation and thus that political action, whether institutional or by civil society, no longer needs to foreground race as an issue (affirmative action, targeted programmes and campaigns, and so on) (Cho 2009). At the heart of the "gay is the new black" analogy is the idea that racism has somehow now been dealt with and the focus must now be on another civil rights issue that is posited as equivalent, when it demonstrably is not. As Nancy Wadsworth points out,

> [i]n the white-dominated LGBT community, fate-linking strategies that express commonality through discourses of equality and civil rights will be empty without attention to the other issues that concern these communities—like race, economics, and other social justice issues. (Wadsworth 2011, 212)

The postracialist position, and deployment of the civil rights analogy, was also used across the border in Canada, where Canadian lesbians and gay men were constructed as nice white people embracing nice white national values, which were posited as progressive in distinction to those of racialised peoples within and outside Canada (Thorpe 2005; Lenon 2011). Suzanne Lenon further argues, through an analysis of affidavits by gay and lesbian couples submitted in Ontario and British Columbia in 2000 and 2001 as part of the campaign for legalisation there, that not only was the civil rights analogy deployed by some couples but they also were at pains to stress their respectability as "ordinary Canadians", fitting a white, middle class, property-owning, taxpaying norm (Lenon 2011).

Other studies on the US investigated the ways in which "black" (and other ethno-racial minority) attitudes towards same-sex marriage were framed by white gay activists, by the media and by ethno-racial minorities themselves. A 2011 study by Negin Ghavami and Kerri Johnson found that apart from hostility to the civil rights analogy and to racist behaviours from the white-dominated movement for same-sex marriage, there existed a higher level of religiosity among African Americans, which is deeply rooted historically, with the Church being a place of refuge, of community and of political and financial support (Ghavami and Johnson 2011, 398 ff.). Another study the same year on Latino attitudes to same-sex marriage also found the role of religion to be important. There, however, the Catholicism of the Latino majority was a far less potent indicator of opposition than the evangelical fundamentalist Protestantism and biblical literalism of a significant Latino minority, and the authors cautioned against assumptions concerning the attitudes of all Latinos. In fact, they found that among the Catholic majority, the less devout, more progressive and younger Latinos, as well as women overall, were more amenable to same-sex marriage, and that the attitudes of the Latino population overall were in "ferment" (Ellison, Acevedo and Ramos-Wada 2011, 52). Scholars further cautioned against monolithic assessments of "black" attitudes to same-sex marriage, pointing out that apart from anything else, a number of African Americans are also LGB. That said, there is no monolithic "black LGB" stance either: while both race and sexual orientation are mutually constitutive and thus equally salient, and many black LGBs are found to support same-sex marriage, a range of other factors impact on attitudes. Those factors include socioeconomic disadvantage, ties to African American community and racism including within the LGBTIQ movement (Lee 2018). Even (some) intersectional analyses were found wanting insofar as they were deployed as predictors of how people might think: "[b]lack gays and lesbians locally and nationally often differ among themselves in their views of same-sex marriage as a civil rights issue; and identity constellations do not determine those differences" (McGuffey 2018).

Of course, as noted above, Kimberlé Crenshaw herself never intended "intersectionality" to become an identity-straightjacket. The point, however, of these various critiques is to highlight that "gayness" and "blackness" (or Latino-ness, and so on) are, first, neither monolithic nor mutually exclusive; second, not a historical progression from a now-fixed civil rights issue of the past to a to-be-fixed equivalent issue in the present; and third, not javelins to be hurled in an Oppression Olympics.

The criticisms of the whiteness of the same-sex marriage campaign have not been limited to North America. In Australia, the civil rights analogy was trotted out again, notably in the mainstream media, but this time in relation to Indigenous Australian civil rights. The analogy left uninterrogated "the historically specific ways that the ongoing project of settler colonialism shapes visions of liberal politics and possibilities for sexual citizenship" within the Australian liberal emancipatory framework (Hegarty et al. 2018, 403). Moreover, the Australian Marriage Equality social media campaign was not only very heterosexualised (with, in addition, those clearly identified as lesbians or gay men fitting heterosexist gender norms), it was also disproportionately white, relative to percentages of people of colour in the overall population (Soller 2019).

The whiteness and (mostly) maleness of media representations of those wanting to same-sex marry (or getting same-sex married), is replicated elsewhere, such as in Argentina's and France's first nationally televised same-sex (white male respectably dressed and groomed) weddings (Winter 2014, 2018b). Even in black-majority South Africa, we saw in Chapter 3 that the model same-sex-married couple is white, male and urban. In the US, the 2015 Supreme Court plaintiff, white 49-year-old IT consultant Jim Obergefell was dubbed the "poster boy" for same-sex marriage by the media (Winter 2018b), and one study showed that people were more likely to be favourable to legalising gay marriage when shown images of white men (Richeson and Van Brunt 2015). However, an earlier study found that television news coverage of gay men and lesbians in the context of the same-sex marriage debate in the first decade of this century featured lesbians as often as gay men and lesbians actually had more speaking time (Moscowitz 2010). The same study found that both lesbians and gay men were more often seen—and seen in conventional couple imagery and fitting normative masculine and feminine stereotypes—than heard, with sound bites being given most often to political and institutional figures. Another area where lesbians feature a little more frequently is in relation to children, as we saw in the case of the French advertisement in Chapter 4, or as in the case of high-profile lesbians and their families such as that of Australian Senate leader and, at the time of writing, shadow foreign minister Penny Wong (Winter 2018b). Wong is also a rare example of a racialised lesbian in both party-political and media prominence.

Finally, what is conspicuously absent from the normative, white property-owning taxpaying image of the ideal gay-married couple is the reality of poverty for many LGBTIQ people, particularly lesbians, with sole mothers being the most at risk of poverty (Albelda et al. 2009; DeFilippis 2016; Schneebaum and Badgett 2019). A 2019 Williams Institute study estimated that some 20 per cent of LGBTIQ people in the United States live in poverty, with the risk being higher than for straight people, higher in some states than in others and higher among racialised groups (Badgett, Choi and Wilson 2019). An earlier study in Australia found that poverty, employment levels and workplace experience for young lesbians belie the assumption that lesbians fare better than heterosexual women in the workplace and in income levels. In fact, the study found, they fare far worse: the results "paint a fairly grim picture of the overall economic well-being of young lesbians in Australia" (Carpenter 2008, 406). In addition, some have argued that the attention given to the same-sex marriage campaign has diverted resources and activist energy from issues of socioeconomic marginalisation facing many members of the LGBTIQ community (DeFilippis, Anderson-Nathe and Panichelli 2015). Although that claim has been disputed by some same-sex marriage advocates (e.g. Badgett 2009), the reality of poverty and marginalisation for many, in the face of the "respectable middle class" framing of the same-sex marriage campaign, often with significant corporate muscle and money behind it, rather tends to support it. In the following chapters, we will look at how these questions of labour, income, inclusion/exclusion and welfare play out for lesbians and gay men and in particular for those with children.

Notes

1 https://www.abs.gov.au/ausstats/abs@.nsf/featurearticlesbyCatalogue/48374764283E7650CA258351001009AA?OpenDocument, accessed 2 January 2020.
2 Australian Bureau of Statistics 2016: https://www.abs.gov.au/ausstats/abs@.nsf/Lookup/by%20Subject/2071.0~2016~Main%20Features~Same-Sex%20Couples~85, accessed 26 January 2020.
3 Ciudad de Buenos Aries statistical table, accessed 18 December 2019. https://drive.google.com/file/d/1N8bkWxhSLAK8dVcQt5DBoelGKGXueDJL/view.
4 Interactive map and charts available at https://williamsinstitute.law.ucla.edu/visualization/lgbt-stats/?topic=SS#demographic, accessed 28 December 2019.
5 Figures sourced from Statista, accessed 30 December 2019. https://www.statista.com/statistics/242074/percentages-of-us-family-households-with-children-by-type/.
6 Information available at https://www.blackdoginstitute.org.au/about-us/news-and-media/mindthefacts. Accessed 5 January 2020.
7 Available online, including notations of subsequent amendments, at https://constitutionus.com/#x14s2, accessed 2 January 2020.
8 American Community Survey website, accessed 2 January 2020. https://www.census.gov/acs/www/about/why-we-ask-each-question/race/.
9 Statistics obtained from the US Census Bureau, accessed 2 January 2020. https://www.census.gov/quickfacts/fact/table/US/PST045219#qf-headnote-b.

PART III

The political economy of "rainbow families"

7

"WORKING FAMILIES"

Parenting, productivity and policy

In this chapter, I look at the rhetorical and policy framing of "working families" by states and employers, and suggest that there is no indication that the economics of state family and welfare policies, or public- or private-sector workplace policies and practices, or the connections between them, have fundamentally changed in the era of same-sex marriage recognition. This is so even when these policies and practices include same-sex couples and parents either explicitly or implicitly (through more neutral language, for example). Nor is there to date any indication that this system has been significantly thrown into question by the presence or actions of "rainbow families", notwithstanding the fact that at least a proportion of the "rainbow family" population is visibly involved in workplace or community social activism. Even those organisations that may challenge at least some aspects of the neoliberal workplace, such as militant trade unions, do not challenge its familialist logics, and may even actively advocate or support them. For the state, the accent remains on maximum social and political advantage with minimum cost, and for business, on worker productivity and maximum profit, also with minimum investment. "Responsible" citizens are the employed, the "hardworking", the fiscally contributing, and, preferably, the married and parenting—regardless of their sexual orientation.

This understanding leaves us in a double bind. On the one hand, we know, historically and still today, that the bulk of parenting and caring labour is done by women (including in the same-sex-married universe), and that workplace laws and social policies that facilitate the participation of carers in the paid workforce thus help to level the workplace playing field for women, while supporting the care of children and others in need of it. On the other hand, the types of support provided are often a poisoned chalice: the logics of "family-friendly" laws and workplaces are still premised on the attribution of primary caring roles to women. Moreover, the question arises of whether workplace flexibility ostensibly designed to benefit workers by increasing their choices can function without simultaneously increasing precariousness in some way. One major way in which precarity is increased is through the normalisation and even "involuntarisation" (my term) of part-time work for women in particular, and its links to the social reproduction of the economy of care (Vosko, MacDonald and Campbell 2009, 14ff.). Moreover, the "flexibility" offered decreases in advantage to the workers the more they deviate from the white-collar professional norm.

Indeed, the emergence of the concept of "family friendly" workplaces is associated with the massive increase in numbers of married women in the professional and white-collar workforces, as women were never really absent from the blue collar, pink collar or rural workforces in the first place (Steedman 1994; Delphy 1998b). It is, further, an economy in which class, race and sex on the one hand, and labour and citizenship on the other, are co-constitutive, in that "labor and citizenship have helped create race and gender [and class] relations, meanings, and identities" (E.N. Glenn 2002, 236). It is thus the professional workforce that became the driver of the introduction of parental leave and of the rhetoric of "work-life balance", into which "rainbow families" are now in the process of being assimilated. So, while I understand all the feminist and rainbow-family arguments that may justify pushing within workplaces, trade unions and so on for such "(rainbow) family-friendliness", the latter invariably comes—like the welfare regime with which it is imbricated—with multiple strings attached.

To take one important example: even provisions that have been encoded in international and regional human rights treaties, such as paid maternity leave (see for example CEDAW, Article 11[2]), have been very difficult to obtain on a national level, and when obtained, are frequently constructed discursively as equivalent to some sort of gift from states or employers. (As a vocabulary litmus test, I performed a quick search in my university library in early June, 2020, of general and business news coverage of employer approaches to maternity leave, and found that good practice in this area was routinely characterised as "generous" by both mainstream and specialist media.) This framing, notwithstanding CEDAW, indicates that maternity and parental leave are still often not considered fundamental rights of workers; the application of maternity and parental leave thus varies considerably from country to country—and in many countries, from employer to employer. The ILO minimum standard for paid maternity leave is 14 weeks, which is not met by many of the countries where same-sex marriage is legal, including, at the time of writing, Argentina (13 weeks, although it meets the ILO standard in the public sector), Iceland, Mexico and Ecuador (each 12 weeks), Taiwan (8 weeks) and the US (zero weeks paid leave and very limited access to unpaid leave). In most countries where paid maternity leave is available, it is either wholly or partially funded by the national social security system.

The European Union is leading the field in this area: in 2019, it adopted a Directive on Work-Life Balance, which sets a legally binding minimum standard for all member states, although many already have higher than those minimum standards. I will discuss this Directive—and the implications of the "work-life balance" framing—more fully below. The uniformisation of family leave on a national level within the EU is enhanced by the strong social protection systems already in place in most EU member countries, such that social protection legislation and contributions cover all or part of paid family leave, health insurance and other benefits. Beyond these EU and national minima, however, and outside the EU, conditions may vary considerably not only from country to country but also—especially in the Anglosphere—from sector to sector and from workplace to workplace, in a context of retreat from strong national worker protection laws and/or collective whole-of-sector workplace bargaining and regulation.

The situation fluctuates even more when it comes to paid paternity or spousal leave, parental leave and carer's leave, where entitlements range from non-existent to more than a year. In a number of countries provisions do not (yet) apply to same-sex couples, even where same-sex marriage is legal, as in Argentina (Cirmi Obon 2017). Moreover, weak parental leave provisions can exacerbate existing income and workplace inequalities, notably in countries with high levels of inequality in the first place, and notably for women (again, in relation to Argentina, see Rodríguez Enriquez and Marzonetto 2015). Paradoxically, poverty alleviation programmes for women with carer responsibilities can exacerbate both the poverty and the imposition of the carer obligation, depending on whether the policy is targeting poor households, women, or building the so-called human capital of children (with concomitant restrictions on women's choices in relation to their households, their children and themselves), and on whether the households are headed by women or not (Bradshaw, Chant and Linneker 2019).

Even though such studies are conducted within a heterosexual framework—where income and power disparities *within* households play out in a different way from within same-sex households (see next chapter)—the broader socioeconomic patterns impact across the board. They all show that higher-income white professional workers are the best-buffered to face the socioeconomic transformations of a neoliberal labour marketplace. Workers with high cultural and social capital (in the Bourdieusian sense) are the most likely to be (a) part of the workplace-regulation conversation in the first place and (b) targeted by employer "inclusivity" and so-called "work-life balance" practices. The lowest-skilled workers and precarious workers, particularly women, are generally the most disadvantaged, both because of their relative lack of cultural and social capital, and the lower likelihood that they will be unionised, or, if unionised, represented by a strong trade union. State policies often reinforce workplace logics in advantaging couples and professional classes while being disadvantageous to the single and the poor, and most especially single parents, the overwhelming majority of whom are women (Albelda 2001, 2011, 2013).

The rhetoric of work and family and its material underpinnings

The ways in which we describe work, working conditions and entitlements (parental leave, flexible working hours and so on), and the interface between work and both personal and domestic life have bearing on how we conceptualise households, individuals and families, and their relationships with workplaces, employers and the state. In the Anglosphere, the phrase "working families" (or in the UK, "hardworking families") has long been popular, as has the expression "work-life balance". Both terms have considerable currency in Anglosphere academic literature focusing on social equality and social in/exclusion (e.g., on "working families": Blau 1999; Burnett, Swan and Cooper 2014; B. Nolan 2018). Outside the Anglosphere, the vocabulary used is a little different: I have not found an exact equivalent for "working families" in French, German, Spanish, Portuguese, Swedish or Dutch, outside neologistic word-for-word translations from English of the term as used in EU, UN or ILO documents (e.g. EU 2019a). Terms used in the languages in national sources found online (such as census documents or news media) usually refer to working or employed individuals, women, parents, work *and* family, families *of* workers, and so on, but no document refers to "working families". As for "work-life balance", either the English term is used with an explanatory paraphrase in the language of the country, or the documents I consulted favour expressions such as "reconciling" or "balancing" work (or working life) and either personal life or family life, or both, but "life" is not used on its own, which is significant for a reason I will explain presently. Sometimes, the foreign language will, under the umbrella English term "work-life balance", focus on a particular issue, such as in the published results of a survey of 1,000 workers conducted by the Austrian office of "big four" accounting firm Ernst & Young. The survey uses the English term, in the header "work-life balance", followed by *Arbeitsbelastung* (workload), which is the actual focus of the report (EY 2019). Another publication, by German think tank Bertelsmann Stiftung (which is undated but refers to data from the first half of the 2010 decade), uses the title "Work-Life-Balance" (all words hyphenated), followed by the phrase *Meilenstein für eine zukunftsfähige Gesellschaft* (Milestone for a sustainable society). The phrase could also translate as "future-oriented" society, as "future-oriented" is a regularly used Bertelsmann Stiftung buzzword.[1] These corporate/private think tank documents are, further, an indication of the interest that corporations take in the "work-life balance" issue, and some research has suggested that the concept is a key part of corporate ideology (Hoffman and Cowan 2008), a point to which I will return presently.

Given the preponderance of these English terms within international institutional documents and EU policy, law and research, their conceptual development and incorporation into corporate and state politics and policy within the Anglosphere warrants some discussion. I stress at the outset that the framing within these various corporate, institutional and policy documents is resolutely heterosexual, and privileges the profile of the "responsible" and "hardworking" married (and usually white) professional. Even the limited "inclusivity" of the stereotypical white middle-class "rainbow family" does not operate.

Working families

The term "working families" is said to spring from the Clinton era in the early 1990s, although I do not think Clinton himself ever used that precise term: he preferred to focus on the "forgotten middle class", who apparently needed more help than the poor. However, Clinton's stump speech in his 1992 presidential campaign included variations on the theme of rewarding people who "work hard and play by the rules", usually coupled with the idea of reforming the welfare system through a "Welfare to work" programme, of the sort that is becoming increasingly common in the capitalist world. An undated and archived presidential webpage on Welfare Reform proclaims that "The President wants welfare reform that reinforces basic American values—work, responsibility, and family —not punishes children for their parents' mistakes".[2]

Barbara Hopkins has pointed out that "working families" has been "a political strategy to counteract the 'welfare queen' narrative in which women have lots of children to receive public assistance" (personal email communication, 7 January 2020). The phrase appealed to both a conservative and a labour union base in Clinton's time, although subsequently it has been most particularly associated with the left, with the splinter party "Working Families Party" (WFP) being formed in 1998. The Party brands itself as "a grassroots, multiracial party of working people coming together across our differences to make our nation work for the many, not the few" (WFP website).[3] It is focused on, among other things, "building a better future for our kids" (WFP website: "About Us").[4] WFP has been lauded by some as a new progressive left (e.g. Ball 2016) and it has tended to support political candidates from the left wing of the Democratic Party. In 2016 it supported Bernie Sanders, and in late 2019 it announced that it was backing Elizabeth Warren in the 2020 Democratic Presidential Primary. This party is, however, somewhat anomalous, as parties that include "family" or "families" in their names are almost always ultra-conservative. The choice of this name by this group indicates that it remains wedded (as it were) to a familialist social model, even if not necessarily to the middle-class white nuclear one, and as such, continues to "think right" (Guillaumin 1986).

The "Welfare Queen" narrative nonetheless held sway in Clinton's US, and continues to do so. In 1996, a Republican-dominated Congress introduced a more punitive Welfare-to-Work law than Clinton had planned. It is the now-notorious Personal Responsibility and Work Opportunities Reconciliation Act (PRWORA) (1996), which Denise Thompson has described as "a piece of vicious thuggery involving some of the most powerful men in the nation bullying the most helpless citizens already victimised by the system that made those men so powerful" (Thompson 2020, 363). The Act reconfigured welfare as Temporary Assistance to Needy Families (TANF), with the accent being on the "Temporary". It was justified by normative "findings" that marriage was "the foundation of a successful society" and "an essential institution of a successful society which promotes the interests of children" (PRWORA Section 101, paras 1 and 2). Congress further found that there were far too many unmarried mothers and too many of them were teenagers; the Act's stated purpose was thus "to end the dependence of needy parents on government benefits by promoting job preparation, work, and marriage" (PRWORA Section 401a, para. 2). The law effectively "singles out low-income women—single mothers, disproportionately of color—for regulation and discipline" (Kornbluh and Mink 2018, 2). It was widely hailed as a success by politicians, business and think tanks alike, because it decreased the numbers of people on welfare from 12.6 million in 1996 to less than a quarter of that number—2.8 million—20 years later (Haskins and Pike 2016). Yet a number of studies have pointed to a connection between PRWORA and a rise in extreme poverty rates and in the working poor, among whom women, especially single mothers, are disproportionately represented (Sawicky 2004). Already at the time of the introduction of PRWORA, unskilled single mothers in the labour force were worse off financially than on welfare, and frequently resorted to various forms of informal work including prostitution (Edin and Lein 1997). (While it would be inaccurate to suggest that poverty is the sole cause of prostitution, because the structural and ideological apparatus that enables and maintains its existence is more complex than that, poverty is nonetheless a major factor in women seeking informal work of various descriptions, including prostitution [Barry 1995].) In short, "employment in a low-wage economy does not lift people out of poverty" (Thompson 2020, 366) and the women targeted by PRWORA are locked into a cycle of impoverishment for which they are indeed rendered "personally responsible".

The idea of "working families" in the US, notwithstanding its association with a self-proclaimed progressive and multiracial political party, is thus an ambiguous one, and the idea of "work" + "family" remains, among the political class at large, anchored in social conservatism and hatred of the poor, the black and the female.

The idea of "working families" resurfaced across the Pond later in the 1990s, as part of Tony Blair's new Labour platform, with a little help from US political consultant Bob Shrum (Freedland 2005). Blair and Clinton were key figures in the Third Way network (Giddens 1998, 2001), which also included Dutch leader Wim Kok (Labour Party), German Chancellor Gerhard Schröder (Social Democratic Party) and Australian Mark Latham (leader of the Federal Labor opposition in 2004 and 2005, and in 2019 elected a member of the NSW Legislative Council [upper house] for the far-right party One Nation.) The ideas of "personal responsibility" and "hard work" and a retreat from state responsibility for welfare were all on Blair's New Labour agenda, marked by a rhetorical shift from the traditional Labour terrain of class to the new social-democrat, far more "slippery" terrain of "community" and community "values" (Reyes 2005, 231–2). The concept has endured, spreading from the centre-left to the rest of the political spectrum: in the 2015 UK national election "politicians from across the political spectrum hardly ever used the word 'families' without prefacing it with two more words: 'hard working'" (Runswick-Cole, Lawthom and Goodley 2016). Katherine Runswick-Cole, Rebecca Lawthom and Dan Goodley see the "hardworking family" discourse as

> conform[ing] to the neoliberal-ableist trope; the "hardworking family" is independent, self-sufficient and, crucially, it does not rely on the state for its survival. As the British Prime Minister [David Cameron] said, these are people who "do the right thing". (Runswick-Cole, Lawthom and Goodley 2016, 257)

The same Prime Minister stated in 2011 that "we've known for years that a relatively small number of families are the source of a large proportion of the problems in society" (cited in Runswick-Cole, Lawthom and Goodley 2016, 258).

Cameron's words demonstrate that "welfare" in the UK has retained the stigma of the 1834 British revision of the 1601 Poor Law, which transformed the poor into "a problem to be contained, controlled and stigmatised out of their state of poverty" rather than a group in need of relief (Charlesworth 2010, 5), and of Bismarck's laws of the 1880s, grounded in social conservatism and a desire to keep workers and the poor "subservient" to the state, thereby undermining socialism (Briggs 1961; Ullmann [1981]2019). "Welfare capitalism" (Esping-Andersen 1990), even at its best (and today it is far from that), was never intended to be emancipatory, only "benevolent", within strict limits of state control.

The following decade in Australia, the term "working families" was mobilised by Prime Minister Kevin Rudd (Labor, elected 2007) and particularly his successor Julia Gillard, who replaced him in a leadership challenge in 2010. In April 2007, Rudd, then Labor opposition leader, and Gillard, then Shadow Minister for Employment and Industrial Relations, presented "Forward With Fairness: Labor's plan for fairer and more productive Australian workplaces" (Rudd and Gillard 2007). In that document, they repeated the phrase "working families" several times, frequently in the same sentence as "fairness", flexibility" and "productivity": all in all, a Third Way style framing that would have kept Clinton or Blair happy. Significantly for the discussion on "work-life balance" that follows below, Rudd and Gillard wrote of "balancing work and family responsibilities" and "family-friendly workplaces". Four years later, as Australia's first (and to date only) female Prime Minister, Gillard used the same framing in the inaugural Whitlam oration at the university Institute of the same name. (Gough Whitlam, Labor Prime Minister from 1972 to 1975 and subsequently Australian ambassador to UNESCO, among other things, was a giant of Australian politics: to deliver the inaugural Whitlam oration was thus a significant honour.) In her oration, Gillard claimed that Labor was "the party of work not welfare":

> We have moved beyond the days of big government and big welfare, to opportunity through education and inclusion through participation. But at every stage in our history fair access to opportunity has been our historic mission. And we have always acknowledged that access to opportunity comes with obligations to seize that opportunity. To work hard, to set your alarm clocks early, to ensure your children are in school. (Gillard 2011)

This framing of "working families" is consistent with a neoliberal system characterised by, first, a re-privatisation of responsibility for care and social welfare; second, a "marketisation" of social policy (Matthies and Uggerhøj 2014; Meagher and Goodwin 2015; Van Berkel et al. 2017); and third, legitimation of the logics of managerialism and employment "flexibility" (Boltanski and Chiapello 1999). Together, these shifts underpin the development of "welfare-to-work" policies, also known as "mutual obligation" (Australia) or "mutual commitment" (Ireland), which penalise the already-marginalised and involve in addition privatisation of welfare and employment agencies (Considine et al. 2015). Neoliberalism "demanded that individuals and families become self-sufficient and able to *choose* and access commercial and voluntary provisions so that the state could be spared the responsibility of ensuring that provisions were made available to all those in need" (Dominelli 2014, 79, italics in original).

In continental Europe, where the legitimacy of systems of social protection and minimum-wage standards is much stronger than in the Anglosphere, many of these neoliberally-driven policies have been introduced more stealthily, "as a means to circumvent existing welfare and labor market institutions, or to discreetly reform them" (Morel, Touzet and Zemmour 2019, 35). In their analysis of the marketisation of the social in France, Nathalie Morel, Chloé Touzet and Michaël Zemmour found that French fiscal welfare strategies operated through four main types of social tax expenditure: 1) tax breaks for employers in subsidised employment programmes (usually at minimum wage, part-time and fixed-term), which significantly diminishes social security revenue; 2) "schemes that are conditional on the situation, status, or income of the recipient" such as cash benefits for low income workers, family benefits (which increase significantly from the third child: an explicitly natalist policy); 3) tax rebates for contributions to private health or retirement insurance funds or the purchase of private home care and other services; 4) tax exemptions for low income earners (Morel, Touzet and Zemmour 2019, 37–8). Although Types 2 and 4 are fairly typical of welfare capitalism, Types 1 and 3, which constitute a shift towards privatisation of welfare and deplete the social security coffers (and thus the state's ability to support its welfare system) have developed considerably in recent decades. Moreover, as the authors pointed out:

> Sums involved are far from negligible: type 1 STEs [social tax expenditures] amount to close to 2 points of gross domestic product (GDP) and 45% of total STEs, while types 2 and 3 put together amount to 1.7 points of GDP and 37% of total STEs. The sheer number of STEs is also noteworthy: Houssoy and Zemmour (2016) recorded no less than 159 STE schemes operating in 2014. (Morel, Touzet and Zemmour 2019, 37)

Moreover, these "privatisation-by-stealth" programmes are not always as stealthy as might be thought. For example, France, like many other capitalist democracies, shifted towards a partial privatisation of (un)employment services and increases in individual monitoring of the unemployed in 2005 following the passage of the

Social Cohesion Act (Lavitry 2017), and since at least the mid-2010s there has been significant social unrest over workplace flexibilisation (e.g. over Loi n° 2016–1088 of 8 August 2016, better known as the El Khomri law).

Apart from making it more difficult for the unemployed to access benefits, through imposing more stringent "accountability" conditions, and thus reducing the unemployment benefit bill overall, another main way states are paying for their privatisation agendas is through reductions of retirement benefits and increasing the age at which one has access to them.

Work-life balance

The term "working families" has come to be imbricated with the idea of "work-life balance" (WLB). In Australia that imbrication is exemplified by the NGO Parents At Work (founded in 2007 as Mums at Work), which in 2019 partnered with commercial parenting support services company Karitane, and not-for-profit employer group APLEN (Advancing Parental Leave Equality Network) to produce the first National Working Families Survey. In her Executive Summary introduction to the survey report, Parents at Work CEO Emma Walsh stressed the idea of family "responsibilities" alongside that of "work-life balance" and concluded that "[t]he future of work must respond to the changing nature of modern family life and increasing caring demands to ensure families, the community and economy can thrive" (Walsh 2019, 7). Like Clinton, like Blair, like Gillard, Walsh harnessed workplaces to dual-heterosexual-parent family models, to the demands of (privatised) caring and to the success of the economy. Interestingly, and somewhat gratuitously, the photographs illustrating the report showed some degree of "ethnic diversity", with the cover photograph being of what appeared to be an Indigenous mother with two children, but the workplaces featured in the imagery where all white-collar professional, with mostly white workers. As for the Parents at Work "team" (that is, its employees), they are all white and youngish, with a majority of women. This imagery of "working families" and "work-life" balance is reproduced throughout a range of marketing literature. I use the term "marketing" advisedly, for reasons I will explain presently.

The European Union's 2019 Directive on Work-Life Balance for Parents and Carers (EU 2019a) was provided for under Principle 9 of the EU's 2017 20-principle Pillar of Social Rights, which is structured around "equal opportunities and access to the labour market; fair working conditions; and social protection and inclusion". Principle 9 reads as follows:

> Parents and people with caring responsibilities have the right to suitable leave, flexible working arrangements and access to care services. Women and men shall have equal access to special leaves of absence in order to fulfil their caring responsibilities and be encouraged to use them in a balanced way.[5]

The Work-Life Balance Directive for Parents and Carers replaced the former Maternity Leave Directive, and foregrounds workplace equality between men and women. It provides for paid parental leave (in the case of both birth and adoption) of at least four months, regardless of sex, while deferring to national law on the amount of pay, and paid carer's leave of up to five days per year. It also provides for flexible working arrangements for those with carer responsibilities, forbids discrimination or dismissal on the basis of the employee having taken parental or carer's leave and forbids any use of the Directive to reduce already-existing pay and other entitlements that are higher than the minimum provided for in the Directive. The recognition of the concept of *members of the same household* for the purpose of carer's leave is particularly important for same-sex couples and indeed all other persons, gay or straight, who do not live in a typical heterofamily unit. This provision is a rare concession to non-family—although the persons being cared for must be *either* relatives *or* in the same household, which means that caring for a lifelong friend (or even a partner) who lives in another household, for example, would not be covered by paid carer's leave.

The Directive further provides for two weeks' "paternity" leave at the time of the birth of a child for fathers or "equivalent second parents" to fathers "where and insofar as recognised by national law" (EU 2019a, Preamble, para. 19). However, it also states that "Member States have the competence to define marital and family status, as well as to establish which persons are to be considered to be a parent, a mother and a father" (EU 2019a, Preamble, para. 18). Many EU member states do not recognise same-sex marriage and at the time of writing, seven of them have constitutionally banned it (but see Chapter 2 on the Coman decision of the ECJ). The Directive further provides several "outs" for employers in approvals of parental or carer's leave or flexible working arrangements. For example, employers can mandate length of service periods before being able to access such leave and have the right "to postpone the granting of parental leave for a reasonable period of time on the grounds that the taking of parental leave at the time requested would seriously disrupt the good functioning of the employer" (EU 2019a, Article 5, para. 5).

This Directive has the weight of law in the EU, which means that all member states are bound to apply it, and litigation on any matter covered by the Directive can be referred to the European Court of Justice for a determination. It is worth noting that at the time of the introduction of the Directive, many EU countries already provided better conditions for maternity leave than provided for in the Directive, with Eastern European countries generally outperforming the Western ones. On the other hand, hardly any EU countries provided paternity leave, and the situation on parental leave varied considerably, going from 13 weeks (unpaid) in Cyprus to 52 weeks at 100 per cent of salary with option for further unpaid leave in Lithuania. Moreover, the differences among EU states reflect the historical diversity of EU welfare-state models. In all member states, however, the social security system provides for part or all of the paid component of leave, where it exists.

The EU could thus be seen, in law at least, to represent best practice concerning "family-friendly" workplaces, and to both outlaw workplace discrimination against women who have children and encourage take-up of parental leave by the spouse or partner of the birth mother such that women have access to better workplace opportunities. However, its use of the term "work-life balance" to name the Directive is significant in that it sends the message that "life outside work" equals "family".

The exact origin of the term "work-life balance" is unclear: it has been claimed that it originated in the US in 1986; it has also been claimed that it comes from the British Women's Liberation movement. The general consensus would appear to be that it came to be preferred over "work-family balance" (although as we saw above, Julia Gillard was still using the latter term in Australia in the 2000s), so as to deflect the presumption that the "balance" only concerned workers with families. However, in practice, as we have just seen in relation to the EU, the new term has taken on more or less the same connotations as the old one, as "the majority of the work–life literature treats, at least implicitly, the 'life' domain as being interchangeable with that of 'family,' particularly as represented by caregiving responsibilities for dependent children" (Lewis and Beauregard 2018, 721; see also Hoffman and Cowan 2008).

The EU Directive nonetheless represents both a big step forward and a best-practice model in comparison with most of Latin America or with Taiwan, which do not provide the same levels of leave as most EU countries already did before the Directive, or the US, which represents worst practice among the countries included in this study. There is no legal requirement at all there for paid maternity or parental leave, only a right to 12 weeks of *unpaid maternity leave* for women employed by companies with 50 or more employees within 75 miles of the worksite (FMLA 1993, Section 101.II.B.ii). Women who do not fit this category—which is most female waged workers—are excluded, and thus have no right to any sort of maternity leave. Moreover, the lowest-paid women and those in precarious employment cannot afford to take unpaid leave, even when they have the right to it. So they either struggle on, or move from work to welfare.

Provisions such as those already existing in EU states and new ones introduced by the Directive are thus to be welcomed. At the same time, the association of "life" with "family" (and nothing else) is problematic, even disturbing. If one has to balance one's "life" (even narrowly defined as "family") with one's "work" then the implication is that "work" is "not-life". Certainly, on one level work in the capitalist system is indeed "not-life", in the Marxian sense that one is alienated from one's own humanity as a wage-earning worker and thus denied agency. However, on another level the separation between "work", where many of us spend over half our waking hours, and "life", which is everything that is left to us in the cracks between "work" (including, presumably, sleep), implies that when we enter our workplace (materially or virtually), we step into a dead zone. We cease to "live". Then, when we are not "at work", we joyfully come to life, like so many Coppelias or Sleeping Beauties. I use these metaphors—one of a clockwork doll, one of an enchanted princess who needs the prince to wake her up and "save" her—advisedly, because, as I noted at the beginning of this chapter, the WLB conversation is invariably had with women, and their domestic "responsibilities", in mind. The work-life dichotomy further suggests that the time we spend in the public sphere (generally associated with the world of "work") is not where our (women's) "real" lives are: it is in the private sphere (code for the family) that we actually "live".

The emergence of the WLB concept thus leaves me ill-at-ease. It returns us to a mindset that configures the public sphere as a world of men and the private sphere as a world of women. Even if much has been made in recent years of men's role in family and caring life in order to at least pay lip-service to workplace equality (and thus men's WLB), it is widely acknowledged, as the above-cited Parents at Work CEO points out, that the domestic sphere remains women's responsibility, even if they delegate some of this responsibility to men or outsource it to paid domestic help (see Chapter 8). So, the idea of WLB, particularly as deployed within corporate literature, for all its inclusive and egalitarian window-dressing, appears as a sinister sleight of rhetoric.

Even the model EU with all its talk of "gender equality" and a discreet nod to same-sex couples in its Work-Life Balance Directive, firmly reproduces in other literature the idea that caring for children is women's responsibility and that when living with a spouse, that spouse is male. In its brochure detailing best-practice examples of WLB from member states, the text of all the entries focuses on women (EU 2019b). Almost all the accompanying imagery shows women with children, with a few images of heterosexual couples and children, and the workplaces featured are mostly white-collar and/or professional. There is the occasional nod to ethno-racial diversity, one photograph of a child with a disability and one photograph of a woman in a "non-traditional" occupation, although it is clear that the photograph, taken on a home construction site, is a carefully posed model. From the immaculate, non-work clothing and the long flowing locks under the hard hat, it is clear that it is not an actual worker. There is not a whiff of anything vaguely gay in any part of the brochure, not even a tokenistic "inclusivity" image.

One publication that does acknowledge that men parent and that some of them are gay is a rather curious British book on "maternity mentoring", designed as a how-to book for white-collar Human Resources departments in medium-sized to large companies, on ensuring diversity in the "talent pipeline" by facilitating women's return to work after childbirth (Seignot and Clutterbuck 2016). Diversity, the authors argue, has been demonstrated to improve a company's financial performance (p. 18), and the general thrust of the book's arguments is about fostering employee retention and engagement at work, reducing absenteeism and "occupational health costs", and ensuring a "gender balance at senior levels". One may wonder why parents need "maternity mentoring" at work as a discrete form of mentoring from any other career mentoring, or why other services or indeed friendship and family networks would not be far better qualified to support women through pregnancy, childbirth and the infancy of children, but the book is clearly designed to promote the idea of a "caring" workplace in order to maximise return for employers on their investment in hiring, paying and training employees. While almost the entire volume focuses on maternity leave and the reinsertion in the workforce of new mothers, presumed to be heterosexual, fathers, same-sex couples and adoptive parents are mentioned from time to time and one chapter is devoted to these three groups. Fathers are assumed to experience greater anxiety about separation from the workplace, isolation at home, and career impacts of taking parental leave (p. 185), a series of concerns that is not articulated as an issue for women. As for same-sex couples, a primary focus of the chapter was on a case study in which the employer "accompanied" a gay father on "the emotional journey undertaken through a complex surrogacy process" (p. 195). Nowhere is the complexity of surrogacy for the women involved discussed: I will return to this case study in Chapters 8 and 9.

To return to the EU "best practice" brochure: much of it has to do with flexible working, home-based work and affordable home-based childcare, often available more or less "on tap". I will return in the next chapter to the family care trap of "outsourcing" care work, but will briefly discuss here the issue of home-based work and flexible hours, presented as positive, whereas the research largely suggests the opposite (e.g. Chung and van der Lippe 2018). Home-based work can undermine rather than support WLB, as work time bleeds into personal time, and "flexibility", apart from the fact that the tendency is for more men than women to take advantage of it, almost always advantages the employers. In their analysis of the corporate rhetoric of WLB in the US, Mary Hoffman and Renee Cowan found "a corporate ideology of work/life characterized by four key ideas":

1 work is the most important element of life;
2 life means family;
3 individuals are responsible for managing the relationship between paid work and the rest of life; and
4 organisations control work/life programs (Hoffman and Cowan 2008, 233–34).

Elaine McCrate (2013) also found that "flexibility" invariably works to the employer's advantage, and the relative advantage to workers decreases in direct proportion to the decrease in their position on the socioeconomic hierarchy (racialised, in lower-skilled employment, and so on) and in union membership and activity, in both the US and Europe. She further found that "[w]orker bargaining power is on the decline in much of Europe and North America", and that "[e]ven European Union directives on working time contain important loopholes that facilitate irregular scheduling" (McCrate 2013, 286). Finally, she pointed out that "irregularity begets irregularity, as workers on flexible or unstable shifts require services themselves" (McCrate 2013, 286). Given the hierarchies of social and cultural capital in the workforce, the most advantaged workers in the stratified system will mitigate the irregularities of their own working lives by "begetting" punishing irregularities in the lives of paid domestic and care workers with fewer socioeconomic resources to hand.

In Europe, Suzan Lewis and Alexandra Beauregard (2018) found, first, that the concept of WLB is formulated with the Western white-collar professional living in a nuclear family arrangement in mind, whereas different understandings among ethno-racial minorities may frame both "work" and "family" differently. They also found that how employers conceptualise WLB—as a right of all workers in healthy workplaces, or as a special favour done to, mainly, mothers (for which the latter are thus made beholden)—can impact substantially both on how WLB is implemented and how it is received and used. Moreover, analysis of post-GFC (global financial crisis) employer practices and rhetoric in the UK showed

> a shift in the understandings and use of the term WLB from an earlier focus on offering "choices" through flexible work arrangements of mutual benefit to employer and employees, toward a reconstruction of WLB as an organizational tool for saving money. New policies such as nonvoluntary remote working were therefore branded as WLB polices. (Lewis and Beauregard 2018, 727)

In Germany, Eckart Hildebrandt found that use of the concept of WLB "shows a weakness in its overemphasis on subjective contribution coupled with an underemphasis on structural aspects" (E. Hildebrandt 2006, 267–68).

Perhaps most tellingly, Kevin Ward et al. linked the emergence of the rhetoric and practices of WLB to the gentrification of formerly working-class urban neighbourhoods. Their description of the transformation of Manchester, which was the world's first industrial city, will be familiar to many in urban centres across the world:

> Run-down properties have been transformed into expensive apartments, with an accompanying growth in the 'consumption infrastructure', such as bars, cafés, gyms, restaurants and museums. New jobs have been created in the 'service economy', although as many have been created at the lower end as at the higher end of the job ladder. In-work poverty remains a real issue, in a city that has failed to arrest deep-seated economic and social inequalities. (Ward et al 2010, 2264–65)

Their study focused on Chorlton, four miles southwest of the city centre, which has shifted from being a primarily working-class/lower middle-class area to being the site of some of the most expensive residential real estate in the UK, and of "a concentrated expression of cosmopolitan liveability" where "aesthetic, employment and housing trajectories are intertwined" (Ward et al. 2010, 2275).

As discussed in Chapter 5, gentrification is also associated—including in Manchester—with the development of gentrified and male-dominated "gay villages", that become both tourist destinations and sites of LGBT sociability and cultural commodification.

Jobs with benefits

Two last aspects of "work-life/worklife" and its strong links with welfare that I would like to discuss in this chapter are spousal retirement and/or superannuation benefits and spousal health benefits. In practically all the countries under study, surviving spouses of deceased pensioners can become reversionary beneficiaries of the deceased's pension, the amount of which is mostly dependent on contributions made to pension funds during the deceased's working life. These benefits are almost always available *only* to spouses and not to partners in civil unions (nor indeed to other nominated beneficiaries), notwithstanding a European Court of Justice ruling in 2008, in a case referred by Germany, that where the surviving civil union partner "is in a situation comparable to that of a spouse who is entitled to the survivor's benefit provided for under the occupational pension scheme", the surviving partner must receive the equivalent pension benefit (ECJ 2018, online). The Court did, however, leave it to the national courts to decide whether the situation *is* equivalent. In France, for example, with regard to both the PaCS and de facto unions, the answer is an emphatic *no*: the situation is not equivalent and thus only married couples have access to transfer of retirement benefit.[6] In Australia, superannuation "defined benefit" (lifetime pension) is transferable to a reversionary beneficiary *if* it can be demonstrated that the beneficiary is a member of the same household and in an intimate partner relationship. However, being married makes the pension reversion a more straightforward process.

However, as Baby Boomers move into retirement and pension funds are becoming more stretched, legislation regarding retirement age and pension allocations is under review in many countries. On 22 October 2019, in a vote hailed as a victory for far-right President Jair Bolsonaro, Brazil's Senate voted to reform the retirement and pension law, which until then had been among the world's most extensive retirement and pension systems, if not *the* most extensive. Among other things, the law increases the retirement age and worker contributions, and lowers the amount payable to the reversionary beneficiary upon the pensioner's death. In the Northern winter of 2019–2020, French workers again mounted a series of strikes in a years-long battle with the government over erosion of retirement and pension rights. Thus, lesbians and gay men, many of whom only recently gained access to the spousal pension reversion system, are seeing the financial benefit of that reversion diminish. They nonetheless, if married, still retain a financial advantage over the non-married.

As concerns health benefits, even though public health systems in many countries, including those concerned by this study, are chronically underfunded, sometimes with long waiting lists for specialist or elective treatment, no one is refused health care because they do not have insurance or cannot afford the treatment fees. The state provides universal healthcare services to individuals and their dependents, sometimes funded via taxation and sometimes through a specific levy on wage earners, often a mix of the two. The system setup, and extent of medical services the state covers, vary from country to country, with Latin American countries being the most diverse, while European countries have, on average, the best public health systems. Almost all of them provide extensive universal public health cover, and most hospitals are public. In addition, residents of EU and European Free Trade Association member countries (the European Economic Area or EEA) benefit from reciprocal cover when travelling within the EEA. Most Latin American countries also provide public universal primary health care, with some specific national variations. In Argentina, for example, healthcare is a mix of state-provided cover for all and union-managed sectoral health funds for workers (Obras sociales) with a small proportion of the population also using private cover. Even the Western Anglosphere—except for the US—has universal public health coverage, although typically patients contribute a proportion of the cost. There may also be other state incentives to take out private health insurance: in Australia in 1997, for example, the government introduced a supplementary levy for public health care for higher income earners, in order to push them to take out private health insurance and reduce pressures and costs in the public system. However, among the countries in this study, the US is by any yardstick the absolute worst place to live if one is in need of healthcare but not independently wealthy; this is why partner health benefits provided by employers have been such an important factor for lesbian and gay couples, as we saw in Chapter 4, and has been used as an argument in favour of same-sex marriage in the US (Badgett 2009).

According to studies by the World Health Organisation, all high income countries have increased health spending as a proportion of GDP (Flores et al. 2017; Xu et al. 2018), "likely responding to higher demand for health care services, ageing populations and technology advances" (Xu et al. 2018, 13). The US, surprisingly, spends 145 per cent of the OECD median on health, but this spending does not reflect greater access to public healthcare. On the contrary, the US has fewer doctors, nurses, new medical school graduates or acute care hospital beds per 1,000 of population than the OECD medians (G. Anderson et al. 2019). What is different about the US is the higher cost of healthcare in a heavily privatised sector, with basic public health cover only available for the most needy, which is why it is an exceptional case, and worthy of a little further discussion here.

The Patient Protection and Affordable Care Act (PPACA), 2010—commonly nicknamed Obamacare, because it was introduced by the first Obama administration—did ease healthcare disadvantage in the US, by, among other things, expanding eligibility for Medicaid. The number of uninsured consequently decreased by some 46.5 million in 2010, or roughly 15 per cent of the population at that time, to 27 million in 2016, or a little over 8 per cent of the population at that time. Since 2017 the Trump administration has been attempting to wind back the PPACA, and affordability problems remain, as a 2012 Supreme Court ruling (*National Federation of Independent Business v. Sebelius*) made it possible for states to refuse to apply the full expansion of Medicaid coverage under the PPACA. In 2018, some 45 per cent of the uninsured cited the cost as a factor in not having health insurance, even with Medicaid (Tolbert et al. 2019).

The Emergency Medical Treatment and Active Labor Act (EMTALA) of 1986 does require hospital emergency departments to provide appropriate medical screening and stabilise all patients, regardless of their health insurance status. However, this emergency treatment requirement is a so-called "unfunded mandate": that is, it is required of hospitals but its cost is not funded by the Federal government. Hospitals thus seek to recover the cost of basic emergency care from all patients, whether insured or not. Other than immediate emergencies, the uninsured or inadequately insured may thus end up delaying or forgoing health care; and medical debt is significant. According to a 2019 study conducted under the auspices of the American Cancer Society research programme, roughly 137 million adults, or some 56 per cent of the adult US population, suffered financial hardship between 2015 and 2017 as a result of medical debt (Yabroff et al. 2019). The 18–34-years-old age-group was particularly vulnerable and the least likely to have health insurance, although a significant albeit lesser degree of financial hardship was also experienced by people with private health insurance. The study also predicted, depressingly, that "[w]ith increasing prevalence of multiple chronic conditions, higher patient cost-sharing, and higher costs of health care, the risk of hardship will likely increase in the future" (Yabroff et al. 2019, 1501).

Public-sector employers in the US offer healthcare plans, with a minority of states funding100 per cent of the coverage, while most public-sector employers charge some level of employee co-payment. In the private sector, some 56 per cent of small firms and 99 per cent of large firms (500+ employees) propose health insurance coverage to their employees, with the overall average being 57 per cent (Claxton et al. 2019). Employees contribute, on average, some 30 per cent of the cost of their health coverage, of which one-quarter, on average, is tax-deductible. The rate of coverage and employee contribution thereto fluctuates according to sector and according to the state in which the employer is located, but the charges for employee contribution have overall increased more than either wages or inflation; the percentage of their contribution to premiums has also increased (Claxton et al. 2019, 7).

Even though employer healthcare plans clearly do not solve all financial stress for all employees, employer-subsidised healthcare benefits for workers, their partners/spouses and families are nonetheless a very big deal in the US, and a significant added value to a job and a wage. So, when in 1996 IBM introduced health benefits for partners of gay and lesbian employees it both advantaged employees materially and enhanced IBM's image with that sector of the population, in a country where prescription drug prices are the highest in the world and a night in a public hospital can cost upwards of US$2,000. Other important employer-subsidised (or trade-union subsidised) schemes in the US are superannuation or retirement benefits, including death benefits to the surviving spouse.

Outside the US, where individual access (and access for dependent children) to universal public health cover is much better—and co-payments by individuals significantly lower, if required at all—family cover is of most benefit to the better-off segments of the population where at least one partner has private health insurance.

Marriage with benefits

One effect of the enduring public-private distinction that lies as the base of the familialist system into which same-sex couples and parents have sought and gained entry is that children's, or spouse's, well-being is seen as a reflection of the socio-economic status of the parents, or of the employed or higher-earning spouse (Lapidus 2004, 232). This distinction is embedded in gendered and generally heteronormative ways within law, policy and workplaces, and advantages those who are seen as "responsible" and "hardworking" citizens while punishing those who deviate from this norm.

As the examples discussed in this chapter show, it is clear that the structure of social protection systems and of employer approaches to employee welfare in (neo) liberal capitalist democracies favours the middle-class married-with-children. Those who deviate from this family or class structure have less access across the board to rights and protections in stratified systems of socioeconomic reproduction. This is so whether these systems are made explicit through policy, as in the case of PRWORA or differential access to retirement benefits, or operate in practice through the reproduction or even exacerbation of existing inequalities by the application of policies that have the superficial appearance of neutrality. This is not a new insight; it is an observation that has been made by a chorus of researchers and social activists for many years. What is striking, however, as concerns the subject of this book, is how (almost) seamlessly the same-sex married-with-children are integrated into these economically unequal, raced and gendered state and workplace logics, where some have entitlements and others have a multiplication of risk.

Notes

1 My thanks to Karin Schönpflug for bringing these documents to my attention.
2 https://clintonwhitehouse1.archives.gov/White_House/Publications/html/briefs/iii-8.html, accessed 6 January 2020.
3 https://workingfamilies.org/, accessed 8 January 2020.
4 https://workingfamilies.org/about-us/, accessed 8 January 2020.
5 https://ec.europa.eu/commission/priorities/deeper-and-fairer-economic-and-monetary-union/european-pillar-social-rights/european-pillar-social-rights-20-principles_en, accessed 12 January 2020.
6 See the relevant articles from the *Code de la sécurité sociale*, accessed 16 January 2020. https://www.legifrance.gouv.fr/affichCode.do?idSectionTA=LEGISCTA000006156098&cidTexte=LEGITEXT000006073189

8

"CARING FAMILIES" AND THE (STILL) GENDERED PRIVATISATION OF RISK

Socioeconomic reproduction and privatisation of risk

Even in the most advanced welfare states, the family has always been, and continues to be, the primary responsibility unit for social and economic welfare. It performs this role within a system of stratified reproduction that operates globally but is primarily regulated by states, including in their deference to what is quaintly termed "market forces", as if "the market" were somehow outside the control of human agency. Shellee Colen defines "stratified reproduction" as follows:

> By stratified reproduction, I mean that physical and social reproduction tasks are accomplished differentially according to inequalities that are based on hierarchies of class, race, ethnicity, gender, place in a global economy ... The reproductive labor of bearing, raising, and socializing children ... is differentially experienced, valued and rewarded according to inequalities of access to material and social resources in particular historical and cultural contexts. (Colen 1995, 78)

The state's need to expand the legal codification of the family accompanies its retreats from social provisioning in the neoliberal age, as the neoliberal economy and its enabling state *depend* on the expansion of privatised and domesticated welfare. A Nicola Barker argues, "[t]he form that the family takes has become less significant to the neoliberal state than the functions it performs on behalf of capitalism" (N. Barker 2012, 162; see also N. Barker 2015). Minh Nguyen, Roberta Zavoretti and Joan Tronto have further argued that the neoliberal project relies on a reframing of the concept of "care" as a moral imperative to be fulfilled by families and local communities. This imperative, they argue, has been strengthened, not weakened, by the "changing practices of marriage, sexuality and kinship ...

familialism, the ideology of the family as a close-knit and caring institution which best provides and care [*sic*] for individuals is gaining greater ground" (Nguyen, Zavoretti and Tronto 2017, 209). The core assumption informing state policies and social attitudes towards families is that the latter are self-sustaining dual-parent systems in a society where one is presumed to be able "to live as one pleases as long as one is successful and operates at one's own risk" (Schönpflug 2008, 33), notwithstanding differences between welfare models or models of capitalism in the societies under discussion.

The privatisation and individualisation of responsibility for welfare corresponds to the exacerbation of gendered risk bias, which Brigitte Young, Isabella Bakker and Diane Elson define as "forms of governance that reduce the extent to which risk is pooled, and measures to protect against it are shared, and instead individualizes [*sic*] risk" (Young, Bakker and Elson 2011, 3).[1] Although they offered this definition in the context of a discussion on macroeconomic policy and finance, their argument on the individualisation and privatisation of risk holds for both the workplace and the care sector. Pat Armstrong and Hugh Armstrong have made a similar point in their discussion of the contrast between, on the one hand, the "medical" model of health care, which renders individuals primarily responsible for their own care and parents responsible for care of children, and according to which health care is "defined in terms of body parts" and regulated by the market, and, on the other hand, the "social model" with "a high level of social protection and the provision of services by the state based on *notions of shared risk and responsibility*" (Armstrong and Armstrong 2009, 257, italics added). The medical/market model of (health)care also makes it "easier to see workers as universally interchangeable and as subject to managerial strategies that divide work into specified, measurable tasks" (Armstrong and Armstrong 2009, 257).

In this chapter, we look at how "rainbow families" are configured as sites of both accumulation of private property and privatisation of care within this overall scenario of privatisation of risk.

"Families we choose"

The above phrase was used in 1991 by Kath Weston to conceptualise a gay and lesbian approach to family that was distinct from heteronormative notions of blood ties and filiation (Weston 1991). This trope has been reproduced extensively in various symbolic ways, from the term "family" being used as code for "fellow homosexuals", to the adoption of the 1979 hit song "We Are Family", by US African American four-sister singing group Sister Sledge, as a frequently played song in Pride Marches and nightclubs. Róisín Ryan-Flood (2014) has argued, however, that attitudes to "family" among LGBTIQ individuals have shifted generationally, as younger generations have grown up with a different history of societal attitudes to homosexuality and in the context of campaigns for, and legalisations of, same-sex marriage. They have also come to the idea of "family" in the wake of the "lesbian baby boom" that was discernible as early as the 1980s, and in the context of the subsequent "gay dads boom" in more recent times. Finally, as Ryan-Flood argues with relation to Irish culture but as can also be argued in relation to other cultural contexts, including ethno-racial minorities (e.g. Wadsworth 2011), connections to "blood-tie" family and associated community take on different levels of importance in different cultural contexts.

What is certain is that over the last two decades, "we are family" has become increasingly aligned, both among vocal, well-organised and often well-funded LGBTIQ activists and in mainstream media and political representations, with the nuclear dual-parent model. Beyond the validation of marriage in terms of symbolic recognition as fulfilling one's citizenship contract, it is assumed that *people get married to have children*. Whether they actually *do* or not is, ideologically speaking, somewhat beside the point: marriage begets family just as parents beget children.

Practically and politically speaking, however, as heterosexuals started marrying less and divorcing more in OECD countries, and having only one to two children, whether hetero-married people have children or not is very much to the point for states. Declines in fertility rates over several decades have prompted many states to introduce incentives to have at least three children, with family benefit increasing proportionally from the third child. There are varied opinions as to the effectiveness of these policies, from assessments that natalist incentives and or strong family benefit policies more generally are effective overall (see e.g. Takayama et al. 2010; Rovny 2011), to assessments that they work sometimes, depending on the policy (Rindfuss and Choe 2016), but often not for that third child so fervently desired by states (Billingsley and Ferrarini 2014), to the conclusion that state natalist policies simply do not work (Togman 2019). Natalist policies have also been criticised as racist, harmful in biopolitical and planetary terms, and contrary to what feminists might envisage as the construction of meaningful affective relationships (Clarke and Haraway 2018).

States remain nonetheless much preoccupied with declining fertility rates and continue to introduce policies and programmes to address them. The concern has even attained supranational level, with the EU developing not only briefing papers and recommendations concerning the "promotion of fertility" in member states (R. Davies 2013) but also, increasingly, a supranational policy framework in which question of fertility are embedded within wider policy frames such as economic growth, gender equality and sustainability (Neyer, Caporali and Sánchez Gassen 2017).

Curiously, this intense preoccupation by states with procreative families has remained largely within a biologising heterosexual frame. The access of same-sex couples to parenting and adoption has remained restricted in many cases or has taken longer to acquire than access to marriage. As marriage became legalised, then, the battle for *family* thus continued—and continues. In some cases, the battles of same-sex couples map onto those of single people wishing to become parents. In France in January 2020, the Senate finally passed in committee a bill adopted by the Assembly the previous September, granting access for lesbians and for single heterosexual women to assisted reproductive technologies (ART) under a complicated and much-amended bioethics law (Cordier 2020). The adoption of this law occurred over six and a half years after same-sex marriage became legal in France. Access for gay men to biological parenting through ART (namely, surrogacy) has called up a far more complex set of ethical issues, in France as elsewhere (outside the US), and the next chapter will focus on them. The ethics of ART, however, are only part of the issue, and not the specific focus of this chapter. Other constraints and complexities arise from the fact that the law only recognises two legal parents. In UK law, for example, one of these parents may be a birth mother who does not raise the child but is formally recognised as biological mother, or a biological father whose main role was to donate sperm, if he did so outside the context of registered donor clinics (Rights of Women 2017). Finally, even where the letter of the law accords the same rights to homosexual as to heterosexual parents, the weight of heteronormavity (and patriarchy) means that the rights are not *applied* equally. Reuters cites the case of a German lesbian who had to jump through administrative hoops for six months in order to be recognised as co-parent of her partner's child: "[h]ad her partner been a man, it would have happened automatically" (Naïr 2019).

All these hurdles, campaigns and legal shifts suggest that legalisation of same-sex marriage, and/or the pre-legalisation sociocultural and political normalisation of "rainbow families", have encouraged a shift from "families we choose" to "families we procreate within a dual-parent model". One significant marker of the mainstreaming of this field is perhaps the creation, in 2007, of the *Journal of GLBT Family Studies*. The primary focus of most contributions to this journal to date is the experience of parenting among white middle class couples living in the US. Findings from a small transnational qualitative survey, "Economics of Same-Sex Marriage and Family Life", which I conducted in 2018 and 2019 and is discussed further below, indicate that marriage was often the moment at which couples chose to enter into new parenting arrangements, and other conversations I have had with lesbians in particular suggest that marriage offers significant legal and financial protections for parents, especially for the parenting role of the non-biological parent. Marriage also protects inheritance rights in many countries. In France, for example, where inheritance laws are quite strict and prioritise biological or adopted children (disinheriting them altogether is not an option under French law) over spouses, and where partners without the recognition of marriage stand to inherit very little at all, if anything, marriage offers protections to surviving partners.

With equal marriage, then, goes equal family, albeit not exactly "same family", as gay men and lesbians wish to procreate on the terms of their own sexuality. As one lesbian responding to my survey put it: "I self-inseminated: no penis-in-vagina sex for me!" Access to ART (either self-organised, as in this case, or through a registered service) thus becomes the means to gain access to "family equality" without having to undergo unwanted sexual relations with the opposite sex. On the face of it, such access appears just, egalitarian and inclusive: and in the case of lesbians using artificial insemination (AI) whether from a known or anonymous sperm donor, is relatively straightforward and with rare, if any, disruptive consequences for the health or lives of those involved, other than the biological mother's pregnancy. However, as we will see in the next chapter, things are far less clear-cut in the case of use of IVF and gestational surrogacy by gay men desiring biological children. Even in the case of women using IVF for their own purposes, the recourse to such techniques, which are invasive and physically testing, often over a period of years, is closely related to intense emotional and societal pressure to become a "real" woman through mothering (e.g. Andrews 2006; Widdows 2006; Throsby 2010). Although these scenarios mainly concern women in heterosexual relationships, the ideology that informs them spills over into, and is amplified by, the surrogacy industry, as we will see.

Much has been written about the motivations of lesbians to become parents, and I will not extensively revisit those discussions here, as my focus is not primarily on the individual motivations of women or individual and couples' parenting choices when the latter have no significant impact on third parties. I am concerned here, rather, with the normative socioeconomic and symbolic constructions of "family", and whether, and to what extent, lesbians and gay men with children or wanting children are able to diverge from these constructions.

Other than those who already have children from a previous heterosexual relationship, lesbians have mostly accessed biological parenting through self-insemination or AI. As to the reasons for choosing biological parenting rather than adoption, it has been suggested that the decision to give birth rather than adopt has been motivated in many cases by the fact that it has been difficult, even impossible, for lesbians to adopt children as a couple or even as single women, until quite recently in most cases in the countries concerned by this book (Sullivan 2004). It has also been suggested, however, that a belief in "a self-evident correspondence between biogenetic and ontological relatedness—that is, a correspondence by which relatedness by blood and genes defines human connection" has motivated many lesbians in choosing biological over adoptive parenting (Sullivan 2004, 57).

In Australia and New Zealand, the "Work, Love and Play" study conducted in 2010—the largest of its kind at that time, and one that remains a reference point—arrives at similar conclusions. Although same-sex marriage was legal in neither country at the time, the authors of the study found that "[i]n large part, the couples in this study were not creating radically new family forms. Around half the participants described their families in terms of a 'two-parent' model" while others spoke of step-parenting their partner's children or of a "blended family" model (both of which essentially fit into a two-parent model as well) (Power et al. 2010, 76). The authors suggest that the reasons for fitting into this model may be primarily pragmatic:

> [a]s most institutions and organisations with which families engage are structured around the expectation that each child will have two (and only two) parents, the legal and logistical negotiations required to parent outside of this model are often complex. (Power et al 2010, 77)

However, they also suggest that other affective and cultural factors come into play: first, fear that the involvement of a third parent or guardian may undermine the autonomy of the couple and its parental authority, and second, that

> while same-sex couples are constructing new patterns of biological (or non-biological) kinship, everyday family life is still practiced in terms of cultural traditions around family—a kind of family *habitus*—that are still dominated by a nuclear family model or ideal. (Power et al 2010, 77)

Over two-fifths of the respondents to Power et al.'s study had biological children within the current same-sex relationship, and most of the rest had biological children from former same-sex or heterosexual relationships. Hardly any had adopted or were fostering children.

Power's use of the descriptor "family *habitus*" is a direct reference to a concept developed by French sociologist Pierre Bourdieu (although the study, surprisingly, does not cite Bourdieu). In his influential 1980 work *Le Sens Pratique* (of which the English translation is titled *The Logic of Practice* [1990]), Bourdieu defines *habitus* as the process of socialisation through which individuals acquire certain *dispositions*, that is, a series of coded responses to the social environment which have generally been deeply internalised. Those dispositions form a series of patterns on which individuals draw to develop adaptive responses to the world around them. Bourdieu famously, and somewhat cryptically, called the system of dispositions that together constitute *habitus* "structured structures intended to function as structuring structures" (Bourdieu 1980b, 88). That is, it is a set of principles that are in turn generative of other principles and representations and enables their organisation, rather than leaving us in a state of perpetual confusion and disorder. *Habitus* is in a way a resolution of the structure vs agency dichotomy, which to my mind has always been a false one in any case: societies and individuals are always shaped by and shape both. Power et al.'s use of the term "family *habitus*" is thus significant: rainbow families do not develop in a sociocultural vacuum. Most especially for that which concerns us here, they do not develop in an economic, legal or biopolitical vacuum, but within and in relation to existing structures, with which they are *disposed* to conform (but also disposed to act upon).

In an attempt to transnationalise insights into the question of the impacts of marriage and child-raising in same-sex couples, I conducted the abovementioned small survey, "Economics of Same-Sex Marriage and Family Life", in 2018 and 2019. I advertised the survey through various international networks, and the respondents self-selected. Only 49 people fully completed the survey, more or less evenly divided between men and women, but they represented a range of birth nationalities, even if those born in the US (of varied ethno-racial backgrounds) represented almost half the respondents (22 people). Other national origins represented were, in alphabetical order, Argentina (2); Belgium (1); Brazil (2); Canada (1); Colombia (1); Fiji (1); Guatemala (1); Iceland (1); Iraq (3); Italy (1); Mexico (2); Netherlands (2); Nigeria (1); Russia (1); South Africa (1); UK (3); and Vietnam (2).

One of the Vietnamese-born was naturalised Canadian and the other was naturalised United Statian. One of the Mexican-born was naturalised Dutch. If one adds in countries of residence or origin of partners to the mix, then we also have Australia (partner of the Fijian woman living with her in Fiji); Israel (Mexican American male); Nepal (UK man living with partner from the Philippines); Peru (Guatemalan male); Switzerland (Russian female). The respondents were aged from their 20s to over 70, with roughly one-third being in their 30s. Almost all were university-educated with over half having some form of postgraduate qualification or currently preparing one. Most were employed fulltime with above-average incomes, although a minority were part-time or precarious workers and some were retired. A number worked from home, and one-fifth of respondents worked long hours: more than 40 per week. The longevity of relationships went from 3 to 42 years.

The patterns of responses concerning marriage, children and domestic labour varied surprisingly little by national context. As concerns division of domestic labour, and caring labour where children were involved, the main factors impacting are similar to those found in other studies: income levels, unequal work commitments or working from home, and whether birth mother or not (some lesbians also had children from previous lesbian or heterosexual partnerships). The gay men with children mostly adopted them although one had a child through surrogacy.

The most fascinating finding was to do with reasons for marrying or not, and the impacts of both desire for children or parenting protections, or attitudes of other family members (both children and parents) on the decision. Some respondents cannot, of course, legally marry in their countries of residence, but among those who can, not all have chosen to. Those who are married mostly cite equality, hard-won right, legal protection, and/or love as their main reasons. A number went on to have children after marrying because they were seen to go together: they either married to have greater parenting protection, or decided to have children as the next rainbow-family step after marriage. One lesbian, who has three children of varying ages, and works part-time at home for a very low wage, also mentioned that her "mother-in-law" was moving in fulltime. Partnering, no doubt particularly for women, may also carry an additional dimension of elder-caring for the "in-laws".

Some of the responses very clearly indicate the societal and legal protections afforded: four cited immigration. One of the Brazilians, a man, also commented that "being married just makes it all easier in terms of bureaucracy, in so many ways". A female Hispanic Texan married to an Anglo woman cited the attitude of her spouse's children. She explained that she got married to "solidify the bond in my step-children's eyes, and ensure a more stable family unit. Their reaction to me as a co-parent shifted as a result of the marriage almost overnight". Family reactions or obligations also impacted on choices *not* to get married. A Caucasian US woman in her 1960s living with her Mexican American partner of 25 years wrote that her partner "does not want to deal with her family about getting married", while a Brazilian woman in her 20s who has been with her partner a little over three years wrote: "my partner is divorced and does not wish to be married again".

Others, living in countries as diverse as Iceland or South Africa, expressed ambivalence towards the institution or simply "hadn't got around to it", suggesting that the institution had little importance in their lives. One white US woman in a relationship with an African American woman who is actively involved in politics cited the material capacity to cohabit as a key factor: "will marry when partner's job location allows us to live together". Finally, a white US man in his 30s gave as the reason for not marrying: "Cost of having ceremony/celebration. Don't want to ask our parents to help pay since we're grown men and since we've lived together for almost 12 years full time". This answer, considered in the light of my discussion in Chapter 5 of the same-sex wedding industry, indicates that for some at least, getting married necessarily involves spending a significant amount of money, which of course is not the case at all.

In the three cases where couples identifiably both filled in the questionnaire (the survey enabled the partners to choose an identifying code and then fill in the questionnaire individually, both using the code), there were some differences of opinion as to how much domestic labour is done by whom. In most cases the respondent gave her or himself a greater share than the partner, with a difference of between 5 and 15 per cent between the responses of each partner. This slight mismatch is unsurprising, but worth noting. Time use had in fact been the original motivator for the survey, but the information it yielded in other areas was far more illuminating.

The consideration for some respondents of marriage as an institutional facilitator (immigration, the "bureaucracy") or as an opening or barrier to family relationships, or indeed as a precursor to having or adopting children, indicates the extent to which legal and societal pressures impact in intimate lesbian and gay partnerships. The relative consistency of these types of responses (along with "equality", "love" and "hard-won right") across different ethno-racial and national contexts is remarkable. Although my study has no statistical validity, being far too small in scale, it is strongly indicative of the range of personal, financial, legal, societal and perhaps even political pressures that lesbians and gay men face in getting married and having children, or not. In most cases they do not map neatly onto hetero-marriage motivators, with the notable exception of having children.

Same-sex marriage and division of domestic labour

One of the major preoccupations of feminist economists working on domestic labour has, understandably, been time use, with divisions of domestic labour remaining profoundly gendered. The question thus inevitably arises: how does time use plays out within same-sex couples? Is there a division of labour that resembles what happens in the straight world, or is something different going on? The short answer to this question is: yes, something a little bit different appears to be going on. The longer answer is: yes *but*, at the same time, "rainbow families" fit within existing legal, economic and societal frameworks that may or may not work to their advantage. Moreover, once again, the bulk of the research has been conducted in and with relation to the US, and even there, some of it has been speculative, considering future impacts of present developments (e.g. Hunter 2012). Elsewhere, national or institutional statistical data-gathering on this topic in same-sex couples is rare. There is thus not yet enough large-scale demographic research to fully understand this question in a transnational context, one exception being the Unions in Context (UNICON) study in the Netherlands, which is a large-scale sampling study of heterosexual and same-sex households without children (Steinmetz and Fischer 2019). Unfortunately the full results of that study are yet to be published at the time of writing, but the authors have commented on sample composition due to self-selection of respondents that could be skewing the results: "people with low-level education are underrepresented in the UNICON data, while women, highly educated people and people who have paid work are overrepresented" (p. 764). The authors do not specify in relation to what yardstick this over- or underrepresentation is occurring: relative to the general population, or relative to the same-sex-coupled population (a demographic that is almost impossible to quantify accurately in any case, as not all same-sex couples are legally partnered or married, or do not identify as such in surveys).

Other time-use studies to date of gay and lesbian households have almost all been conducted in the Anglosphere, and most are qualitative, which could be indicative of the lack of funding available to conduct large-scale studies and/or the lack of institutional data on this topic. Many of the existing studies have an internal-couple focus: that is, they examine how domestic labour is performed and negotiated within couples, with some comparison between gay male and lesbian households but little attention to broader socioeconomic and institutional contexts (e.g. Kurdek 2007; Barrett 2015; Kelly and Hauck 2015). These studies suggest that gay men and lesbians largely do not gender-conform—that is, that something different is indeed going on—but that the household division of labour (DoL) can be a bone of contention in some relationships. Some of these studies also suggest that income and hours spent in paid work are significant factors impacting on household DoL.

Lisa Giddings, however, in a small study conducted among lesbians in the US in the 1990s, found that lesbian households do *not* necessarily do things differently, but that gendered societal patterns *do* impact:

> lesbian couples exhibit a variety of different divisions of labor ranging from those that parallel the most unequal heterosexual stereotypes in which one household member performs all of the dirty, repetitive and relatively unstimulating household labor while relying on another household member for income, to those that resemble the more purposefully egalitarian relationships. In addition, many couples reached these agreements in a similar fashion to their heterosexual counterparts. That is, income, wealth, and gender-role ideology served as integral components (whether implicitly or explicitly) of their labor contract. (Giddings 1998, 97–8)

Around the same time as Giddings' study was published, Sarah Oerton, writing within a UK context, called for a better theoretical and methodological approach to research into domestic labour in lesbian and gay households. She argued that it was "time to move beyond" explanations of DoL in same-sex households that are "couched in terms of individuals' preferences, abilities, time schedules, physical limitations, energies, different expectations of 'standards,' 'tolerance levels' and so on" (Oerton 1997, 429). She called for research that would undertake comparative analysis of different types of households within a broader societal context, in order to better understand "the ways in which gendering processes inform the division of domestic labour and child care in lesbian and gay households" (Oerton 1997, 429).

A larger scale study of the type Oerton called for, which drew on American Time Use Survey data from 2003 to 2013, did indeed find some gendered differences between lesbian and gay households, partly related to the income demographics discussed in Chapter 6. However, the study also found that bargaining models that were developed in a context of power inequalities within heterosexual households (Agarwal 1994, 1997) are of limited use in analysing DoL within same-sex partnerships (Roncolato and Martell 2016). They echoed the argument made in 2009 by Suzanne Bergeron that feminist analyses of household and care work were premised on heteronormative bargaining models that "tend to reify stereotypical gendered notions in the household division of labor [and] presume an inherent gender-role binary that maps heteronormative affective relations, child-raising, and domestic life together" (Bergeron 2009, 59). These arguments are, however, contradicted by Alyssa Schneebaum (2019), who suggests that "bargaining power plays an important role in determining the household DoL in same-sex couples, since same-sex couples are more likely than different sex couples to be interracial and mixed ethnicity" (Schneebaum 2019, 5). That is, the power differential in same-sex couples that leads to bargaining behaviours is more likely to be ethno-racial rather than gendered (although presumably it could also have a dimension of socioeconomic class attached in some cases).

However, Leanne Roncolato and Michael Martell found that in lesbian households in particular, the amount of time spent on domestic labour within the couple had a "concave" relationship to earnings. Domestic labour time share did not show a compensatory increase among lower earning partners, while higher-earning partners contributed equally to domestic labour (although this DoL shifts slightly in the case of couples with children, if the primary carer is doing fewer hours paid work). Overall, the total household and caring labour in coupled lesbian households in the US appears to be higher than in heterosexual households. In another paper drawing on the same US Time Use data, the authors suggest that

> One hypothesis is that lesbians may be "preforming [*sic*] their gender" and fulfilling expectations of what it is to be a woman, despite the fact that they also have partners who are taking on "women's responsibilities". [Their] results suggest that the socialization of women to be caregivers continues to influence behavior even when they are members of households whose composition does

> not conform to a conventional heterosexual structure. (Martell and Roncolato 2016, 390)

They also found that gay men with children spend more time on domestic labour than heterosexual men, but in households without children the quantum of male labour was the same. They suggested that perhaps "gay men are more likely to purchase household services or market substitutes for household services, such as prepared meals" (Martell and Roncolato 2016, 389). However, they concluded that "time-use differences by sexual orientation are driven by characteristics, namely parenthood, rather than a 'homosexual lifestyle'" (Martell and Roncolato 2016, 390).

Few studies take into account the impact of *marital status* on domestic labour in same-sex couples, in part, no doubt, because of relative recency of legalisation. In her study of same-sex marriage and household DoL in the US, Alyssa Schneebaum found that "[i]nstitutional settings and social norms play an important role in sorting groups of individuals into particular types of work" (Schneebaum 2019, 33). She focused in particular on the impact of US taxation and alimony regimes. Entry into a legal marriage appeared to impact negatively on household DoL—that is, the division of labour between partners increased rather than decreased, and this was so whether or not there were children in the household. She further found a greater degree of domestic labour specialisation in households with children, comparable to that in heterosexual couples. "The DoL comes with the economic, financial, and social implications of joint taxation, alimony, and marriage rights above and beyond their relationship to having children in the household")Schneebaum 2019, 32). Income disparities between the partners play a significant role, but it appears that fiscal arrangements and societal norms impact just as significantly.

The transnational political economy of care

For parents to be able to fulfil the "responsible citizen" obligation of being "working families" at the same time as they develop professionally as individuals, and for them to enjoy other activities that involve neither paid work nor parenting (socialising with friends, pursuing hobbies, going to the theatre or cinema and so on), some level of outsourcing of domestic labour is needed, from household cleaning to creches to babysitting and possibly live-in "help".

Care work, both waged and unwaged, has long been a preoccupation in both feminist sociology and feminist economics, given its core function in perpetuating male supremacist social and economic systems. "Care" is now so mainstream—not only in feminist economics but across a range of disciplines and sub-disciplines in the social sciences—and applicable beyond the home to areas such as age, disability or palliative care, that the term has become a field-marker even in languages other than English (notably the romance languages).

When paid labour is employed to do this work within heterosexual households, it is conceptualised as the "subcontracting" of this domestic work that somehow "belongs" to women (Galerand and Kergoat 2013)—and this mindset remains even when the state provides incentives to outsource domestic work (Windebank 2009). It also, unfortunately, continues to characterise much feminist discussion of the exploitation of migrant domestic labour within global care chains (e.g. Hochschild 2000; Triandafyllidou 2013). Much of this literature presumes an entirely female universe of domestic work and responsibility therefor. It is not "households" or "couples" or "families" or "parents" who free themselves up from caring and cleaning tasks by employing racialised female domestic labour: it is other, richer, whiter women, framed as individual deciders, supervisors and payers of wages. The exploiter and the exploited are both female, locked into a subcontracting arrangement within the marriage contract, where the more privileged female "owner" of the domestic labour outsources it to the "help". It is "a exceptional form of work, one subjected to cultures of protection focused on the consequences of its perceived difference as intimate labor in private spaces done for low wages, but outside the purview of public interference" (Boris and Fish 2015, 534). Throughout the postwar decades, neither states nor the International Labour Organisation (ILO) even considered such labour to be "work" (which highlights, once again, its "intimate" connection to domestic labour more generally).

State programmes can even reinforce systems of exploitation of migrant domestic labour within entirely legal frameworks. In their analysis of working conditions of Philippine women performing live-in domestic labour under the Canadian Live-In Caregiver Program (LCP, part of its Temporary Foreign Worker Program, but discontinued for new arrivals after 2014), Elsa Galerand, Martin Gallié and Jeanne Ollivier-Gobeil found systematic and multiple violations of workplace rights and of various other fundamental rights and freedoms (among others: privacy, freedom of movement and freedom of association) (Galerand, Gallié and Ollivier-Gobeil 2015, 35; see also Galerand and Gallié 2018). These violations constituted breaches of both Canadian and international law, including the ILO's Domestic Workers Convention of 2011 (ILO 2011). The latter was the result of a long campaign by the workers themselves and ally-advocates, notably the YWCA (Young Women's Christian Association): their victory "illustrates the significance of transnational networks and activist practices forged in more localized struggles, but applied to an international campaign" (Boris and Fish 2015, 541–2). (I use the term "Philippine" here rather than "Filipina", because, as Shirlita Espinosa has pointed out, "the very name 'Filipina' is almost synonymous with debased femininity" in a global economic order that profits from the sexualised labour of Philippine women [Espinosa 2017, 6].) The situation in which these women found themselves was exacerbated by the fact that one of the conditions of their visa under this programme, which ostensibly provided a pathway to permanent residency after a qualifying period, was that they must remain with the same employer and in the same type of work.

This is one example of a global care industry characterised by low-paid and precarious work largely performed by women, on whom the extent of demand and expectation made is generally in direct proportion to the degree to which they are racialised (Hochschild and Ehrenreich 2002; Parreñas 2006; Gutiérrez

Rodríguez and Brites 2014). Yet the professionalisation of domestic work has a long history (Meagher 1997), and has been the focus of various international and state measures such as the above-mentioned ILO Domestic Workers' Convention or Argentine Law 26.844 regulating the working conditions of paid domestic workers (Régimen Especial de Contrato de Trabajo para el Personal de Casas Particulares, 2013, see also Pereyra 2018). These legal and policy instruments are designed to protect domestic workers' human rights and working conditions and raise consciousness among both workers and employers about domestic workers' rights, but it nonetheless remains a precarious and heavily raced-gendered employment sector characterised by both legal (but often restricted, as in the Canadian case cited above) and, often, irregular migration.

Paid domestic care work is even often considered to be a qualitatively different workplace to others, due to the privatised and strongly affective components of the work, such that considering this work solely or primarily through an economic lens (Hochschild's [2000] global care chain model being derived from that of the global commodity chain) is inadequate to account for the complexity of the labour and affective relationships involved (e.g. Yeates 2012; Gutiérrez Rodríguez and Brites 2014; Brown 2016). Yet even this analysis can lead to a trap, as the affective component is then often used to consider domestic caring work as somehow sitting outside the framework of workplace regulation, an attitude of which Galerand and Gallié found ample evidence in their Canadian study.

The assumption that domestic employment exists within an unregulated and wholly privatised and individualised labour market has in any case been demonstrated to be false, such as in Vera Pavlou's study of the relevance and applications of European workplace law in this area (Pavlou 2016). The European Union has also given institutional and financial support to trade union efforts to organise domestic workers, such as the "Getting Organised" project of the European Federation of Food, Agriculture and Tourism Trade Unions (EFFAT) (Mather 2015). At the same time, the EU, through brochures such as the Work-Life Balance publication discussed in Chapter 7 (EU 2019b), proudly boasts the availability of 24/7 on-tap in-home childcare (performed by women) as a (partially) state-sponsored resource available to other women to free them up for other and presumably better paid employment outside the home.

Care labour has thus always been a paradoxical area for feminists, and it is unsurprising that it has occupied such a significant place in the field of feminist economics (e.g. Folbre 1994, 2001; Folbre and Bittman 2004; Nelson 2013). Women remain trapped in a care chain, however conceptualised, both materially and analytically. Drucilla Barker has argued that "feminist economics work on care, including the empirical work, leaves it in the realm of the economic and leaves in place the public (market)/private (households) distinction" in which caring remains conceptualised as women's work within a heteronormative framework (D. Barker 2012, 588). Drawing on the queer critique (and critique of queer) of Cathy Cohen (1997), Barker emphasises that "heteronormativity does not simply regulate same-sex desires, but persons across a whole spectrum of familial and sexual arrangements that do not conform to the hegemonic ideal" (D. Barker 2012, 580). Thus, the poor African American so-called "welfare queen" who leaves paid work to care for her children does not conform to the heteronormative model, even if she is herself heterosexual, nor does the migrant care worker whose own children are perhaps thousands of kilometres away, whereas a well-off married woman who performs the same domestic care work without having to rely on welfare fits the model perfectly (Cohen 1997; D. Barker 2012). Similarly, the gay or lesbian married couple with children who are purchasing a house and are financially independent through work or other income sources, also fit the model perfectly.

Barker suggests reframing the feminist analysis to consider care work as a site of global biopolitcs, in which the paid caring labour is largely performed by migrant populations, "often cast as dangerous, disenfranchised, disposable, and undeserving of the rights and privileges of human dignity" (D. Barker 2012, 575). Drawing on Hardt and Negri's conceptualisation of biopolitics within Empire (Hardt and Negri 2000), itself inspired by Foucault's original notion of biopower (Foucault 1976), Barker situates regulation of populations within international economic and financial institutions and "political regimes regulating the flows of capital and people". She further situates disciplines of the body within "heteronormative cultural inscriptions of ideal citizens, families, and workers" that are "enforced by regulatory practices of the state and internalized by subjects" (D. Barker 2012, 581).

As Barker and others such as Nicola Yeates (2012) note, not all care work is done by women, and sometimes it is done by men who are also marginalised because deemed less "respectable"—although I would argue that racialised men doing care work are assimilated to the class of women for whom such work is "normal". Unfortunately, the heteronorm prevails: a 2013 report by the ILO, the research for which is mostly based on the decade to 2010, stresses that domestic work remains an overwhelmingly feminised field. Eighty-three per cent of all paid domestic work worldwide is performed by women—or to put it another way, "[g] lobally, one in every 13 female wage workers is a domestic worker" and those men in domestic work are mostly performing masculinised tasks such as gardening or chauffeuring (ILO 2013, 19).

The ILO data, while disaggregated by country where the domestic workers are employed, does not disaggregate employer data by race, sexual orientation and so on. Moreover,the ILO data can surprise: the region employing the fewest domestic workers in the period covered by the report is the West (7 per cent of the world's total), and the region employing the most is Asia-Pacific (41 per cent), followed by Latin America and the Caribbean (37 per cent) (ILO 2013, 24). These statistics rather give the lie to the imagery of Empire in which the West is the largest consumer of this largely transnationalised and largely feminised workforce. For example, the 2019 survey on Overseas Filipino Workers (OFWs) conducted by the Philippine Statistics Authority shows that the majority of OFWs are working in East Asia (18 per cent), Saudi Arabia (22.44 per cent) or the United Arab Emirates (a little under 13 per cent) (Philippine Statistics Authority 2019). The lower figure for the West may be due to a number of factors, including gendered sociocultural attitudes concerning the "appropriateness" of hiring domestic labour, even in households that have the means to do so (Baxter, Hewitt and Western 2009). It may also be due to the fact that a great deal of domestic care work is outsourced to care institutions, staffed by precariously employed and low-paid workers, such that a significant proportion of "domestic work" is not actually performed in the household. Empire has many faces, and the COVID-19 pandemic has shone harsh light on some of them. In egalitarian and social-protectionist Sweden, for example, "[a]t the start of the pandemic in March, 40 per cent of homecare workers in Stockholm [catering primarily to an elderly population] were employed on hourly contracts" (Pelling 2020). This in a country that has bucked the European lock-down trend (with resulting high death rate per capita) and where for-profit elder companies have multiplied since the 1990s thanks to a "free choice" voucher system—another element that undermines the generous welfare-state image that the country has long enjoyed (Pelling 2020).

But what does all this have to do with same-sex marriage and rainbow families? How do they participate in these global and local care chains? *Do* they participate? The short answer is: we know they participate but we do not know to what extent. Already, available data on domestic workers more generally is patchy, as much of the research is qualitative, and the ILO quantitative study, which is probably the largest, notes that precise statistics are hard to come by due to undercounting, different ways in which countries categorise domestic workers, and the proportion of irregular migrants among them (ILO 2013). Moreover, available data is mostly not disaggregated by type of employer beyond the country or city in which they live, and not at all disaggregated by sexual orientation (nor, for that matter, by other demographics such as race/ethnicity).

As concerns same-sex households in particular, we mainly have small and qualitative studies (and even those are thin on the ground) and anecdotal evidence to go by. Existing research does suggest that gay men in particular are quite likely to employ domestic labour, especially when they have children (e.g. Bergman et al. 2010). Dana Berkowitz argues that

> although many gay fathers challenge stereotypes of men as primary caregivers, many are also able to buy their way out of domesticity, a finding intimately tied to both their class position in society and their ability as male bodied parents to continue to rely on the privilege granted to the traditional father-as-breadwinner status. (Berkowitz 2013, 80)

In their Human Resources guide on "maternity mentoring", discussed in Chapter 7, Nicki Seignot and David Clutterbuck discuss a case study of a gay male couple who became parents of twins through a South African surrogacy service. They couple report benefiting from "a full time maternity nurse for 5 months, which helped immensely. She knew how to do everything!" (cited in Seignot and Clutterbuck 2016, 196). They added that "a brilliant friend who is a grandmother of 14 children" frequently performed the typical grandmother role in providing free childcare "in the absence of close family" living nearby (cited in Seignot and Clutterbuck 2016, 196). The story is narrated positively, without any commentary on the different and intersectional levels of gender, race and age exploitation involved in providing these men with their desired family.

As concerns lesbian households, evidence to date appears to be largely anecdotal, but it suggests that some financially comfortable and professionally employed white lesbians do employ racialised domestic help (both male and female). One example I recall vividly from my own experience of several years ago is of a lesbian (without children) telling me about "our little Asians" who came to do the household cleaning.

Although we lack precise statistics, qualitative and anecdotal evidence does suggest that some lesbian and gay households exactly reproduce the socially stratified uses of transnational reproductive and caring labour which with we have become, sadly, all too familiar. In the last section of this chapter, I discuss how that process of social stratification is exemplified through housing.

Housing we "choose"

The very structuring of our societies and economies pushes us towards traditional family forms and actually makes it very difficult to live outside them, even when one fervently wishes to. One particularly salient aspect of this question has to do with housing, services and other property (owned or rented) or utilities in common: from living arrangements to owning a car or having a telephone line installed. For example, in many countries, such as the one I live in, Australia, it is impossible for two unrelated adults who are not married and not incorporated as a company to formally co-own a car and register it in both names. While this is a relatively trivial example, it is indicative of the difficulties. In many countries it can be very difficult to sign a tenancy agreement under more than one name when the tenants are unrelated by blood and not married to each other. Or, to seek to migrate to the country of a person with whom one is in an intimate relationship, one must usually show evidence of being exclusively, legally and financially bound to that person, through marriage, joint bank accounts and so on. Everything forces us into the couple-family model and it is sometimes extraordinarily difficult to organise living arrangements outside it without facing marginalisation and even legal prohibition and censure.

A case in point is local zoning laws in the US, many of which impose normative definitions of what a "household" is, tying that definition to some conceptualisation of cohabiting family in which children are either biologically related to the parents or formally adopted—which is not the situation of a significant and growing minority of US households (Redburn 2019). Such regulations have, somewhat alarmingly, been found not to violate the Constitution and have resulted in some protracted local zoning disputes (Redburn 2019). Even some rainbow families are falling into lockstep with these laws and, in some cases, actively seeking their enforcement. In 2014, two such families were involved in a zoning dispute waged both by their neighbours and by the City of Hartford, Connecticut, who brought a lawsuit in March 2015 against a group household that became known as the "Scarborough 11". The nickname combined the name of the street in an upmarket area, and the number of members of the household, comprising three straight married couples, three children, the adult son of one of the other men, and a single woman. The 8 adults had joined together to buy a house on that wealthy street, upscaling their already-existing 11-member household to a bigger house in a more upmarket area, not thinking they were contravening zoning laws. Their neighbours disagreed. One of them, a married lesbian mother, published an op-ed in a local newspaper in which she wrote that she and her partner had

> found a perfect house to renovate on Scarborough Street, which is in a R-8 zone for single families and is currently the focus of a dispute because 11 people are living in a house on the street, in violation of city rules. (Skenderian, cited in The Scarborough Family and Yarbrough, 2019)

In October 2016, the City of Hartford withdrew its lawsuit and began work on revising its zoning laws (De La Torre). The Scarborough case was all the more striking in that by most yardsticks, the residents of the Scarborough house fit perfectly well within normative criteria: mostly married heterosexuals with biological children, and all white and comfortably middle class.

Yet—notwithstanding the objection by gay and lesbian neighbours—the Scarborough Street dispute got folded into the debate on same-sex marriage and family diversity that was raging in the US at the time, and the Scarborough 11, perhaps a little bizarrely, found considerable support among same-sex marriage advocates. This particular story demonstrates that the institutionalisation of same-sex marriage and rainbow families can have a range of impacts in people's lives, and both normative and non-normative understandings of "rainbow family" or "diverse family forms" can be mobilised at different moments and/or for different reasons. However, it is telling that among those objecting to this somewhat non-traditional household were two gay-couple households, at least one of which also had children, and that those people were on the side of the City and its law. In short, they considered themselves to be more "normal", and certainly more law-abiding, than the Scarborough 11 household.

Although zoning regulations in the US are, as in so many other US examples cited in this book, an exceptional case in relation to the other countries under discussion, they are revealing of a deeper problem that characterises cities in capitalist countries, where most LGBTIQ populations tend to live. As we saw in the previous chapter, as well as in Chapter 5, "gayness" (and white male gayness in particular) has become associated with gentrification of inner-city areas that once were working class, ethnic minority or immigrant. To add two other examples: the inner-city Parisian area of the Marais (which literally means "marsh", as the present-day Marais was originally a marshy area on the river plain of the Seine), has had various fortunes throughout history but following the Revolution became largely working class, with a significant Jewish population (both wealthy and less so). Over recent decades it has become regentrified, and is characterised by the development of a "gay village". The area is now fashionable and upmarket, and many of the traditional Jewish sites, including a bathhouse and many kosher cafes, restaurants and other food outlets, have disappeared. In Madrid, a similar process happened in the inner-city area of Chueca, within the Justicia district that was "traditionally the home of the poor working classes and those living on the wrong side of the law" (Robbins 2011, 3)—although for somewhat different historical reasons to the Parisian renewal. The area continued to be a site of resistance under Franco, notwithstanding the dictator's attempt to tame the area, and from 1975, it became a quasi-carnivalesque site as part of the *movida madrileña*, the transformational countercultural movement that developed after the end of the dictatorship (Robbins 2011; see also Martinez and Dodge 2010). In Sydney, the former working class and marginal areas around Darlinghust, Surry Hills and Kings Cross became synonymous with gay (male) and subsequently LGBTIQ culture: "Oxford Street" (Darlinghurst) has for decades been code for "gay nightlife".

These scenarios are replicated across global and not-so-global cities, but their downside is rarely considered: the moneyed urban gay villages are also created at the expense of poorer urban populations who are displaced and squeezed in an ever more expensive housing rental market. Housing affordability and rent and mortgage stress are impacting increasingly in all the countries concerned by this study, particularly in the major urban areas in which most gay people live (Salvi del Pero et al. 2016; OECD 2018). Gay gentrification and both the imagery and reality of the respectable rainbow family with its married parents who own or are buying their own home serve to hide the fact that LGBTIQ populations, particularly the under-30s and particularly lesbians, are at severe risk of poverty and homelessness (see e.g. NCOSS 2015). They also marginalise older LGBTIQ people, who face specific social, financial and health challenges (Choi and Meyer 2016). As Nancy Knauer has argued,

> marriage equality fails to address some of the most pressing issues facing LGBT elders, such the legal fragility of their extended chosen families, *their disproportionately high levels of financial insecurity*, and their fear of encountering anti-LGBT bias across a wide range of senior services. (Knauer 2016, 105, italics added)

She stresses that "LGBT elders" are all the less well represented in that "they do not fit within the prevailing advocacy paradigm that works hard to portray LGBT individual [*sic*] as not only a deserving minority but also *the same* as non-LGBT individuals" (Knauer 2016, 105, italics in original). This paradigm is based on a claim not only of shared group identity but a group *sameness*, both internally and with a dominant image of heterosexual normality. That assumption of sameness does not serve elders well, especially the current generation who have a significantly different experience of living as lesbian, gay or transsexual (the term transgender was not used when they were young). And it particularly does not serve lesbians well: Jane Traies has pointed out that even research on LGBT ageing largely invisibilises lesbians and fails to understand the specificities of lesbian networks and relationships, or the particular challenges that older lesbians face in a masculinist and heterosexist world of ageing and aged care (Traies 2016).

It is not only the very old and very young demographics (whether white or not) that the homonormative home-owning rainbow-family paradigm does not serve well. To return to the issue of housing, let us consider New Orleans, where the Mardi Gras carnival has also become imbricated with upmarket gay nightlife, although perhaps not to the same level of explicitness as in Sydney's Mardi Gras, given that Pride is a midyear festival elsewhere in the US, and New Orleans' Mardi Gras is strongly connected to its French and Creole Catholic heritage. New Orleans is also, however, the poorest of the US's 50 largest cities (although other areas of the state of Louisiana are even poorer), and has one of the country's largest urban African American populations. The devastation of Hurricane Katrina in 2005 further displaced and disenfranchised the city's black poor, who continue to suffer the impacts of both the hurricane and insufficient government response. As Alecia Long put it in 2007, in an article discussing the dislocation of black urban poor and the "redevelopment" of social housing by commercial developers in the wake of Hurricane Katrina:

> In a nation that loathes poverty and prefers to deny its existence, just being poor is an affront to the lies told by politicians—conservative and liberal—about the supposed successes of welfare reform and the benefits of a free-market economy. (Long 2007, 803)

The retreat of states from social housing—although that retreat is more marked in the Americas and the Anglosphere than in continental Europe (André and Chalaux 2018; Whitehead 2018)—is part of the wider trend of retreat from welfare across the capitalist world. Long's article is titled, tellingly, "Poverty is the new prostitution": the poor are the new undesirable class, to be shunned by respectable people. Being poor, being unemployed, underemployed or simply badly paid, being homeless, being a "welfare mother", and being any of these things while not being white: these are the crimes of the third millennium in neoliberal capitalist democracies. Race and sex are of far greater structural importance here than sexual orientation per se, notwithstanding widespread accounts of ongoing discrimination, violence and bullying experienced by LGBTIQ populations (e.g. FRA 2020). Unfortunately, as we saw above in the case of the lesbian objector to the Scarborough 11, rainbow families wish to position themselves, or are being positioned regardless of their own desiderata, within the assimilative logic of marriage and dual-parent families, on the side of the respectable and not the undesirable. With the family *habitus* of dominant society goes the class *habitus*.

Conclusion: differently equal

Feminist and gendered analyses of families, households and household and caring labour, which presuppose heterosexual female mother/wife-subjects, both are and are not transferable to analyses of "rainbow families". Heterosexual power dynamics such as household bargaining are less present, if at all, while institutional frameworks and sociocultural expectations have a homonormatising impact—particularly in the case of couples with children. As Lee Badgett commented in a 2013 interview, in economic terms, "same-sex couples with children resemble heterosexual couples with children much more than they resemble childless same-sex couples" (cited in Mundy 2013, comment paraphrased by the interviewer). The interviewer added that one "might say that gay parents are simultaneously departing from traditional family structures and leading the way back toward them" (Mundy 2013). This last comment pretty much sums up what available research and anecdotal evidence have demonstrated. We have seen throughout this book that to be married and to become a parent is to fulfil a core sociopolitical and economic expectation in constructing that "fundamental group unit of society": the family. We have seen further in this chapter that this assimilation is as much if not more a question of structural constraint as a matter of personal desire to straighten out gayness, particularly as concerns the establishment of households and families. Again, these structural constraints impact more significantly on lesbians, who have lower incomes and are more likely to have children, either with the same-sex spouse or, often, prior to same-sex marrying. As in the straight world, men almost always have more freedom, higher social capital and access to greater financial resources than women—other demographic factors being equal. As we will see in the next chapter, one significant way in which gay men are now deploying those resources is in the procurement of biological children.

Note

1 I am grateful to Mansour Omeira for drawing attention to this important analysis in the context of a discussion within the International Association of Feminist Economics on collective versus individual risk in modes of participation in public political debate (January 2020).

9

GAY DADS

The "queered" political economy of surrogacy

Since 2015, when same-sex marriage was legalised in the US, the US organisation Menhavingbabies has organised, along with a number of European partners, an annual conference in Brussels on "parenting options for European gay men" seeking surrogacy arrangements in North America.[1] The association claims to provide "unbiased" advice on surrogacy.[2] Almost all EU member states have banned surrogacy in any form and those that have not done so have placed restrictions such as availability only for nationals of the country or only for heterosexual couples with some sort of "medical" need, and even in such cases have generally restricted it to so-called "altruistic" surrogacy, that is, non-remunerated. In the US, laws vary considerably from one state to another, but commercial surrogacy is legal in a number of states, including, now, for married same-sex couples. In many countries outside the EU, such as Ukraine, where surrogacy is a booming business that bears all the hallmarks of the "escort" industry, surrogacy is only available to married heterosexual couples. It is thus unsurprising that the US beckons to gay male clients of surrogacy, and a number of surrogacy agencies have sprung up in recent years in the US and elsewhere, catering specifically to gay men both in the US and transnationally.

At the same time, European campaigns for access to medically assisted procreation for lesbians (MAP) potentially provide for a backdoor reopening of the surrogacy debate, as gay men begin to claim equal access to Assisted Reproductive Technologies (ART). France, for example, held an Estates General on Bioethics in 2018 with a view to revisiting the law prohibiting access for single women and lesbians to MAP (legalised in 2019). Its report of the debates included discussion of surrogacy for gay men, with divided opinions among participants, although almost all were opposed to commercial surrogacy (Comité Consultatif national d'éthique 2018). However, the report noted that some contributors to the deliberations of the Estates General advanced the argument that "equal access to MAP [for lesbian couples and single women] could constitute discrimination between female and male couples" (Comité Consultatif national d'éthique 2018, 128; my translation). Surrogacy is currently banned in France, with French public opinion being relatively equally divided albeit fluctuating on the issue, although slightly more favourable in recent years (e.g. IFOP 2013, 2017). The above-cited observation by the Comité d'éthique suggests that gay men's "equal rights" claims may have been behind this slight shift in opinion, especially considered in the context of the European activities of groups such as Menhavingbabies.

In this final chapter, then, we will look at the business (I use the word advisedly) of surrogacy in general and for homosexual men in particular in a transnational market dubbed "Fertility Inc." by *New York Times* journalist Gina Kolata (Kolata 2002). Although as noted above, access to ART also concerns lesbians, and the discussion on lesbian access has, along with the legalisation of same-sex marriage and adoption, become a springboard for campaigns for gay men's access, the ethical, legal, political and financial issues associated with the use of surrogacy normally do not arise for lesbians, so the conversation is quite different. Certainly, in both cases one can make the same or similar challenges to arguments that assert some sort of right to a *biological* child (rather than a fostered or adopted one, for example), as no such rights is formally encoded in any human rights instrument or UN development goals. More generally, one can extend that challenge to question the logic of homonormativised and reproductively essentialist family structures among lesbians and gay men. Yet there are significant material differences between ART for lesbians and ART for gay men. Donating sperm through one ejaculation is not quite the same thing as renting out (or "lending") one's uterus for the term of a pregnancy (and/or donating or selling one's eggs), and certainly does not have the same physical and psychological impacts on the sperm donor as egg extraction and carrying a pregnancy to term have on women. The client-service provider relationship is thus quite different, as are the socioeconomic and cultural power relationships. I am thus, in this chapter, going to leave aside the already much-discussed lesbian baby boom that has been with us since at least the late 1980s (Patterson 1995; Sullivan 2004; Ryan-Flood 2009), and focus on the more ethically and politically challenging discussion of gay men's demands for parenting through surrogacy.

These demands have been fuelled not only by a rhetoric of equal rights to marriage and family but also by the medicalisation of (in)fertility. Some such as Gabriele Werner-Felmayer—who is nonetheless cautiously critical of the overuse and marketisation of ARTs—infer from the inclusion of "reproductive health" in the UN Millennium Development Goals (MDGs) that infertility is perceived as a "global health issue" (Werner-Felmayer 2015, 15). In fact, MDG 5 is explicitly about *maternal health*, and not about infertility at all (other than infertility caused by poor health support for women in pregnancy), and most certainly does not, either explicitly or implicitly, support any claim to access to the bodies of women to produce children that those women then relinquish to others.[3] In fact, surrogacy, which demonstrably carries significant risks for both egg and gestation-providers, *undermines* the goal of achieving good maternal health so is contrary to MDG 5.

Moreover, there is evidence that the medicalising of infertility (whether the latter is biological or situational, as in the case of homosexual couples) has fostered a normalisation of the practice of surrogacy such that the "cure" leads to an increase in the "disease" by swelling the numbers of "patients". Astridur Stefansdottir found that in the UK, which in 1985 was the first country to develop specific legislation on surrogacy (but limited it to "altruistic" surrogacy), there was an expectation that demand would stabilise after an initial surge. In fact, the opposite has happened:

> Using new technological solutions to overcome childlessness not only satisfies desires and demands but also increases the pressure to have children. Groups that generally were neither considered to have any health problems nor to have any reason to seek healthcare service due to not having a child, such as childless individuals or two men living together, now experience a need for healthcare service due to new possibilities and a change in the culture of reproductive behaviour. (Stefansdottir 2018, 76)

Having children thus now becomes an expectation, with affluent societies now characterised by a "new norm for reproduction" (Stefansdottir 2018, 76) that completes the new norm of marriage and family for all. The medicalisation of reproduction as a problem to be technologically solved through access to the medical marketplace has also impacted on the processes adopted by LGBTIQ persons or couples wishing to raise children, which, "despite the tremendous variety … are all shaped by and within an era of fertility biomedicine marked by a global set of technoscientific practices and transnational flows" (Mamo and Alston-Stepnitz 2015, 520). This era is further marked by national and transnational medical marketisation characterised by socioeconomic stratification and commodification of reproduction. It is, in short, a "baby business", as Deborah Spar has famously put it (Spar 2006).

Here, I examine access to surrogacy as a contractual relationship in a patriarchal capitalist economy, in which the intending parents are the clients; the egg-providers and surrogates (both biological and gestational) are the service-providers, framed as independent contractors leasing out their bodies or selling organic matter produced by those bodies; and the children are the commodity purchased. Or, to put it more crudely, adapting a familiar idiomatic expression, the eggs are the dough and the surrogate is the oven in which the bun (the child) is cooked. Surrogacy agencies, within that contractual model, are the service-delivery intermediaries or agents. (Ekman [2013, ch. 6] has also called the agents "uterus pimps".) My use of the language of capitalist exchange is not intended to dehumanise the women or children concerned. On the contrary, my intent is make explicit the relationship of stratification and commodification within a capitalist logic, in which the "service" is the appropriation of women's bodies and production therefrom (Guillaumin 1992), and the commodity procured via this service is a human being. This is why surrogacy has often—and from the outset—been compared to prostitution and to trafficking in women (Stone 1988; Raymond 1993; Ekman 2013; Klein 2017), although that comparison is not my focus here.

The logic of capitalist exchange informs much of the framing and vocabulary used in pro-surrogacy or ostensibly more "neutral" medical literature. Most particularly, egg- and gestational service-providers are disappeared as subjects through references to access to enabling technologies to fulfil the needs, desires, and "procreative rights" of the client-parents (Sperling 2011 being a startling example of such framing), and guidelines for checking the fitness of the gestational carrier, all of which are discussed below. At times, even more terre-à-terre terms are used, such as references to the "commissioning" of a child through commercial surrogacy (e.g. ESHRE Task Force on Ethics and Law 2005; Norton, Hudson and Culley 2013). Also noteworthy is both client-parents and some researchers' strong association of the father's genetic material with creation of children and family within a heteronormed couple, while the egg-provider's genetic material is on the contrary readily dissociated in the minds of the commissioning clients from the person who provided it (Riggs 2018, 154). Similarly, some literature reproduces some medical institutions' dissociation of wombs and pregnancies from the women themselves, including, for example, the US Centers for Disease Control and Prevention's definition of the surrogate not as a person but as a "host uterus", cited in one of the increasing number of articles preoccupied with the costs and obstacles that gay men face in accessing surrogacy (May and Tenzek 2016, 433).

As gay men's access to surrogacy functions, in market terms, in quite similar ways to heterosexual men's (and indeed women's) access to surrogacy, I will first provide an analysis of the political economy of surrogacy today more generally, and its health impacts for women, before going on to look specifically at gay men's rights claims to parenting by surrogacy, the sorts of surrogacy networks and markets in which they are involved, and the academic arguments in support of them.

From Baby M to a global industry

In discussing the Baby M case in 1987, Katha Pollitt wrote that

> so-called surrogacy agreements are so unprecedented that the resulting human arrangements bear no resemblance to adoption, illegitimacy, custody after divorce, or any other relationship involving parents and children, yet, at the same time, bear an uncanny resemblance to the all-sales-final style of a used-car lot. (Pollitt 1987, 667)

Some three decades later, surrogacy agreements have become at once more familiar, more complex and more transnationalised, not to mention the focus of an increasing body of statutory legislation, case law, and legal and medical opinions. They have in consequence been heatedly debated within and outside academe. However, the "uncanny resemblance to the all-sales-final style of a used car lot" remains very much with us, as surrogacy agreements continue to take the form of contractual arrangements made in a global free-market economy, with the surrogate and egg-providers producing the child-commodity in exchange for a fee and/or for payment of expenses, as the result of a purchase or donation-procuration order placed by those who aspire to being the child's sole and legal parents. Although some surrogacy arrangements are made directly with friends or family members, the majority of baby-orders and accompanying terms of delivery are usually negotiated by surrogacy brokers, who may be private individuals, medical professionals or lawyers, but more often than not these days are agencies set up precisely for the purpose of handling surrogacy and IVF (in vitro fertilisation) arrangements—much as a real estate agent handles property sales and rentals, a travel agent handles travel (and there is often a travel component in surrogacy brokerage as well), or indeed, as a used car dealer buys and sells cars from and to private individuals.

The Baby M case was certainly not the first case of surrogacy in the world, as there is a long history of women in servitude or slavery producing children for their masters, more often than not as a result of rape. Pamela Bridgewater has noted that during the period of slavery in the United States, reproduction operated as a "successful subindustry", the slave "breeders" producing a constant new supply of labour (Bridgewater 2007, 1222). She argues that "the slavery reproduction market should continue to serve as the worst case scenario against which we gauge the functioning of a modem market for reproductive services and material", and that "the history of the exploitation of enslaved women's reproductive capacities provides us with a particular historical context" from which to undertake an analysis of the contemporary reproductive industry (pp. 1223–4).

The legendary archetype of the slave-surrogate is Hagar, the Egyptian slave of Abraham, who bore him the son Ishmael (apparently at his wife Sarah's bidding as she was unable to bear him a son) (book of Genesis, Old Testament; see also Brinsden 2016, 1; Whetstine and Beach 2016, 33). Subsequently, Sarah miraculously conceived and bore Isaac, and then had Abraham cast out Hagar and Ishmael. However, God told Abraham that Ishmael would found a great nation, because he also was Abraham's son. Thus, legend has it, began the history of conflict between Arabs and Jews. The story of Abraham, Hagar and Sarah is also emblematic of the contemporary operation of surrogacy: the DNA of the father is determinant, while the biological mother is disposable. Tellingly, a surrogacy agency set up in Topeka, Kansas, in the 1980s was originally called The Hagar Institute (Johnson 1987). There is also, of course, a related history of women in slavery or service performing postnatal reproductive care as, for example, wet nurses (Spar 2006, 73) and an ancient history of "medical" surrogacy being legally encoded through the Babylonian Code of Laws drawn up by King Hammurabi (Brinsden 2016, 1).

Nor is the Baby M case the first to form the object of a legal contract between surrogacy service-provider and client. The first known contract was in the US in 1976—three years after the first IVF pregnancy (1973, not carried to term). The contract was drawn up by Dearborn, Michigan lawyer Noel Keane, an enthusiast of ART, and arguably the world's first known professional surrogacy broker, on behalf of a single male acquaintance. He advertised in university papers for a surrogate and the woman who answered the ad bore the client a child in 1978, the same year the first IVF baby Louise Brown was born in London. By the time of his death in 1997 Keane had, according to his son, negotiated some 600 surrogacy arrangements worldwide (Van Gelder 1997).

Most famously, Keane was the lawyer for client William Stern in the 1986–88 Baby M case. That case involved Stern contracting to pay Mary Beth Whitehead US$10,000 to produce a child for him and his wife Elizabeth using traditional surrogacy methods (where the surrogate is both biological and gestational parent). Upon the child's birth, however, Whitehead refused to hand her over, taking her to Florida (an action routinely reported as "kidnapping"), and the Sterns sued to be recognised as the baby girl's legal parents. In 1987, the New Jersey Superior Court recognised the surrogacy contract as valid and awarded custody to the Sterns; the judge was "overtly critical" of Whitehead's behaviour, her educational level and her socioeconomic situation (Whetstine and Beach 2016, 33). By contrast, the Sterns were comfortable middle class professionals with higher-level university education. The following year, the New Jersey Supreme Court overruled the lower court's recognition of the surrogacy contract, stating that it conflicted with public policy and statutory law on adoption at that time, in particular as concerns subjecting the latter to a financial transaction. It noted, among other things, that "baby-selling potentially results in the exploitation of all parties involved" and that "contractual surrender of parental rights is not provided for in our statutes as now written" (Supreme Court of New Jersey, 1988). The Court recognised the equal parental rights of both biological parents and referred the custody issue back to the New Jersey Family Court. Using the yardstick of the "best interests of the child", as interpreted by the courts, which may well have involved both class and personal prejudice (Stone 1988), the Family Court awarded custody to the Sterns with visitation rights for Whitehead. That decision was influenced by Whitehead's behaviour throughout the custody battle, including alleged threats against the Sterns or threats to kill herself and/or Baby M. In 2004, Melissa Stern (Baby M), upon reaching the legal age of adulthood, legally terminated Whitehead's parental rights and had her adoption by Elizabeth Stern legally encoded.

The Baby M case thus set the scene for the many political and legal complexities that have surrounded surrogacy ever since, and it is pretty much *de rigueur* to cite it within discussions of surrogacy, as indeed I have here. Most aspects of the ongoing framing of the surrogacy relationship and its attendant moral, political, legal, bioethical and indeed financial dilemmas were already present in that case. They include: the systematic media framing of the biological father as "parent" and of the gestational (and in this case also biological) mother as "surrogate" (Raymond 1993, 34), with associated attention to the fathering needs of the male client; the question of whether or not procreation should be the object of contracted remuneration; whether and to what extent biological and/or gestational parenting confers parental rights (particularly if the surrogacy service-provider is framed as less worthy that the client parent, as Whitehead was); what is the appropriate feminist position to take on surrogacy (for two conflicting contemporaneous views in the case of Baby M, see Stone 1988; Younger 1988); how to protect the rights of children born through surrogacy arrangements; and the presentation of the issue as some sort of "wicked problem" (Rittel and Webber 1973)—although that term did not have the same widespread currency at that time as it does today (e.g. Younger 1988, who did not herself use that precise term).

Those elements of today's surrogacy debate that developed later—largely in response to the introduction of legal restrictions in Western countries, themselves introduced in response to the Baby M case and subsequent case law—are, first, the distinction between gestational and traditional surrogacy (although the first gestational surrogacy was around the same time as the Baby M case, also in the US, and also brokered by Keane); and second, arguments over the ethics of "altruistic" surrogacy versus commercial surrogacy. The other new elements in today's debate developed as a result of the emergence of a lucrative transnational surrogacy market, namely: transnational exploitation of women; the nationality status of children purchased transnationally (including agreement by the country of client-parents to accept the children); and what happens when the child-commodity purchased turns out to be "defective" (such as the notorious "Baby Gammy" case in Australia and Thailand in 2014–16, discussed below)—although this last issue can also arise within a single national context, as we will see. The most recent new development, in the wake of gay rights campaigns and in particular the legalisation of same-sex marriage in capitalist democracies, is gay men's reframing of access to surrogacy arrangements as an equal rights and justice issue, often accompanied by a discourse of challenge to traditional gender roles—a challenge posited as inherently progressive and even "feminist" (e.g. Cory 2015; S. Lewis 2017).

These new elements and the national, transnational and supranational legal debate to which they have given rise, especially since 2010, have generated a considerable amount of legal literature in the form of briefing documents, reports and recommendations. Most recently, they have led to a project to draft an international Convention, pursued by an expert committee of the Hague Conference on Private International Law (HCCH: standing for the English and French names Hague Conference/Conférence de la Haye), which meets biannually. HCCH is an intergovernmental institution comprising 82 members, including all EU member states and the EU itself. A body of scholarly literature debating the legal issues has emerged over the same period; some of it discusses the ramifications of a possible Hague Convention (e.g. McLeod and Botterell 2014; Gerber and O'Byrne 2015; Pol 2017). The issue has also been debated by the European parliament, which has published briefing notes on transnational surrogacy arrangements and the adoption and rights of children born through such arrangements, as well as on European Court of Human Rights case law (see for example Rigon and Chateau 2016).

In their introduction to their 2015 anthology, Paula Gerber and Katie O'Byrne wrote that "the advent of surrogacy may be said to have contributed to a fundamental redefinition of motherhood, parentage and the family itself—for better or for worse, depending on the perspective adopted" (2015: 5–6). The assumption seems to be that surrogacy is now with us, it is already "done" worldwide (including, increasingly, for gay male client-parents), it therefore cannot be undone. Which on one level is perfectly true. What has already been "done" cannot be undone; but what is to be done, or not done, next is far more open to debate.

Surrogacy in the global medical tourism marketplace

Surrogacy today is big business. Although precise figures on the value of the surrogacy trade worldwide as a subset of so-called "medical tourism" or "reproductive tourism" are hard to come by, it was estimated in 2008 that the global surrogacy market was worth US$6 billion (Deonandan 2015; Werner-Felmayer 2015, 22), while a 2013 estimate placed the total value of the US overall ART market at US $3 billion (Knoche 2014, 183). In 2018, the website Global Market Insights estimated the surrogacy industry alone to be worth US$5.5 billion.[4] In 2015, the my-MED-holiday website cited a general estimate that nine children are born through surrogacy each year in every US state, while in the UK surrogate baby numbers rose by 255 per cent between 2008 and 2014 (my-MED-holiday 2015). In India, births through surrogacy doubled between 2003 and 2006 and "about 2000 babies were born to carriers [*sic*] in India in 2011 alone. Investigators estimate that as many as 1000 of those births could be attributed to British customers" (Knoche 2014, 184).

Surrogacy markets have become increasingly transnationalised for both legal and financial reasons (commercial surrogacy is either allowed, unregulated or poorly regulated, and surrogacy services come far more cheaply in the so-called Third World or non-EU Eastern Europe), with India and, increasingly, Ukraine routinely cited as surrogacy market hotspots. India in particular has been the focus of a wealth of feminist study on the transnational exploitation of women in the surrogacy industry (e.g. Deomampo 2013; Twine 2015, ch. VI; Fellowes 2017; Saravanan 2018; Gupta 2018). The Indian government prohibited surrogacy for foreign nationals in 2015 and in 2017 it banned commercial surrogacy. It was already banned for gay couples in 2012, the year before homosexuality was recriminalised (having been decriminalised in 2009; it is now once again decriminalised, since 2018). Surrogacy agencies have, however, found ways around the bans, for example by moving the gestational surrogate across a border to a neighbouring country such as Nepal once she becomes pregnant (Rudrappa 2017). Other Asian countries, such as Thailand, have also introduced bans on commercial surrogacy and surrogacy for foreign nationals in recent years, but the trade has either continued via loopholes, as in the case of India, or simply shifted to a new location.

It has been suggested in response to bans that the industry should be regulated rather than banned, the argument being that it is happening anyway and regulation would afford some protections to the women rather than driving the practice underground (and often overseas) where regulation is impossible (e.g. Fellowes

2017). Similar arguments have been made concerning the legal regulation of prostitution. However, I believe such arguments to be flawed, as not only does regulation legitimise the practice it regulates, but it also fails to eradicate the unregulated varieties of the practice, including cheaper offshore versions, which flourish in a climate of legal legitimation. In the case of surrogacy, the default commercial relationship is a private business model in which the egg- and gestational service-providers are not waged employees but contracted, more often than not via some sort of pimping intermediary in a reproductive "gig economy". It is that model that is legitimated through the regulation of commercial surrogacy.

National and transnational surrogacy agencies have proliferated in the three decades since the Baby M case, and their websites are set up like those of any business in search of clients. For example, the US website Surrogacy.com, under the heading "About Surrogacy", suggests the seven questions clients and service-providers in search of an agency should ask (note the use of the frame of service provision):

1. What is your screening process for intended parents and prospective surrogates?
2. What are the services that you offer intended parents and surrogates?
3. What is your agency's history?
4. What kind of legal assistance do you provide?
5. What are your agency costs for surrogacy?
6. How involved will I be in the surrogacy process?
7. What are your requirements for joining your agency?[5]

At the time I visited the site, it featured above its header a posed photograph of a young, slim, light-skinned heterosexual couple, dressed in light-coloured clothing and seated on a sofa against a light background, seriously studying a prospectus. The site's pages for prospective surrogates show similar imagery: smilingly pregnant women (occasionally not white, but generally slim, light-skinned rather than very dark-skinned and normatively pretty, with what looks like costly dental work), sometimes in equally smiling conversation with client-mothers. Surrogacy agencies invariably contain such imagery, almost certainly shot using models rather than actual clients or surrogacy service-providers. They also invariably pitch their "world-class" or "international" standards and their mission to "build families" and help client-parents "realise their dreams". The sites present headshots of potential surrogacy service-providers for the clients to choose from, often with a warm-and-fuzzy statement from the woman who is framed as selfless, generous and honoured to help, for example:

> Being able to provide the gift of parenthood to another family is a selfless act that I have wanted to fulfill for some time … I would be honored to be given the opportunity to embark on this journey with you in hopes of completing the missing link to your story (from American Surrogacy website).[6]

Many agencies based in the US, Eastern Europe and Asia propose transnational surrogacy arrangements, but as concerns surrogacy for gay men, most dedicated agencies for national or transnational surrogacy are based in the US. The oldest of them, Growing Generations, which operates transnationally, promises to "deliver dreams" to its client-parents. Set up in 1996, the agency subsequently opened up to straight couples as well, because "dreams don't have sexual orientation".[7] The agency had served as intermediary for the production of 297 babies by 2004, 1,000 by 2012 and 1,813 by 2019, which indicates a rapid and increasing growth rate in the "gayby" business. The website shows the total cost of obtaining an egg, including agency fees, egg donor fee (some of which surely goes to the medical facility organising the egg harvest), legal fees and various incidentals, to start at around US$23,000–25,000. As for the surrogacy fee, the total starts at around US $130,000 but can go above $200,000. The agency offers to facilitate loan arrangements for those seeking surrogacy, but even here, as Dana Berkowitz (2013), among others, has noted, only the most privileged of men are able to have children through surrogacy, which is also by far the most expensive way for them to become parents.

In short, procuring children by surrogacy definitely sits at the luxury end of the global medical marketplace. By comparison, agency-brokered transnational adoption costs between US$20,000 and $40,000. By way of further comparison with procedures that do not involve human beings giving birth to other human beings but simply the skills and labour of medical professionals: a "budget" facelift in Argentina costs circa US$2,500 according to Argentinian medical business Sublimis,[8] or having dental work done in Thailand is less than half the cost of having it done in Australia (but the medical risks are far greater, according to travel advice site Traveller).[9] One reason the transnational surrogacy market has flourished—beyond legal restrictions or prohibitions—is also related to lower cost. Like the Argentinian facelift or the Thai dental work, Eastern European, South American or Asian surrogacy services are far cheaper.

Product checking in the surrogacy saleyard

The Thai surrogacy ban was prompted by the abovementioned Baby Gammy case of 2014. Gestational service-providers are more often than not implanted with more than one embryo to increase the chance of a successful pregnancy; in general, the "extra" fœtuses are then selectively aborted. However, in the case of Gammy, who was discovered to have Down syndrome, the gestational service-provider, Pattharamon Chanbua, who took on the surrogacy to pay off family debts and was implanted with eggs purchased from an anonymous Australian woman, had refused a selective abortion because of her Buddhist beliefs, and said she would raise the boy on her own. The Australian clients, David and Wendy Farnell, left the country with Gammy's twin sister Pipah—somewhat hurriedly, following Australian embassy advice, due to political unrest in Thailand at the time—and Chanbua appealed to international donors for support to raise Gammy, which brought the story into the international press. She also appealed to Western Australia's Family Court to have Pipah returned to her. International outrage was exacerbated when client-parent David Farnell was discovered to be a formerly convicted sex offender, and Australian authorities responded by looking into the welfare of the purchased daughter (Whitaker 2016). However, no evidence of Farnell re-offending since 1999 came to light. What did come to light at the time of the Baby Gammy hearing was that Farnell had found his Chinese wife Wendy Li via the Zhanjiang Happy Marriage Agency, a so-called "mail-order bride" agency. At the time of commissioning Pipah, David Farnell was in his mid-50s and Wendy Li Farnell was in her late 40s.

The Western Australian Family Court ruled, first, that the Farnells did not abandon Gammy but wanted to take him too, and second, that Pipah should continue to live with the Farnells. However, Justice Thackray, in delivering his ruling, expressed considerable sympathy for Chanbua and strong reservations concerning commercial surrogacy. He referred to Chanbua as "birth mother" rather than "gestational carrier" because he considered that the use of the latter term

> runs the risk of dehumanising a woman who carries a baby for another. I accept that Mrs Chanbua fell in love with the twins before their birth, and that her role in giving them life extended well beyond that of a 'carrier'. (Family Court of Western Australia 2016; see also ABC News 2016)

He further commented that:

> Quite apart from the separation of the twins, this case serves to highlight the dilemmas that arise when the reproductive capacities of women are turned into saleable commodities, with all the usual fallout when contracts go wrong. The facts also demonstrate the conflicts of interest that arise when middlemen rush to profit from the demand of a market in which the comparatively rich benefit from the preparedness of the poor to provide a service that the rich either cannot or will not perform.
>
> … It is noteworthy that no evidence was provided about the long-term impact on mothers of giving up children they carried, and there was no evidence of the impact on the children themselves. (Family Court of Western Australia 2016, paras 756 and 757)

Thus, even though the ruling appeared to favour the Farnells, due to the judge's interpretation of the best interests of the child Pipah at that time, his commentary in handing down that decision unequivocally condemned the practice of surrogacy. Over the same period as those legal proceedings, some AU$250,000, including a donation by the Farnells, were raised to help support Gammy and his gestational mother, with whom he continues to live. He was granted Australian citizenship in 2015, on the basis that his biological father is Australian.

The Chief Justice of the Australian Family Court at that time, Diana Bryant, took a different position from Justice Thackray. She called for the Australian government to legalise commercial surrogacy in Australia because "current laws were driving couples to enter into unethical arrangements overseas" (cited in B. Brennan 2015). However, it is unlikely that such legalisations would solve the problem, as the growth of the medical tourism industry more generally shows, with Thailand, Singapore and Malaysia in particular having capitalised on this industry in Australia's neighbourhood. Transnational commercial surrogacy would still be cheaper than Australian commercial surrogacy, and in a global capitalist market, the cost of services and return on one's investment are major considerations.

The Gammy case is not an isolated one. Later the same year in the UK, a woman refused to take a severely disabled twin from a surrogacy service-provider (also based in the UK), who reported that the client-mother had called the baby girl a "fucking dribbling cabbage", but took the baby's healthy twin brother (cited in Perry 2014). In the wake of the Baby Gammy case, which was cited in UK media reports on the British case, this refusal of a "defective" product sparked outrage in the British press (e.g. G. Fraser 2014).

The risks of such "defective" child-products are exacerbated in gestational surrogacy, in part because of the absence of any pre-existing biological connection between the surrogate and the embryo, particularly when the surrogate has already had multiple pregnancies or when multiple embryos are implanted (Söderström-Anttila et al. 2016). Fœtuses produced through ART including surrogacy run a greater risk of pre-term births, lower birth weight, and perinatal mortality (Simopoulou et al. 2018, 5). A 2016 Norwegian study also suggested that, partly because of the greater incidence of pre-term births and lower birth weight, children produced from ART run a higher risk of developing cancer (Reigstad et al. 2016).

Fœtal risks are further exacerbated by unnecessary pre-term cæsarean births (C-sections). The use of C-sections has been steadily increasing since the early 1990s (Baker 2006, 99 ff.), but almost doubled globally between 2000 and 2015 (Boerma et al. 2018, 1341), with a corresponding increase in the number of unnecessary interventions (Betrán et al. 2018). In their contribution to a series published in *The Lancet* on the "global cæsarean section epidemic" (Betrán et al. 2018), Ana Pilar Betrán et al. (2018) noted that the increase, contrary to popular perceptions, was due to choices made not by the women themselves but by the health professionals who either imposed them or persuaded women to accept them. They further noted that private health providers were more likely to use C-sections than public ones, citing the example of Brazil, where "80–90% of all babies in the private sector are born by CS, compared with 30–40% in the public sector" (Betrán et al. 2018, 1360). In their contribution to the same series, Jane Sandall et al. (2018) detailed a number of risks to both infants and birth mothers arising from pre-term C-sections: severe respiratory difficulties and hypoglycæmia in infants, along with more general lifetime poor health, and an increased risk of mortality and severe morbidity for the mothers.

Fœtal risks, however, serious as they are, pale into insignificance beside the risks to the egg and gestation-providers—including those from unnecessary C-sections as noted above. Sandall et al. define "severe maternal morbidity" associated with C-sections as:

> the presence of complications such as a hæmorrhage, requiring hysterectomy or blood transfusion, any hysterectomy, uterine rupture, complications associated with anæsthetic (including those arising from the administration of a general or local anæsthetic, analgesic, or other sedation during labour and delivery), obstetric shock, cardiac arrest, acute renal failure, assisted ventilation or intubation, puerperal venous thromboembolism, major puerperal infection, inhospital wound disruption, and hæmatoma. (Sandall et al 2018, 1350)

Studies have shown that gestational service-providers, particularly in the case of multiple pregnancies or implantations, are also at greater risk of conditions such as hypertension, pre-eclampsia (hypertension with organ damage, usually liver or kidneys: symptoms include severe headaches, impaired vision and shortness of breath), cholestasis (blockage of bile flow), hyperemesis gravidarum (violent and repeated vomiting), postpartum hæmorrhage, gestational diabetes and venous thromboembolism (blood clots that start in veins), and may be more likely to undergo C-section deliveries and hysterectomies (Knoche 2014, 184; Klein 2017, ch. 2; Simopoulou et al. 2018, 5). Egg providers, for their part, run a significant risk of ovarian hyperstimulation syndrome (OHSS)

> which, in severe cases, may cause renal failure, hypovolemic shock secondary to intravascular volume depletion (severe dehydration and risk of organ failure resulting from fluid depletion in the blood), acute respiratory distress syndrome, pulmonary thromboembolism (blood clot in lungs), and in some cases, death. (Simopoulou et al 2018, 5)

Egg-providers and gestational service-providers have to undergo multiple health checks and repeated reproductive "treatments" over several months, including regulation of ovulation and conception to foster development of parallel ovulation and menstrual cycles in both women, thus maximising the chances that the gestation-provider's body will accept the implanted embryo(s). In addition, both egg- and gestation-providers are subjected to rigorous policing of their behaviour during the period of egg generation and implantation and pregnancy: they are not allowed to have sexual relations (with men in any case) during the "treatment", and health guidelines recommended for any pregnant woman (no drugs or alcohol, no smoking, regular sleep patterns and a healthy diet) are strictly imposed for egg- and gestation-providers. Although these conditions are not imposed by law in countries that allow surrogacy, they are recommended by professional societies or required by surrogacy agencies. However, the concern of these societies and agencies in imposing them is less to do with the physical and emotional well-being of the service-providers than with the successful realisation of the surrogacy contract: delivery of a product in good condition (i.e. a healthy child) to the client-parents. Even biomedical research on the risks of surrogacy takes a similar tone. For example, Söderström-Anttila et al. in reviewing research on "outcomes for surrogate mothers, children and the resulting families" in 2015, stated that:

> One of the cornerstones in surrogacy arrangements is the importance of choosing the surrogate mother with extreme caution. To minimise the medical risks to the surrogate mother recommendations drawn up by expert groups in ESHRE, ASRM and FIGO should be followed … To avoid unnecessary endangerment of the health of the surrogate and the future child it is strongly recommended that only one embryo at a time is transferred to the surrogate. (Söderström-Anttila et al 2016, 272)

Even though such research acknowledges that surrogates do encounter health risks, it mostly does not take an ethical position in opposition to surrogacy, but rather advocates the conditions in which optimum "results" may be obtained with minimal harm.

The guidelines for choice of gestational service-providers are set out by the above-cited ASRM (American Society of Reproductive Medicine) in a Fact Sheet available on its website. The Fact Sheet states that

> The ideal GC [gestational carrier] is a healthy woman between the ages of 21 and 45 who has had a successful term pregnancy and has a supportive family environment to help her cope with the added stress of pregnancy. The carrier should have no more than five previous vaginal deliveries or two previous cesarean deliveries. Prior to becoming pregnant, the GC should talk about the risks of pregnancy with her healthcare provider. (ASRM 2012)

ASRM further recommends a complete physical health check including tests for sexually transmitted diseases and other viral infections such as hepatitis, and a mental health evaluation. It is interesting that ASRM acknowledges that pregnancy does place physical and emotional stress on women (however rewarding or unrewarding it may otherwise be), and does carry physical risks at the best of times. "Ideally", ASRM advocates stress minimisation through "a supportive family environment", thus both collectivising and privatising the risk management among a family for whom the gestational service-provider is at least one of the breadwinners, and removing the responsibility for managing that risk from the clients or the agents.

A 2018 study in the US further detailed the prescriptive conditions set out by surrogacy agencies, which include: surrogates must have a body mass index between 18 and 34 (31 in some cases, although the threshold for obesity is 30); they must not be on welfare and be in a financially stable situation; must not take drugs or smoke; must have health insurance; must have no history of mental or severe physical illness; and must have a clean bill of obstetric/gynæcological health (Islam 2018). I am eerily reminded of cattle auctions or indeed slave auctions; the used-car-lot metaphor also once again comes to mind. The gestational "car" must already have some "mileage" on her odometer (through previous pregnancy/ies) but not too much (not to the extent of risking a clapped-out "engine"), and be in good overall condition, for the dealer to consider brokering a sale.

As concerns the experience of the egg- and gestation-providers, women have recounted being "groomed" to perform these services. One *cause célèbre* is that of Maggie Eastman, a woman from the US city of Seattle, who told her story in the 2011 film *Eggsploitation* (directed by Justin Baird and Jennifer Lahl) and subsequently to the press and in a 2019 anti-surrogacy book (Eastman and Ridley 2015; Maggie 2019). Eastman tells of being encouraged into surrogacy when she was 21 years old by a woman some 20 years her senior, who worked as a nurse at a fertility clinic and whom she met at a party in 2002:

> In a relatively short time, this woman knew I liked kids, was a struggling college student working several part-time jobs and still taking out loans. I'm sure she could tell I was naïve, sheltered, and insecure … I was struggling with depression, felt awkward in my body, was silently confused about my sexuality, and desperately wanted to be liked and fit in. In many ways, I wasn't that different from other young women my age. (Maggie 2019, 28)

Eastman's interlocutor flattered her, telling her how beautiful and intelligent she was, appealing to her need to be liked. Later on in the evening, after having spent some time "grooming" Eastman, the nurse suggested she think about egg donation, as both an altruistic gesture to help others and to help her pay off her student loans, reassuring her that the procedure was virtually risk-free. Through this grooming process, Eastman became an egg-provider and continued over the next decade, with post-"donation" abdominal discomfort increasing after each time. All the while, however, she was reassured that she was doing a wonderful job and giving a great gift. Shortly after her tenth donation at the age of 32, she was diagnosed with stage four breast cancer that had metastasised to her liver and bones, which was almost unheard-of for a fit white woman her age who did not drink or smoke. Eastman blamed the hormone treatments dispensed to her during her years of egg provision. While medical opinions are divided on the topic (e.g. those cited in Eastman and Ridley 2015), other cases of metastatic cancer developing in otherwise perfectly healthy and quite young women who have participated several times in egg harvesting have been cited (e.g. Vera 2016; Brody 2017).

In our societies where women are trained from an early age to associate their worth, first with their looks, second, with their sexual availability, third, with their capacity to produce children, and fourth with their capacity for altruism—that feminised quality *par excellence*—it appears all too easy to groom women to give the "gift" of a child.

When the altruism becomes overlaid with the discourse of equality and rights in a rainbowed world, the production of the child-gift becomes framed as not only altruistic but as politically essential, even feminist, as we are about to see.

Homonormative reproductive freedom in a gay man's world

What is interesting about arguments in favour of the practice of surrogacy and for its regulation where gay male clients are concerned is that these clients claim to be challenging heteronormative, biologically deterministic approaches to parenting and to "family", even as they remain resolutely within a nuclear family model. Gay dads using surrogacy services claim to challenge and disrupt gendered and biologising norms of nurturing, yet in doing so, they reproduce deterministic approaches to family-making in that the biological link of baby to one of the fathers is seen to be of paramount importance. The genetic material of the gay fathers (or indeed straight fathers, for that matter) is almost always the key factor in surrogacy arrangements. The egg and the womb are provided by two different women (for the most part), neither of whom will be an adoptive parent and both of whom are thus considered to be interchangeable and dispensable—but the sperm is definitely Dad's. The father is almost always (always in the case of gay dads) the only biological parent to lay claim to ownership of the child-commodity in surrogacy arrangements, which returns us directly to the centre of biologising—and masculinist—norms about parenting and transmission. Race-matching of the egg-provider with the client-fathers is also often a priority so as to produce appropriately coloured babies, but the race of the gestational service-provider is irrelevant as she is simply a vessel.

A number of studies have shown that a DNA-link between one of the gay client-fathers and the "commissioned" child is perceived as important for gay men to develop meaningful and socially validated kinship relationships that fit in with dominant family models. Such arguments stand in stark contrast to the earlier gay- and particularly lesbian-liberation framings of "families we choose", and are the clearest articulation of the homonormative ideology informing the logic of "rainbow families". Even though gay male parents having commissioned children through surrogacy often have ambiguous relationships to biological links (Murphy 2013), and sometimes claim that "biology doesn't matter", those same men introduce other markers of biological connection to their commissioned child such as references to "bio'" and "non-bio" dads (Riggs 2018, 153). Moreover, even as they claim that families are "about love, and it really doesn't matter about biology", such statements are belied by the fact that they have entered into a surrogacy arrangement, which "it could be argued, is by default to make genetic matter matter" (Riggs 2018, 153). Other studies show the sociocultural importance of biological family for gay men in hetero/homonormative family frameworks, such that "the presence of a genetic relationship is the most oft cited reason that gay men choose surrogacy" (Berkowitz 2013, 76; see also Dempsey 2013; Gondouin 2018; Nebeling Petersen 2018).

Fitting in to the respectable heterosexual family model extends to fitting in to the national family as well. To be accepted into the national family, the gay family needs not only to match normative family structures but also to fit in with cultural and racial norms, such as in Israel, where "the Jewish family" is the microcosm of the nation (Tsfati and Adital 2018b, 4), or in Sweden, where "[w]anting a child that 'blends in' also concerns ideas of regional and national identity and what it means to be Swedish" (Gondouin 2018, 113–4).

Other literature promotes both women's "choice" to become surrogates and gay men's access to surrogacy as emancipatory and liberating for all concerned. Much of this literature positively foregrounds men's parenting through surrogacy as challenging gender stereotypes (e.g. Cory 2015; Tsfati and Ben-Ari 2018a; Fantus and Newman 2019), and as creating greater self-esteem and stronger links with the gay dads' own families (Bergman et al. 2010). However, such changing approaches to parenting and improved self-esteem do not in themselves necessitate access to the procurement of children through surrogacy. Some of this literature also posits gestational service-providers who bear and then hand over children to others as similarly challenging stereotypes of maternal bonding: "surrogate narratives challenge heteronormative family structures and resist hegemonic femininity that has dictated women's normative reproductive decision-making" (Fantus and Newman 2019, 10; see also Cory 2015). Some scholars take a more nuanced approach. Dana Berkowitz, for example, in an article that does not foreground arguments around surrogacy per se but focuses on gay men's narratives of parenting, found that gay men's "challenges" to gender roles in parenting are themselves gendered. As liminally positioned parents, they frequently resort to heterosexual scripts and "maternal" tropes such as "biological clock" and "soccer mom" in describing their desire for children and experience of parenting (Berkowitz 2011). Other research focuses on the "roadblocks" gay men face in accessing surrogacy (Koh 2016, 44; see also Lustenberger 2017) and/or the support that they need from institutions and employers through the "emotional journey" of procuring a child through surrogacy (e.g. Seignot and Clutterbuck. 2016, 195).

The "feminist" justifications of surrogacy bear some resemblance to "feminist" justifications of prostitution, with which surrogacy is often compared by both its defenders and its critics (see, e.g. for the former, S. Lewis 2017; and for the latter, Ekman 2013). The basic argument is that women have agency and exercise choice; we therefore should not criticise their choices. The problem with such arguments is that they are individualistic and thus remove choices from the social, political, cultural and economic contexts in which they are made. The "agency" argument in particular is a straw-figure one, as sentient beings have agency by definition, and it thus cannot be removed simply by criticising the practices in which agents engage. In other words, the agency of women, individually or collectively, as social actors within given situations of constraint or relative lack thereof is a separate set of considerations from the ways in which systems, structures and ideologies operate more globally to enable or constrain the capacity to make free choices, or to shape the conceptual frameworks within which "choice" is understood.

Although structure and agency are necessarily interdependent, as they feed each other reciprocally (c.f. Bourdieu's concept of *habitus*, discussed in Chapter 8 [Bourdieu 1980b]), they are not the same. *Of course* women (and men for that matter) make choices, but they do so within both a material and an ideological context. For many, particularly women, it is a context of considerable economic, psychological and sociocultural constraint. In our societies in which women's bodies and their reproductive functions are conceptualised as objects of appropriation and exchange (Guillaumin 1992)—such that even the most privileged women are impacted by these processes and their justifying ideology—choices to sell, rent out or donate parts of one's body or its sexual or reproductive functions do not happen in a power vacuum. On an individual level, other things being equal, any sentient being has the right to do anything to her own body that she wishes, even if others may consider those actions harmful to the individual making those choices. The problem with such a position is first, that other things are *not* equal, and second, because of this inequality, individual "choices" have broader social, cultural or economic ramifications that not only affect the individuals concerned but go far beyond them. This is not to say that an individual acting under constraint or pressure is responsible for harms done to others; it is rather to say that individualistic and decontextualised framings create an illusion of unfettered agency that bears no correspondence to the material reality. We have understood such mechanisms in relation to, for example, factory work, or domestic violence, or anonymous conscripted foot soldiers without whom wars could not happen, and so on. But prostitution and surrogacy are somehow placed off limits from considerations of structure and ideology in a (neo)liberal conceptualisation of free individual choice in an open marketplace.

This argument is all the more insidious in that the idea of a woman's right over her body, so strongly advanced by feminists in the area of women's reproductive rights, is used by surrogacy-defenders as presenting an opening for feminists and gay men to agree about surrogacy. It is argued, in an article explicitly focused on gay men's desires and motivations, that gestational service-providers to these men, in "choosing" to decouple pregnancy from maternity and "re-experience" pregnancy on its own, are able to exercise "reproductive freedom and procreative liberty" (Fantus and Newman 2019, 10). Unfortunately, the authors do not explain exactly how the experience of producing offspring for gay male clients constitutes the freedom and liberty being asserted. Women's campaigns for reproductive rights have been centred *precisely* on removing women's bodies from the control of men and servicing of male desires. Surrogacy, on the contrary, reinstates that control.

Connor Cory even goes so far as to suggest that "feminists *should* advocate for responsible surrogacy as part of a larger project of undermining the nexus between biological and social roles", which, he assumes, would also help to prevent exploitation in the transnational surrogacy industry (Cory 2015, 134, emphasis added). He criticises feminist focus on the experience of egg- and gestation-providers, rather than on the experience and desires of the client-parents, as too "exclusive" and "narrow" (Cory 2015, 135). Although he does acknowledge that the egg- and gestational service-providers "assume all of the health and safety risks" his priority is ensuring a more straightforward regulatory framework for gay male client-parents, who face a "legal landscape for surrogacy [that] varies dramatically from [US] state to state" and thus "have to invest significant resources in the initial stage of their family creation simply to decide where they can trust that the legal regime will respect their families and their rights" (Cory 2015, 150).

This "obstacle course" facing gay men wishing to procure biological children through surrogacy is a focus of much of the literature, and periodically crops up in news reports as well (e.g. Hider 2015: the article is titled "Gay couple trapped in surrogacy row"). Sibylle Lustenberger, for example, in her article on the experience of Israeli gay men faced with bureaucratic complications and "a chain of [unreliable] intermediaries" in India, wrote of their uncertainties and insecurities, discussed "during dinners and … hours at the pool" at their hotel (Lustenberger 2017, 399). The legal, institutional and practical obstacles they encountered apparently left them feeling "vulnerable and threatened" (p. 400). While Lustenberger acknowledges the privilege that these men enjoy, she also claims that as gay men they are rendered "vulnerable", including in Israel—notorious for its pinkwashing—where having children is culturally important. She sees gay men's exclusion from legal access to surrogacy in Israel as tantamount to considering them "second-class citizens" (p. 396). A somewhat more nuanced account is offered by Michael Nebeling Petersen, who argues that although gay mean accessing surrogacy are "economically and racially privileged … the new procreative forms create new stratifications among gay men who have to work affectively within institutionalized White heterosexuality" while not having the same level of ease of access to surrogacy as married heterosexual couples (Nebeling Petersen 2018, 713). Nebeling Petersen also acknowledges, however, that "[g]lobal and racialized inequalities [between client-parents and egg- and gestation-providers] are made invisible by neoliberal discourses that stage intended parents and surrogate mothers as free, individual, and rational agents" (p. 696).

Conclusion: buying babies, buying family

As we have seen, surrogacy is expensive, and only the most affluent of clients can afford it. Those lobbies for gay men who demand access to surrogacy as a matter of equal right and claim to be discriminated against are in fact exercising considerable class and, more often than not, race privilege in "buy[ing] their way out of discriminatory adoptive policies and stak[ing] out a 9-month lease on a surrogate mother's womb to construct a genetically related, and sometimes a genetically engineered, child" (Berkowitz 2013, 73). Although Berkowitz is accurate in describing the privilege and the relationship of exchange, she underestimates both the time involved and the number of women involved. Usually, the wombs of two women are involved: the one producing the eggs and the one carrying the pregnancy to term. Both women, as we have seen above, have to undergo rigorous medical screening and complex and potentially harmful procedures to both harvest the eggs and ensure the gestational carrier will receive them. In addition, the physical and psychological effects of a pregnancy do not end at the birth of the child but continue for some time afterwards. The time and physical commitments, and impacts for the egg- and gestation-providers, thus last much longer than the term of the pregnancy.

What is telling in the "gay dads" discourse that bizarrely brushes a revolutionary queer veneer over a normative happy-families narrative is the extent to which the surrogate is absent from the image and from the conversation. The narrative even directly depends on the surrogates' absence as people and certainly as parents of any sort, as Ekman (2013) notes (notwithstanding some happy-families narratives by gay dads where the so-called altruistic surrogate is claimed to have maintained a relationship with them and with the child).[10] Surrogates become reduced to wombs, or rather, separated from their wombs, as if the wombs were some tool external to their person that they used to provide a service, much as a carpenter might employ a saw, chisel and sander to cut and shape pieces of wood for furniture. Surrogates are the assembly line workers in the baby trade, whether they donate or sell their labour. Indeed, Pamela Bridgewater has noted the flawed logic behind "the default notion that so long as the woman providing the service or material is not paid, then the arrangement is acceptable and free from coercion" (2007, 1226). Yet, unlike assembly line workers, the tools *are them*: a pregnancy is an intimately embodied practice, operating physical changes in both the egg- and the gestation-providers and carrying risks to their own health.

Notwithstanding normative societal notions about what constitutes "family", there remains no legal right to have a *biological* child encoded in any national or international law. It is worrying that gay men's demands for children by surrogacy, which are dependent on the construction of women's bodies as alienable objects that can be hired out, have been folded into both the LGBTIQ rights and the "reproductive freedom" agendas. Their relatively uncritical adoption by LGBTIQ rights groups and indeed some professional associations that issue advice to intending gay male parents (e.g. Australian Psychological Society n.d.) is yet again, and sadly, evidence that what men want will invariably trump what women need in our societies and economies.

Notes

1 See for example the page advertising the 2020 conference, accessed 10 February 2020. https://www.menhavingbabies.org/surrogacy-seminars/brussels/program/

2 Main menhavingbabies website, accessed 10 February 2020. https://www.menhavingbabies.org/

3 The MDGs and supporting reports and literature are available at https://www.un.org/millenniumgoals/, accessed 27 February 2020.

4 https://www.gminsights.com/industry-analysis/surrogacy-market, accessed 10 February 2020.

5 https://surrogate.com/about-surrogacy/surrogacy-professionals/find-a-surrogacy-agency/, accessed 26 April 2019.

6 https://www.americansurrogacy.com/parents/available_surrogates, accessed 11 February 2020.
7 Growing Dreams website, "About Us" page, accessed 1 March 2020. https://www.growinggenerations.com/about-us/history/.
8 https://www.sublimis.com/plastic-surgery-argentina/facelift-abroad.html, accessed 1 March 2020.
9 "The risky rise of dental holidays". Traveller website, n.d., accessed 1 March 2020. https://www.traveller.com.au/the-risky-rise-of-dental-holidays-blv7
10 In the mid-2000s in Montreal I had a long conversation with a gay male couple who recounted precisely this narrative: the birth mother apparently lived nearby and all was well. I did not have the opportunity to meet or talk with the birth mother and do not know what has transpired since, but to this day I only have the fathers' word to go by. The mother, even here, remained absent.

CONCLUSION

In December 2019, the lesbian marriage of Bogotá, Colombia's first female mayor made international headlines. A prominent anti-corruption campaigner and an out lesbian, Claudia López Hernández married her partner Angélica Lozano a few days before taking office. The press featured several photographs of the couple in matching white designer pantsuits holding identical bouquets of white flowers, which López had posted to Twitter with the comment "¡Gracias a la vida por este año maravilloso: me gradué del doctorado, gané la Alcaldía y me casé con el amor de mi vida!" (translated by Associated Press as "Thank *you* life for this marvelous year! I graduated with my doctorate, won mayoral office and married the love of my life!") (Associated Press 2019, my italics added to highlight a slight but significant mistranslation in this context).

The tweet says it all: López's year is "marvellous" because it combines three significant marks of success: obtaining a doctorate (cultural capital), which she obtained in political science at Northwestern University in Chicago (a clear mark of the "been-to" credentials of Global South elites who study in the Global North); being elected to political office (particularly with her profile), in a country marked by conflict and corruption, where the rate of violence against women is high, and which is one of the worst performers in Latin America as concerns women's representation in parliament and government; and marrying "the love of her life", which, although a stereotypically "feminine" aspiration as women are still largely defined by their marital status, becomes revolutionary in that her spouse is a woman. Even the imagery combines tradition and modernity: married in white with flowers, but in tailored pantsuits not bridal gowns.

The Associated Press framing of the story is typical of the Anglosphere reports (although some other stories draw even more attention to López's looks). Two aspects of that framing are troubling, in that they simultaneously globalise/Anglicise López's story, ignoring key contextual specificities, and essentialise Latin America.

First, López's being "openly lesbian" is considered all the more revolutionary in that she is elected in a "traditionally conservative, Catholic country" (Associated Press 2019). This framing is gratingly stereotypical when one considers that anti-gay religious conservatism in Latin American countries is being fuelled more by evangelical Protestantism than by Catholicism at this time—which is, as we saw in Chapter 6, also the case in Latino communities in the US. Such tropes of "traditionalist" Catholic Latin America serve an Anglo-dominated, WASP (white Anglo-Saxon Protestant) worldview, in which "Catholic Latin America" is locked into a reified traditionalism. In fact, if López's election is groundbreaking, it is as much because she is female and a vocal anti-corruption campaigner in a country marked by ongoing misogyny and corruption, as because she is homosexual. Same-sex marriage was, after all, legalised in Colombia in 2016.

The other troubling aspect of the Associated Press story is the fact that the author missed the obvious reference in López's cited tweet to the celebrated song by Violeta Parra "Gracias a la vida (que me ha dado tanto)" (thanks to life, which has given me so much), which has become a liberatory hymn in Latin America. Parra and her music were part of the Nueva canción movement, which combined folk-style music with social justice lyrics during revolutionary and human rights struggles of the 1970s and 1980s. One cannot say "gracias a la vida" in Latin America without referencing that song and all it symbolises in terms of both campaigns for and celebrations of social justice, democracy and human and women's rights within contemporary Latin American history. López is thus tacitly—and indeed justifiably—positioning herself within that history.

López's story, then, is both extraordinary and ordinary. She both breaks barriers and conforms. She is in many ways the personification of what same-sex marriage has come to symbolise—and the Anglosphere representation of her story reinforces the globalisation and homogenisation of that symbolism.

Whatever else it may be, same-sex marriage today represents a claim to legitimacy—social, political, economic and cultural—both of the lives of homosexuals and of the states that legislate for or against same-sex marriage. Same-sex marriage sells, wins votes and positions nation-states among the world's human rights avant-garde. The very nomenclature routinely used in activist and institutional parlance—"equal marriage", "egalitarian marriage", "marriage equality" or "marriage for all", the variants depending on the country and the language spoken—reflects a political framing in which equality, inclusivity and indeed the globalisation of rights and culture are foregrounded. States and markets alike have used this equality-inclusion-rights frame as a branding exercise that garners political capital, and profit, at little cost. The poster-people for same-sex marriage are, with few exceptions, white, attractive, between 20 and 40 years old and often with young children attached in a perfectly homonormative image of family.

Maurice Tomlinson, on whose words I opened this book, sees the legalisation of same-sex marriage as a way of normalising homosexuality, making it socioculturally acceptable, and thus enabling lesbians and gay men to lead lives and have relationships that are just as "unremarkable" as those of any heterosexual (Tomlinson

2020, online). He argues that same-sex marriage can be mobilised in this way in his native Jamaica as a means to another end: decriminalisation and societal integration of LGBTIQ people more generally, thus ensuring equal "sexual citizenship" across the board. Usually, same-sex marriage and family rights are considered a positive-rights endpoint in a staged process, following the obtention of negative rights such as decriminalisation and anti-discrimination laws. Tomlinson advocates turning this logic on its head, challenging "the established formula for achieving LGBT equality" (Tomlinson 2020, online).

David Evans first theorised the concept of sexual citizenship in 1993, using it to describe a process of ideological and biopolitical control. "To the extent that it guarantees differential market access, commodification of sexual immorality within 'private' environments", he argued, sexual citizenship has "served to largely maintain the purity of the moral community and fragment and distract potential dissent, and to quite clear material and ideological ends" (Evans 1993, 8). Almost 25 years later, Diane Richardson argued that "privatisation of sexual citizenship can obscure the workings of power associated with forms of citizenship recognition … that are typically seen as about privatised 'choices' such as, for instance, equal marriage, in addition to marginalising economic dimensions of sexual citizenship" (Richardson 2017, 220). Although Richardson was critiquing the idea of "citizenship" within the liberal capitalist democracies of the Global North, the critique is applicable throughout the (neo)liberal world.

The same year, Gilly Hartal and Orna Sasson-Levy analysed the links between sexual citizenship and nationalism in Israeli context, arguing that "LGBT individuals' inclusion within national boundaries is always accompanied by an adoption of nationalistic discourse and continuous marking of internal boundaries of belonging. These boundaries signify who is a good homo-citizen and who is not" (Hartal and Sasson-Levy 2017, 757). Even though they were writing about the general mainstreaming of LGBT rights and identities within the homonationalistically charged Israeli context, the argument is applicable to the institutionalisation of same-sex marriage as well. A good homo-citizen is a married homo-citizen, and preferably a double-income two-kids type of one. A Johanna Gondouin put it in her discussion of homonormative parenthood and transnational surrogacy in Sweden,

> []l]ove appears to be a key component in a process through which homosexuality is managed by being inscribed into the socially acceptable order. A nuclear family is formed through two individuals meeting, falling in love, having children and living happily ever after. (Gondouin 2018, 112)

Good homo-citizens are also good homo-workers and consumers, and can reap rewards both economically and in terms of social capital, in the Bourdieusian sense (Bourdieu 1980a). Whatever else marriage is or is not, it marks the individuals within it, legally, socially and economically, often albeit not always conferring socio-economic and sociocultural advantage. Economically speaking, if one follows Nicola Barker's argument that "law uses recognition and non-recognition to control access to economic justice" (N. Barker 2011, 460), then lesbian and gay entry into the system of legitimation through marriage is equivalent to accepting the rules by which access to economic advantage is allowed or denied (N. Barker 2012, 193).

I have argued in this book that the very idea of "family" is rooted in masculinist and nationalist ideologies, and as such, bound up with their normative relations of ruling, which renders futile any attempt to revolutionise the institution. One can at best modify it to make it more inclusive, egalitarian and so on, which is in fact the substance of the arguments of most same-sex marriage advocates. This is undoubtedly a defensible objective, given the importance of "family" in shaping both social and economic organisation and the lives of individuals. Moreover, the institution of marriage *has* evolved; to suggest that it has not or that this evolution has not had some positive impacts for large groups of people (women for a start) would be to fly in the face of demonstrable fact. That said, the ideological premises of the institution and its socioeconomic functions remain entirely intact. If they did not, marriage would no longer, in fact, be marriage.

Same-sex marriage advocate Lee Badgett has argued that "gay people will not change marriage in any significant way on their own" (2009, Kindle, Introduction, 3 of 288). "As a deeply rooted social and cultural institution", she writes, "marriage is powerful in ways that we might not always appreciate and in ways that we certainly cannot control" (Badgett 2009, Kindle, Introduction, 3 of 288). Indeed. However, Badgett and I come from quite different perspectives in our analysis of the ways in which the power of marriage operates.

As I have argued in this book, the power of marriage lies primarily in its imbrication with state and the market as an institution of socioeconomic and cultural reproduction. Sexual orientation, in fact, now matters far less in that system of reproduction in the countries discussed in this book than sex, race and class—or, for that matter, country of origin and residence, and native language. Or rather, it matters insofar as it can serve to reinforce the system through adapting it to the inclusion of new participants. We have seen that it is easy to honomormalise marriage without changing any other aspect of malestream structures and processes of social stratification, and with minimal modification to their justifying ideologies. In fact, the institutionalisation of same-sex marriage works a dream in co-opting sections of the LGBTIQ population into its hierarchies of privilege and exclusion.

Clare Chambers has advocated for a "marriage-free state", because she sees "even reformed marriage" as creating "unjustified inequalities between married and unmarried people and their children" (Chambers 2017, 201). The state she envisages would not rule out weddings or love or expressions of commitment, but would rule out the state imposing or privileging a particular format for relationships "in such a way as to disadvantage, discriminate against, or stigmatize those whose families are not structured according to that format … Marriage must be neither prerequisite nor hindrance" (Chambers 2017, 204).

Interestingly, however, Chambers retains the idea of family, and family structures, which she hopes to decouple from the idea of marriage. Whether she can decouple either or both from malestream capitalism is another question.

REFERENCES

ABC News (Australian Broadcasting Corporation). 2011. "Pilots slam Qantas chief's pay packet". 7 September. Accessed 24 December 2019. https://www.abc.net.au/news/2011-09-07/pilots-slam-qantas-chiefs-pay-rise/2875530

ABC News. 2015. "Gay marriage: Australia's businesses take out full-page ad backing same-sex partnerships". 29 May. Accessed 22 December 2019. https://www.abc.net.au/news/2015-05-29/corporations-behind-same-sex-marriage/6505758

ABC News. 2016. "Baby Gammy: Surrogacy row family cleared of abandoning child with Down syndrome in Thailand". 14 April. Accessed 25 April 2019. https://www.abc.net.au/news/2016-04-14/baby-gammy-twin-must-remain-with-family-wa-court-rules/7326196

ABC News. 2019. "Jetstar strike cancels flights in Sydney, Melbourne, Brisbane and Adelaide". 14 December. Accessed 24 December 2019. https://www.abc.net.au/news/2019-12-13/jetstar-strike-causes-flight-cancellations-around-australia/11795788

ABC Radio National. 2020. "Is there a moral case against the COVID-19 'shutdown'?". *The Minefield*, 13 May. Accessed 31 May 2020. https://www.abc.net.au/radionational/programs/theminefield/philosophical-case-against-the-shutdown/12241372

Abramovitz, Mimi. 1988. *Regulating the Lives of Women: Social Welfare Policy from Colonial Times to the Present.* New York: Routledge.

Adlam, Geoff. 2018. "The 2018 legal workplace environment survey". New Zealand Law Society, 29 June. Accessed 27 December 2019. https://www.lawsociety.org.nz/practice-resources/the-business-of-law/workplace-environment/the-2018-legal-workplace-environment-survey

Agamben, Giorgio. 2020. "Una voce di Giorgio Agamben". *Quodlibet*, 26 February–11 May. Accessed 31 May 2020. https://www.quodlibet.it/una-voce-giorgioagamben

Agarwal, Bina. 1988. *Structures of Patriarchy: The State, the Community, and the Household.* London: Zed Books.

Agarwal, Bina. 1994. *A Field of One's Own: Gender and Land Rights in South Asia.* Cambridge and New York: Cambridge University Press.

Agarwal, Bina. 1997. "'Bargaining' and gender relations: Within and beyond the household". International Food Policy Research Institute, Food Consumption and Nutrition Division, Washington, Discussion Paper No. 27.

Ainsworth, Susan, Andi Pekarek and Peter Ghin. 2018. "What Australia's marriage equality vote says about corporate activism". *Inside Business*, 15 November, University of Melbourne. Accessed 23 December 2019. https://pursuit.unimelb.edu.au/articles/what-australia-s-marriage-equality-vote-says-about-corporate-activism

Aksoy, Cevat G., Christopher S. Carpenter and Jeff Frank. 2018. "Sexual orientation and earnings: New evidence from the United Kingdom". *Industrial and Labor Relations Review* 7 (1): 242–272. doi:10.1177/0019793916687759

Albelda, Randy. 2001. "Welfare-to-work, farewell to families? US welfare reform and work/family debates". *Feminist Economics* 7 (1): 119–135.

Albelda, Randy. 2011. "Time binds: US antipoverty policies, poverty, and the well-being of single mothers". *Feminist Economics* 17 (4): 189–214.

Albelda, Randy. 2013. "Low-Wage Mothers on the Edge in the US". In *Handbook of Research on Gender and Economic Life*, edited by Deborah M. Figart and Tonia L. Warnecke, 257–272. Northampton, MA: Edward Elgar.

Albelda, Randyet al. 2009. *Poverty in the Lesbian, Gay and Bisexual Community*. Los Angeles: The Williams Institute.

Aldén, Linaet al. 2015. "Effect of registered partnership on labor earnings and fertility for same-sex couples: Evidence from Swedish register data". *Demography* 52 (4): 1243–1268.

Aldrich, Robert. 2003. *Colonialism and Homosexuality*. London and New York: Routledge.

Aliansi Masyarakat Adat Nusantaraet al. 2012. "Civil society denounces adoption of flawed ASEAN human rights declaration". 19 November. Accessed 18 November 2019. https://www.hrw.org/news/2012/11/19/civil-society-denounces-adoption-flawed-asean-human-rights-declaration

Amari, Salima. 2018. *Lesbiennes de l'immigration. Construction de soi et relations familiales*. Vulaines-sur-Seine: Éditions du Croquant.

Amnesty International. 2018. "Business leaders and employers show their support for equal marriage in Northern Ireland – open letter". Press release, 11 September. Accessed 18 December 2019. https://www.amnesty.org.uk/press-releases/business-leaders-and-employers-show-their-support-equal-marriage-northern-ireland

ANC (African National Congress). 1993. "A Bill of Rights for a New South Africa". Accessed 21 November 2019. https://web.archive.org/web/20150319202442/http://anc.org.za/show.php?id=231

Anderson, Benedict. 1983. *Imagined Communities: Reflections on the Origin and Spread of Nationalism*. London: Verso.

Anderson, Bridget. 2000. *Doing the Dirty Work? The Global Politics of Domestic Labour*. London: Zed Books.

Anderson, Bridget and Isabel Shutes (eds). 2014. *Care and Migrant Labour: Theory, Policy and Politics*. London: Palgrave.

Anderson, Fleur and Michael Smith. 2017. "Dutton blasts CEOs' same-sex push". *The Australian Financial Review*, 17 March, 10.

Anderson, Gerard F., Peter Hussey and Varduhi Petrosyan. 2019. "It's still the prices, stupid: Why the US spends so much on health care". *Health Affairs* 38 (1): 87–95. doi:10.1377/hlthaff.2018.05144

Andersson, Gunnaret al. 2006. "The demographics of same-sex marriages in Norway and Sweden". *Demography* 43 (1): 79–98. doi:10.1353/dem.2006.0001

André, Christophe and Thomas Chalaux. 2018. "Building a typology of housing systems to inform policies in OECD and EU member States". *Economie et Statistique / Economics and Statistics*. doi:10.187/ecostat.2018.500t.1943

Andrews, Lori B. 2006. "How is Technology Changing the Meaning of Motherhood for Western Women". In *Women's Reproductive Rights*, edited by Heather Widdows, ltziar Alkorta Idiakez and Aitziber Emaldi Cirión, 124–139. Basingstoke and New York: Palgrave Macmillan.

Anthias, Floyaand NiraYuval-Davis. 1989. "Introduction". In *Woman-Nation-State*, edited by NiraYuval-Davis and FloyaAnthias, 1–15. London:Macmillan.

Aristotle. 350 BCE. *Politics*. Translated by Benjamin Jowett. Internet Classics Archive. Accessed 15 September 2019. http://classics.mit.edu/Aristotle/politics.html

Armstrong, Pat and Hugh Armstrong. 2009. "Precarious Employment in the Health-care Sector." In *Gender and the Contours of Precarious Employment*, edited by Leah F. Vosko, Martha MacDonald and Iain Campbell, 256–270. London and New York: Routledge.

ASRM (American Society of Reproductive Medicine). 2012. "Gestational carrier (surrogate) fact sheet". Accessed26 April 2019. https://www.reproductivefacts.org/news-and-publications/patient-fact-sheets-and-booklets/documents/fact-sheets-and-info-booklets/gestational-carrier-surrogate/

Associated Press. 2019. "Colombia: Bogotá's first female mayor marries same-sex partner". *The Guardian*, 18 December. Accessed 18 June 2020. https://www.theguardian.com/world/2019/dec/17/colombia-bogota-claudia-lopez-first-female-mayor-marries-same-sex-partner

Australian, The. 2017. "Do as I say, not as I do! Mutti Merkel puts The Donald over her knee for refugee ban". (Editorial). 31 January, 13.

Australian Psychological Society. n.d. "Information sheet: Gay men and surrogacy". Accessed 1 March 2020. https://www.psychology.org.au/for-the-public/Psychology-topics/LGBTI/LGBTI-Parenting/Gay-men-and-surrogacy

Avins, Jenni. 2015. "Marriage equality in the US is about to create a $2.6 billion wedding boom". *Quartz*, 27 June. Accessed 4 December 2019. https://qz.com/438868/same-sex-marriage-billion-dollar-wedding-economy-boom/

Avraham, Doron. 2016. "The religious and moral origins of German conservative social policy". *Journal of Policy History* 28 (1): 133–161.

Bacon, Jen. 2012. "Until death do us part: Lesbian rhetorics of relational divorce". *Women's Studies in Communication* 35 (2): 158–177. doi:10.1080/07491409.2012.724523

Badgett, M.V. Lee. 1995. "Gender, sexuality, and sexual orientation: All in the feminist family?". *Feminist Economics* 1 (1): 121–139. doi:10.1080/714042217

Badgett, M.V. Lee. 2009. *When Gay People Get Married: What Happens When Societies Legalize Same-Sex Marriage*. New York and London: New York University Press (Kindle edition).

Badgett, M.V. Lee. 2020. *The Economic Case for LGBT Equality: Why Fair and Equal Treatment Benefits Us All*. Boston: Beacon Press.

Badgett, M.V. Lee and Christy Mallory. 2014. *Patterns of Relationship Recognition for Same-Sex Couples: Divorce and Terminations*. Los Angeles: The Williams Institute.

Badgett, M.V. Lee, Laura E. Durso, Angeliki Kastanis and Christy Mallory. 2013. *The Business Impact of LGBT-Supportive Workplace Policies*. Los Angeles: The Williams Institute.

Badgett, M.V. Lee, Soon Kyu Choi and Bianca D.M. Wilson. 2019. *LGBT Poverty in the United States: A Study of Differences between Sexual Orientation and Gender Identity Groups*. Los Angeles: The Williams Institute.

Badgett, M.V. Lee, Kees Waaldijk and Yana van der Meulen Rodgers. 2019. "The relationship between LGBT inclusion and economic development: Macro-level evidence". *World Development* 120: 1–14. doi:10.1016/j.worlddev.2019.03.011

Baker, Maureen. 2006. *Restructuring Family Policies: Convergences and Divergences*. Toronto: University of Toronto Press.

Ball, Molly. 2016. "The pugnacious, relentless progressive party that wants to remake America". *The Atlantic*, 7 January. Accessed 8 January 2020. https://www.theatlantic.com/politics/archive/2016/01/working-families-party/422949/

Ballent, Anahi. 2010. "Unforgettable Kitsch: Images around Eva Perón" (translated by Beatrice D. Gurwitz). In *The New Cultural History of Peronism: Power and Identity in Mid-Twentieth-Century Argentina*, edited by Matthew B. Karush and Oscar Chamosa. Durham, NC: Duke University Press. doi:10.1215/9780822392866-006

Balsam, Kimberley F., Esther D. Rothblum and Robert E. Wickham. 2017. "Longitudinal predictors of relationship dissolution among same-sex and heterosexual couples". *Couple and Family Psychology: Research and Practice* 5 (4): 247–257. doi:10.1037/cfp0000091

Bariola, Emily, Anthony Lyons and William Leonard. 2015. "The mental health benefits of relationship formalisation among lesbians and gay men in same-sex relationships". *Australian and New Zealand Journal of Public Health* 39 (6): 530–535. doi:10.1111/1753-6405.12432

Barker, Drucilla. 2012. "Querying the paradox of caring labor". *Rethinking Marxism* 24 (4): 574–591. doi:10.1080/08935696.2012.711065

Barker, Nicola. 2011. "Ambiguous symbolisms: Recognising customary marriage and same-sex marriage in South Africa". *International Journal of Law in Context* 7 (4): 447–466. doi:10.1017/S1744552311000243

Barker, Nicola. 2012. *Not the Marrying Kind: A Feminist Critique of Same-Sex Marriage*. London: Palgrave Macmillan.

Barker, Nicola. 2015. "After the Wedding, What Next? Conservatism and Conjugality". In *From Civil Partnership to Same-Sex Marriage: Interdisciplinary Reflections*, edited by Nicola Barker and Daniel Monk, 220–237. London: Routledge.

Barker, Nicola and Daniel Monk (eds). 2015. *From Civil Partnership to Same-Sex Marriage: Interdisciplinary Reflections*. London: Routledge.

Barker, Vanessa. 2018. *Nordic Nationalism and Penal Order: Walling the Welfare State*. London and New York: Routledge.

Barnard, Mason. 2013. "Ecotourism's hidden cost: 'Green' tourism's colonial toll". *Harvard International Review* 35 (2): 8–9.

Barrett, Carla. 2015. 'Queering the home: The domestic labor of lesbian and gay couples in contemporary England". *Home Cultures* 12 (2): 193–211.

Barrientos, Armando. 2004. "Latin America: Towards a Liberal-Informal Welfare Regime". In *Insecurity and Welfare Regimes in Asia, Africa and Latin America: Social Policy in Development Contexts*, edited by Ian Gough and Geof Wood, 121–168. Cambridge: Cambridge University Press.

Barry, Kathleen. 1995. *The Prostitution of Sexuality*. New York: New York University Press.

Baxter, Janeen, Belinda Hewitt and Mark Western. 2009. "Who uses paid domestic labor in Australia? Choice and constraint in hiring household help". *Feminist Economics* 15 (1): 1–26. doi:10.1080/13545700802248989

Bazley, DameMargaret. 2018. "Independent review of Russell McVeagh". May–June 2018. Accessed 27 December 2019. https://www.russellmcveagh.com/getmedia/cc682d64-46a1-40e3-987b-cd82223bea24/Independent-Review-of-Russell-McVeagh-2018.pdf/

Beachy, Robert. 2012. "To Police and Protect: The Surveillance of Homosexuality in Imperial Berlin". In *After the History of Sexuality: German Genealogies with and beyond*

Foucault, edited by Scott Spector, Helmut Puff and Dagmar Herzog, 109–123. Oxford and New York: Berghahn Books.

Beachy, Robert. 2014. *Gay Berlin: Birthplace of a Modern Identity*. New York: Alfred A. Knopf.

de Beauvoir, Simone. 1949. *Le Deuxième Sexe*. Paris: Gallimard.

Belgrano Rawson, Milagros. 2012. "Ley de matrimonio igualitario y aborto en Argentina: notas sobre una revolución incompleta". *Estudos Feministas* 20 (1): 173–188.

Bell, Mark. 2017. "Analysis and comparative review of equality data collection practices in the European Union: Data collection in relation to LGBTI People". European Commission Directorate-General for Justice and Consumers. Luxembourg: European Union. doi:10.2838/522787

Belot, Henry. 2017. "Qantas to continue advocating for same-sex marriage despite criticism from Peter Dutton". *ABC News*, 18 March. Accessed 22 December 2019. https://www.abc.net.au/news/2017-03-18/qantas-continue-same-sex-marriage-support-peter-dutton-criticism/8366306

Bergeron, Suzanne. 2009. "An interpretive analytics to move caring labor off the straight path". *Frontiers: A Journal of Women Studies* 30 (1): 55–64.

Bergman, Kimet al. 2010. "Gay men who become fathers via surrogacy: The transition to parenthood". *Journal of GLBT Family Studies* 6 (2) 111–141. doi:10.1080/15504281003704940

Berkowitz, Dana. 2011. "Maternal instincts, biological clocks, and soccer moms: Gay men's parenting and family narratives". *Symbolic Interaction* 34 (4): 514–535.

Berkowitz, Dana. 2013. "Gay Men and Surrogacy". In *LGBT-Parent Families: Innovations in Research and Implications for Practice*, edited by Abbie E. Goldberg and Katherine R. Allen, 71–86. New York: Springer.

Bernhard, Market al. 2017. "Joint letter from Australian business leaders in support of marriage equality". March. Accessed 18 December 2019. https://qnews.com.au/read-the-marriage-equality-letter-aussie-ceos-wrote-to-the-pm/

Bernstein, Mary and Brenna Harvey. 2018. "The Movement towards Marriage Equality in Advanced Industrialized Countries". In *Handbook on Gender and Social Policy*, edited by Sheila Shaver, 307–323. Northampton, MA: Edward Elgar.

Bernstein, Mary and Verta Taylor (eds). 2013. *The Marrying Kind? Debating Same-Sex Marriage within the Lesbian and Gay Movement*. Minneapolis: University of Minnesota Press.

Bertelsmann Stiftung. n.d. *Work-Life-Balance: Meilenstein für eine zukunftsfähige Gesellschaft*. Gütersloh: Bertelsmann Stiftung.

Berthelot, Benoît. 2018. "Amazon: un rapport alarmant sur les conditions de travail à Montélimar". *Capital*, 27 April. Accessed 5 June 2020. https://www.capital.fr/entreprises-marches/amazon-un-rapport-alarmant-sur-les-conditions-de-travail-a-montelimar-1285393

Besoky, Juan Luis. 2018. "Los muchachos peronistas antijudíos. A propósito del antisemitismo en el movimiento peronista". *Trabajos y Comunicaciones* 47, doi:10.24215/23468971e057

Betrán, Ana Pilaret al. 2018. "Interventions to reduce unnecessary caesarean sections in healthy women and babies". *The Lancet* 392 (10155): 1358–1368.

Bible, Jacquelineet al. 2018. "A content analysis of the first decade of the *Journal of GLBT Family Studies*". *Journal of GLBT Family Studies* 14 (4): 337–355. doi:10.1080/1550428X.2017.1349626

Bilchit, David and Melanie Judge. 2007. "For whom does the bell toll? The challenges and possibilities of the Civil Union Act for family law in South Africa". *South African Journal on Human Rights* 23 (3): 466–499. doi:10.1080/19962126.2007.11864930

Bilge, Sirma. 2015. "Le blanchiment de l'intersectionnalité". *Recherches Féministes* 28 (2): 9–32.

Billingsley, Sunnee and Tommy Ferrarini. 2014. "Family policy and fertility intentions in 21 European countries". *Journal of Marriage and Family* 76: 428–445. doi:10.1111/jomf.12097

Björnsson, Thorbjörn and Yuval Shany. 2014. "The Court of Justice of the European Union". In *Assessing the Effectiveness of International Courts*, edited by Yuval Shany. doi:10.1093/acprof:oso/9780199643295.003.0012

Blau, Joel. 1999. *Illusions of Prosperity: America's Working Families in an Age of Economic Insecurity*. New York: Oxford University Press.

Boele-Woelki, Katharina and Angelika Fuchs. 2017. *Same-Sex Relationships and Beyond: Gender Matters in the EU*. Cambridge: Intersentia.

Boerma, Tieset al. 2018. "Global epidemiology of use of and disparities in caesarean sections". *The Lancet* 392 (10155): 1341–1348.

Boltanski, Luc and Eve Chiapello. 1999. *Le Nouvel Esprit du capitalisme*. Paris: Gallimard.

Boniol, Mathieu, Michelle McIsaac, Lihui Xu, Tana Wuliji, Khassoum Diallo and Jim Campbell. 2019. "Gender equity in the health workforce: Analysis of 104 countries". Health Workforce Working Paper 1. Geneva: World Health Organization.

Bonthuy, Elsje. 2007. "Race and gender in the Civil Union Act". *South African Journal on Human Rights* 23 (3): 526–542, doi:10.1080/19962126.2007.11864935

Booth, Robert. 2010. "Cruise ships still find a Haitian berth". *The Guardian*, 18 January. Accessed 16 December 2019. https://www.theguardian.com/world/2010/jan/17/cruise-ships-haiti-earthquake

Borer, Tristan Anne. 2009. "Gendered war and gendered peace: Truth commissions and postconflict gender violence: Lessons from South Africa". *Violence Against Women* 15 (10): 1169–1193. doi:10.1177/1077801209344676

Borgia, Valence, Alice Remy and Olivia Roche. 2018. *Rapport sur le harcèlement sexuel au sein de la profession d'avocat*. Paris: Union des Jeunes Avocats de Paris.

Boris, Eileen and Jennifer N. Fish. 2015. "Decent Work for Domestics: Feminist Organizing, Worker Empowerment and the ILO". In *Towards a Global History of Domestic and Caregiving Workers*, edited by Dirk Hoerder, Elise van Nederveen Meerkerk and Silke Neunsinger, 530–552. Leiden: Brill.

Boswell, Randy. 2012. "Feds touted gay-wedding tourism ads in 2006". *Postmedia News*, 13 January. Accessed via Proquest, 13 November 2019. http://ezproxy.library.usyd.edu.au/login?url=https://search.proquest.com/docview/916125800?accountid=14757

Bourdieu, Pierre. 1980a. "Le Capital social". *Actes de la recherche en sciences sociales* 31 (1): 2–3.

Bourdieu, Pierre. 1980b. *Le Sens pratique*. Paris: Minuit.

Bourdieu, Pierre. 1990. *The Logic of Practice*, translated by Richard Nice. Stanford: Stanford University Press.

Bourque, André. 2017. "Technology profit and pivots in the $300 billion wedding space". *Huffpost*, 6 December (updated). Accessed 13 May 2019. https://www.huffpost.com/entry/technology-profit-and-piv_b_7193112

Bowen, Howard. 2013. *Social Responsibilities of the Businessman*. Iowa City: University of Iowa Press.

Boyd, Nan Alamilla. 2008. "Sex and tourism: The economic implications of the gay marriage movement". *Radical History Review* 100: 223–235. doi:10.1215/01636545-2007-032

Bradshaw, Sarah, Sylvia Chant and Brian Linneker. 2019. "Challenges and changes in gendered poverty: The feminization, de-feminization, and Re-feminization of poverty in Latin America". *Feminist Economics* 25 (1): 119–144. doi:10.1080/13545701.2018.1529417

Brennan, Bridget. 2015. "Commercial surrogacy should be legalised, Family Court Chief Justice Diana Bryant says". *ABC News*, 18 April. Accessed 29 April 2019. https://www.

abc.net.au/news/2015-04-18/commercial-surrogacy-should-be-legalised-family-court-justice/6402924

Brennan, Christopher. 2014. "Backpackers or working holiday makers? Working tourists in Australia". *Qualitative Sociology Review* 10 (3): 94–114.

Brennan, Christopher. 2018. "Northern lights instead of workers' rights: Volunteer working tourists in Finnish Lapland". *Nordic Journal of Working Life Studies* 8 (2): 43–61.

Bresser-Pereira, Luiz Carlos. 2011. "From Old to New Developmentalism in Latin America". In *The Oxford Handbook of Latin America Economics*, edited by Jose Antonio Ocampo and Jaime Ros, 108–129. Oxford and New York: Oxford University Press. doi:10.1093/Oxfordhb/9780199571048.013.0005

Bridgewater, Pamela D. 2007. "Reconstructing rationality: Towards a critical economic theory of reproduction". *Emory Law Journal* 56: 1215–1234.

Briggs, Asa. 1961. "The welfare state in historical perspective". *European Journal of Sociology/Archives Européennes de Sociologie* 2 (2): 221–258. doi:10.1017/S0003975600000412

Brinsden, Peter R. 2016. "Surrogacy's Past, Present, and Future". In *Handbook of Gestational Surrogacy: International Clinical Practice and Policy Issues*, edited by E. Scott Sills, 1–8. Cambridge and New York: Cambridge University Press.

Brody, Jane E. 2017. "Do egg donors face long-term risks?". *The New York Times*, 10 July. Accessed 10 February 2020. https://www.nytimes.com/2017/07/10/well/live/are-there-long-term-risks-to-egg-donors.html

Brooks, Richard. 2018. "The financial scandal no one is talking about". *The Guardian*, 29 May. Accessed 29 December 2019. https://www.theguardian.com/news/2018/may/29/the-financial-scandal-no-one-is-talking-about-big-four-accountancy-firms

Brown, Rachel H. 2016. "Re-examining the transnational nanny". *International Feminist Journal of Politics* 18 (2): 210–229. doi:10.1080/14616742.2015.1007728

Bucher, Nathalie Rosa. 2009. "South Africa: Law failing lesbians on 'corrective rape'". *Inter Press Service*, 31 August. Accessed 30 November 2019. www.ipsnews.net/2009/08/south-africa-law-failing-lesbians-on-corrective-rape/

Burnes, Theodore R. and Mindy M. Chen. 2012. "The Multiple Identities of Transgender Individuals: Incorporating a Framework of Intersectionality to Gender Crossing". In *Navigating Multiple Identities: Race, Gender, Culture, Nationality, and Roles*, edited by Ruthellen Josselson and Michele Harway, 113–128. New York: Oxford University Press.

Burnett, Simon B., Jonathan Swan and Cary Cooper. 2014. "Working Families: Who Cares?". In *Contemporary Issues in Family Studies: Global Perspectives on Partnerships, Parenting and Support in a Changing World*, edited by Angela Abela and Janet Walker, 215–226. Chichester: Wiley Blackwell.

Butcher, Jim. 2007. *Ecotourism, NGOs and Development: A Critical Analysis*. London: Routledge.

Butler, Ben. 2020a. "'Outrageous': Qantas criticised for standing down 20,000 workers without pay". *The Guardian*, 19 March. Accessed 5 June 2020. https://www.theguardian.com/business/2020/mar/19/coronavirus-qantas-and-jetstar-to-suspend-international-flights-and-stand-down-20000-workers

Butler, Ben. 2020b. "Qantas to cut 6,000 jobs and keep 15,000 stood down in bid to survive coronavirus downturn". *The Guardian*, 25 June. Accessed 29 June 2020. https://www.theguardian.com/business/2020/jun/25/qantas-to-cut-6000-jobs-and-keep-15000-stood-down-in-bid-to-survive-coronavirus-downturn

Butler, Martha and Cynthia Kirkby. 2013. *Same-Sex Marriage, Divorce and Families: Selected Recent Developments*. Ottawa: Parliament of Canada House of Commons. Accessed 4 January 2020. https://lop.parl.ca/sites/PublicWebsite/default/en_CA/ResearchPublications/201374E#a10

Cadei, Emily. 2015. "How corporate America propelled same-sex marriage". *Newsweek*, 30 June. Accessed 18 December 2019. https://www.newsweek.com/2015/07/10/shift-corporate-america-social-issues-become-good-business-348458.html

Cameron, David. 2011. "David Cameron's Conservative Party conference speech in full". *The Guardian*, 5 October. Accessed 13 February 2012. www.guardian.co.uk/politics/2011/oct/05/david-cameronconservative-party-speech

Cantamutto, Francisco J. 2016. "Kirchnerism in Argentina: A populist dispute for hegemony". *International Critical Thought* 6 (2): 227–244.

Cantamutto, Francisco J. 2017. "Fases del kirchnerismo: de la ruptura a la afirmación particularista". *Convergencia: Revista de Ciencias Sociales* 74: 63–89.

Carlson, Marifran. 1988. *¡Feminismo!: The Woman's Movement in Argentina from its Beginnings to Eva Perón*. Chicago: Academy Chicago Press.

Carmingnani, Fabrizio. 2017. "This is what economics tells us about gay marriage". *World Economic Forum/The Conversation*, 5 October. Accessed 27 December 2019. https://www.weforum.org/agenda/2017/10/this-is-what-economics-tells-us-about-gay-marriage/

Carpenter, Christopher. 2008. "Sexual orientation, income, and non-pecuniary economic outcomes: New evidence from young lesbians in Australia". *Review of Economics of the Household* 6 (4): 391–408. doi:10.1007/s11150-008-9034-5.

CEANA (Comisión para el Esclarecimiento de las Actividades del Nazismo en la Argentina). 1998a. *Primer informe de avance*. Buenos Aires: CEANA.

CEANA. 1998b. *Segundo informe de avance*. Buenos Aires: CEANA.

Carville, Olivia. 2019. "IBM fired as many as 100,000 in recent years, lawsuit shows". *Bloomberg*, 1 August. Accessed 24 December 2019. https://www.bloomberg.com/news/articles/2019-07-31/ibm-fired-as-many-as-100-000-in-recent-years-court-case-shows

Cattero, Bruno and Marta D'Onofrio. 2018. "Organizing and Collective Bargaining in the Digitized 'Tertiary Factories' of Amazon: A Comparison between Germany and Italy". In *Working in Digital and Smart Organizations: Legal, Economic and Organizational Perspectives on the Digitalization of Labour Relations*, edited by Edoardo Aleset *al.*, 141–164. Cham: Palgrave Macmillan.

Centraal Bureau voor de Statistiek. 2016. "Lesbian couples likelier to break up than male couples". The Hague: CBS. Accessed 4 January 2020. https://www.cbs.nl/en-gb/news/2016/13/lesbian-couples-likelier-to-break-up-than-male-couples

Centraal Bureau voor de Statistiek. 2019. "Gay male couples have the highest incomes". The Hague: CBS. Accessed 18 December 2019. https://www.cbs.nl/en-gb/news/2019/41/gay-male-couples-have-the-highest-incomes

Chambers, Clare. 2017. *Against Marriage: An Egalitarian Defense of the Marriage-Free State*. Oxford and New York: Oxford University Press.

Charlesworth, Lorie. 2010. *Welfare's Forgotten Past: A Socio-Legal History of the Poor Law*. Abingdon and New York: Routledge.

Chasin, Alexandra. 2000. *Selling Out: The Gay and Lesbian Movement Goes to Market*. New York: Palgrave.

Chauvin, Kelsey. 2018. "The best same-sex wedding destinations around the world". *Fodor's Travel*, 8 February. Accessed 28 May 2019. https://www.fodors.com/news/photos/best-same-sex-wedding-destinations-around-the-world

Chemin, Anne. 2007. "L'Annulation du mariage gay de Bègles confirmée en cassation". *Le Monde*, 14March. Accessed 8 December. 2019. https://www.lemonde.fr/societe/article/2007/03/14/l-annulation-du-mariage-gay-de-begles-confirmee-en-cassation_882918_3224.html

Chetcuti, Natacha. 2010. *Se dire lesbienne. Vie de couple, sexualité, repreésentation de soi*. Paris: Payot.

Chisholm, Dianne. 2004. *Queer Constellations: Subcultural Space in the Wake of the City*. Minneapolis:University of Minnesota Press.

Cho, Sumi. 2009. "Post-racialism". *Iowa Law Review* 94: 1589–1649.

Choi, Soon Kyu and Ilan H. Meyer. 2016. *LGBT Aging: A Review of Research Findings, Needs, and Policy Implications*. Los Angeles: The Williams Institute, UCLA.

Christie, Jane L. 2015. *Negotiating Gendered Discourses: Michelle Bachelet and Cristina Fernández de Kirchner*. Lanham, MD: Lexington Books.

Chung, Heejung and Tanja van der Lippe. 2018. "Flexible working, work–life balance, and gender equality: Introduction". *Social Indicators Research*. doi:10.1007/s11205-018-2025-x

Cirmi Obon, Lucia. 2017. "Who flies the kite? Argentinean parental leave design: Care penalties for the included and the excluded families". Research Paper, Master of Arts in Development Studies, International Institute of Social Studies, The Hague.

Clark, Andrew. 2017. "Behind the 'yes' business campaign". *Australian Financial Review*, 16 November, 56.

Clarke, Adele E. and Donna Jeanne Haraway (eds). 2018. *Making Kin not Population*. Chicago: Prickly Paradigm Press.

Clavel, Geoffroy. 2013. "Mariage gay: Apple et les entreprises 'gay-friendly' dans le collimateur du Printemps français". *Huffington Post France*, 16 May. Accessed 24 December 2019. https://www.huffingtonpost.fr/2013/05/16/mariage-gay-apple-entreprises-gay-friendly-collimateur-printemps-francais_n_3284643.html

Claxton, Garyet al. 2019. *Employer Health Benefits 2019: Annual Survey*. San Francisco: Kaiser Family Foundation.

CLIA (Cruise Lines Industry Association). 2020. *2020 State of the Cruise Industry Outlook*. Washington: CLIA.

CMI (Community Marketing & Insights), Gay Wedding Institute, Gay Weddings and WeddingWire. 2016. "2016 survey of contemporary couples & current wedding trends". Accessed 5 December 2019. http://publications.weddingwire.com/i/687417-2016-contemporary-couples-current-wedding-trends-report/21?m4=

Cockburn, Paige. 2017. "Same-sex marriage: Qantas CEO Alan Joyce urges 'good businesses' to support 'yes' vote". *ABC News*, 25 August. Accessed 21 December 2019. https://www.abc.net.au/news/2017-08-25/alan-joyce-calls-for-businesses-to-support-same-sex-marriage/8842332

Cohen, Cathy J. 1997. "Punks, buldaggers and welfare queens: The radical potential of queer politics?" *GLQ* 3: 437–465.

Cohn, D'Vera. 2010. "Census history: Counting Hispanics". Pew Research Center, 3 March. Accessed 2 January 2020. https://www.pewsocialtrends.org/2010/03/03/census-history-counting-hispanics-2/

Colen, Shellee. 1995. "Like a Mother to Them: Stratified Reproduction and West Indian Childcare Workers and Employers in New York". In *Conceiving the New World Order: The Global Politics of Reproduction*, edited by Faye D. Ginsburg and Rayna Rapp, 78–102. Berkeley: University of California Press.

Comité Consultatif national d'éthique. 2018. *Bio-éthique: états généraux. Rapport de synthèse*. Les Ulis: EDP Sciences.

Connell, John and Barbara Rugendyke (eds). 2008. *Tourism at the Grassroots Villagers and visitors in the Asia-Pacific*. London and New York: Routledge.

Considine, Mark. 2015. *Getting Welfare to Work: Street-Level Governance in Australia, the UK, and the Netherlands*. Oxford: Oxford University Press.

Coon, David R. 2012. "Sun, sand, and citizenship: The marketing of gay tourism". *Journal of Homosexuality*, 59 (4) 511–534. doi:10.1080/00918369.2012.648883

Cordier, Solène. 2020. "Bioéthique: la PMA pour toutes adoptée en commission au Sénat". *Le Monde*, 9 January. Accessed 15 June 2020. https://www.lemonde.fr/societe/article/2020/01/09/bioethique-la-pma-pour-toutes-adoptee-en-commission-au-senat_6025288_3224.html

Cortina, Clara and Patrick Festy. 2014. "Identification of same-sex couples and families in censuses, registers and surveys". Families and Societies Working Paper Series 8. Brussels: European Union.

Cory, Connor. 2015. "Access and exploitation: Can gay men and feminists agree on surrogacy policy?" *Georgetown Journal on Poverty Law and Policy* 23 (1): 133–160.

Costa, Carlos, Fiona Eva Bakas, Zélia Breda, Marília Durão, Inês Carvalho and Sandra Caçador. 2017. "Gender, flexibility and the 'ideal tourism worker'". *Annals of Tourism Research* 64: 64–75.

Craig, Paul P. and Gráinne De Búrca. 2015. *EU Law: Text, Cases, and Materials*. Oxford and New York: Oxford University Press (6th edition).

Craze, Kirsten. 2012. "The seven tribes of Sydney". *The Daily Telegraph*, 11 July. Accessed 22 December 2019. https://www.dailytelegraph.com.au/news/opinion/the-seven-tribes-of-Sydney/news-story/4c5eeb12def11a4e40b160d03859125f?sv=4d672c10f24d5d5b0054edc384eaab79

Crenshaw, Kimberlé. 1989. "Demarginalizing the intersection of race and sex: A black feminist critique of antidiscrimination doctrine, feminist theory, and antiracist politics". *University of Chicago Legal Forum* 139–167.

Crenshaw, Kimberlé. 1991. "Mapping the margins: Intersectionality, identity politics and violence against women of color". *Stanford Law Review* 43: 1241–1299.

Crenshaw, Kimberlé. 2016. Keynote address at the Women of the World festival, Southbank Centre, London, 8–13 March. Accessed 13 October 2017. https://world.secret-paths.com/533/its-important-kimberly-crenshaw-on-intersectionality/

Cunningham-Parmeter, Keith. 2016. "From Amazon to Uber: Defining employment in the modern economy". *Boston University Law Review* 96: 1673–1728.

Currier, Ashley and Julie Moreau. 2018. "Understanding Same-Sex Marriage Debates in Malawi and South Africa". In *Global Perspectives on Same-Sex Marriage: A Neo-Institutional Approach*, edited by Bronwyn Winter, Maxime Forest and Réjane Sénac, 81–104. Basingstoke and New York: Palgrave.

Davidson-Schmich, Louise K. 2017. "LGBT politics in Germany: Unification as a catalyst for change". *German Politics* 26 (4): 534–555. doi:10.1080/09644008.2017.1370705

Davies, Caroline. 2015. "Wedding industry gives same-sex marriages a mixed reception". *The Guardian*, 21 October. Accessed 13 July 2018. https://www.theguardian.com/world/2015/oct/20/uk-same-sex-marriages-15000-lucrative-market

Davies, Ron. 2013. *Promoting Fertility in the EU: Social Policy Options for Member States*. Brussels: Library of the European Parliament.

Davis, Kathy. 2008. "Intersectionality as buzzword: A sociology of science perspective on what makes a feminist theory successful". *Feminist Theory* 9 (1): 67–85. doi:10.1177/1464700108086364

Davis, Kierrynn and Nel Glass. 2011. "Reframing the Heteronormative Constructions of Lesbian Partner Violence: An Australian Case Study". In *Intimate Partner Violence in LGBTQ Lives*, edited by Janice L. Ristock, 13–36. New York: Routledge.

Davis, Lewis S. and Claudia R. Williamson. 2019. "Does individualism promote gender equality?" *World Development* 123: 104627–104642. doi:10.1016/j.worlddev.2019.104627

Dawson, Mark, Bruno De Witte and Elise Muir (eds). 2013. *Judicial Activism at the European Court of Justice*. Cheltenham: Edward Elgar.

Declaration of Montreal. 2006. Accessed 18 November 2019. www.declarationofmontreal.org/

DeFilippis, Joseph Nicholas. 2016. "'What about the rest of us?' An overview of LGBT poverty issues and a call to action". *Journal of Progressive Human Services* 27 (3): 143–174. doi:10.1080/10428232.2016.1198673

DeFilippis, Joseph Nicholas, Ben Anderson-Nathe and Meg Panichelli. 2015. "Notes on same-sex marriage: Concerns for feminist social workers". *Affilia: Journal of Women and Social Work* 30 (4): 461–475.

Deloitte/AHRC (Australian Human Rights Commission). 2017. *Missing out: The Business Case for Customer Diversity*. Sydney: Deloitte.

Del Río, Coral and Olga Alonso-Villar. 2019a. "Occupational achievements of same-sex couples in the United States by gender and race". *Industrial Relations* 58 (4): 704–731. doi:10.1111/irel.12246

Del Río, Coral and Olga Alonso-Villar. 2019b. "Occupational segregation by sexual orientation in the U.S.: Exploring its economic effects on same-sex couples". *Review of Economics of the Household* 17 (2): 439–467. doi:10.1007/s11150-018-9421-5.

Delphy, Christine. 1998a. "L'Ennemi principal". In *L'Ennemi principal 1: Economie politique du patriarcat*, edited by Christine Delphy, 31–56. Paris: Syllepse.

Delphy, Christine. 1998b. "Travail ménager ou travail domestique?". In *L'Ennemi principal 1: Economie politique du patriarcat*, edited by Christine Delphy, 57–73. Paris: Syllepse.

Delphy, Christine and Diana Leonard. 1992. *Familiar Exploitation: A New Analysis of Marriage in Contemporary Western Societies*. Cambridge: Polity Press.

Dempsey, Deborah. 2013. "Surrogacy, gay male couples and the significance of biogenetic paternity". *New Genetics and Society* 32 (1): 37–53. doi:10.1080/14636778.2012.735859

Deomampo, Daisy. 2013. "Gendered geographies of reproductive tourism". *Gender and Society* 27 (4): 514–537. doi:10.1177/0891243213486832

Deonandan, Raywat. 2015. "Recent trends in reproductive tourism and international surrogacy: Ethical considerations and challenges for policy". *Risk Management and Healthcare Policy* 8: 111–119. doi:10.2147/RMHP.S63862

Deringil, Selim. 2007. "The Turks and 'Europe': The argument from history". *Middle Eastern Studies* 43 (5): 709–723. doi:10.1080/00263200701422600

De Ruyter, Alex and Martyn Brown. 2019. *The Gig Economy*. Newcastle-Upon-Tyne: Agenda Publishing.

De la Torre, Vanessa. 2016. "City of Hartford withdraws suit in 'Scarborough 11' case". *Hartford Courant*, 27 October. Accessed 26 January 2020. https://www.courant.com/community/hartford/hc-hartford-scarborough11-withdrawal-1028-20161027-story.html

De Vos, Pierre. 2007. "The 'inevitability' of same-sex marriage in South Africa's post-apartheid state". *South African Journal on Human Rights* 23 (3): 432–465, doi:10.1080/19962126.2007.11864931

Diegues, Antonio Carlos. 2001. "Regional and Domestic Mass Tourism in Brazil: An Overview". In *The Native Tourist: Mass Tourism within Developing Countries*, edited by Krishna B. Ghimire, 55–85. London and New York: Earthscan.

Dominelli, Lena. 2014. "The Age of Austerity in Welfare Services: Impact upon Social Work and Marginalized People". In *Participation, Marginalization and Welfare Services: Concepts, Politics and Practices across European Countries*, edited by Aila-Lena Matthies and Lars Uggerhøj, 79–93. Farnham: Ashgate.

Donovan, Catherine. 2004. "Why reach for the moon? Because the stars aren't enough". *Feminism & Psychology* 14 (1): 24–29. doi:10.1177/0959353504040298

Dose, Ralf. 2014. *Magnus Hirschfeld: The Origins of the Gay Liberation Movement*, translated by Edward H. Willis. New York: New York University Press.

Duff, Angus. 2017. "Corporate social responsibility as a legitimacy maintenance strategy in the professional accountancy firm". *The British Accounting Review* 49: 513–531.

Duff, Brian. 2010. *Parent as Citizen: A Democratic Dilemma*. Minneapolis: University of Minnesota Press.

Duffy, Nick. 2017. "Couple accidentally become first to marry in Faroe Islands". *Pink News*, 8 September. Accessed 4 December 2019. https://www.pinknews.co.uk/2017/09/08/couple-accidentally-become-first-to-marry-in-faroe-islands/

Duggan, Lisa. 2002. "The New Homonormativity: The Sexual Politics of Neoliberalism". In *Materializing Democracy: Toward a Revitalized Cultural Politics*, ed. Russ Castronovo and Dana D. Nelson, 175–194. Durham, NC: Duke University Press.

Dulitzky, Ariel E. 2019. "An Inter-American Constitutional Court? The invention of the conventionality control by the Inter-American Court of Human Rights". *Texas International Law Journal* 50 (1): 45–93.

Du Toit, Louise. 2005. "A Phenomenology of Rape: Forging a New Vocabulary for Action". In *(Un)thinking Citizenship: Feminist Debates in Contemporary South Africa*, 253–274. London and New York: Routledge.

Du Toit, Louise. 2014. "Shifting meanings of postconflict sexual violence in South Africa". *Signs: Journal of Women in Culture and Society* 40 (1): 101–123.

Duxbury, Alison and Hsien-Li Tan. 2019. *Can ASEAN Take Human Rights Seriously?*. Cambridge: Cambridge University Press.

Duyvendak, Jan Willem. 2016. "The Pitfalls of Normalization: The Dutch Case and the Future of Equality". In *After Marriage Equality: The Future of LGBT Rights*, edited by Carlos A. Ball, 288–305. New York: New York University Press.

Eastman, Maggie and Jane Ridley. 2015. "'Donating my eggs gave me cancer': After receiving a terminal diagnosis, Maggie Eastman wants to warn other women of the risks of surrogacy". *New York Post*, 3 December, 40.

ECJ (European Court of Justice). 2018. *Judgment of the Court (Grand Chamber) of 5 June 2018. Relu Adrian Coman and Others v Inspectoratul General pentru Imigrări and Ministerul Afacerilor Interne. Case C-673/16*. Accessed 18 November 2019. http://curia.europa.eu/juris/celex.jsf?celex=62016CJ0673&lang1=en&type=TXT&ancre=

ECtHR (European Court of Human Rights). 2012. *Affaire Gas et Dubois c. France. (Requête N° 25951/07). Arrêt. 15 mars 2012*. Accessed 16 May 2020. https://hudoc.echr.coe.int/eng#{%22itemid%22:[%22001-109571%22]}

ECtHR. 2013. *Case of X and others v. Austria (Application no. 19010/07). Judgment. 19 February 2013*. Accessed 16 May 2020. https://hudoc.echr.coe.int/fre#{%22itemid%22:[%22001-116735%22]}

ECtHR. 2016. *Affaire Chapin et Charpentier c. France (Requête n° 40183/07). Arrêt définitif. 9 juin 2016*. Accessed 18 November 2019. https://hudoc.echr.coe.int/eng#{%22itemid%22:[%22001-163436%22]}

Edelman, Lee. 2004. *No Future: Queer Theory and the Death Drive*. Durham, NC: Duke University Press.

Edin, Kathryn and Laura Lein. 1997. *Making Ends Meet: How Single Mothers Survive Welfare and Low-Wage Work*. New York: Russell Sage Foundation.

Ekman, Kajsa. 2013. *Being and Being Bought: Prostitution, Surrogacy and the Split Self*, translated by Suzanne Martin Cheadle. Melbourne: Spinifex Press.

Eliassi, Barzoo. 2015. "Constructing cultural otherness within the Swedish welfare state: The cases of social workers in Sweden". *Qualitative Social Work* 14 (4): 554–571. doi:10.1177/1473325014559091

Ellison, Christopher G., Gabriel A. Acevedo and Aida I. Ramos-Wada. 2011. "Religion and attitudes toward same-sex marriage among U.S. Latinos". *Social Science Quarterly* 92 (1): 35–56.

Elliston, Deborah. 2014. "Queer History and Its Discontents at Tahiti: The Contested Politics of Modernity and Sexual Subjectivity". In *Gender on the Edge: Transgender, Gay, and Other Pacific Islanders*, edited by Niko Besnier and Kalissa Alexeyeff, 33–55. Honolulu: University of Hawai'i Press.

Encarción, Omar G. 2016. *Out in the Periphery: Latin America's Gay Rights Revolution*. Oxford and New York: Oxford Scholarship online. doi:10.1093/acprof:oso/9780199356645.001.0001

Enloe, Cynthia. 1990. *Bananas, Beaches and Bases: Making Feminist Sense of International Politics*. Berkeley, CA: University of California Press.

Enloe, Cynthia. 2000. *Maneuvers: The International Politics of Militarizing Women's Lives*. Berkeley, CA: University of California Press.

Epstein, Robert P. and Jeffrey Friedman. 2000. *Paragraph 175*. Montreal: Films Transit.

Eriksen, Tine Rask. 2018. *Dilemmas of Care in the Nordic Welfare State: Continuity and Change*. London: Routledge.

Erlangsen, Annetteet al. 2020. "Suicide among persons who entered same-sex and opposite-sex marriage in Denmark and Sweden, 1989–2016: A binational, register-based cohort study". *Journal of Epidemiology and Community Health* 74: 78–83.

Escudé, Carlos. 2007. *Kirchner y la Cooptación de Piqueteros 2003–2007*. Buenos Aires: Universidad del CEMA, Serie Documentos de Trabajo Nro. 359.

ESHRE (European Society of Human Reproduction and Embryology) Task Force on Ethics and Law. 2005. "ESHRE task force on ethics and law 10: Surrogacy". *Human Reproduction* 20 (10): 2705–2707.

Esping-Andersen, Gøsta. 1990. *The Three Worlds of Welfare Capitalism*. Princeton, NJ: Princeton University Press.

Esping-Andersen, Gøsta. 1999. *Social Foundations of Post-Industrial Economies*. Oxford: Oxford University Press.

Esping-Andersen, Gøsta. 2009. *The Incomplete Revolution: Adapting to Women's New Roles*. Cambridge: Polity.

Espinosa, Shirlita Africa. 2017. *Sexualised Citizenship: A Cultural History of Philippine-s-Australian Migration*. Singapore: Palgrave Macmillan.

Estatísticas Socials. 2019. "Registro Civil 2018: casamentos entre pessoas do mesmo sexo aumentam 61,7% em um ano". Rio de Janeiro: Instituto Brasileiro de Geografia e Estatística. Accessed 18 December 2019. https://agenciadenoticias.ibge.gov.br/agencia-sala-de-imprensa/2013-agencia-de-noticias/releases/26195-registro-civil-2018-casamentos-entre-pessoas-do-mesmo-sexo-aumentam-61-7-em-um-ano

Estévez-Abe, M. 2009. "Gender, inequality, and capitalism: The 'varieties of capitalism' and women". *Social Politics* 16 (2): 182–191.

EU (European Union). 2000. *Council Directive 2000/43/EC of 29 June 2000 implementing the principle of equal treatment between persons irrespective of racial or ethnic origin* (The Racial Equality Directive). Accessed 2 January 2020. https://eur-lex.europa.eu/legal-content/EN/TXT/?uri=CELEX%3A32000L0043

EU. 2019a. *Directive (EU) 2019/1158 of the European Parliament and of the Council of 20 June 2019 on work-life balance for parents and carers and repealing Council Directive 2010/18/EU: PE/20/2019/REV/1*. Accessed 12 January 2020. https://eur-lex.europa.eu/legal-content/EN/TXT/?qid=1578804588216&uri=CELEX:32019L1158

EU. 2019b. "Work-life balance for all: Best practice examples from EU Member States". Luxembourg: EU.

Eurostat. 2019. "Marriage and divorce statistics". Accessed 19 June 2020. https://ec.europa.eu/eurostat/statistics-explained/index.php/Marriage_and_divorce_statistics#Fewer_marriages.2C_more_divorces

Evans, David T. 1993. *Sexual Citizenship: The Material Construction of Sexualities*. New York: Routledge.

Evans, Jennifer V. 2010. "Decriminalization, seduction and 'unnatural desire' in East Germany". *Feminist Studies* 36 (3): 553–577.

Evans, R.J.W. 2008. *Austria, Hungary, and the Habsburgs: Central Europe c. 1683–1867*. Oxford: Oxford University Press. doi:10.1093/acprof:oso/9780199541621.003.0003

EY (Ernst & Young). 2019. "*Work-Life-Balance / Arbeitsbelastung*". Vienna: EY Austria.

Fairfield, Tasha. 2011. "Business power and protest: Argentina's agricultural producers protest in comparative context". *Studies in Comparative International Development* 46: 424–453.

Falleti, Tulia G. and Emilio A. Parrado. 2017. *Latin America since the Left Turn*. Philadelphia: University of Pennsylvania Press.

Family Court of Western Australia. 2016. *Farnell & Anor and Chanbua [2016] FCWA 17*. Accessed 26 April 2019. assets.documentcloud.org/documents/2802498/Family-Court-of-WA-Judgment-Farnell-amp-Anor-and.pdf.

Fantus, Sophia and Peter A. Newman. 2019. "Motivations to pursue surrogacy for gay fathers in Canada: A qualitative investigation". *Journal of GLBT Family Studies*. doi:10.1080/1550428X.2018.1546156

Farkas, Lilla. 2017. "The meaning of racial or ethnic origin in EU law: Between stereotypes and identities". European Commission Directorate-General for Justice and Consumers. Luxembourg: European Union. doi:10.2838/83148

Federal Republic of Germany. 1949. *Basic Law* (Constitution). Accessed 13 October 2019. https://www.bundesregierung.de/breg-en/chancellor/basic-law-470510

Féliz, Mariano. 2016. "Till Death Do Us Part? Kirchnerism, Neodevelopmentalism and the Struggle for Hegemony in Argentina". In *The Three Worlds of Social Democracy: A Global View*, edited by Ingo Schmidt, 91–106. London: Pluto Press.

Fellowes, Melanie G. 2017. "Commercial surrogacy in India: The presumption of adaptive preference formation, the possibility of autonomy and the persistence of exploitation". *Medical Law International* 17 (4): 249–272.

Fernández de Kirchner, Cristina. 2010a. "Televised statement in support of Marriage Equality Bill", 12 July. Accessed 7 December 2016. https://www.youtube.com/watch?v=ixVrmrQg9AM

Fernández de Kirchner, Cristina. 2010b. "Discurso en el acto de promulgación de la ley de Matrimonio Igualitario". 21 July 2010. Accessed 15 October 2019. Video: https://www.youtube.com/watch?v=rxlatNJni4s. Text: https://es.wikisource.org/wiki/Discurso_de_Cristina_Fern%C3%A1ndez_en_el_acto_de_promulgaci%C3%B3n_de_la_ley_de_Matrimonio_Igualitario

Ferree, Myra Marx. 1994. "'The time of chaos was the best': Feminist mobilization and demobilization in East Germany". *Gender and Society* 8 (4): 597–623.

Fetner, Tinaand MelanieHeath. 2016. "Do same-sex and straight weddings aspire to the fairytale? Women's conformity and resistance to traditional weddings". *Sociological Perspectives* 59(4):721–742. doi:10.1177/0731121415601269

Filgueira, Fernando. 1998. "El nuevo modelo de prestaciones sociales en America Latina; residualismo y ciudadania estratificada". In *Citidadanta y politica social*, edited by Brian Roberts. San Jose: FLACSO/SSRC, 71–116.

Fleury, Sonia. 2017. "The welfare state in Latin America: Reform, innovation and fatigue". *Cadernos de Saúde Pública/Reports in Public Health*. doi:10.1590/0102-311X00058116

Flores, Gabrielaet al. 2017. *Tracking Universal Health Coverage: 2017 Global Monitoring Report*. Geneva: World Health Organization and World Bank.

FMLA (Family and Medical Leave Act). 1993. Washington: US Department of Labor. Accessed 12 January 2020. https://www.dol.gov/agencies/whd/laws-and-regulations/laws/fmla

Folbre, Nancy. 1994. *Who Pays for the Kids? Gender and the Structures of Constraint.* New York: Routledge.

Folbre, Nancy. 2001. *The Invisible Heart: Economics and Family Values.* New York: The New Press.

Folbre, Nancy and Michael Bittman (eds). 2004. *Family Time: The Social Organization of Care.* London and New York: Routledge.

Forest, Maxime. 2018. "Europeanizing vs. Nationalizing the issue of Same-Sex Marriage in Central Europe: A Comparative Analysis of Framing Processes in Croatia, Hungary, Slovakia and Slovenia". In *Global Perspectives on Same-Sex Marriage: A Neo-Institutional Approach*, edited by Bronwyn Winter, Maxime Forest and Réjane Sénac, 127–148. New York: Palgrave Macmillan.

Foucault, Michel. 1976. *Histoire de la Sexualité I: La volonté de savoir.* Paris: Gallimard.

Fourie and Another v. Minister of Home Affairs and Another. 2005. *Constitutional Court of the Republic of South Africa, CCT 60/04.*

FRA (European Agency for Fundamental Rights). 2014. *EU LGBT Survey: European Union Lesbian, Gay, Bisexual and Transgender Survey: Main Results.* Vienna: FRA.

FRA. 2020. *EU-LGBTI II: A Long Way to Go for LGBTI Equality.* Vienna: FRA.

Fraser, Derek. 2019. "The English Poor Law and the Origins of the British Welfare State". In *The Emergence of the Welfare State in Britain and Germany 1850–1950*, edited by W.J. Mommsen, 9–31. London and New York: Routledge (2nd edition).

Fraser, Giles. 2014. "A baby must never become a 'faulty product' if surrogacy doesn't go to plan". *The Guardian*, 5 September. Accessed 26 April 2019. https://www.theguardian.com/commentisfree/belief/2014/sep/05/baby-must-not-become-faulty-product-when-surrogacy-doesnt-go-plan

Freedland, Jonathan. 2005. "Something for everyone". *The Guardian*, 23 April. Accessed 6 January 2020. https://www.theguardian.com/politics/2005/apr/23/election2005.politicalcolumnists1

French, Steve. 2018. "Between globalisation and Brexit: Migration, pay and the road to modern slavery in the UK hospitality industry". *Research in Hospitality Management* 8 (1)*: 23–32.* doi:10.1080/22243534.2018.1501185".

Fridman, Viviana. 2010. "Les Transformations de l'icône d'Eva Perón dans l'imaginaire politique argentin". *Canadian Journal of Latin American and Caribbean Studies / Revue canadienne desétudes latino-américaines et caraïbes* 35 (70): 197–219.

Friedman, Elisabeth Jay. 2019. *Seeking Rights from the Left: Gender, Sexuality, and the Latin American Pink Tide.* Durham, NC: Duke University Press.

Fulli-Lemaire, Samuel. 2017. "Legal Recognition of Same-Sex Relationships in Central Europe: Steady Progress". In *Same-Sex Relationships and Beyond: Gender Matters in the EU*, edited by Katharina Boele-Woelki and Angelika Fuchs, 19–38. Cambridge: Cambridge University Press.

Gabbaccia, Donna and Katharine Donato. 2016. *Gender and Migration: From the Slavery Era to the Global Age.* New York: Russell Sage Foundation.

Galerand, Elsa and Danièle Kergoat. 2013. "Le Travail comme enjeu des rapports sociaux (de sexe)". In *Travail et genre dans le monde: l'état des savoirs*, edited by Margaret Maruani, 44–51. Paris: La Découverte.

Galerand, Elsa and Martin Gallié. 2018. "Travail non libre et rapports sociaux de sexe – À propos des programmes canadiens d'immigration temporaire". *Canadian Journal of Law and Society / Revue Canadienne Droit et Société* 33 (2): 223–241. doi:10.1017/cls.2018.20

Galerand, Elsa, Martin Gallié and Jeanne Ollivier-Gobeil, with PINAY: Filipino Women's Organization in Quebec/Organisation des femmes Philippines du Québec. 2015. "Travail domestique et exploitation: le cas des travailleuses domestiques philippines au Canada (PAFR)". Rapport de Recherche SAC-PINAY. Montréal: Université du Québec à Montréal. Accessed 1 February 2020. www.mcgill.ca/lldrl/labourlaw-and-developm ent-researchlaboratory

Gálvez-Muñoz, Lina, Paula Rodríguez-Modroño and Mónica Domínguez-Serrano. 2011. "Work and time use by gender: A new clustering of European welfare systems". *Feminist Economics* 17 (4): 125–157. doi:10.1080/13545701.2011.620975

Garcia-Blanco, Iñaki and Karin Wahl-Jorgensen. 2012. "The discursive construction of women politicians in the European press". *Feminist Media Studies* 12 (3): 422–441. doi:10.1080/14680777.2011.615636

García-Sayán, Diego. 2011. "The Inter-American Court and constitutionalism in Latin America". *Texas Law Review* 89 (7): 1835–1862.

Garrison, Cassandra. 2019. "Comeback queen: Argentina's fiery 'Cristina' stages remarkable return as VP". *Reuters*, 28 October.

Geidner, Chris. 2015. "Internal report: Major diversity, organizational problems at human rights campaign". *Buzzfeed News*, 3 June. Accessed 24 December 2019. https://www.buzzfeednews.com/article/chrisgeidner/internal-report-major-diversity-organizational-problems-at-h#.cbAygzDnY

Gerber, Paula. 2012. "ASEAN human rights declaration: A step forward or a slide backwards?". *The Conversation*, 21 November. Accessed 18 November. 2019. http://theconversation.com/asean-human-rights-declaration-a-step-forward-or-a-slide-backwards-10895

Gerdes, Stefanie. 2016. "700 German churches vote to marry same-sex couples." *Gaystarnews*, 15 January. Accessed13 November 2019. https://www.gaystarnews.com/article/700/

Gezmiş, Hilal. 2018. "From neoliberalism to neo-developmentalism? The political economy of post-crisis Argentina (2002–2015)". *New Political Economy* 23 (1): 66–87.

Ghavami, Negin and Kerri L. Johnson. 2011. "Comparing sexual and ethnic minority perspectives on same-sex marriage". *Journal of Social Issues* 67 (2): 394–412.

Giddens, Anthony. 1998. *The Third Way: The Renewal of Social Democracy*. Cambridge: Polity.

Giddens, Anthony. 2001 (ed.). *The Global Third Way Debate*. Cambridge: Polity.

Giddings, Lisa. 1998. "Political economy and the construction of gender: The example of housework within same-sex households". *Feminist Economics* 4 (2): 97–106.

Gill, Stephen and A. Claire Cutler. 2014. *New Constitutionalism and World Order*. Cambridge: Cambridge University Press.

Gillard, Julia. 2011. "Speech to the Inaugural Whitlam Institute Gough Whitlam Oration, Sydney". Accessed 11 January 2020. https://pmtranscripts.pmc.gov.au/release/transcrip t-17771

Glenn, Clinton. 2017. "In homonational times: Nationalist mythology and LGBT inclusivity/Au temps de l'homonationalisme: Mythologie nationale et inclusivité LGBT". *Esse: Arts + Opinions* 91: 8–15.

Glenn, Evelyn Nakano. 2002. *Unequal Freedom: How Race and Gender Shaped American Citizenship and Labor*. Cambridge, MA: Harvard University Press.

Godin, Romaric. 2019. *La Guerre sociale en France. Aux sources économiques de la démocratie autoritaire*. Paris: La Découverte.

Gondouin, Johanna. 2018. "Reproducing heteronormativity: Gay Parenthood and Transnational Surrogacy in Sweden". In *Transnationalising Reproduction: Third Party Conception in a Globalised World*, edited by Róisín Ryan-Flood and Jenny Gunnarsson Payne, 107–121. London: Routledge.

Gordon-Murray, A. 2017. "SSM: New Zealand's experience shows how Yes vote could boost our economy". *The Conversation*, 20 November. https://www.abc.net.au/news/2017-11-21/same-sex-marriage-nz-economic-boost-and-australia/9171498

Goulds, Sharon, with Amy Ashlee, Isobel Fergus, Jacqui Gallinetti and Sophie Tanner. 2019. *Rewrite Her Story: The State of the World's Girls 2019*. Woking, UK, and Los Angeles, CA: Plan International and Geena Davis Institute on Gender and Media.

Grau, Günter. 1999. "Return of the past". *Journal of Homosexuality* 37 (4): 1–21, doi:10.1300/J082v37n04_02

Gray, Joanne. 2016. "Outstanding 50 LGBTI executives: Cover story". *The Australian Financial Review*, 2 December, 14. Accessed 23 December 2019. http://ezproxy.library.usyd.edu.au/login?url=https://search-proquest-com.ezproxy1.library.usyd.edu.au/docview/1844857663?accountid=14757

Gross, Michael Joseph. 2008. "Gay is the new black?". *The Advocate*, 16 November. Accessed 20 December 2019. https://www.advocate.com/news/2008/11/16/gay-new-black#article-content

Guaracino, Jeff. 2007. *Gay and Lesbian Tourism: The Essential Guide for Marketing*. Oxford and Burlington, MA: Butterworth Heinemann.

Guigou, Elisabeth. 1999. "Déclaration de Mme Elisabeth Guigou, ministre de la justice, sur la proposition de loi relative au Pacs, le droit de la famille et le mariage, notamment les modifications techniques apportées par l'Assemblée nationale en seconde lecture, Paris le 30 mars 1999". Paris: Assemblée Nationale. Accessed 20 October 2019. http://discours.vie-publique.fr/notices/993000996.html

Guillaumin, Colette. 1986. "Le sexisme, pensée de 'la' droite? ou pensée de droite?". *Amazones d'Hier, Lesbiennes d'Aujourd'Hui* 5 (1): 38–41.

Guillaumin, Colette. 1992. "Pratique du pouvoir et idée de Nature". In *Sexe, Race et Pratique du pouvoir. L'Idée de Nature*, 14–82. Paris: côté-femmes.

Gupta, Jyotsna Agnihotri. 2018. "Reproductive Labour or Reproductive Trafficking? Indian Women's Reproductive Bodies in the Globalised Bioeconomy". In *Transnationalising Reproduction: Third Party Conception in a Globalised World*, edited by Róisín Ryan-Flood and Jenny Gunnarsson Payne, 85–106. London: Routledge.

Gutiérrez Rodríguez, Encarnación and Jurema Brites (eds). 2014. "Special issue on domestic work between regulation and intimacy". *Women's Studies International Forum* 46.

Guzmán, Víctor Humberto. 2016. "Una 'ley de medios' en los medios. La Ley de Servicios de Comunicación Audiovisual argentina en el espacio público mediatizado". *Estudios Sobre el Mensaje Periodistico* 22 (2): 1019–1037.

Hadler, Simon. 2017. "Europe's other? The Turks and shifting borders of memory". *European Review of History/Revue européenne d'histoire* 24 (4): 507–526. doi:10.1080/13507486.2017.1307814

Hals, Tom. 2019. "Royal Caribbean liability for volcano deaths may turn on 'act of God' defense". *Reuters*, 13 December. Accessed 16 December 2019. https://www.reuters.com/article/us-newzealand-volcano-lawsuits-analysis/royal-caribbean-liability-for-volcano-deaths-may-turn-on-act-of-god-defense-idUSKBN1YG2NX

Hamlyn, Charlotte. 2017. "Perth couple poised to become first in Australia to file for same-sex divorce". *ABC News*, 11 December. Accessed 4 January 2020. https://www.abc.net.au/news/2017-12-11/couple-to-become-first-in-australia-to-file-for-same-sex-divorce/9244828

Hancock, Ange Marie. 2004. *The Politics of Disgust: The Public Identity of the Welfare Queen*. New York: New York University Press.

Hänninen, Sakari, Kirsi-Marja Lehtelä and Paula Saikkonen (eds). 2019. *The Relational Nordic Welfare State: Between Utopia and Ideology*. Cheltenham: Edward Elgar.

Hara, Kotaro*et al.*2017. "A Data-driven analysis of workers' earnings on Amazon Mechanical Turk". Ithaca, NY:Cornell University. Accessed2 January 2020. http://arxiv.org/abs/1712.05796

Hardt, Michael and Antonio Negri. 2000. *Empire*. Cambridge, MA: Harvard University Press.

Hartal, Gilly and Orna Sasson-Levy. 2017. "Being [in] the center: Sexual citizenship and homonationalism at Tel Aviv's gay-center". *Sexualities* 20 (5–6): 738–761.

Haskins, Justin and Logan Pike. 2016. "Twenty years later, welfare reform remains wildly successful and oddly controversial". *Forbes*, 22 August. Accessed 8 January 2020. https://www.forbes.com/sites/realspin/2016/08/22/twenty-years-later-welfare-reform-remains-wildly-successful-and-oddly-controversial/#53d1ec4a7390

Hechler, Jeannette. 1991. "Global spotlight: Notes from an East German lesbian". *Gay Community News* 18 (32): 16.

Hegarty, Benjaminet al. 2018. "Heterosexuality and race in the Australian same-sex marriage postal survey". *Australian Feminist Studies* 33 (97): 400–416. doi:10.1080/08164649.2018.1536441

Hersher, Rebecca. 2017. "You probably don't want to know about Haiti's sewage problems". *NPR*, 29 July. Accessed 16 December 2019. https://www.npr.org/sections/goatsandsoda/2017/07/29/537945957/you-probably-dont-want-to-know-about-haitis-sewage-problems

Hider, James. 2015. "Gay couple trapped in surrogacy row". *The Times*, 26 February, 33.

Hie, Luiza. 2018. "Romanian constitutional ban on same sex marriage fails on low vote turnout". *Reuters*, 8 October. Accessed 16 May 2020. https://www.reuters.com/article/us-romania-referendum/romanian-constitutional-ban-on-same-sex-marriage-fails-on-low-vote-turnout-idUSKCN1MH0XI

Hildebrandt, Achim, Eva-Maria Trüdinger and Dominik Wyss. 2019. "The missing link? Modernization, tolerance, and legislation on homosexuality". *Political Research Quarterly* 72 (3): 539–553.

Hildebrandt, Eckart. 2006. "Balance between work and life – New corporate impositions through flexible working time or opportunity for time sovereignty?". *European Societies* 8 (2): 251–271. doi:10.1080/14616690600645001

Hillhouse, Raelynn J. 1990. "Out of the closet behind the wall: Sexual politics and social change in the GDR". *Slavic Review* 49 (4): 585–596.

Hirschfeld, Magnus. 1914. *Die Homosexualität des Mannes und des Weibes*. Forgotten Books. Accessed 3 December 2019. https://www.forgottenbooks.com/de/books/DieHomosexualitatdesMannesunddesWeibes_11044447

Hochschild, Arlie R. 2000. "Global Care Chains and Emotional Surplus Value". In *On the Edge: Living with Global Capitalism*, edited by Will Hutton and Anthony Giddens, 130–146. London: Jonathan Cape.

Hochschild, Arlie R. 2012. *The Managed Heart: Commercialization of Human Feeling*. Berkeley: University of California Press online.

Hochschild, Arlie R. and Barbara Ehrenreich (eds). 2002. *Global Woman: Nannies, Maids and Sex Workers in the New Economy*. New York: Metropolitan Press.

Hoffman, Mary F. and Renee L. Cowan. 2008. "The meaning of work/life: A corporate ideology of work/life balance". *Communication Quarterly* 56 (3): 227–246. doi:10.1080/01463370802251053

Holmes, Cindy. 2011. "Troubling Normalcy Examining 'Healthy Relationships' in Lesbian Domestic Violence Prevention". In *Intimate Partner Violence in LGBTQ Lives*, edited by Janice L. Ristock, 209–231. New York: Routledge.

hooks, bell. 1984. *Feminist Theory from Margin to Center.* Boston: South End Press.

Hopkins, Barbara E. 2013. "Gender and Provisioning under Different Capitalisms". In *Handbook of Research on Gender and Economic Life*, edited by Deborah M. Figart and Tonia L. Warnecke, 93–112. Northampton, MA: Edward Elgar.

Hossain, Mohammed, Muhammad Atif, Ammad Ahmed and Lokman Mia. 2019. "Do LGBT workplace diversity policies create value for firms?". *Journal of Business Ethics.* doi:10.1007/s10551-019-04158-z

HRC (Human Rights Campaign). 2018a. *Corporate Equality Index 2018.* Washington: HRC.

HRC. 2018b. *Top Law Firms for Equality 2018.* Washington: HRC.

HRC. 2020. *Corporate Equality Index 2020.* Washington: HRC.

HRW(Human Rights Watch) and IGLHRC (International Gay and Lesbian Human Rights Commission). 2003. *More than a Name: State-Sponsored Homophobia and Its Consequences in Southern Africa.* New York: Human Rights Watch.

Humpert, Stephan. 2016. "Somewhere over the rainbow: Sexual orientation and earnings in Germany". *International Journal of Manpower* 31 (1): 69–98. doi:10.1108/IJM-03-2014-0080.

Humphery-Jenner, Mark. 2016. "Why Australia legalising same-sex marriage makes good business sense". *The Conversation*, 17 May. Accessed 23 December 2019. https://theconversation.com/why-australia-legalising-same-sex-marriage-makes-good-business-sense-59462

Hunter, Nan D. 2012. "The future impact of same-sex marriage: More questions than answers". *Georgetown Law Journal* 100: 1855–1879.

Hutchinson, Darren Lenard. 2000. "Gay rights for gay whites: Race, sexual identity, and equal protection discourse". *Cornell Law Review* 85: 1358–1391.

IACtHR/CIDH (Inter American Court of Human Rights/Corte Interamericana de Derechos Humanos). 2017. *Opinión Consultiva Oc-24/17 de 24 de noviembre de 2017. Solicitada Por La República De Costa Rica. Identidad De Género, E Igualdad Y No Discriminación A Parejas Del Mismo Sexo.* San José, Costa Rica, IACtHR.

Ibrahim, Abadir M. 2015. "LGBT rights in Africa and the discursive role of international human rights law". *African Human Rights Law Journal* 15: 263–281. doi:10.17159/1996-2096/2015/v15n2a2

IFOP (Institut français d'opinion publique). 2013. "Les Français face à la PMA, la GPA et l'homoparentalité". Survey N° 111105. Paris: IFOP/Femme Actuelle.

IFOP. 2017. "Les Français et les questions liées à la bioéthique". Survey N° 115159. Paris: IFOP/La Croix/Forum européen de Bioéthique.

ILGA-Europe. 2019. *Annual Review of the Human Rights Situation of Lesbian, Gay, Bisexual, Trans and Intersex People.* Brussels: ILGA-Europe. Accessed 18 November 2019. https://www.ilga-europe.org/annualreview/2019

ILO (International Labour Organization). 2011. *Domestic Workers Convention. Document C189.* Geneva: ILO. Accessed 15 May 2016. https://www.ilo.org/dyn/normlex/en/f?p=NORMLEXPUB:12100:0::NO::P12100_ILO_CODE:C189

ILO. 2013. *Domestic Workers across the World: Global and Regional Statistics and the Extent of Legal Protection.* Geneva: ILO.

ILOSTAT. 2019. "Statistics on union membership". Accessed 24 December 2019. https://ilostat.ilo.org/topics/union-membership/

IMF (International Monetary Fund). 2016. "Argentina: Financial system stability assessment. IMF Country Report N° 16/64". Washington: IMF.

Ingraham, Chrys. 1999. *White Weddings: Romancing Heterosexuality in Popular Culture*. New York and London: Routledge.

Ingraham, Chrys. 2011. "One is Not Born a Bride: How Weddings Regulate Heterosexuality". In *Introducing the New Sexuality Studies*, edited by Steven Seidman *et al.*, 303–307. London and New York: Routledge (2nd edition).

INSEE (Institut National de la Statistique et des Études Économiques). 2019. *Tableaux de l'économie française: édition 2019*. Montrouge: INSEE.

Islam, Deepan. 2018. "Outsourcing embryos: An examination of the maternal surrogacy market". *Journal of Social and Administrative Sciences* 5 (2): 100–115.

Jacobs, Sam. 2017. "Same-sex marriage could be a $650 million boost to the Australian economy". *Business Insider*, 18 September. Accessed 4 December 2019. https://www.businessinsider.com.au/same-sex-marriage-could-be-a-650-million-boost-to-the-australian-economy-2017-9

Jennings, Ann L. 1993. "Public or Private? Institutional Economics and Feminism". In *Beyond Economic Man: Feminist Theory and Economics*, edited by Marianne A. Ferber and Julie A. Nelson, 111–129. Chicago: University of Chicago Press.

Jewkes, Rachel and Naeema Abrahams. 2002. "The epidemiology of rape and sexual coercion in South Africa: An overview". *Social Science & Medicine* 55: 1231–1244.

Johnson, Bonnie. 1987. "And baby makes four: For the first time a surrogate bears a child genetically not her own". *People*, 4 May. Accessed 25 April 2019. https://people.com/archive/and-baby-makes-four-for-the-first-time-a-surrogate-bears-a-child-genetically-not-her-own-vol-27-no-18/

Johnson, Gary R. 1987. "In the name of the fatherland: An analysis of kin term usage in patriotic speech and literature". *International Political Science Review / Revue internationale de science politique* 8 (2): 165–174.

Johnson, Kecia R. and Karyn Loscocco. 2015. "Black marriage through the prism of gender, race, and class". *Journal of Black Studies* 46 (2): 142–171.

Jones, Kathleen B. 1993. *Compassionate Authority: Democracy and the Representation of Women*. London and New York: Routledge.

Jordhus-Lier, David and Anders Underthun. 2015. "Introduction: The Spatialities of Hotels and Tourism Workplaces". In *A Hospitable World? Organising Work and Workers in Hotels and Tourist Resorts*, edited by David Jordhus-Lier and Anders Underthun, 1–10. London and New York: Routledge.

Joshi, Devin K., Meseret F. Hailu and Lauren J. Reising. 2019. "Violators, virtuous, or victims? How global newspapers represent the female member of parliament". *Feminist Media Studies*. doi:10.1080/14680777.2019.1642225

Joshi, Yuvraj. 2012. "Respectable queerness". *Columbia Human Rights Law Review* 43 (2): 415–467

Judge, Melanie. 2014. "For better or worse? Same-sex marriage and the (re)making of hegemonic masculinities and femininities in South Africa". *Agenda* 28 (2): 67–73. doi:10.1080/10130950.2014.928491

Kaese, Fynn and Jonas Wolff. 2016. "Piqueteros after the hype: Unemployed movements in Argentina, 2008–2015". *European Review of Latin American and Caribbean Studies / Revista Europea de Estudios Latinoamericanos y del Caribe* 102: 47–68.

Kahn, Miriam. 2011. "Illusion and reality in Tahiti's tourist cocoons". *Journal of Tourism and Cultural Change* 9 (3): 201–216.

Kail, Ben Lennox, Katie L. Acosta and Eric R. Wright. 2015. "State-level marriage equality and the health of same-sex couples". *The American Journal of Public* Health 105 (6): 1101–1105. doi:10.2105/AJPH.2015.302589

Kaiser, Anna Jean. 2018. "Brazil: Same-sex couples rush to the altar ahead of Bolsonaro inauguration". *The Guardian*, 13 December. Accessed 18 December 2019. https://www.theguardian.com/world/2018/dec/12/brazil-same-sex-marriage-increase-bolsonaro

Kara, Siddarth. 2019. *Tainted Garments: The Exploitation of Women and Girls in India's Home-based Garment Sector*. Berkeley: Blum Center for Developing Economies, University of California Berkeley.

Karp, Paul. 2017. "Marriage equality: Lots of support but little funding from corporate Australia". *The Guardian*, 2 September. Accessed 18 December 2019. https://www.theguardian.com/australia-news/2017/sep/02/marriage-equality-lots-of-support-but-little-funding-from-corporate-australia

Karp, Paul. 2018. "Coalition stacking Fair Work Commission with mates, Labor says". *The Guardian*, 7 December. Accessed 19 March 2020. https://www.theguardian.com/australia-news/2018/dec/07/coalition-stacking-fair-work-commission-with-mates-labor-says

Karpov, Vyacheslav and Kimmo Kääriäinen. 2005. "'Abortion culture' in Russia: Its origins, scope, and challenge to social development". *Sociological Practice* 7 (2): 13–33.

Kaysen, Susanna, 1993. *Girl, Interrupted*. New York: Vintage Books.

Kearl, Michelle Kelsey. 2015. "'Is gay the new black?': An intersectional perspective on social movement rhetoric in California's Proposition 8 debate". *Communication and Critical/Cultural Studies* 12 (1): 63–82. doi:10.1080/14791420.2014.995684

Kelly, Maura and Elizabeth Hauck. 2015. "Doing housework, redoing gender: Queer couples negotiate the household division of labor". *Journal of GLBT Family Studies* 11 (5): 438–464. doi:10.1080/1550428X.2015.1006750

Kincaid, Jamaica. 2018. *A Small Place*. London: Daunt Books (English edition).

King, Debra and Gabrielle Meagher. 2009. *Paid Care in Australia: Politics, Profits, Practices*. Sydney: Sydney University Press.

Klare, Karl E. 1998. "Legal culture and transformative constitutionalism". *South African Journal on Human* Rights 14 (1): 146–188. doi:10.1080/02587203.1998.11834974

Klein, Renate. 2017. *Surrogacy: A Human Rights Violation*. Melbourne: Spinifex Press.

Klimmer, Rudolf. 1965. *Die Homosexualität als biologisch-soziologische Zeitfrage*. Hamburg: Kriminalistik (3rd edition).

Knauer, Nancy J. 2016. "LGBT Elders: Making the Case for Equity in Aging". In *After Marriage Equality: The Future of LGBT Rights*, edited by Carlos A. Ball, 105–126. New York: New York University Press.

Knoche, Jonathan W. 2014. "Health concerns and ethical considerations regarding international surrogacy". *International Journal of Gynecology and Obstetrics* 126: 183–186.

Koh, Tabitha L. 2016. "Obstacle course: Roadblocks gay men face on the path to surrogacy". *Family Advocate* 38 (4): 44–45.

Kolata, Gina. 2002. "Fertility Inc.: Clinics race to lure clients". *New York Times*, 1 January, F1. Accessed 29 February 2020. *Gale Academic OneFile*. https://link-gale-com.ezproxy1.library.usyd.edu.au/apps/doc/A81202189/AONE?u=usyd&sid=AONE&xid=9ef788c6

Kolk, Martin and Gunnar Andersson. 2018. "Two decades of same-sex marriage in Sweden: A demographic account of developments in marriage, childbearing and divorce". Stockholm: Stockholm University Linnaeus Center on Social Policy and Family Dynamics in Europe, Working Paper 2018: 2. Accessed 6 January 2020. https://www.su.se/polopoly_fs/1.77756.1521221452!/menu/standard/file/WP_2018_02.pdf

Koraan, Rene and Alison Geduld. 2015. "Corrective rape of lesbians in the era of transformative constitutionalism in South Africa". *Potchefstroom Electronic Law Journal* 18 (5): 1931–1953.

Kornbluh, Felicia and Gwendolyn Mink. 2018. *Ensuring Poverty: Welfare Reform in Feminist Perspective*. Philadelphia: University of Pennsylvania Press.

Koziol, Michael. 2017. "Turnbull government 'won't be bullied' by CEOs on same-sex marriage, says Peter Dutton". *The Sydney Morning Herald*, 18 March. Accessed 22 December 2019. https://www.smh.com.au/politics/federal/turnbull-government-wont-be-bullied-by-ceos-on-samesex-marriage-says-peter-dutton-20170318-gv11uh.html

von Krafft-Ebing, Richard. 1939. *Psychopathia Sexualis: A Medico-Forensic Study*. New York: Pioneer Publications.

Kramer, Stephanie. 2019. "U.S. has world's highest rate of children living in single-parent households". *Pew Research Center*, 12 December. Accessed 19 June 2020. https://www.pewresearch.org/fact-tank/2019/12/12/u-s-children-more-likely-than-children-in-other-countries-to-live-with-just-one-parent/

Krieger, Daniel. 2014. "Denmark's civil unions: One giant leap for mankind". *The Wilson Quarterly*, Fall. Accessed 26 October 2019. https://www.wilsonquarterly.com/quarterly/summer-2014-1989-and-the-making-of-our-modern-world/denmarks-civil-unions-one-giant-leap-for-mankind/

Krook, Mona Lena and Fiona Mackay. 2011. "Introduction: Gender, Politics, and Institutions". In *Gender, Politics, and Institutions: Towards a Feminist Institutionalism*, edited by Mona Lena Krook and Fiona Mackay, 1–20. New York: Palgrave Macmillan.

Kuhar, Roman and David Paternotte (eds). 2017. *Anti-Gender Campaigns in Europe: Mobilizing against Equality*. New York: Rowman & Littlefield.

Kunert, Paul. 2016. "IBM union: OK guys, you've beaten us down, we give in". *The Register*, 6 January. Accessed 24 December 2019. https://www.theregister.co.uk/2016/01/06/alliance_at_ibm_suspends_organised_campaigns/

Kurdek, Lawrence A. 2007. "The allocation of household labor by partners in gay and lesbian couples". *Journal of Family Issues* 28 (1): 132–148.

Kvist, Jonet al. 2011. *Changing Social Equality: The Nordic Welfare Model in the 21st Century*. Bristol: Policy Press.

Laclau, Ernesto. 2008. *La Raison populiste*. Paris: Le Seuil.

Lacombe, Philippe. 2008. "Les Identités sexuées et 'le troisième sexe' à Tahiti". *Cahiers du Genre* 45 (2): 177–197.

Lacombe, Philippe. 2013. "Mahu et rae rae de Tahiti: de la singularité des contextes locaux à l'universalité des questions sur le genre". *Hermès* 65 (1): 89–90.

Laing, Lesley. 2017. "Secondary victimization: Domestic violence survivors navigating the family law system". *Violence Against Women* 23 (11): 1314–1335.

Lakoff, George. 1996. *Moral Politics: What Conservatives Know that Liberals Don't*. Chicago: University of Chicago Press.

Lakoff, George. 2002. *Moral Politics: How Liberals and Conservatives Think*. Chicago: University of Chicago Press (2nd edition).

Lakoff, George. 2004. "What's in a word? Plenty, if the word is 'marriage'". *UC Berkeley News*, 2 March. Accessed 12 September 2019. https://www.berkeley.edu/news/media/releases/2004/02/20_lakoff.shtml

Lapidus, June. 2004. "All the lesbian mothers are coupled, all the single mothers are straight, and all of us are tired: Reflections on being a single lesbian mom". *Feminist Economics* 10 (2): 227–236. doi:10.1080/1354570042000217784

Lauder, Simon. 2011. "Qantas to fly again after Fair Work terminates dispute". *ABC News*, 31 October. Accessed 24 December 2019. https://www.abc.net.au/news/2011-10-31/qantas-action-terminated-fair-work-rules/3609158

Lavitry, Lynda. 2017. "Back-to-Work Services in France and the Flexibility Edict". In *Frontline Delivery of Welfare-to-Work Policies in Europe: Activating the Unemployed*, edited by Rik Van Berkel*et al.*, 70–87. London and New York: Routledge.

Lazala, Mauricio and Joe Bardwell. 2015. "'What human rights?' Why some companies speak out while others don't". *Open Democracy*, 17 June. Accessed 18 December 2019. https://www.opendemocracy.net/en/openglobalrights-openpage/what-human-rights-why-some-companies-speak-out-while/

L.D. 2008. "L'Annulation du mariage pour non-virginité rejetée en appel". *Le Figaro*, 18 November. Accessed 21 May 2020. https://www.lefigaro.fr/actualite-france/2008/11/17/01016-20081117ARTFIG00496-l-annulation-du-mariage-pour-non-virginite-rejetee-en-appel-.php

Le Monde. 2013. "Premier divorce d'un couple homosexuel en France". Accessed 4 January 2020. https://www.lemonde.fr/societe/article/2013/10/31/premier-divorce-d-un-couple-homosexuel-en-france_3505844_3224.html

Lee, Donna, Mark Hampton and Julia Jeyachey. 2015. "The political economy of precarious work in the tourism industry in small island developing states". *Review of International Political Economy* 22 (1): 194–223. doi:10.1080/09692290.2014.887590

Lee, Jess. 2018. "Black LGB identities and perceptions of same-sex marriage". *Journal of Homosexuality* 65 (14): 2005–2027. doi:10.1080/00918369.2017.1423214

Lemke, Jürgen. 1993. "Gay and lesbian life in East German society before and after 1989". *The Oral History Review* 21 (2): 31–40.

Lenon, Suzanne. 2011. "'Why is our love an issue?': Same-sex marriage and the racial politics of the ordinary". *Social Identities* 17 (3): 351–372. doi:10.1080/13504630.2011.570975

Lewis, Jane. 1997. "Gender and welfare regimes: Further thoughts". *Social Politics* 4 (2): 160–177.

Lewis, Sophie. 2017. "Defending intimacy against what? Limits of antisurrogacy feminisms". *Signs: Journal of Women in Culture and Society* 43 (1): 97–125.

Lewis, Suzan and T. Alexandra Beauregard. 2018, "The Meanings of Work–Life Balance: A Cultural Perspective". In *The Cambridge Handbook of the Global Work-Family Interface*, edited by Kristen M. Shockley, Winny Shen and Ryan C. Johnson, 720–732. Cambridge and New York: Cambridge University Press.

Li, Feng and Venky Nagar. 2013. "Diversity and performance". *Management Science* 59 (3): 529–544. doi:10.1287/mnsc.1120.1548

Lind, Amy and Cricket Keating. 2013. "Navigating the left turn: Sexual justice and the citizen revolution in Ecuador". *International Feminist Journal of Politics* 15 (4): 515–533. doi:10.1080/14616742.2013.813162

Lindhorst, Commas, Jeffrey L. Edleson and Taryn Lindhorst. 2012. *Battered Women, Their Children, and International Law: The Unintended Consequences of the Hague Child Abduction Convention*. Boston: Northeastern University Press.

Livingston, Gretchen and Anna Brown. 2017. "Intermarriage in the U.S. 50 years after Loving v. Virginia: 1. Trends and patterns in intermarriage". *Pew Research Center*, 18 May. Accessed 30 December 2019. https://www.pewsocialtrends.org/2017/05/18/1-trends-and-patterns-in-intermarriage/

Lofquist, Daphneet al. 2012. *Households and Families: 2010 Census Briefs*. Suitland, MD: U.S. Census Bureau.

Long, Alecia P. 2007. "Poverty is the new prostitution: Race, poverty, and public housing in post-Katrina New Orleans". *Journal of American History* 94 (3): 795–803. doi:10.2307/25095141

López, Nancy. 2018. "The US Census Bureau keeps confusing race and ethnicity". *The Conversation*, 28 February. Accessed 2 January 2020. http://theconversation.com/the-us-census-bureau-keeps-confusing-race-and-ethnicity-89649

López, Nancyet al. 2018. "What's your 'street race'? Leveraging multidimensional measures of race and intersectionality for examining physical and mental health status among Latinxs". *Sociology of Race and Ethnicity* 4 (1). doi:10.1177/2332649217708798

López-Morales, Ernesto, Hyun Bang Shin and Loretta Lees. 2016. "Latin American gentrifications". *Urban Geography* 37 (8): 1091–1108, doi:10.1080/02723638.2016.1200335

Lorde, Audré. 1984. "The Master's Tools Will Never Dismantle the Master's House". In *Sister Outsider*, 110–113. Freedom, CA: The Crossing Press.

Lowrey, Annie. 2018. "Jeff Bezos's $150 billion fortune is a policy failure". *The Atlantic*, 1 August. Accessed 5 June 2020. https://www.theatlantic.com/business/archive/2018/08/the-problem-with-bezos-billions/566552/

Lozano, Esther. 2019. "Eva Perón, una mujer que sigue polarizando a la sociedad argentina". *SBS Spanish*, 16 May. Accessed 23 October 2019. https://www.sbs.com.au/language/english/audio/eva-peron-una-mujer-que-sigue-polarizando-a-la-sociedad-argentina

Lustenberger, Sibylle. 2017. "'We are citizens'—Vulnerability and privilege in the experiences of Israeli gay men with surrogacy in India". *Journal of Comparative Family Studies* 48 (3): 393–403.

McClymont, Kate and Jacqueline Maley. 2020. "High Court inquiry finds former justice Dyson Heydon sexually harassed associates". *The Sydney Morning Herald*, 22 June. Accessed 23 June 2020. https://www.smh.com.au/national/high-court-inquiry-finds-former-justice-dyson-heydon-sexually-harassed-associates-20200622-p5550w.html

McCrate, Elaine. 2013. "Employer-Oriented Schedule Flexibility, Gender and Family Care". In *Handbook of Research on Gender and Economic Life*, edited by Deborah M. Figart and Tonia L. Warnecke, 273–289. Northampton, MA: Edward Elgar.

McGuffey, C. Shawn. 2018. "Intersectionality, cognition, disclosure and black lGBT Views on civil rights and marriage equality: Is gay the new black?". *Du Bois Review* 15 (2): 441–465.

Mackay, Fiona, Meryl Kenny and Louise Chappell. 2010. "New institutionalism through a gender lens: Towards a feminist institutionalism?". *International Political Science Review* 31 (5): 573–588.

MacKinnon, Catharine A. 1989. *Toward a Feminist Theory of the State.* Cambridge, MA: Harvard University Press.

MacKinnon, Catharine A. 1990. "Legal Perspectives on Sexual Difference". In *Theoretical Perspectives on Sexual Difference*, edited by Deborah L. Rhode, 213–225. New Haven: Yale University Press.

MacKinnon, Catharine A. and Reva B. Siegel. 2004. *Directions in Sexual Harassment Law.* New Haven: Yale University Press.

McLeod, Carolynand AndrewBotterell. 2014. "A Hague convention on contract pregnancy (or "surrogacy"): Avoiding ethical inconsistencies with the Convention on Adoption". *International Journal of Feminist Approaches to Bioethics*7 (2):219–235.

McNicholas Smith, Kate and Imogen Tyler. 2017. "Lesbian brides: Post-queer popular culture". *Feminist Media Studies* 17 (3): 315–331. doi:10.1080/14680777.2017.1282883

Maggie. 2019. "Anonymous No More: How I Was Groomed to Be a Multiple Egg Donor". In *Broken Bonds: Surrogate Mothers Speak Out*, edited by Jennifer Lahl, Melinda Tankard-Reist and Renate Klein, 27–35. Melbourne: Spinifex.

Mallol, Christophe Serra. 2014. "Exclusion et dispositifs sociaux dans l'outre-mer du Pacifique. L'Exemple de la prostitution de rue en Polynésie Française". *Revue française des affaires sociales* 2014 (4): 90–113.

Mallory, Christy and Brad Sears. 2016. *Estimating the Economic Impact of Marriage for Same-Sex Couples One Year after Obergefell.* Los Angeles: The Williams Institute.

Mamo, Laura and Eli Alston-Stepnitz. 2015. "Queer intimacies and structural inequalities: New directions in stratified reproduction". *Journal of Family Issues* 36 (4): 519–540.

Mangan, Lucy. 2013. "Weekend: STARTERS: In years to come, we'll look back at Amazon's employment practices as the good old days". *The Guardian*, 30 November. Accessed 22 December 2019. http://ezproxy.library.usyd.edu.au/login?url=https://search-proquest-com.ezproxy1.library.usyd.edu.au/docview/1462525401?accountid=14757

Marhoefer, Laurie. 2015a. "'The book was a revelation, I recognized myself in it': Lesbian sexuality, censorship, and the queer press in Weimar-era Germany". *Journal of Women's History* 27 (2): 62–86. doi:10.1353/jowh.2015.0016

Marhoefer, Laurie. 2015b. *Sex and the Weimar Republic: German Homosexual Emancipation and the Rise of the Nazis*. Toronto: University of Toronto Press.

Markens, Susan. 2012. "The global reproductive health market: U.S. media framings and public discourses about transnational surrogacy". *Social Science & Medicine* 74: 1745–1753.

Martell, Michael E. and Leanne Roncolato. 2016. "The homosexual lifestyle: Time use in same-sex households". *Journal of Demographic Economics* 82: 365–398. doi:10.1017/dem.2016.14

Martin, Andrew, Annie Kelly, Laura Turquet and Stephanie Ross. 2009. *Hate Crimes: The Rise of 'Corrective' Rape in South Africa*. London: Action Aid.

Martinez, Omar and Brian Dodge. 2010. "El barrio de La Chueca of Madrid, Spain: An emerging epicenter of the global LGBT civil rights movement". *Journal of Homosexuality* 57 (2): 226–248. doi:10.1080/00918360903488913

Martínez Franzoni, Juliana. 2008. "Welfare regimes in Latin America: Capturing constellations of markets, families, and policies". *Latin American Politics and Society* 50 (2): 67–100. https://doi.org/10. 1111/j. 1548-2456. 2008. 0001

Martinsson, Lena, Gabrielle Griffin and Katarina Giritli Nygren (eds). 2016. *Challenging the Myth of Gender Equality in Sweden*. Bristol: Policy Press.

Mather, Celia. 2015. *Domestic Workers in Europe: Getting Organised!*Brussels: EFFAT (European Federation of Food, Agriculture and Tourism Trade Unions).

Matousek, Mark. 2019. "Cruise-ship workers reveal how much money they make". *Business Insider*, 4 June. Accessed 13 December 2019. https://www.businessinsider.com.au/cruise-ship-workers-reveal-how-much-money-they-make-2019-5?r=US&IR=T

Matthies, Aila-Lena and Lars Uggerhøj. 2014. *Participation, Marginalization and Welfare Services: Concepts, Politics and Practices across European Countries*. Farnham: Ashgate.

May, Amy and Kelly Tenzek. 2016. "'A gift we are unable to create ourselves': Uncertainty reduction in online classified ads posted by gay men pursuing surrogacy". *Journal of GLBT Family Studies* 12 (5): 430–450/ doi:10.1080/1550428X.2015.1128860

Meagher, Gabrielle. 1997. "Recreating 'domestic service': Institutional cultures and the evolution of paid household work". *Feminist Economics* 3 (2): 1–27. doi:10.1080/135457097338681

Meagher, Gabrielle and Susan Goodwin (eds). 2015. *Markets, Rights and Power in Australian Social Policy*. Sydney: Sydney University Press.

Menasce Horowitz, Juliana, Nikki Graf and Gretchen Livingston. 2019. "Marriage and cohabitation in the U.S. 1: The landscape of marriage and cohabitation in the U.S". *Pew Research Center*, 6 November. Accessed 2 January 2020. https://www.pewsocialtrends.org/2019/11/06/the-landscape-of-marriage-and-cohabitation-in-the-u-s/

Meyer, Tamar. 2000. "Gender Ironies of Nationalism: Setting the Stage". In *Gender Ironies of Nationalism: Sexing the Nation*, edited by Tamar Meyer, 1–24. London and New York: Routledge.

Meyer-Stabley, Bertrand. 2017. *Eva Peron: L'Argentine adulée et décriée*. Paris:La Boîte à Pandore.

Mildenberger, Florian. 2012. "Socialist Eugenics and Homosexuality in the GDR: The Case of Günter Dörner". In *After The History of Sexuality: German Genealogies with and beyond Foucault*, edited by ScottSpector, HelmutPuff and DagmarHerzog, 216–230. Oxford andNew York:Berghahn Books.

Millett, Kate. 1978. *Sexual Politics*. New York: Ballantine Books.

Misthos, Luke. 2017. "Wedding industry gets ready for a surge in same-sex marriages". *Financial Review*, 8 December. Accessed 4 December 2019. https://www.afr.com/politics/wedding-industry-gets-ready-for-a-surge-in-samesex-marriages-20171208-h01hqe

Modine, Austin. 2008. "IBM hits back against over-timers with pay cut". *The Register*, 23 January. Accessed 18 December 2019. https://www.theregister.co.uk/2008/01/23/ibm_techies_get_pay_cut_overtime/

Moeller, Hero. 1950. "Liberalismus". *Jahrbücher für Nationalökonomie und Statistik* 162: 214–240.

Moeller, Robert G. 1994. ""The homosexual man is a "man," the homosexual woman is a "woman"": Sex, society, and the law in postwar West Germany". *Journal of the History of Sexuality* 4 (3): 395–429.

Moghadam, Valentine M.(ed.) 1994. *Identity Politics and Women: Cultural Reassertions and Feminisms in International Perspective*. Boulder, CO:Westview Press.

Mohanty, Chandra Talpade. 2013. "Transnational feminist crossings: On neoliberalism and radical critique". *Signs* 38 (4): 967–991.

Moran, Rachel F. 2012. "Beyond the Loving Analogy: The Independent Logic of Same-Sex Marriage". In *Loving v. Virginia in a Post-Racial World: Rethinking Race, Sex, and Marriage*, edited by Kevin Noble Maillard and Rose Cuison Villazor, 242–252. Cambridge and New York: Cambridge University Press.

Morel, Nathalie, Chloé Touzet and Michaël Zemmour. 2019. "From the hidden welfare state to the hidden part of welfare state reform: Analyzing the uses and effects of fiscal welfare in France". *Social Policy and Administration* 53 (1): 34–48.

Morgan, Robin. 1970. *Sisterhood is Powerful: An Anthology of Writings from the Women's Liberation Movement*. New York: Vintage Books.

Morgan, Robin. 1984. *Sisterhood is Global: The International Women's Movement Anthology*. New York: Anchor Press/Doubleday.

Morgan, Robin. 2003. *Sisterhood Is Forever: The Women's Anthology for a New Millennium*. New York: Washington Square Press/Simon & Schuster.

Morrison, Adele M. 2007. "Same-sex *loving*: Subverting white supremacy through same-sex marriage". *Michigan Journal of Race and Law* 13 (1): 177–225.

Morrissey, Megan E. 2013. "Rape as a weapon of hate: Discursive constructions and material consequences of black lesbianism in South Africa". *Women's Studies in Communication* 36 (1): 72–91. doi:10.1080/07491409.2013.755450

Moscowitz, Leigh M. 2010. "Gay marriage in television news: Voice and visual representation in the same-sex marriage debate". *Journal of Broadcasting & Electronic Media* 54 (1): 24–39. doi:10.1080/08838150903550360

Movement Advancement Project. n.d. "Where we call home: LGBT people in rural America". Accessed 26 January 2020. http://lgbtmap.org/rural-lgbt

Mucciaroni, Gary. 2008. *Same Sex, Different Politics Success and Failure in the Struggles over Gay Rights*. Chicago: University of Chicago Press.

Muir, Elise. 2013. "The Court of Justice: A Fundamental Rights Institution among Others". In *Judicial Activism at the European Court of Justice*, edited by Mark Dawson, Bruno De Witte and Elise Muir, 76–101. Cheltenham: Edward Elgar.

Mundy, Liza. 2013. "The gay guide to wedded bliss". *The Atlantic*, June. Accessed 15 January 2020. https://www.theatlantic.com/magazine/archive/2013/06/the-gay-guide-to-wedded-bliss/309317/

Murphy, Dean A. 2013. "The desire for parenthood: Gay men choosing to become parents through surrogacy". *Journal of Family Issues* 34 (8): 1104–1124.

Mushaben, Joyce Marie. 2017. *Becoming Madam Chancellor: Angela Merkel and the Berlin Republic*. Cambridge and New York: Cambridge University Press.

My-MED-tourism. 2015. "Surrogacy statistics: numbers and success rates worldwide". Accessed 25 April 2019. www.mymedholiday.com/article-info/50/639/surrogacy-statistics-numbers-success-rates-worldwide

Naidoo, Kamban and Michelle Karels. 2012a. "Hate crimes against black lesbian South Africans: Where race, sexual orientation and gender collide (Part I)". *Obiter* 33 (2): 236–259.

Naidoo, Kamban and Michelle Karels. 2012b. "Hate crimes against black lesbian South Africans: Where race, sexual orientation and gender collide (Part II)". *Obiter* 33 (3): 600–624.

Naidoo, Kamban and Michelle Karels. 2016. "Prosecuting 'hate': An overview of problem areas relating to hate crimes and challenges to criminal litigation". *Journal for Juridical Science* 41 (1): 65–82. doi:10.18820/24150517/JJS41.v1.4

Naïr, Prathap. 2019. "After equal marriage, LGBT+ Germans fight for the right to a family". *Reuters*, 5 June. Accessed 15 June 2020. https://www.reuters.com/article/us-germany-lgbt-youth/after-equal-marriage-lgbt-germans-fight-for-the-right-to-a-family-idUSKCN1T602T

Nathan, Mathias and Ignacio Pardo. 2018. "Demografía de las parejas del mismo sexo en Uruguay". Programa de Población, Documentos de Trabajo, Universidad de la República. Accessed 20 December 2019. http://cienciassociales.edu.uy/unidadmultidisciplinaria/wp-content/uploads/sites/6/2019/04/Documento-de-trabajo-N%C2%BA2-PP-FINAL.pdf

National Coalition for Gay and Lesbian Equality v. Minister of Justice. 1998. *Constitutional Court of South Africa, Case CCT 11/98*.

National Records of Scotland. 2019. *Scotland's Population: The Registrar General's Annual Review of Demographic Trends 2018*, 164th edition. Edinburgh:National Records of Scotland.

Navarro, Marysa. 2012. "Evita, Historia y Mitología". *Caravelle* 98: 113–133.

NCOSS (NSW Council of Social Services). 2015. *Beyond the Myth of "Pink Privilege": Poverty, Disadvantage and LGBTI People in NSW: A Scoping Review of the Evidence*. Sydney: NCOSS.

Nebeling Petersen, Michael. 2018. "Becoming gay fathers through transnational commercial surrogacy". *Journal of Family Issues* 39 (3): 693–719.

Neidhardt, Alberto-Horst. 2018. "The Coman case: Extending free movement rights to same sex couples or protecting marital status?" *European University Institute Blog*, 13 December. Accessed 18 November 2019. https://me.eui.eu/alberto-horst-neidhardt/blog/the-coman-case-enhancing-free-movement-rights-for-same-sex-couples-or-protecting-the-status-of-marriage/

Nelson, Julie. 2013. "Gender and Caring". In *Handbook of Research on Gender and Economic Life*, edited by Deborah M. Figart and Tonia L. Warnecke. 62–76. Northampton, MA: Edward Elgar.

Neyer, Gerda, Arianna Caporali and Nora Sánchez Gassen. 2017. *EU-Policies and Fertility: The Emergence of Fertility-Related Family Policies at the Supra-National Level*. Stockholm: Stockholm University Linnaeus Center on Social Policy and Family Dynamics in Europe, Working Paper 2017: 01.

Nguyen, Minh T.N., Roberta Zavoretti and Joan Tronto. 2017. "Beyond the global care chain: Boundaries, institutions and ethics of care". *Ethics and Social Welfare* 11 (3): 199–212. doi:10.1080/17496535.2017.1300308

Nolan, Brian. 2018. *Generating Prosperity for Working Families in Affluent Countries*. Oxford and New York: Oxford University Press.

Nolan, Mary. 2011. "Gender and utopian visions in a post-utopian era: Americanism, human rights, market fundamentalism". *Central European History* 44: 13–36. doi:10.1017/S0008938910001160

Nolte, Detlef and Almut Schilling-Vacaflor. 2012. *New Constitutionalism in Latin America: Promises and Practices*. Farnham: Ashgate.

Norton, Wendy, Nicky Hudson and Lorraine Culley. 2013. "Gay men seeking surrogacy to achieve parenthood". *Reproductive BioMedicine Online* 27: 271–279.

Oakley, Ann. 1974. *The Sociology of Housework*. Bristol: Policy Press.

O'Brien, Anne. 2020. "Punitive welfare is never a good idea: It's time to leave it in the past". *ABC Religion and Ethics*, 21 May. Accessed 11 June 2020. https://www.abc.net.au/religion/its-time-to-leave-punitive-welfare-in-the-past/12272176

O'Brien, Mary. 1981. *The Politics of Reproduction*. Boston: Routledge & Kegan Paul.

O'Byrne, Katieand PaulaGerber. 2015. "Surrogacy and Human Rights: Contemporary, Complex, Contested and Controversial". In *Surrogacy, Law and Human Rights*, edited by PaulaGerber and KatieO'Byrne, 1–7. Farnham:Ashgate Publishing.

O'Connor, Julia S., Ann Shola Orloff and Sheila Shaver. 1999. *States, Markets, Families: Gender, Liberalism, and Social Policy in Australia, Canada, Great Britain, and the United States*. Cambridge: Cambridge University Press.

OECD (Organization for Economic Cooperation and Development). 2017. "Sustaining nature-based tourism in Iceland". OECD Economic Surveys, issue 15 of 2017.

OECD. 2018. "Affordable housing database". Accessed 27 January 2020. https://www.oecd.org/social/affordable-housing-database/

OECD. 2019. "SF3.1: Marriage and divorce rates". Accessed 13 October 2019. https://www.oecd.org/els/family/SF_3_1_Marriage_and_divorce_rates.pdf

Oerton, Sarah. 1997. "'Queer housewives?': Some problems in theorising the division of domestic labour in lesbian and gay households". *Women's Studies International Forum* 20 (3): 421–430.

Office for National Statistics. 2018. *Divorces in England and Wales: 2017*. London: ONS.

Office for National Statistics. 2019a. *Sexual Orientation, UK: 2017. Statistical Bulletin*, 21 January. London: ONS.

Office for National Statistics. 2019b. *Marriages in England and Wales: 2016. Statistical Bulletin*, 28 March. London: ONS.

Office for National Statistics. 2019c. *Research Report on Population Estimates by Ethnic Group and Religion*. London: ONS.

Okin, Susan Moller. 1979. *Women in Western Political Thought*. Princeton, NJ: Princeton University Press.

Óladóttir, Oddny Þora. 2018. *Tourism in Iceland in Figures*. Reykjavik: Icelandic Tourist Board.

Orloff, Ann Shola. 1993. "Gender and the social rights of citizenship: The comparative analysis of gender relations and welfare states". *American Sociological Review* 58: 303–328.

Orloff, Ann Shola. 1997. "Comment on Jane Lewis's 'Gender and Welfare Regimes: Further Thoughts'". *Social Politics* 4 (2): 188–202.

Orwell, George. 2001. *Animal Farm. Project Gutenberg Australia*. Accessed 27 December 2019. http://gutenberg.net.au/ebooks01/0100011h.html

Other Foundation, The and HSRC (Human Sciences Research Council). 2016. *Progressive Prudes*. Johannesburg:The Other Foundationand HSRC.

Outinen, Sami. 2012. "Labour market activation in Finland in the 1990s: Workfare reforms and labour market flexibilisation". *Local Economy* 27(5–6): 629–636. doi:10.1177/0269094212445353

Parreñas, Rachel. 2006. "Migrant Filipina Domestic Workers and International Division of Reproductive Labor". In *Global Dimensions of Gender and Carework*, edited by Mary K. Zimmerman, Jacquelyn S. Litt and Christine E. Bose, 48–64. Stanford, CA: Stanford University Press.

Pateman,Carole. 1988. *The Sexual Contract*. Cambridge: Polity Press.

Pateman,Carole. 1989. *The Disorder of Women: Democracy, Feminism and Political Theory*. Cambridge: Polity Press.

Patterson, Charlotte J. 1995. "Families of the lesbian baby boom: Parents' division of labor and children's adjustment". *Developmental Psychology* 31 (1): 115–123. doi:10.1037/0012-1649.31.1.115

Pavlou, Vera. 2016. "Domestic work in EU law: The relevance of EU employment law in challenging domestic workers' vulnerability". *European Law Review* 41 (3): 379–398.

Pelling, Lisa. 2020. "Sweden, the pandemic and precarious working conditions". *Social Europe*, 10 June. Accessed 11 June 2020. https://www.socialeurope.eu/sweden-the-pandemic-and-precarious-working-conditions

Pender, Kieran. 2019. *Us Too? Bullying and Sexual Harassment in the Legal Profession*. London: International Bar Association.

Pengelly, Martin. 2019. "Trump calls Ocasio-Cortez 'Evita' in new book American Carnage". *The Guardian*, 8 July. Accessed 25 October 2019. https://www.theguardian.com/us-news/2019/jul/07/donald-trump-alexandria-ocasio-cortez-evita-american-carnage

Perales, Francisco and Alice Campbell. 2017. "Revealed: Who supports marriage equality in Australia—and who doesn't". *The Conversation*, 31 August. Accessed 23 December 2019. https://theconversation.com/revealed-who-supports-marriage-equality-in-australia-and-who-doesnt-82988

Pereyra, Francisca. 2018. *Cuando la expansión de derechos es posible: el diálogo social de las trabajadoras domésticas en Argentina*. Buenos Aires: Oficina de País de la Organización Internacional del Trajabo para la Argentina, Serie Documentos de Trabajo 26.

Pérez, Germán J. and Ana Natalucci. 2010. "La Matriz Movimientista de Acción Colectiva en Argentina: La Experiencia del Espacio Militante Kirchnerista". *América Latina Hoy* 54: 97–112.

Perry, Keith. 2014. "British mother rejected disabled twin because she was a 'dribbling cabbage,' says surrogate". *The Telegraph*, 26 August. Accessed 25 April 2019. https://www.telegraph.co.uk/news/health/children/11055643/British-mother-rejected-disabled-twin-because-she-was-a-dribbling-cabbage-says-surrogate.html

Petersen, Klaus and Jørn Henrik Petersen. 2013. "Confusion and divergence: Origins and meanings of the term 'welfare state' in Germany and Britain, 1840–1940". *Journal of European Social Policy* 23 (1): 37–51. doi:10.1177/0958928712463160

Peterson, V. Spike. 2013. "The intended and unintended queering of states/nations". *Studies in Ethnicity and Nationalism* 13 (1): 57–68.

PFAW (People For the American Way). 2010. *The Rise of the Corporate Court: How the Supreme Court is Putting Business First*. Washington: PFAW.

Philippine Statistics Authority. 2020. *Survey on Overseas Filipinos Statistical Tables*. Accessed19 September 2020. https://psa.gov.ph/statistics/survey/labor-and-employment/survey-overseas-filipinos

Phillips, Tom. 2011. "Brazil census shows African-Brazilians in the majority for the first time". *The Guardian*, 18 November. Accessed 21 June 2020. https://www.theguardian.com/world/2011/nov/17/brazil-census-african-brazilians-majority

Pierson, Paul and Theda Skocpol. 2002. "Historical Institutionalism in Contemporary Political Science". In *Political Science: The State of the Discipline*, edited by Ira Katznelson and Helen Milner, 693–721. New York: Norton.

Pine, B. JosephII and James H. Gilmore. 2011. *The Experience Economy*. Cambridge, MA: Harvard Business Review Press.

Pinto, Mónica. 1997. "El principio pro homine: criterios de hermenéutica y pautas para la regulación de los derechos humanos". In *La Aplicación de los tratados internacionales sobre derechos humanos por los tribunales locales*, edited by Martin Abregú and Christian Courtis, 163–172. Buenos Aires: Editores del Puerto.

Piquard, Alexandre. 2020. "Amazon et la France: 'Je t'aime, moi non plus'". *Le Monde*, 15 May, 15.

Plantenga, Janneke and Chantal Remery. 2013. "Work-Family Reconciliation Policies in Europe". In *Handbook of Research on Gender and Economic Life*, edited by Deborah M. Figart and Tonia L. Warnecke, 290–306. Northampton, MA: Edward Elgar.

Plato. 360 BCE. *The Republic*. Translated by Benjamin Jowett. The Internet Classics Archive. Accessed 15 September 2019. http://classics.mit.edu/Plato/republic.html

Pol, Rutuja. 2017. "Proposing an international instrument to address issues arising out of international surrogacy arrangements". *Georgetown Journal of International Law* 48: 1309–1335.

Pollitt, Katha. 1987. "Contracts and apple pie; the strange case of Baby M". *The Nation*, 244, 23 May, 667–673.

Poon, Maurice K.L. 2011. "Beyond Good and Evil: The Social Construction of Violence in Intimate Gay Relationships". In *Intimate Partner Violence in LGBTQ Lives*, edited by Janice L. Ristock, 102–130. New York: Routledge.

Potter, SirMark. 2006. *Judgement in the case of Wilkinson v Kitzinger [2006] EWHC 2022 (Fam)*. Accessed 22 April 2017. www.familylawweek.co.uk/site.aspx?i=ed2118

Power, Jenniferet al. 2010. "Diversity, tradition and family: Australian same-sex attracted parents and their families". *Gay & Lesbian Issues and Psychology Review* 6 (2): 66–81.

PR Newswire. 2006. "Canada sends an open 'Wedding Invitation' to gay and lesbian couples; Canadian Tourism Commission launches new integrated marketing program". 2 June. Accessed via Proquest, 13 November 2019. http://ezproxy.library.usyd.edu.au/login?url=https://search.proquest.com/docview/447654724?accountid=14757

Prasad, Ajnesh. 2008. "On the potential and perils of same-sex marriage: A perspective from queer theory". *Journal of Bisexuality* 7 (3–4): 91–215. doi:10.1080/15299710802170813

Prasad, Praatika. 2018. "More color more pride: Addressing structural barriers to interracial LGBTQ loving". *Fordham Law Review* 87, Article 16. Accessed 30 December 2019. https://ir.lawnet.fordham.edu/flro/vol87/iss1/16

Prassl, Jeremias. 2018. *Humans as a Service: The Promise and Perils of Work in the Gig Economy*. Oxford: Oxford Scholarship online. doi:10.1093/oso/9780198797012.001.0001

Pretzel, Andreas. 2012. "Homosexuality in the Sexual Ethics of the 1930s: A Values Debate in the Culture Wars between Conservatism, Liberalism, and Moral-National Renewal," translated by William Seth Howes and Erik Huneke. In *After the History of Sexuality: German Genealogies with and beyond Foucault*, edited by Scott Spector, Helmut Puff and Dagmar Herzog, 202–215. Oxford and New York: Berghahn Books.

Pritchard, Annette, Nigel Morgan and Diane Sedgley. 2007. "In Search of Lesbian Space? Manchester's Gay Village". In *Tourism and Gender: Embodiment, Sensuality and Experience*, edited by Annette Pritchard*et al.*, 273–289. Wallingford: CABI.

PRWORA (*Personal Responsibility and Work Opportunities Reconciliation Act*). 1996. *H.R. 3734*. Washington: 104th Congress. Accessed 9 January 2020. https://www.congress.gov/bill/104th-congress/house-bill/3734/text

Puar, Jasbir K. 2002a. "Circuits of queer mobility: Tourism, travel, and globalization". *GLQ: A Journal of Lesbian and Gay Studies* 8 (12): 101–137.

Puar, Jasbir K. 2002b. "A transnational feminist critique of queer tourism". *Antipode* 34 (5): 935–946. doi:10.1111/1467-8330.00283

Puar, Jasbir K. 2007. *Terrorist Assemblages: Homonationalism in Queer Times*. Durham, NC: Duke University Press.

Puhle, Hans-Jurgen. 1978. "Conservatism in modern German history". *Journal of Contemporary History* 13 (4): 689–720.

Quadagno, Jill. 1994. *The Color of Welfare: How Racism Undermined the War on Poverty*. Oxford and New York: Oxford University Press.

Quiroga, María Virginia, Marcela Brizzio and Nicolas Forlani. 2018. "Las organizaciones piqueteras y los virajes políticos en Argentina del siglo XXI". *Cuaderno Venezolano de Sociología* 27 (3): 27–48.

Raymond, Janice. 1993. *Women as Wombs: Reproductive Technologies and the Battle over Women's Freedom*. San Francisco/Melbourne/Munich: Harper/Spinifex/Frauenoffensive.

Redburn, Kate. 2019. "Zoned out: How zoning law undermines family law's functional turn". *Yale Law Journal* 128 (8): 2412–2473.

Régimen Especial de Contrato de Trabajo para el Personal de Casas Particulares. 2013. Ley 26.844. Buenos Aires: Presidencia de la Nación. Accessed 31 January 2020. http://servicios.infoleg.gob.ar/infolegInternet/anexos/210000-214999/210489/norma.htm

Reigstad, Marte Myhreet al. 2016. "Risk of cancer in children conceived by assisted reproductive technology". *Pediatrics* 137 (3). doi:10.1542/peds.2015-2061

Renan, Ernest. 1882. "Qu'est-ce qu'une nation?". Lecture delivered at the Sorbonne, 11 March. Accessed 22 September 2019. www.bmlisieux.com/archives/nation01.htm

Renshaw, Catherine. 2013. "The ASEAN Human Rights Declaration—Cause for celebration?". *Asiapacific.anu.edu.au.*, 25 January. Accessed 18 November 2019. http://asiapacific.anu.edu.au/regarding-rights/2013/01/25/the-asean-human-rights-declaration-cause-for-celebration/

Repoll, Jeronimo. 2010. "Politica y medios de comunicación en Argentina. Kirchner, Clarín y la Ley". *Andamios* 7 (14): 35–67.

Republic of South Africa. 1996. *Constitution of the Republic of South Africa*. ISBN ISBN: 978-0-621-39063-6.

Reyes, Oscar. 2005. "New Labour's Politics of the Hard-working Family". In *Discourse Theory in European Politics*, edited by David R. Howarth and Jacob Torfing, 231–254. Basingstoke and New York: Palgrave Macmillan.

Rhodes, Carl. 2017. "The market for virtue: Why companies like Qantas are campaigning for marriage equality". *The Conversation*, 28 August. Accessed 23 December 2019. https://theconversation.com/the-market-for-virtue-why-companies-like-qantas-are-campaigning-for-marriage-equality-82905

Rich, Adrienne. 1980. "Compulsory heterosexuality and lesbian existence". *Signs: Journal of Women in Culture and Society* 5 (4): 631–660.

Richardson, Diane. 2017. "Rethinking sexual citizenship". *Sociology* 51 (2): 208–224.

Richardson-Self, Louise. 2015. *Justifying Same-Sex Marriage: A Philosophical Investigation*. New York: Rowman & Littlefield.

Richeson, Jennifer and Alexa Van Brunt. 2015. "Same-sex marriage and the case of race". *The Hill*, 20 April. http://thehill.com/blogs/congress-blog/judicial/240417-same-sex-marriage-and-the-case-of-race. Accessed 20 June 2016

Riggs, Damien W. 2018. "Making matter matter: Meanings accorded to genetic material among Australian gay men". *Reproductive Biomedicine & Society Online* 7: 150–157.

Rights of Women. 2017. *Children and the Law: Lesbian Parenting*. London: Rights of Women. Accessed 15 June 2020. https://rightsofwomen.org.uk/get-information/family-law/lesbian-parenting-and-the-law/

Rigon, Amalia and Céline Chateau. 2016. *Regulating International Surrogacy Arrangements – State of Play*. Brussels: European Parliament Policy Department C: Citizens' Rights and Constitutional Affairs.

Rindfuss, Ronald R. and Minja Kim Choe (eds). 2016. *Low Fertility, Institutions, and their Policies: Variations across Industrialized Countries*. Cham: Springer.

Ristock, Janice L. (ed.). 2011. *Intimate Partner Violence in LGBTQ Lives*. New York: Routledge.

Rittel, Horst J. and Melvin M. Webber. 1973. "Dilemmas in a general theory of planning". *Policy Sciences* 4 (2): 155–169.

RNZ (Radio New Zealand). 2019. "Box ticking: Are rainbow tick workplaces really safe for LGBTQI staff?". 29 May. Accessed 26 December 2019. https://www.rnz.co.nz/news/national/390787/box-ticking-are-rainbow-tick-workplaces-really-safe-for-lgbtqi-staff

Robbins, Jill. 2011. *Crossing through Chueca: Lesbian Literary Culture in Queer Madrid*. Minneapolis: University of Minnesota Press.

Robinson, Nathan J. 2018. "The 'human rights campaign' has totally betrayed its constituents". *Current Affairs*, 7 September. Accessed 27 December 2019. https://www.currentaffairs.org/2018/09/the-human-rights-campaign-has-totally-betrayed-its-constituents

Robinson, Prue and John Connell. 2008. "'Everything is Truthful Here': Custom Village Tourism in Tanna, Vanuatu". In *Tourism at the Grassroots Villagers and visitors in the Asia-Pacific*, edited by John Connell and Barbara Rugendyke, 77–97. London and New York: Routledge.

Robinson, Russell K. 2014. "Marriage equality and postracialism". *UCLA Law Review* 61: 1010–1076.

Robson, Ruthann. 2007. "Sexual democracy". *South African Journal on Human Rights* 23 (3): 409–431. doi:10.1080/19962126.2007.11864934

Rodarte Berbera, Hayde. 2017. "The pro personae principle and its application by Mexican courts". *Queen Mary Human Rights Law Review* 4 (1). Accessed 19 November 2019. https://www.qmul.ac.uk/law/humanrights/hrlr/human-rights-law-review-vol-4/

Rodiles, Alejandro. 2016. "The Law and Politics of the Pro Persona Principle in Latin America". In *The Interpretation of International Law by Domestic Courts*, edited by Helmut Philipp Aust and Georg Nolte, 153–174. Oxford and New York: Oxford University Press.

Rodríguez Enriquez, Corina and Gabriela Marzonetto. 2015. "Organización social del cuidado y desigualdad: el déficit de políticas públicas de cuidado en Argentina". *Revista Perspectivas de Políticas Públicas* 4 (8): 103–134.

Romano, Flavio. 2006. *Clinton and Blair: The Political Economy of the Third Way*. London: Routledge.

Roncolato, Leanne and Michael E. Martell. 2016. "*Modern Families: Bargaining and Time-Use in Same-Sex Households*". Conference paper delivered at the 2017 Conference of the American Economic Association (paper dated 28 December 2016). Accessed 13 February 2020. https://www.aeaweb.org/conference/2017/preliminary/paper/8R42rkQt

Rosano, Susana. 2005a. "Rostros y Máscaras de Eva Perón: Imaginario Populista y Representación (Argentina, 1951–2003)". PhD dissertation, University of Pittsburgh.

Rosano, Susana. 2005b. "Imaginario femenino en el populismo argentino. Género y nación en 'La razón de mi vida', de Eva Perón". *Iberoamericana Nueva época* 5 (19): 51–63.

Ross, Karen and Margie Comrie. 2012. "The rules of the (leadership) game: Gender, politics and news". *Journalism* 13 (8): 969–984.

Rothschild, Cynthia, with Scott Long and Susana T. Fried. 2005. *Written Out: How Sexuality is Used to Attack Women's Organizing*. New York and New Brunswick, NJ: International

Gay and Lesbian Human Rights Commission and the Center for Women's Global Leadership (revised edition).

Rouban, Luc. 2018. *Le paradoxe du macronisme*. Paris: Presses de Sciences Po.

Rousseau, Jean-Jacques. 1755. "Discours sur l'origine et les fondements de l'inégalité parmi les hommes". In public domain. Available online at *Wikisource*. Accessed 28 August 2019. https://fr.wikisource.org/wiki/Discours_sur_l'origine_et_les_fondements_de_l'inégalité_parmi_les_hommes

Rousseau, Jean-Jacques. 1782. *Émile, ou De l'éducation*. Accessed 28 August 2019. https://fr.wikisource.org/Émile,_ou_De_léducation/Édition_1782

Rovny, Allison E. 2011. "Welfare state policy determinants of fertility level: A comparative analysis". *Journal of European Social Policy* 21 (4): 335–347. doi:10.1177/0958928711412221

Royce, Mark R. 2017. *The Political Theology of European Integration: Comparing the Influence of Religious Histories on European Policies*. Cham: Palgrave Macmillan.

Rudd, Kevin and Julia Gillard. 2007. "Forward with fairness: Labor's plan for fairer and more productive Australian workplaces". Accessed 11 January 2020. https://parlinfo.aph.gov.au/parlInfo/search/display/display.w3p;query=Id:%22library/partypol/WTWM6%22

Rudra, Nita. 2007. "Welfare regimes in developing countries: Unique or universal?". *Journal of Politics* 69 (2): 378–396.

Rudrappa, Sharmila. 2017. "India outlawed commercial surrogacy – clinics are finding loopholes". *The Conversation*, 23 October. Accessed 25 April 2019. https://theconversation.com/india-outlawed-commercial-surrogacy-clinics-are-finding-loopholes-81784

Ruiz-Ballesteros, Esteban and Macarena Hernández-Ramírez. 2010. "Tourism that empowers? Commodification and appropriation in Ecuador's *Turismo Comunitario*". *Critique of Anthropology* 30 (2): 201–229. doi:10.1177/0308275X09345426

Runswick-Cole, Katherine, Rebecca Lawthom and Dan Goodley. 2016. "The trouble with 'hard working families". *Community, Work & Family* 19 (2): 257–260, doi:10.1080/13668803.2016.1134153

Rydstrom, J. 2011. *Odd Couples: A History of Gay Marriage in Scandinavia*. Amsterdam. Amsterdam University Press.

Ryan, Patrick. 2019. "Women going backwards at the top of corporate Australia". *ABC News*, 10 September. Accessed 22 December 2019. https://www.abc.net.au/news/2019-09-10/female-ceo-top-200-australian-companies-gender-equality/11493864

Ryan-Flood, Róisín. 2009. *Lesbian Motherhood: Gender, Families and Sexual Citizenship*. London and New York: Palgrave Macmillan.

Ryan-Flood, Róisín. 2014. "Staying Connected: Lesbian and Gay Narratives of Family". In *The 'Irish' Family*, edited by Linda Connolly, 173–187. London: Routledge.

Ryan-Flood, Róisín and Jenny Gunnarsson Payne (eds). 2018. *Transnationalising Reproduction: Third Party Conception in a Globalised World*. London: Routledge.

Sainato, Michael. 2019. "'We are not robots': Amazon warehouse employees push to unionize". *The Guardian*, 1 January. Accessed 20 December 2019. https://www.theguardian.com/technology/2019/jan/01/amazon-fulfillment-center-warehouse-employees-union-new-york-minnesota

Sainsbury, Diane (ed.). 1994. *Gendering Welfare States*. London and Thousand Oaks, CA: Sage Publications.

Sainsbury, Diane. 1996. *Gender, Equality and Welfare States*. Cambridge: Cambridge University Press.

Sainsbury, Diane (ed.). 1999. *Gender and Welfare State Regimes*. Oxford: Oxford University Press.

Sainsbury, Diane (ed.). 2006. "Immigrants' social rights in comparative perspective: Welfare regimes, forms of immigration and immigration policy regimes". *Journal of European Social Policy* 16 (3): 229–244. doi:10.1177/0958928706065594

Sala Constitucional de la Corte Suprema de Justicia de Costa Rica. 2018. *Resolución N° 12782–2018. Minorías. Matrimonio Entre Personas Del Mismo Sexo. Artículo 14.6 del Código de Familia.* Accessed 16 May 2019. https://nexuspj.poder-judicial.go.cr/document/sen-1-0007-875801

SALRC (South African Law Reform Commission). 2003. *Discussion Paper 104: Project 118: Domestic Partnerships.* Pretoria: SALRC.

Salvi del Pero, Angelica*et al.*2016. *Policies to Promote Access to Good-quality Affordable Housing in OECD Countries.* OECD Social, Employment and Migration Working Papers No. 176. Paris:OECD. doi:10.1787/5jm3p5gl4djd-en

Sandall, Janeet al. 2018. "Short-term and long-term effects of caesarean section on the health of women and children". *The Lancet* 392: 1349–1357.

Sansone, Dario. 2019. "Pink work: Same-sex marriage, employment and discrimination". *Journal of Public Economics*180. doi:10.1016/j.jpubeco.2019.104086

Saravanan, Sheela. 2018. *A Transnational Feminist View of Surrogacy Biomarkets in India.* Singapore: Springer.

Sardone, Susan Breslow. 2109. "Wedding statistics and honeymoon facts & figures". *Tripsavvy*, 26 June. Accessed 6 December 2019. https://www.tripsavvy.com/wedding-statistics-and-honeymoon-facts-1860546

Sawer, Marian. 1996. "Gender, metaphor and the state". *Feminist Review* 52: 118–134.

Sawicky, Max B. 2004. "The Mirage of Welfare Reform". In *Welfare, the Working Poor, and Labor*, edited by Louise B. Simmons, 11–23. London and New York: Routledge.

SBS (Special Broadcasting Service). 2015. "Unions 'trashing' Qantas brand: Joyce". *SBS News*, 25 February. Accessed 24 December 2019. https://www.sbs.com.au/news/unions-trashing-qantas-brand-joyce

Scarborough Family, The and Michael W. Yarbrough. 2019. "'Zoning is a Way of Sorting People.' An interview with the Scarborough Family". In *Queer Families and Relationships after Marriage Equality*, edited by Michael W. Yarbrough, Angela Jones and Joseph Nicholas DeFilippis, 150–167. London and New York: Routledge.

Schließ, Gero. 2017. "Opinion: Angela Merkel's calculated change of heart on gay marriage". *Deutsche Welle*, 27 June. Accessed 13 January 2020. https://www.dw.com/en/opinion-angela-merkels-calculated-change-of-heart-on-gay-marriage/a-39440996-0

Schmidt, Vivien A. 2008. "Discursive institutionalism: The explanatory power of ideas and discourse". *Annual Review of Political Science* 11: 303–326.

Schmidt, Vivien A. 2010. "Taking ideas and discourse seriously: Explaining change through discursive institutionalism as the fourth 'new institutionalism'". *European Political Science Review* 2 (1): 1–25.

Schneebaum, Alyssa. 2019. *Partnership Recognition Rights and the Household Division of Labor.* Pre-publication copy.

Schneebaum, Alyssa and M.V. Lee Badgett. 2019. "Poverty in US lesbian and gay couple households". *Feminist Economics* 25 (1): 1–30. doi:10.1080/13545701.2018.1441533

Schönpflug, Karin. 2008. *Feminism, Economics and Utopia: Time Travelling through Paradigms.* London: Routledge.

Schor, Paul. 2017. *Counting Americans: How the US Census Classified the Nation.* Oxford and New York: Oxford University Press.

Schwartz, Oscar. 2019. "Untold history of AI: How Amazon's Mechanical Turkers got squeezed inside the machine". *Spectrum* (Institute of Electrical and Electronics Engineers),

22 April. Accessed 26 December 2019. https://spectrum.ieee.org/tech-talk/tech-history/dawn-of-electronics/untold-history-of-ai-mechanical-turk-revisited-tktkt

Scott, Jessica. 2013. "The distance between death and marriage". *International Feminist Journal of Politics* 15 (4): 534–551. doi:10.1080/14616742.2013.832891

Seekings, Jeremy and Nicoli Nattrass. 2005. *Class, Race, and Inequality in South Africa*. New Haven: Yale University Press.

Seignot, Nicki and David Clutterbuck. 2016. *Mentoring New Parents at Work: A Guide for Businesses and Organisations*. London: Routledge.

Sel, Susana and Pablo Gasloli. 2014. "Audiovisual Services Law No. 26.522: Cultural Practices, Power and Communication". In *The International Political Economy of Communication: Media and Power in South America*, edited by Cheryl Martens, Ernesto Vivares and Robert W. McChesney, 84–99. Basingstoke and New York: Palgrave Macmillan.

Semuels, Alana. 2018. "The Internet is enabling a new kind of poorly paid hell". *The Atlantic*, 23 January. Accessed 24 December 2019. https://www.theatlantic.com/business/archive/2018/01/amazon-mechanical-turk/551192/

Sénac, Réjane. 2018. "Same-Sex Marriage in France and Spain: Comparing Resistance in a Centralized Secular Republic and the Dynamics of Change in a 'Quasi-Federal' Constitutional Monarchy". In *Global Perspectives on Same-Sex Marriage: A Neo-Institutional Approach*, edited by Bronwyn Winter, Maxime Forest and Réjane Sénac, 105–125. Basingstoke and New York: Palgrave Macmillan.

Shanahan, Dennis. 2017. "Sparks fly as chiefs tell PM 'marriage equality good for business, so do it'". *The Australian*, 16 March. Accessed 22 December 2019. http://ezproxy.library.usyd.edu.au/login?url=https://search-proquest-com.ezproxy1.library.usyd.edu.au/docview/1877587556?accountid=14757

Siaroff, Alan. 1994. "Work, Welfare and Gender Equality: A New Typology". In *Gendering Welfare States*, edited by Diane Sainsbury, 82–100. London: Sage.

Siim, Beate. 2002. *Gender and Citizenship: Politics and Agency in France, Britain and Denmark*. Cambridge: Cambridge University Press.

Silverman, Jay G., Cynthia M. Mesh, Carrie V. Cuthbert, Kim Slote and Lundy Bancroft. 2004. "Child custody determinations in cases involving intimate partner violence: A human rights analysis". *American Journal of Public Health* 94 (6): 951–957.

Simopoulou, M., K. Sfakianoudis, P. Tsioulou, A. Rapani, G. Anifandis, A. Pantou, S. Bolaris, P. Bakas, E. Deligeoroglou, K. Pantos and M. Koutsilieris. 2018. "Risks in surrogacy considering the embryo: From the preimplantation to the gestational and neonatal period". *BioMed Research International*, Article ID 6287507. doi:10.1155/2018/6287507

Simpson, Rachel and Honor Figgis. 1997. *The Age of Consent. Briefing Paper N° 21/97*. Sydney: NSW Parliamentary Library Research Service.

Sinclair, M. Thea (ed.). 1997. *Gender, Work and Tourism*. London: Routledge.

Singh, Prachi. 2016. "Summing up: Inside the big fat global wedding industry". *Fashion United UK*, 24 June. Accessed 14 May 2019. https://fashionunited.uk/news/business/summing-up-inside-the-big-fat-global-wedding-industry/2016062420874

Smith, Michael. 2017. "Rare victory for the big end of town". *The Australian Financial Review*, 16 November, 38. Accessed 23 December 2019. http://ezproxy.library.usyd.edu.au/login?url=https://search-proquest-com.ezproxy1.library.usyd.edu.au/docview/1963877293?accountid=14757

Smith, Miriam. 2018. "Historical Institutionalism and Same-Sex Marriage: A Comparative Analysis of the USA and Canada". In *Global Perspectives on Same-Sex Marriage: A Neo-Institutional Approach*, edited by Bronwyn Winter, Maxime Forest and Réjane Sénac, 161–179. Basingstoke and New York: Palgrave.

Sobel-Read, Kevin B. and Georgia Monaghan. 2017. "Why the fashion industry keeps failing to fix labour exploitation". *The Conversation*, 20 November. Accessed 24 December 2019. https://theconversation.com/why-the-fashion-industry-keeps-failing-to-fix-la bour-exploitation-87356

Söderström-Anttila, Vivecaet al. 2016. "Surrogacy: Outcomes for surrogate mothers, children and the resulting families—a systematic review". *Human Reproduction Update* 22 (2): 260–276. doi:10.1093/humupd/dmv046

Soller, Tate. 2019. "Straightening out same-sex marriage for 'all' Australians: A content analysis study of prejudices in Australia's campaign for marriage equality". London: Media@LSE Working Paper Series.

Spar, Deborah. 2006. *The Baby Business: How Money, Science, and Politics Drive the Commerce of Conception*. Cambridge, MA: Harvard Business Review Press.

Sperling, Daniel. 2011. "'Male and female he created them': Procreative liberty, its conceptual deficiencies and the legal right to access fertility care of males". *International Journal of Law in Context* 7 (3): 375–400.

SRVAW (Special Rapporteur on Violence Against Women). 2009. *15 Years of the United Nations Special Rapporteur on Violence Against Women (1994–2009)—A Critical Review*. Geneva: UNSRVAW.

Standing, Guy. 2016. *The Precariat: The New Dangerous Class*. London: Bloomsbury Publishing.

Staudenmeier, Rebecca. 2018. "Could Germany get a gender-neutral national anthem?". *Deutsche Welle*, 6 March. Accessed 22 May 2020. https://www.dw.com/en/could-germa ny-get-a-gender-neutral-national-anthem/a-42823170

Stauffer, Brian. 2018. "'Soon there won't be much to hide': Transparency in the apparel industry". *Human Rights Watch*. Accessed 24 December 2019. https://www.hrw.org/ world-report/2018/essay/transparency-in-apparel-industry

Steedman, Carolyn, 1994. "The price of experience: Women and the making of the English working class". *Radical History Review* 59: 108–119.

Stefansdottir, Astridur. 2018. "Is 'surrogacy⊠ an infertility treatment?". *Clinical Ethics* 13 (2): 75–81.

Stein, Arlene. 2013. "What's the Matter with Newark? Race, Class, Marriage Politics, and the Limits of Queer Liberalism". In *The Marrying Kind? Debating Same-Sex Marriage with the Lesbian and Gay Movement*, edited by Mary Bernstein and Verta Taylor. Minneapolis: University of Minnesota Press.

Steinmetz, Stephanie and Mirjam Fischer. 2019. "Surveying persons in same-sex relationships in a probabilistic way— An example from the Netherlands". *Journal of Official Statistics* 35 (4): 753–776. doi:10.2478/JOS-2019-0032

Stilinovic, Milly. 2018. "From demonstration to dividend: How Sydney's Mardi Gras has become big business". *Forbes*, 2 March. Accessed 8 December 2019. https://www.forbes. com/sites/millystilinovic/2018/03/02/from-demonstration-to-divi
dend-how-Sydneys-mardi-gras-has-become-big-business/#7f58149e4cc8

Stone, Amy L. and Jane Ward. 2011. "From 'black people are not a homosexual act' to 'gay is the new black': Mapping white uses of blackness in modern gay rights campaigns in the United States". *Social Identities* 17 (5): 605–624. doi:10.1080/13504630.2011.595204

Stone, Lorraine. 1988. "Neoslavery - Surrogate motherhood contracts v. The Thirteenth Amendment". *Law & Inequality: A Journal of Theory and Practice* 6 (2): 63–73.

Sulla, Victor and Precious Zikhali. 2018. *Overcoming Poverty and Inequality in South Africa: An Assessment of Drivers, Constraints and Opportunities*. Washington, DC: The World Bank Group.

Sullivan, Maureen. 2004. *The Family of Woman: Lesbian Mothers, Their Children, and the Undoing of Gender*. Berkeley: University of California Press.

Supreme Court of New Jersey. 1988. *In re Baby M, 537 A.2d 1227, 109 N.J. 396*. Accessed 24 April 2019. https://law.justia.com/cases/new-jersey/supreme-court/1988/109-n-j-396-1.html

Swarr, Amanda Lock. 2012. "Paradoxes of butchness: Lesbian masculinities and sexual violence in contemporary South Africa". *Signs: Journal of Women in Culture and Society* 37 (4): 961–988.

Sylvestre, Anne. 2017. "Anne Sylvestre, 60 ans de carrière: La reine de la chanson française se confié à Têtu". Interview with Adrien Naselli. *Têtu*, 13 December. Accessed 8 December 2019. https://tetu.com/2017/12/13/anne-sylvestre-60-ans-de-chanson-rencontre-reine-chanson-francaise/

Tabbush, Constanza, María Constanza Díaz, Catlina Trebisacce and Victoria Keller. 2019. "LGBT Rights Yes, Abortion No: Explaining Uneven Trajectories in Argentina under Kirchnerism (2003–2015)". In *Seeking Rights from the Left: Gender, Sexuality, and the Latin American Pink Tide*, edited by Elisabeth Jay Friedman, 82–114. Durham, NC: Duke University Press.

Tadros, Edmund. 2018a. "Deloitte, EY, KPMG, PwC deny promoting tax avoidance schemes". *The Australian Financial Review*, 9 October. Accessed 29 December 2019. https://www.afr.com/companies/professional-services/deloitte-ey-kpmg-pwc-deny-promoting-tax-avoidance-schemes-20181009-h16dv6

Tadros, Edmund. 2018b. "Deloitte, EY, KPMG and PwC win $3.4b in federal contracts". *The Australian Financial Review*, 13 November. Accessed 29 December 2019. https://www.afr.com/politics/federal-contracts-with-big-four-deloitte-ey-kpmg-and-pwc-reach-34b-20181113-h17une

Tadros, Edmund. 2019. "Deloitte, EY, KPMG and PwC a 'systemic' tax risk: ATO". *The Australian Financial Review*, 12 September. Accessed 29 December 2019. https://www.afr.com/companies/professional-services/deloitte-ey-kpmg-and-pwc-a-systemic-tax-risk-ato-20190911-p52qbi

Takayama, Noriyukiet al. 2010. *Fertility and Public Policy: How to Reverse the Trend of Declining Birth Rates*. Cambridge, MA: MIT Press.

Tang, Caroline. 2017. "Banking on equality". *The Mosman Daily*, 12 October, 10.

Taylor, Greg. 2014. "The East German contribution to equal gay and lesbian rights in Germany". *American Journal of Legal History* 54 (3): 303–350.

Taylor, Paulet al. 2012. "When labels don't fit: Hispanics and their views of identity II: Identity, pan-ethnicity and race". *Pew Research Center*, 4 April. Accessed 3 January 2020. https://www.pewresearch.org/hispanic/2012/04/04/ii-identity-pan-ethnicity-and-race/

Taylor, Tiffany and Katrina Bloch (eds). 2018. *Marginalized Mothers: Mothering from the Margins*. Bingley, West Yorkshire: Emerald Publishers.

Taylor-Gooby, Peter, Benjamin Leruth and Heejung Chung (eds). 2017. *After Austerity: Welfare State Transformation in Europe after the Great Recession*. Oxford: Oxford University Press.

Taylor Mill, Harriet. 1970. "The Enfranchisement of Women". In *Essays on Sex Equality by John Stuart Mill and Harriet Taylor Mill*, edited by Alice S. Rossi, 89–121. Chicago: The University of Chicago Press.

TeleSUR. 2014. "Eva Perón at the heart of women's vote in Argentina". 10 November. Accessed 23 October 2019. https://www.telesurenglish.net/analysis/Eva-Peron-at-the-Heart-of-Womens-Vote-in-Argentina-20141110-0041.html

Telles, Edward. 2018. "Latinos, race, and the U.S. Census". *Annals of the American Academy of Political and Social Science* 677: 153–164.

Terry, Rodney L. and Marissa Fond. 2013. "Experimental U.S. Census Bureau race and Hispanic origin survey questions: Reactions from Spanish speakers". *Hispanic Journal of Behavioral Sciences* 35 (4): 524–541. doi:10.1177/0739986313499007

Terry, William. 2016. "Workers on the Move: Global Labour Sourcing in the Cruise Industry". In *Tourism and Leisure Mobilities: Politics, Work, and Play*, edited by JillianRickly, KevinHannam and Mary Mostafanezhad, 121–133. London and New York: Routledge.

Terry, William. 2018. "Precarity and guest work in U.S. tourism: J-1 and H-2B visa programs". *Tourism Geographies* 20 (1): 85–106. doi:10.1080/14616688.2017.1336784

Tetreault, Mary Ann. 1992. "Women and Revolution: A Framework for Analysis". In *Gendered States: Feminist (Re)Visions of International Relations Theory*, edited by V. Spike Peterson, 99–121. Boulder, CO: Lynne Rienner Publishers.

The Local (Germany). 2016. "First gay 'wedding' happens in Berlin Protestant church". 12 August. Accessed 13 January 2020. https://www.thelocal.de/20160812/first-gay-wedding-in-berlin-protestant-church

Therkelson, Anetteet al. 2013. "'I am very straight in my gay life': Approaching an understanding of lesbian tourists' identity construction". *Journal of Vacation Marketing* 19 (4): 317–327. doi:10.1177/1356766712474449

Thompson, Denise. 2020. *Masculinity and the Ruling of the World*. Sydney: Self-published.

Thorpe, Jocelyn. 2005. "Redrawing national boundaries: Gender, race, class, and same-sex marriage discourse in Canada". *Canadian Woman Studies* 24 (2–3): 15–21.

Throsby, Karen. 2010. "'Doing What Comes Naturally …': Negotiating Normality in Accounts of IVF Failure". In *Governing the Female Body: Gender, Health, and Networks of Power*, edited by Lori Reed and Paula Saukko, 233–252. New York: State University of New York Press.

Togman, Richard. 2019. *Nationalizing Sex: Fertility, Fear, and Power*. Oxford: Oxford University Press.

Tolbert, Jennifer, Kendal Orgera, Natalie Singer and Anthony Damico. 2019. "Key facts about the uninsured population". *Kaiser Family Foundation*, 13 December. Accessed 17 December 2019. https://www.kff.org/uninsured/issue-brief/key-facts-about-the-uninsured-population/

Tomlinson, Maurice. 2020. "Decriminalization or marriage, where should Caribbean LGBT people focus?" *Erasing 76 Crimes*, 15 May. Accessed 18 May 2020. https://76crimes.com/2020/05/15/decriminalization-or-marriage-where-should-caribbean-lgbt-people-focus/?fbclid=IwAR1FrEYro_F7Ux8CBUvDy5pCliPH9VcswjtRotPKTYORmQzTAlwMpAolGVo

Trade Arabia. 2017. "Luxury weddings a 'key segment of the tourism sector'". 4 May. Accessed 6 December 2019. www.tradearabia.com/news/TTN_324513.html

Traies, Jane. 2016. "Becoming Visible: De-Marginalising Older Lesbians in LGBT Ageing Discourse". In *Ageing and Sexualities: Interdisciplinary Perspectives*, edited by Rosie Harding and Elizabeth Peel, 77–96. London and New York: Routledge.

Tresch, John. 2011. "The machine awakens: The science and politics of the fantastic automaton". *French Historical Studies* 34 (1): 87–123. doi:10.1215/00161071-2010-024

Triandafyllidou, Anna (ed.). 2013. *Irregular Migrant Domestic Workers in Europe. Who Cares?*. Farnham, UK, and Burlington, VT: Ashgate.

Tribunal Judiciaire de Nanterre. 2020. *Ordonnance de référé rendue le 14 avril 2020. N° 20/00503*. Accessed 5 June 2020. https://www.doctrine.fr/d/TJ/Nanterre/2020/U5313E2393E5EACB45021

Tryfonidou, Alina. 2018. "Free movement of same-sex spouses within the EU: The ECJ's Coman judgment". *European Law Blog*, 19 June 2018. Accessed 18 November 2019. https://europeanlawblog.eu/2018/06/19/free-movement-of-same-sex-spouses-within-the-eu-the-ecjs-coman-judgment/

Tsfati, Maya and Adital Ben-Ari. 2018a. "Between the social and the personal: Israeli male gay parents, surrogacy and socio-political concepts of parenthood and gender". *Journal of GLBT Family Studies*. doi:10.1080/1550428X.2017.1413475

Tsfati, Maya and Adital Ben-Ari. 2018b. "Dualism, tension, and integration: Dialectics as a theme of integration in daily lives of Israeli gay men who became fathers through overseas surrogacy". *Journal of Homosexuality*. doi:10.1080/00918369.2018.1500781

Tsoukala, Philomena. 2010. "Marrying family law to the nation". *The American Journal of Comparative Law* 58. doi:10.5131/ajcl.2010.0005

Twine, France Winddance. 2015. *Outsourcing the Womb: Race, Class, and Gestational Surrogacy in a Global Market*. London and New York: Routledge (2nd edition).

UKSC (United Kingdom Supreme Court). 2018. *JUDGMENT R (on the application of Steinfeld and Keidan) (Appellants) v Secretary of State for International Development (in substitution for the Home Secretary and the Education Secretary) (Respondent). Trinity Term [2018] UKSC 32*. London: UKSC.

Ullmann, Hans Peter. 2019. "German Industry and Bismarck's Social Security System". In *The Emergence of the Welfare State in Britain and Germany 1850–1950*, edited by W.J. Mommsen, 133–149. London and New York: Routledge.

Underthun, Andres. 2015. "Stretching Liminal Spaces of Work? Temporality, Displacement and Precariousness among Transient Hotel Workers". In *A Hospitable World? Organising Work and Workers in Hotels and Tourist Resorts*, edited by David Jordhus-Lier and Anders Underthun, 27–38. London and New York: Routledge.

UNDP (United Nations Development Programme). 2019. *Human Development Report 2019: Beyond Income, beyond Averages, beyond Today: Inequalities in Human Development in the 21st Century*. New York: UNDP.

UNHRC (UN Human Rights Council). 2011. *Discriminatory Laws and Practices and Acts of Violence against Individuals Based on their Sexual Orientation and Gender Identity. Report of the United Nations High Commissioner for Human Rights*. UN Document A/HRC/19/41, 17 November. Accessed 17 May 2020. https://www.ohchr.org/Documents/Issues/Discrimination/A.HRC.19.41_English.pdf

UNWTO and IGLTA (United Nations World Tourism Organization and International Gay and Lesbian Travel Association). 2017. *Second Global Report on LGBT Tourism*. Madrid: UNWTO.

Unión Informática. 2017. "Final judgment: IBM forced to admit labor union 'Unión Informática'". 24 August. Accessed 24 December 2019. https://unioninformatica.org/final-judgment-ibm-forced-to-admit-labor-union-union-informatica/

Urry, John and Jonas Larsen. 2011. *The Tourist Gave 3.0*. London: Sage.

Valverde, Mariana. 2006. "A new entity in the history of sexuality: The respectable same-sex couple". *Feminist Studies* 32 (1): 155–162.

Van Berkel, Riket al. (eds). 2017. *Frontline Delivery of Welfare-to-Work Policies in Europe: Activating the Unemployed*. London and New York: Routledge.

Van Eeden-Moorefield, Bradet al. 2011. "Same-sex relationships and dissolution: The connection between heteronormativity and homonormativity". *Family Relations* 60 (5): 562–571.

Van Gelder, Lawrence. 1997. "Noel Keane, 58, lawyer in surrogate mother cases, is dead". *The New York Times*, 28 January. Accessed 24 April 2019. https://www.nytimes.com/1997/01/28/nyregion/noel-keane-58-lawyer-in-surrogate-mother-cases-is-dead.html

Vandegrift, Darcie. 2008. "'This isn't paradise—I work here': Global restructuring, the tourism industry, and women workers in Caribbean Costa Rica". *Gender and Society* 22 (6): 778–798. doi:10.1177/0891243208324999

Vašák, Karel. 1977. "Human rights: A thirty-year struggle: The sustained efforts to give force of law to the Universal Declaration of Human Rights". *UNESCO Courier* 30, 11.

Vázquez, Pablo A. 2007. "Evita and women's participation in politics". Instituto Nacional de Investigaciones Históricas Eva Perón. Accessed 31 October 2019. www.evitaperon.org/evita_peron_instituto.htm

Vásquez Castillo, Maria Teresa. 2004. *Land Privatization in Mexico: Urbanization, Formation of Regions and Globalization in Ejidos*. London and New York: Routledge.

Vera, Danielle A. 2016. "R-egg-ulation: A call for greater regulation of the big business of human egg harvesting". *Michigan Journal of Gender and Law* 23 (2): 391–424.

Vetten, Lisa. 2011. "Paradox and Policy: Addressing Rape in Post-apartheid South Africa". In *International Approaches to Rape*, edited by Nicole Westmarland and Geetanjali Gangoli. Bristol: Bristol University Press.

Vicuña Gonzalez, Vernadette. 2015. "Making Aloha: Lei and the Cultural Labor of Hospitality". In *Making the Empire Work: Labor and United States Imperialism*, edited by Daniel E. Bender and Jana K. Lipman, 161–182. New York: New York University Press.

Villarreal, Daniel. 2017. "The world's largest LGBTQ travel network is endorsing Trump hotels and people are pissed". *Hornet*, 11 July. Accessed18 November 2019. https://hornet.com/stories/lgbtq-travel-trump-hotels/

Visser, Jelle. 2019. *Trade Unions in the Balance*. ILO ACTRAV Working Paper. Geneva: International Labour Organization.

Vogel, David. 2006. *The Market for Virtue: The Potential and Limits of Corporate Social Responsibility*. Washington: Brookings Institution Press (revised edition).

Vosko, Leah F., Martha MacDonald and Iain Campbell. 2009. "Introduction". In *Gender and the Contours of Precarious Employment*, edited by Leah F. Vosko, Martha MacDonald and Iain Campbell, 1–25. London and New York: Routledge.

Voskuhl, Adelheid. 2013. *Androids in the Enlightenment: Mechanics, Artisans, and Cultures of the Self.* Chicago: University of Chicago Press.

Wadsworth, Nancy D. 2011. "Intersectionality in California's same-sex marriage battles: A complex proposition". *Political Research Quarterly* 64 (1): 200–216. doi:10.1177/1065912910376386

Waitt, Gordon and Kevin Markwell. 2014. *Gay Tourism: Culture and Context*. London and New York: Routledge (2nd edition).

Walby, Sylvia. 1994. "Is citizenship gendered?". *Sociology* 28 (2): 379–395.

Walsh, Emma. 2019. "Executive Summary". In *National Working Families Report 2019, by Parents at Work, Karitane and APLEN*. Crows Nest, NSW: Parents at Work.

Wang, Chin Chin, Carl Cater and Tiffany Low. 2016. "Political challenges in community-based ecotourism". *Journal of Sustainable Tourism* 24 (11): 1555–1568. doi:10.1080/09669582.2015.1125908

Ward, Kevin, Colette Fagan, Linda McDowell, Diane Perrons and Kath Ray. 2010. "Class transformation and work–life balance in urban Britain: The case of Manchester". *Urban Studies* 47 (11): 2259–2278. doi:10.1177/0042098009359030

Waring, Marilyn. 1988. *Counting for Nothing: What Men Value & What Women are Worth*. Wellington, New Zealand: Allen & Unwin.

Webster, Jennica. 2018. *Examining the Impact of LGBT Senior Leadership Representation on Business Outcomes*. Milwaukee: Wisconsin LGBT Chamber of Commerce.

WEF (World Economic Forum). 2018. *The Global Gender Gap Report 2018*. Geneva: WEF.

Werner-Felmayer, Gabriele. 2015. "Globalisation and Market Orientation: A Challenge within Reproductive Medicine". *In Cross-Cultural Comparisons on Surrogacy and Egg Donation: Interdisciplinary Perspectives from India, Germany and Israel*, edited by Sayani Mitra, Silke Schicktanz and Tulsi Patel, 13–34. Cham: Palgrave Macmillan.

Weston, Kath. 1991. *Families We Choose: Lesbians, Gays, Kinship*. New York: Columbia University Press.

Whetstine, Leslie M.and Bradley G.Beach. 2016. "Surrogacy's Changing Social Profile". In *Handbook of Gestational Surrogacy*, edited by E. ScottSills, 33–40. Cambridge:Cambridge University Press.

Whisnant, Clayton J. 2016. *Queer Identities and Politics in Germany: A History 1880–1945*. New York: Harrington Park Press.

Whitaker, Andrea. 2016. "From 'Mung Ming' to 'Baby Gammy': A local history of assisted reproduction in Thailand". *Reproductive Biomedicine and Society Online*. doi:10.1016/j.rbms.2016.05.005

Whitehead, Christine M.E. 2018. "Comment – On building typologies of housing systems in the OECD". *Economie et Statistique / Economics and Statistics*. doi:10.187/ecostat.2018.500t.1944

Widdows, Heather. 2006. "The Impact of New Reproductive Technologies on Concepts of Genetic Relatedness and Non-relatedness". In *Women's Reproductive Rights*, edited by Heather Widdows, ltziar Alkorta Idiakez and Aitziber Emaldi Cirión, 151–164. Basingstoke and New York: Palgrave Macmillan.

Wilkes, Karen. 2016. *Whiteness, Weddings and Tourism in the Caribbean: Paradise for Sale*. New York: Palgrave Macmillan.

Williamson, Emma, Nancy Lombard and Oona Brooks-Hay. 2020. "'Coronavirus murders': Media narrative about domestic abuse during lockdown is wrong and harmful". *The Conversation*, 15 May. Accessed 31 May 2020. https://theconversation.com/coronavirus-murders-media-narrative-about-domestic-abuse-during-lockdown-is-wrong-and-harmful-137011

Windebank, Jan. 2009. "State support for domestic services: A comparison of the outsourcing of domestic cleaning in France and Britain". *Journal of Contemporary European Studies* 17 (3): 437–449. doi:10.1080/14782800903339370

Winsor, Ben. 2017. "Coopers says sorry and endorses marriage equality after mounting boycott". *SBS News*, 15 March. Accessed 22 December 2019. https://www.sbs.com.au/news/coopers-says-sorry-and-endorses-marriage-equality-after-mounting-boycott. https://www.sbs.com.au/news/coopers-says-sorry-and-endorses-marriage-equality-after-mounting-boycott

Winter, Bronwyn. 2006. "The Social Foundations of the Sacred: Feminists and the Politics of Religion". In *Handbook of Gender and Women's Studies*, edited by Kathy Davis, Mary Evans and Judith Lorber, 92–108. London: Sage.

Winter, Bronwyn. 2014. "The ties that bind us: The hidden tangles of gay marriage". *Portal: Journal of Multidisciplinary International Studies* 11 (1): special issue on 'Stigma'. doi:10.5130/portal.v11i1.3296

Winter, Bronwyn. 2017. *Women, Insecurity, and Violence in a Post-9/11 World*. Syracuse, NY: Syracuse University Press.

Winter, Bronwyn. 2018a. "Preserving the Social Fabric: Debates over the Meaning of the Family in the United Kingdom, the Republic of Ireland and Australia". In *Global Perspectives on Same-Sex Marriage: A Neo-Institutional Approach*, edited by Bronwyn Winter, Maxime Forest and Réjane Sénac, 149–170. Basingstoke and New York: Palgrave.

Winter, Bronwyn. 2018b. "'Tampering with Society's DNA' or 'Making Society Stronger': Family, Religion and Gay Rights in the Construction of the Nation". In *Gendering Nationalism: Intersections of Nation, Gender and Sexuality in the 21st Century*, ed. Jon Mulholland, Nicola Montagna and Erin Sanders-McDonagh, 109–126. Basingstoke: Palgrave Macmillan.

Winter, Bronwyn. 2018c. "Conclusion". In *Global Perspectives on Same-Sex Marriage: A Neo-Institutional Approach*, edited by Bronwyn Winter, Maxime Forest and Réjane Sénac, 221–227. Basingstoke and New York: Palgrave Macmillan.

Winter, Bronwyn, Maxime Forest and Réjane Sénac. 2018. *Global Perspectives on Same-Sex Marriage: A Neo-Institutional Approach*. New York: Palgrave Macmillan.

WTTC (World Travel and Tourism Council). 2019a. *World, Transformed: Megatrends and their Implications for Travel and Tourism*. London: WTTC.

WTTC. 2019b. *Travel and Tourism: Economic Impact 2019: World*. London: WTTC.

Xu, Keet al. 2018. *Public Spending on Health: A Closer Look at Global Trends*. WHO/HIS/HGF/HF Working Paper 18.3. Geneva: World Health Organization.

Yabroff, K. Robin, Jingxuan Zhao, Xuesong Han and Zhiyuan Zheng. 2019. "Prevalence and correlates of medical financial hardship in the USA". *Journal of General Internal Medicine* 34 (8): 1494–1502. doi:10.1007/s11606-019-05002-w

Yeates, Nicola. 2012. "Global care chains: A state-of-the-art review and future directions in transnationalization research". *Global Networks* 12 (2): 135–154.

Yogyakarta Principles, The. 2007. Accessed 16 May 2020. https://yogyakartaprinciples.org/

Yogyakarta+10. 2017. Accessed 16 May 2020. https://yogyakartaprinciples.org/principles-en/yp10/

Young, Brigitte, IsabellaBakker and DianeElson. 2011. "Introduction". In *Questioning Financial Governance from a Feminist Perspective*, 1–10. LondonandNew York:Routledge.

Younge, Gary. 2003. "Gay is the new black". *The Guardian*, 16 June. Accessed 16 December 2019. https://www.theguardian.com/world/2003/jun/16/gayrights.usa

Younger, Judith T. 1988. "What the Baby M case is really all about". *Law & Inequality: A Journal of Theory and Practice* 6 (2): 75–82.

Yuval-Davis, Nira. 2006. "Intersectionality and feminist politics". *European Journal of Women's Studies* 13 (3): 193–209. doi:10.1177/1350506806065752

Zaglul, Layla. 2018. "Costa Rican politics looks divided, but its people are hopeful". *The Conversation*, 24 April. Accessed 19 November 2019. https://theconversation.com/costa-rican-politics-looks-divided-but-its-people-are-hopeful-94941

Zampoukos, Kristina and Dimitri Iaonnides. 2011. "The tourism labour conundrum: Agenda for new research in the geography of hospitality workers". *Hospitality & Society* 1 (1). doi:10.1386/hosp.1.1.25_1

Zeoli, April M., Echo Rivera, Cris M. Sullivan and Sheryl Kubiak. 2013. "Post-separation abuse of women and their children: Boundary-setting and family court utilization among victimized mothers". *Journal of Family Violence* 28 (6): 547–560.

Zimmerman, Karla. 2019. "Top 10 gay wedding destinations". *Lonely Planet*, 21 August. Accessed 28 May 2019. https://www.lonelyplanet.com/articles/top-10-gay-wedding-destinations

INDEX

For Product Safety Concerns and Information please contact our EU representative GPSR@taylorandfrancis.com
Taylor & Francis Verlag GmbH, Kaufingerstraße 24, 80331 München, Germany

www.ingramcontent.com/pod-product-compliance
Lightning Source LLC
LaVergne TN
LVHW021123300926
849160LV00010B/841

* 9 7 8 1 1 3 8 5 0 2 6 8 0 *